Organizational Excellence Through Total Quality Management

A Practical Approach

Organizational Excellence Through Total Quality Management

A Practical Approach

H Lal
Director General
Quality Forum
Federation of Indian Chambers of Commerce and Industry (FICCI)
and
Technical Advisor
United Nations Industrial Development Organization (UNIDO)
New Delhi

NEW AGE MANAGEMENT
An Imprint of
NEW AGE INTERNATIONAL (P) LIMITED, PUBLISHERS
New Delhi • Bangalore • Chennai • Cochin • Guwahati
Hyderabad • Kolkata • Lucknow • Mumbai
Visit us at **www.newagepublishers.com**

Published by New Age International (P) Ltd., Publishers
First Edition: 2008
Reprint: 2015

BRANCHES

- **Bangalore** 37/10, 8th Cross (Near Hanuman Temple), Azad Nagar, Chamarajpet Bangalore-560 018, Tel.: (080) 26756823, Telefax: 26756820 **E-mail: bangalore@newagepublishers.com**
- **Chennai** 26, Damodaran Street, T. Nagar, Chennai-600 017, Tel.: (044) 24353401 Telefax: 24351463, **E-mail: chennai@newagepublishers.com**
- **Cochin** CC-39/1016, Carrier Station Road, Ernakulam South, Cochin-682 016 Tel.: (0484) 2377303, Telefax: 4051303 **E-mail: cochin@newagepublishers.com**
- **Guwahati** Hemsen Complex, Mohd. Shah Road, Paltan Bazar, Near Starline Hotel Guwahati-781 008 Tel.: (0361) 2513881, Telefax: 2543669 **E-mail: guwahati@newagepublishers.com**
- **Hyderabad** 105, 1st Floor, Madhiray Kaveri Tower, 3-2-19, Azam Jahi Road, Near Kumar Theater Nimboliadda, Kachiguda, Hyderabad-500 027, Tel.: (040) 24652456 Telefax: 24652457 **E-mail: hyderabad@newagepublishers.com**
- **Kolkata** RDB Chambers (Formerly Lotus Cinema) 106A, 1st Floor, S N Banerjee Road Kolkata-700 014 Tel.: (033) 22273773, Telefax: 22275247 **E-mail: kolkata@newagepublishers.com**
- **Lucknow** 16-A, Jopling Road, Lucknow-226 001, Tel.: (0522) 2209578, 4045297 Telefax: 2204098, **E-mail:lucknow@newagepublishers.com**
- **Mumbai** 142C, Victor House, Ground Floor, N.M. Joshi Marg, Lower Parel Mumbai-400 013, Tel.: (022) 24927869, Telefax: 24915415 **E-mail: mumbai@newagepublishers.com**
- **New Delhi** 22, Golden House, Daryaganj, New Delhi-110 002 Tel.: (011) 23262368, 23262370, Telefax: 43551305 **E-mail: sales@newagepublishers.com**

ISBN: 978-81-224-2289-4

₹ 350.00
(No Tax on books)
C-15-07-8619

Printed in India at Ajit Printing Press, New Delhi.
Typeset at In-house, New Delhi.

PUBLISHING GLOBALLY
NEW AGE INTERNATIONAL (P) LIMITED, PUBLISHERS
7/30 A, Daryaganj, New Delhi - 110002
Visit us at **www.newagepublishers.com**

Dedicated to

my wife

SUSHMA

who sacrificed so much

for all my success

Foreword

Quality has become a priority national strategy. It has major technical, economic and human implications, which influence competitiveness, employment, exports and overall economic growth of any country. In the first phase of our economic development in the last four decades the emphasis had to be on creation of capacities, import substitution and attaining self-reliance. While we are pursuing these goals, there has been a major transformation in global economy, especially in the industrial sector. Rapid technological developments especially advances in micro-electronics, computers and controls; globalisation of technologies production facilities and markets and the national drive for total quality management initiated in Japan and now being adopted almost world over have their lessons for us in our future programmes. The Indian economy will also have to reorient its basic priorities and quality must be accorded its rightful place.

World over the strategic sectors have provided new techniques, and approaches to quality management, safety and reliability. The environment and demands on weapon systems, nuclear power plant and systems and equipment for space programmes have stretched technologies to their limits and resulted in the most exacting specifications and management systems.

Yet another trend in the recent decades has been the shift from inspection of final product to remove defects to building quality into the product. This has led to evolution of standards for Quality Management Systems in the form of ISO-9000 series of standards. In addition, a number of new concepts and tools have been developed for managing quality and achieving organizational excellence. With explosion of quality related knowledge, managers and quality professionals find it difficult to decide as to which of the competing approaches and tools should be adopted.

In this context, this Book by General H. Lal is very useful and timely. The Book explains in detail the basic quality management structure and system in an organization. In addition the Book takes the reader through essential elements of new quality management concepts and tools, developed during last decade and provides practical guidance on how and in what situation various quality tools and techniques can be employed. This will help managers to make an informed judgment in developing appropriate strategy for improving competitiveness and moving towards organizational excellence.

I know General Lal for over two decades. He started his quality profession in 1964 when he joined Indian Defence Quality Organization (DGQA). He has spent over 40 years in the field and has held top positions in quality in the country. He headed DGQA, the largest organization in the world with over 20,000 quality professionals. Then he took over Bureau of Indian Standards, one of the largest National Standards Organization in the world. He was member of ISO Committee which developed ISO-9000:2000 version, and he is still Chairman of Management and systems Divisional Council of Bureau of Indian Standards which interacts with ISO in all quality related standards. He is author of many Books including the one on ISO-9000 which was published by ISO and WTO in English, French and Spanish and subsequently translated in many national languages. At present, he is the Director General of FICCI Quality Forum and Quality Adviser to United Nations Industrial Development Organization. His crowning glory is that he has been appointed Chairman of National Board for Quality Promotion, set up by Quality Council of India, which has got wide charter of promoting quality in all sections of national life. Even at age of 75 years, he has strong passion for quality which is reflected in the way he conducts the affairs of National Board for Quality Promotion.

This Book has been written by him based on his long experience in India and abroad. The Book will be a good addition to quality literature in India when the country is moving on its quality journey to become a global superpower.

Girdhar Gyani
Secretary General
Quality Council of India

Preface

The word excellence is widely used to denote superlative performance in any activity in which an individual or organization is engaged. In the context of organizations excellence may refer to some aspects of their activities or it may also be used for their overall performance. It is difficult to define organizational excellence because some of its elements are intangible which cannot be quantified or measured. Excellence must really be seen in terms of competition. The competition has been an integral part of evolution itself. It manifests itself in fights among males and females of the species in trying to win the best mates for procreation. In business, there has always been a competition among organizations to win customers and investors.

If we analyse organisational excellence, it is more about attitude of mind and behaviour pattern of its people. It is journey towards creating superior sustainable organization rather than a destination. There is no absolute value for excellence. Just like Olympic records, the standards of excellence keep on improving. At a point in time goalpost may be the 'Best' in its class. Another word which has been traditionally used as a parameter in relation to excellence is Quality. Higher the quality in an organization near it reaches towards excellence. Thus better we manage quality nearer we move towards excellence. Here the word "Quality" has been used in its broader sense of overall performance rather than quality of products and services.

Although a number of new tools and techniques have been developed in recent years, in effect all these are subsets of broader concept of quality management called "Total Quality Management." In this, the word, 'Total' signifies that it involves all departments at all levels and it may also cover customers, suppliers and even society at large. The word Management implied that it is a management function. TQM is a broad concept covering management approaches for improvement of organizational performance aimed to achieve excellence. Thus emergence of new tools has not made TQM obsolete. In fact, it has enriched the body of knowledge of TQM.

No single management tool can succeed unless it is integrated in overall management of Quality in an organization.

This book has been written to interpret TQM in the new light embracing all the new quality management concepts and tools which have been developed in the last two decades. To make the book self contained, all these concepts and tools have been covered at some length in different chapters so that the reader is aware of all the weapons in the armory which he can use in the war of competition in the globalised world.

This is the second edition of the book "TQM a Practical Approach" which was published by Wiley Eastern in 1989. The intrinsic value of the Book can be judged from the fact that 17 years after its publication, it is still being sold and many reprints have been made. Seventeen years is a long time particularly in this era of rapid technological development and explosion of knowledge. This edition of the Book has been totally revised and enlarged. It incorporates modern concept of TQM embracing current management practices and quality tools and techniques which have been developed during this period. The book has been organized in three parts. Part I deals with the basic structure of quality management which were already covered in the first edition of the book. Some of the chapters in this part such as Human Factor in Quality and Economics of Quality have been totally revised in the light of new developments. As services are coming into increasing prominence, Part I also contains an additional Chapter on Management of Service Quality. Part II is a totally new addition. It contains the Philosophy of TQM and twelve chapters on new quality management concepts and tools such as Six Sigma, Lean Production, CRM, Balanced Score Card, etc. and tools developed during last two decades. In addition, a comprehensive guidance has been given on implementation of TQM in the last Chapter of Part II which includes an elaborate questionnaire for carrying out quality health check of an organization. Part III contains various statistical and non-statistical tools which have been traditionally used for managing quality in an organization.

The Book has been primarily written for quality professionals and managers of various functions both in manufacturing and service sectors. The Book is admirably suited for students of MBA courses which provides guidance on quality and related issues which are important for today's managers and to make reader aware of all the quality tools and techniques. Care has been taken to explain various tools in a simple language avoiding use of advanced mathematics and statistics. It can be easily understood by persons who do not have mathematical background so that they can apply these tools in manufacturing and service industries for enhancing customer satisfaction and cost competitiveness.

H.LAL

Contents

PART-III

PART-1

1

Product Quality and its Control

WHAT IS QUALITY ?

The term quality is often used loosely and it conveys different meanings to different people. When referring to a product, it generally signifies the degree of its excellence. However, when examined closely, this meaning of quality is found to be misleading. For instance, a Buick or a Mercedes may be an excellent car in Europe or America, but it obviously is a poor vehicle for use in the jungle tracks of Africa or India. Similarly a good walking shoe makes unsuitable footwear for sports. Thus there can be no absolute quality rating for a product, without relation to its intended use. The quality of a product can therefore be defined as, "fitness for the purpose." The more fully it serves its intended purpose, the higher is its quality. Definition of Quality as per ISO 9000:2005 is given below:

"Degree to which a set of inherent characteristics (distinguishing features) fulfills requirements *i.e.*, needs or expectations that are stated, generally implied or obligatory."

QUALITY CHARACTERISTICS

The quality of a product consists of a number of elements, each of which has a definite function that contributes to making the product fit for its intended use. These elements, such as shape, size, or physical, chemical or sensory properties are the building blocks of product quality and are called quality characteristics. Although some of the quality characteristics can be specified in quantitative terms, no single characteristic can be used to measure the quality of a product on an absolute scale. The overall quality of the product depends on the sum total of all the characteristics and attributes which have a bearing on its end use.

QUALITY CONTROL

The term 'Control' in the context of management is a function whereby performance is measured against the planned objectives, and in case of deficiency, necessary remedial measures are taken to ensure the achievement of the stipulated objectives.

When applied to the quality of a product, the term "Quality Control" denotes all those activities which are directed to maintaining and improving it. In specific terms it involves:-

(a) Setting of quality targets

(b) Appraisal of conformance

(c) Taking corrective action where, any deviation is noticed

(d) Planning for improvements in quality.

EVOLUTION OF QUALITY CONTROL

The concept of quality control is not new. It can be traced back to the stone age man who examined the point of his rough-hewn stone tool to see whether it was sharp enough for his purse. In present day terminology, he was assessing the quality of the tool which he had chiseled by comparing it with his mental picture of a good tool. Our stone age man had one distinct advantage over the present day quality engineer; since he himself was the manufacturer as well as user, he knew exactly what he wanted and thus made efforts to attain the quality which would meet this purpose. This situation changed with social progress. For better efficiency, jobs were divided and various people specialised in the production of different goods and services. For instance, potters made all the pots and weavers wove the cloth required by every one in the village. Further progress continued along these lines and was characterised by growth in size and specialisation to meet the changing requirements of society. Along with the changing production system, quality control practices also evolved to suit the products and methods of production. Important steps in this evolution are briefly described below:

(a) ***Craftsmanship:*** From early civilisation to the industrial revolution, the craftman himself, or the master craftsman who guided a group of craftsmen exercised quality control. The reputation for craft-

manship and the incentive of better price for a superior product were the main governing factors of product quality. This situation prevailed until the nineteenth century.

(b) ***Supervisor's Control:*** With the expansion of manufacture during the industrial revolution, large factories were established to meet the increasing demands of the consumers. This gave rise to the need of supervisors to control the work of a large number of workers. Usually, supervisors were picked up from among the elder workers who had thorough knowledge of the job, and thus were able to guide and administer the other workers. Among other functions, the checking of the quality of jobs produced in the shop was also the responsibility of the supervisor or the foreman. This was usually by visual check of jobs, for which he mainly relied on his subjective experience.

(c) ***Inspection:*** With the advent of the manufacture of interchangeable components on a mass scale in the early part of last century it became essential to critically examine each component with the aid of measuring instruments or gauges. Obviously this job could not be performed by the shop supervisor, who was fully occupied with other problems concerning production. Thus a full-time inspector came on the scene and the quality function was separated from production. With these developments a new discipline, "Engineering Inspection", came into being and elaborate inspection organisations were created in large manufacturing companies.

(d) ***Statistical Quality Control:*** World War II generated a great upsurge in industrial activity. The tremendous requirements of defence stores necessitated mass production on an unprecedented scale. As conventional inspection methods were inadequate for this purpose, statistical methods like sampling tables and control charts were introduced, which reduced the burden on the inspection organisation, and enabled it to cope with mass production. Although, statistical quality control did increase the efficiency of the inspection organisation and enlarge the area of control to include in-process check, it still remained an extension of inspection, as it tackled the quality problem only at the shop floor level by the physical inspection of a part or whole of the product. It could not view the problem from the overall company perspective as the management saw it.

CHANGING QUALITY CONCEPTS

Upto the late nineteen forties, product quality was generally considered in terms of functional efficiency and aesthetic appeal. Rapid technological advancement during the post-war period has led to the emergence of a new concept of product quality. It has been realised that there is more to any product than streamlined appearance and ability to function well at the time of purchase. There are attributes such as continued fault-free service and maintenance costs which are equally important from the customer's point of view.

Since quality is a measure of the user satisfaction provided by a product, it should include the following characteristics:

- Functional efficiency
- Appearance
- Ease of installation and operation
- Safety
- Reliability
- Maintainability
- Running and maintenance cost

The above mentioned quality features do not just occur in the product. They have to be specially incorporated in the design and a conscious effort is required during manufacture, to achieve them in the actual product. This brings us to the two facets of quality; namely "Quality of Design" and "Quality of Conformance." Quality is initially created by the designer in the form of product specifications and manufacturing instructions. The extent to which the design is inherently capable of providing user satisfaction can be termed as "Quality of Design." On the other hand, Quality of conformance relates to the fidelity with which the product conforms to the design. The control of both these aspects of quality is important if the end product is to meet customer acceptance.

QUALITY MANAGEMENT

It has been realized that inspection alone cannot build quality into a product unless quality has been designed and manufactured into it. Therefore, quality awareness must begin at the very conception of the product and continue during the various stages of its development and manufacture and even during its usage, to provide feedback from the users which is so essential for quality improvement. To distinguish this "Cradle-to-grave" concept from the traditional concept of quality control, various new terms such as "company wide quality control", "Quality Assurance", and the "Quality Management" have been coined in quality control literature. The quality of products in a company is determined by the philosophy, commitment and the quality policy of the top management and the extent to which this policy can be put in actual practice. Since this is basically a management function, involving direction by top management and coordination of all quality related activities in different departments of a company.

Quality Management deals with the product in its totality. It has been recognized that quality is determined by the combined efforts of various departments such as Design, Engineering, Purchase, Production and Quality Control. Various activities of different departments which are specifically aimed at building quality into the production are given in Table 1. The departments primarily responsible for the activities as well as those having contributory responsibility are also shown against respective activities. Thus Quality Management is an across-the-company management function which coordinates and controls widespread quality activities with a view to achieving the desired quality of the end-product. This concept of quality management is illustrated in Fig. 1. This configuration signifies the Integrated Quality System covering all quality control activities during various phases of product development. The quality cycle begins and ends with the customer. It starts when the customer's need is analyzed to design a product for its fulfillment. During the development and manufacture of the product, various departments and sections of the company make their contribution in building quality into it. The cycle ends with the user, because the final proof of product quality comes during its service with the customer, whose satisfaction is the ultimate aim. In this concept, Quality is no longer the exclusive domain of quality inspectors. Designers, process planners, production engineers and even sales personnel have their role to play in the achievement of the primary quality objective, which is 'MAXIMUM CUSTOMER SATISFACTION AT MINIMUM COST.'

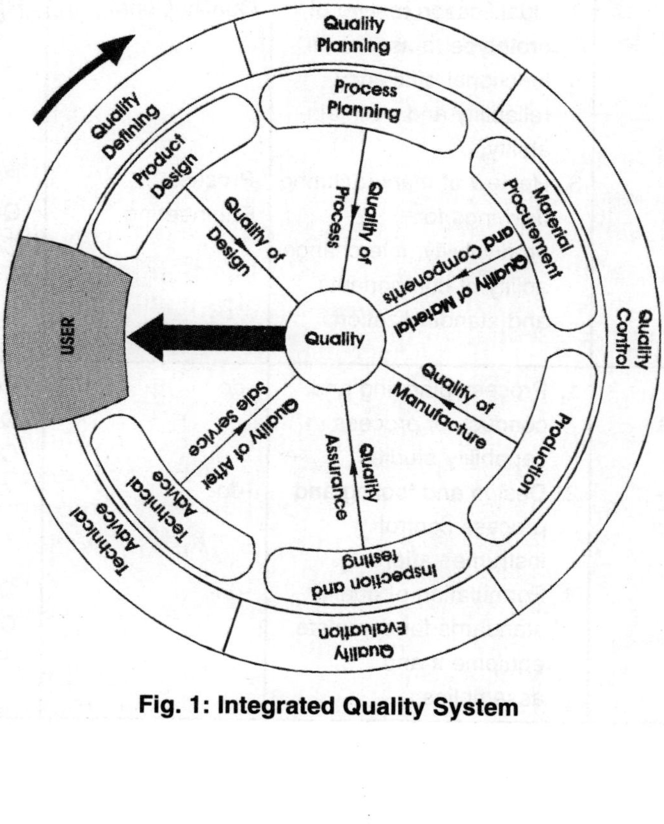

Fig. 1: Integrated Quality System

Table 1. Quality Activities

Phase	*Activity*	*Department having primary responsibility*	*Department having contributory responsibility*
CONCEPT	1. Market research to study user needs and preferences.	Marketing	R & D
	2. Analysis of customer complaints of existing product.	Quality Control	Marketing
	3. Study of competitive product quality.	R & D	Quality Control
	4. Formulation of qualitative requirements of the new product.	R & D	Marketing, Quality Control
DEVELOPMENT	1. Review of prototype design and value analysis to see that it meets user's requirement at minimum cost.	R&D	Quality Control, Marketing
	2. Qualification testing of prototype to assess its functional efficiency, reliability and maintainability.	Quality Control	R&D
	3. Review of manufacturing drawings for producibility, interchangeability of components and standardization.	Process Engineering	R&D, Quality Control
PROCESS PLANNING	1. Process planning and conduct of process capability studies.	-do-	Production, Quality Control
	2. Design and tooling and process control instrumentation.	-do-	-do-
	3. Formulation of quality standards for complete equipment and assemblies.	-do-	Quality Control, R&D

Contd...

	4. Preparation of procurement ment specification for materials and bought out components.	-do-	Purchase, R&D
	5. Formulation of inspection procedures.	Quality Control	Production, Process Engineering
	6. Design/procurement of special test equipments.	-do-	-do-
MATERIAL PROCURE-MENT	1. Capacity verification of vendors.	Purchase	Quality Control
	2. Incorporation of quality requirements in purchase orders.	-do-	-do-
	3. Surveillance of quality at vendor's works.	Quality Control	Purchase
	4. Quality assurance of incoming material.	-do-	-do-
PRODUCTION	1. Operation of process control and data feed back for improvement.	Production	Process Engg. and Quality Control
	2. Process surveillance and inspection/testing of product.	Quality Control	Production
	3. Investigation of defects and causes of out of control process.	-do-	Production and Process Engg.
	4. Analysis of quality data for improvement in the process products.	-do-	Production, Process Engg. and R&D
USAGE AND MAINTE-NANCE	1. Technical advice for proper operation and maintenance	Marketing/ Service	—
	2. Performance feed back on reliability	Marketing	Quality Control
	3. Failure analysis	Quality Control	Process Engg., R&D and Production.

2

Creating Quality by Design

Design is the basic function for the creation of product quality. Unless quality is designed into product, it cannot be achieved during manufacture. The prime aim of the designer is to create a product that will satisfy a customer's need at a price which he is willing to pay. With the introduction of newer and better products as a result of technological progress, the customer is becoming increasingly well-informed and discriminating. Sweeping quality claims made in sales promotion campaigns by aggressive salesmen have aroused the expectations of consumers to fairly high levels and they are not prepared to accept the products which do not come up to their expectations. In a competitive market, the designers have to keep on striving for higher and higher quality levels if their companies are to remain in business.

PRODUCT DEVELOPMENT CYCLE

The product development cycle starts with the assessment of the customer's needs and ends when the design is finally released for bulk production. The main steps in the development cycle are enumerated below:

1. Market survey and analysis of customer's needs.
2. Formulation of design specification.
3. Preliminary design of the product.
4. Design review.

5. Manufacture and evaluation of the prototype.
6. Preparation of manufacturing drawings and product specifications.
7. Pilot production run and adjustment of the design.
8. Release of design for bulk production.

There is no rigid line of demarcation between the various steps mentioned above. Some of the steps may overlap and certain others may be skipped, or may occur in a different sequence.

ASSESSMENT OF CUSTOMER'S NEEDS

The starting point of any design is the user's demand. The more fully this demand is understood, the better is the chance for a design meeting the approval of the user's, often, the customer's themselves are not very clear about what exactly they want from a product. It is here that the quality engineers of the company can help them in deciding about what is required of the product. This can be done by explaining to the prospective customers the variety of features which can be provided in the product and eliciting information about their preferences. Sometimes, a prior market survey cannot be conducted for fear of leaking the information about the new product to competitors. In such cases, the designers, the marketing organisation and the quality engineers have themselves to assume the role of the customer and decide about the desirable features in the proposed product. This exercise of noting customer reaction, even a simulated one, is considered necessary to ensure a reasonable chance of customer acceptance of the product.

FORMULATION OF DESIGN SPECIFICATION

Once the requirements and expectations of the prospective customers have been analyzed, they must be translated into a design specification, which lays down feature targets to be achieved along with constraints, if any. Although a design specification is normally the prerogative of the designers it is always advisable to formulate it in consultation with the quality engineers. They can advise on the technical failings of the previous product of which a newer version is to be designed, so that those drawbacks could be avoided in the new design. A design specification should be a comprehensive document which fully reflects the demands and expectations of the users. All the quality characteristics of the proposed product should be clearly defined, so that the designer knows exactly what is to be achieved.

PRELIMINARY DESIGN

Having given the guidelines in the form of design specifications the designer should be given a free hand in developing the preliminary design of the product. However, if during the process of design it is felt by the designer that a particular feature or characteristic cannot be achieved within the existing framework of the design specification or other constraints, the fact should be brought to the notice of the management. The management can then take one of the following decisions to overcome the difficulty.

(a) Scaling down of the required feature target.
(b) Removal or modification of the constraint preventing realization of the subject feature.
(c) Attempting alternative design.
(d) Incorporation of other features to compensate for the feature which cannot be provided.

Such decision will inevitably involve consolation with quality engineers and the marketing organizations, to analyze its repercussions on other quality parameters of the product and its saleability.

GENERAL CONSIDERATION FOR A GOOD DESIGN

Although functional requirements and methods of their achievement in design will be different for products belonging to different fields of technology, there are certain general requirements which are more or less universal in nature and are applicable in varying degrees to almost all industrial products. These requirements and their methods of achievement are discussed below:

APPEARANCE

To the down-to-earth, practical-minded person, appearance may not be of much importance as long as a product works, but the designer should keep in mind the normal reaction of an average customer when styling the external shape and finish. It should be remembered that first contact of the product with the prospective customer is through its shape and finish, including that of its packing. He is not going to be impressed by a rough and poorly finished product, even if he is told that it works beautifully. The chances are, that he is not going to bother to see it work. At the same time, overemphasis on the shape and finish is also not desirable, as it increases the cost. The styling and finish of the product should be compatible with its function. Generally, it is worthwhile to invest in visual appeal for consumer goods, such as household appliances and automobiles, whereas industrial goods can do with functional styling and essential protective finish. For a good visual effect, sharp lines, corners and abrupt changes of contour should be avoided in the external shape. The surface finish should be smooth and of a soil pleasing colour.

FUNCTIONAL EFFICIENCY

Next to the outwar appearance, functional performance is the only characteristic which a customer looks for in a product at the time of purchase. It hardly needs to be emphasized that the designer has to ensure that the product performs its intended function to the satisfaction of the user.

SAFETY

Safety is a requirement of which the user is not normally aware, until the lack of it is proved to him by an accident causing damage or injury. For certain types of products such as armaments, explosives, aircraft and equipments using high voltages, the importance of safety is well recognized and is given due consideration during design. For certain others, like household appliances, industrial machinery, automobiles, chemicals etc., which are also potentially dangerous, the safety requirement is not so well appreciated. These products can also be made safer if a conscious effort is made during design. The designer should assume that the user of the product is careless, (and occasionally, who is not?) and try to design the product to be accident-proof, as far as possible. Sockets for domestic electrical connections which automatically remain covered when not in use, or machine guards, which switch off the machine when removed, are cases in point. Designers have a very heavy responsibility in the prevention of accidents involving machinery. All power-operated machines and equipments should have built-in safety devices and should be designed on fail-safe principle, *i.e.* when any failure of the equipment occurs it should automatically be brought to safe condition, and should not cause an accident. All indicating devices where incorrect indication can cause accidents, should be designed to error on the safe side and in case of failure, should indicate in the safe direction, as is provided in railway signal equipment. Attention to the minor details of safety feature during design can considerably reduce the accident rate.

RELIABILITY

Any device or equipment should not only function when it is sold, but it should continue to function satisfactorily during its intended life. This ability of continued functioning is called reliability. Reliability, like safety, is not appreciated until unreliability manifests itself in the form of frequent failures. Unfortunately, reliability cannot be readily checked or measured at the time of purchase, yet nothing is more frustrating to the user than an equipment or appliance which is unreliable. Like other quality parameters, reliability also is essentially built-in during design. To design a reliable equipment, careful consideration has to be given to the factors affecting reliability. Basically the reliability of an equipment depends upon the number of components and their own reliability. The lesser the number of components the lesser will be the chance of any one of them failing and the more reliable will be the equipment. The effect of component reliability on the overall reliability of the equipment is obvious. If any of the components are failure-prone, the equipment cannot be reliable. The designer has therefore to keep the number of components to a minimum, and use only components with proved reliability.

MAINTAINABILITY

In spite of all the care in designing for reliability, certain failures are bound to take place during service. The equipment should be so designed that when a failure does take place it can easily be repaired and put back into service. It often happens, that the life of certain components used in the design is much less than the intended life of the equipment. It should be ensured that such components are easily accessible in the product, and their securing and positioning arrangements are such that the components can easily be replaced. The variety of component should be kept to a minimum to ease the spares problem. The tolerances should be so designed that components are interchangeable without requiring any fitting during assembly. In complex equipment, efforts should be made to provide some means by which an indication is automatically given when a system or subsystem fails. This alerts the operator who may be able to take quick remedial measures or at least switch off the equipment to avoid possible further damage. Temperature and oil pressure gauges fitted on the dashboard of vehicles are examples of such indicating devices.

EASE OF PRODUCTION

So far we have been looking at the problem from the user's point of view and trying to provide for his requirements. Now we should look at it from the other side *i.e.* from manufacturing viewpoint. However, excellent a design may be, it may not be possible to exploit it, if it cannot be easily manufactured at a reasonable cost. This is one aspect which designers tend to ignore in the early stages of design, until it is too late. Any design basically consists of a number of components which are grouped in sub-assemblies and assemblies to form the complete equipment. While the detailed design of individual components is being prepared, a thought should be given to the process by which the component will be manufactured during bulk production. For example, if a component is to be produced by die-casting, consideration should be given to metal flow, die draft, location of bosses, fillets and radii etc. before the design is finalized. For components requiring metal finishing, intricate patterns, blind holes, deep cavities and other shapes which may be inaccessible to the scurfing and polishing wheels or where solutions may be trapped, have to be avoided. Facilities should be provided for holding the components during polishing as well as for suspension and good electrical contact during plating. While the production-oriented design of components is important, it is also found that most production difficulties arise during assembly. The design should minimize this problem by having a fewer number of parts with compatible tolerances to ensure easy assembly. When possible, the mating parts should include locating holes and lugs for self-alignment. The provision of elongated holes instead of round holes avoids the build-up of tolerances and facilitates assembly without distortion. To this extent, some knowledge of production processes is essential for the designers. If this is not possible due to the specialized nature of the processes involved, a production engineer should be incorporated in the designs team at least on a part time basis, so that expert advice on production matters is easily available from the earliest stage of design.

STANDARDIZATION

This is a discipline, whose potentialities have been realized only lately. A substantial improvement in quality and economy can be achieved if this aspect is given due consideration during design. The designer should make a conscious effort to keep the variety of the components to the minimum. For example, in a particular place a 5 mm bolt may be adequate from strength considerations, but if at most other places standard 6 mm bolts have been used, it would be advisable to use a 6 mm bolt even in this application. The slight additional cost due to the bigger size will be more than offset by savings resulting from standardization. While designing a system, every effort should be made to use as many components as possible from the existing design of the previous model or other similar standard products used for other applications. Such standard parts will normally be available in the market at a cost much less than that at which they can be manufactured in the company. This will also save time in design, and avoid extended testing to assess their reliability. This incidentally will also help in improving maintainability as discussed earlier.

REVIEW OF DESIGN

Before the preliminary design has progressed further, it should be subjected to a critical review by all those who are connected with the product, such as quality engineers, production engineers and sales personnel. The design review would cover the following activities:

1. To advise the designer regarding components or mechanisms which have not performed satisfactorily, in the earlier models of the design so that these shortcomings can be eliminated in the new design.

2. To identify critical features which are likely to cause problems during bulk manufacture, so as to initiate design changes to avoid manufacturing difficulties.
3. To identify quality characteristics which are likely to require special equipment, so that necessary testing facilities can be created before the product is manufactured.
4. Evaluation of reliability of design by competent engineers, so that design changes, if necessary, can be incorporated before the prototype is produced.
5. Review of test programme for the evaluation of the prototype with particular reference to the environmental conditions, it is to encounter in service.

OTHER DESIGN ACTIVITIES

Once the design review has been undertaken, following residual activities are carried out before production of the prototype.

1. Simulated testing of critical system.
2. Incorporating changes in the design to eliminate shortcomings observed during the evaluation of the prototype.
3. Formulation of testing procedures for bulk production, based on experience gained during the testing of the prototype. Where required, special test equipment is designed or procured for process control during bulk production.
4. While final manufacturing drawings are being prepared, tolerance analysis is undertaken, preferably by a team of production engineers and designers to arrive at the tolerances which are functionally acceptable and can be achieved during bulk production.
5. In case of major equipment, essential documents such as product specification, operator's manual, part list, and servicing and repair instructions should also be prepared after the design is finalized. The quality of these documents enhances the value of the equipment on which the customers often have to invest a considerable amount.
6. Where required, suitable packaging should also be carefully designed, because packaging adds to the customer appeal of the product, and also serves to protect the product during transit.
7. Release of design for production of prototype.

Although the design control procedure discussed above is quite exhaustive, it must be followed for major products to avoid quality problems during actual production or still worse, during usage with customers. However, in case of minor products, certain steps may be omitted and certain others telescoped, to shorten the product development cycle.

Design review may look cumbersome but it is a valuable tool for ensuring quality of a product. Design review may make some changes in the design desirable. These changes or modifications can easily be incorporated at the early stages when the design is on the drawing board. At a later stage, major changes in design are very difficult and may upset the entire time schedule, besides entailing extra cost. In some companies, the preliminary design is also subjected to "value analysis", with a view to reducing the cost of the product without sacrificing its quality. The application of this technique is discussed in chapter 32.

EVALUATION OF THE PROTOTYPE

At this stage of design, the designer will invariably be under tremendous pressure to quickly finish the design and pass it on for production. This is so, because even with the best of forecasting, planning and vigorous progressing of design, the target dates of completion generally arrive too soon. Therefore, there is often a tendency to dispense with detailed evaluation of design and the prototype. It is argued that after all the designer with all his experience, knows what he has done and anyone can see for himself that the prototype functions satisfactorily. Thus there is nothing more to be seen in a formal evaluation. It will be a shortsighted policy to accept such a view, otherwise in trying to save time on evaluation, much more time may be lost and greater difficulties faced later, during production or in service. Some of the snags may be so serious that the whole project or the product may be a failure, resulting in attendant losses and loss of reputation. Therefore, if any thing, the evaluation should be as thorough as time and resources permit. Although the general functioning of a product can be seen by casual observation, it does not provide answers to such questions as its behaviour under diverse environmental conditions, its inherent safety, reliability and the ease of maintaining the required quality level. For instance there is a case where, a new type of viewing equipment was developed for a particular organisation. Due to the urgency of requirement, the equipment was accepted by the organisation without detailed technical trials. During the short period of its service with the users, it was revealed that the equipment had serious functional drawbacks and a very low level of reliability. A major redesign project was undertaken to remove these snags, which along with subsequent evaluation studies took about two years to complete. Thus in trying to save a couple of months, over 2 years were wasted. This could have been avoided, if proper evaluation had been carried out in the first instance.

The evaluation of the prototype should be carried out according to a well-planned evaluation programme, which should clearly lay down aspects to be studied and specific points on which information is required.

It is advisable that evaluation programme be coordinated by an agency different from the designer, so that objectivity of evaluation can be maintained. Generally, the task of coordinating the evaluation programme is entrusted to the Quality Manager. Besides the Design and Quality departments, representatives of other related departments, such as Production and Marketing may also be associated with evaluation programme to achieve breadth of view. As a result of evaluation, certain changes or modifications may be necessary in the design. After these changes and modifications have been carried out, those and other related features should again be subjected to confirmatory evaluation to ensure that the shortcomings of the design observed earlier, have been eliminated. This process of the adjustment of design and evaluation should be continued until a fully satisfactory design is evolved.

PREPARATION OF MANUFACTURING DRAWINGS

This is one of the most tedious and difficult phases of design, yet quality literally depends upon the correctness and completeness of the manufacturing drawings and specifications, because the production agencies manufacture the product according to these documents. If there is any inaccuracy in the drawings, it will obviously be reflected in the product, since the manufacturers take guidance from the drawings and not from the approved prototype. Therefore, it is imperative that the drawings truly reflect the final design as it has emerged after evaluation studies.

Even if the drawings are a precise reflection of the approved prototype, the matter does not end here. With the best of technology and machines, no two products can be exactly alike, which brings us to the problem of tolerances, which are an essential part of the manufacturing drawings. It is generally assumed, that the tolerances of various components are selected for sound technological reasons and are as wide as possible. Unfortunately, this is not always the case. Designers tend to specify closer tolerances than are really necessary, just to be on the safe side. Similar is the tendency in the choice of materials and surface finishes. Much thought and diligence is necessary in arriving at correct tolerances. Although tolerancing is primarily the designers prerogative. Production and Quality engineers with their intimate knowledge of the capabilities of various production processes, can be of immense help. The use of tolerance data on similar previous products and the statistical analysis of tolerances discussed in Chapter 30 can help to provide a rational solution to the tolerancing problem.

FORMULATION OF PRODUCT SPECIFICATION

Specification is an important quality document for the product because it is here that quality of the product as a whole is defined in precise technical terms. Although the user's requirements and design specifications give some indication of the quality features which are desirable in the product, it is the product specification which precisely lays the quality levels which are to be achieved in the bulk production. The specification forms the basis for all trade enquires for the manufacture and supply of the product. It also forms the standard of reference for all subsequent stages of quality management, during manufacture, inspection and shipment. Without imposing undue restrictions on the exact method of manufacture to be followed, the specification should clearly define all the important characteristics to be achieved and also lay down general guidelines as to how these characteristics will be measured, to ensure that these have actually been achieved. Rather than giving details of every test or procedure of measurement, reference should be made to the organisational or national standards, wherever possible. However, if a particular measurement is peculiar to the product and is not covered in widely used standards, details of such tests or other means of quality assurance should be given for the guidance of the production and inspection staff.

Draft Specification is normally prepared by the Design Department on the standard format used by the company. As far as possible this draft should be discussed with Quality Engineering and Manufacturing Departments and their views should be incorporated. Final specification should be issued by the Quality Department, as quality defining is one of their primary tasks.

DESIGN CHANGES DURING PRODUCTION

Even when the design has been released for production, it cannot be considered to be absolutely final, requiring no further changes. Certain problems may be faced during production which may call for changes in design. However, before these changes are approved, their implication and repercussions on quality parameters should be thoroughly gone into by the design and quality engineering departments. Once it is decided to incorporate the design changes, necessary amendments should be carried out in all the affected drawings and specifications. Normally the copies of drawings and specifications are held by various departments of the company. A suitable procedure should be evolved, and communicated to all concerned. Generally, whenever any drawing is amended, the amended copies of the drawing are issued to the concerned sections, who are asked to return the old copies to the design office. A number of quality problems arise where there is no proper system of the updating of drawings. The production operator may continue to carry out machining operations as per the old drawings which have since been amended and the discrepancy may be revealed only in assembly or in final inspection. It is therefore, advisable to have effective control over the distribution of drawings and specifications.

3

Quality Control of the Purchased Product

Every organisation whether a manufacturing company or a consumer organisation needs to purchase a variety of raw materials and products for further processing or consumption. In either case quality of the product is an important factor which has to be given due consideration during purchase. If the store is required for consumption or usage, its quality determines the user satisfaction. If the purchased material is required for further processing, its quality will influence the quality of end product. For example, the physical properties of a metal will determine the durability of the component made from it. Therefore, control over the quality of the purchased product is essential for any organisation. The degree and nature of control will depend upon the needs of the particular organisation. All manufacturing companies in any case have some form of quality control set up for assuring the quality of their own products. The same set up (with some additional help if required) can be utilised to exercise control over the quality of the purchased stores. If the purchaser is a non-manufacturing organisation, such as a sales agency, a government department or a service organisation, it has to have a special organisation for quality assurance of purchased products.

It is generally thought that consumer's quality control organisations is merely an inspection agency and comes in to picture only when the material is being delivered. This is no longer true in the present day context when the products have multiplied in diversity and complexity. No doubt inspection is still an important function of the purchaser's quality organisation, but its main activity lies before the purchase order is negotiated. It is seen from actual experience in many fields that over 70% of the quality problems in the purchased product are caused by vague specifications or misunderstanding of the purchaser's requirement by the producer. Hardly any producer worth the name would knowingly like to supply a product which will not meet the customer's requirement. Therefore, unless the producer is made aware of the exact requirements of the purchaser, quality problems are bound to arise when the product is put up for acceptance inspection, or worse still when the product is being actually used. To avoid these problems the concept of quality management or total quality control can be applied to the purchased product also. Quality control tasks which are to be carried out in various phases of procurement of the product are discussed in this chapter.

QUALITY ADVICE ON THE PRODUCT TO BE PURCHASED

Requirement of the material or product to be procured is generally initiated by the production control in the case of manufacturing concerns, and by the actual user or the stockholder in the case of non-manufacturing concerns. In either case quality organisation can make positive contribution by assisting the indenter in selection of actual product to be procured.

PROCUREMENT OF TRADITIONAL ITEMS

Even if the requirement is of traditional items which the company has been using in the past, it is still worthwhile to refer it to quality control organisation before placing actual order. A well-run quality control organisation will keep itself abreast with the latest developments in the materials and products of interest to the company. It is possible that a new or improved material may have been introduced which may serve the need of the company better than the traditional item which the company has been using. Further there may have been quality problems in the use of the particular material. It may therefore be advisable to make some change in the product specifications or include special warranty clauses in the tender documents to safeguard the company's interest. Unless this aspect is looked into at this stage, it may be difficult to control the quality of the purchased product.

PROCUREMENT OF NEW PRODUCTS

When the product is being purchased for the first time the indenter will normally indicate his requirement in general terms, though he may also give the specific product to be purchased based on manufacturers advertisements or sales brochures. It is the quality control organisation which can make comparative evaluation of the products which can meet the general requirements of the company by analysis of the technical specifications of competing products. Further it may also happen that none of the existing products in the market meet all the company's requirements fully. In such cases manufactures may have to be asked, whether they can provide additional features to meet the special requirement of the company. Study of such problem can best be carried out by the quality engineers of the company.

PROCUREMENT OF PRODUCTS AS PER PURCHASER'S DESIGNS

No manufacturer can afford to manufacture every single item which goes into making of his products. It is often more economical to get some of the components as per their own design manufactured by ancillary companies or subcontractors. In such cases the specifications of such components have to be prepared by the quality control organisation in consultation with company's design engineers. The manufacturing facilities available with the likely ancillary industries have to be kept in view while finalising the product specifications. Some of the major user organisations such as Defence and Railways have their own design element to meet their special requirements. To get stores of a particular design manufactured from trade, it is essential to prepare detailed specification covering all important quality characteristics to enable the prospective manufacturers to submit their quotations. Attention to such details at this stage will avoid protracted correspondence with the contractors seeking clarifications about the product and thus ensure speedy procurement.

DETERMINING QUANTITY TO BE PROCURED

Normally quantity of store to be procured is indicated by the actual user or the stockholder depending upon expected consumption or requirement. While deciding on the actual quantity to be purchased at a time, consideration is also given to the economy which can be achieved by bulk purchase, *e.g.*, by purchasing whole year's requirements at a time rather than making quarterly or half yearly purchases. Against this must be balanced the cost of additional storage space and inventory cost. From these factors optimum quantity to be purchased at a time is worked out. At this stage consideration should also be given to the possible deterioration of the product quality during storage. In some cases this factor may nullify the economic advantage of bulk purchase. To avoid such eventuality, delivery of the product may have to be phased in accordance with the actual consumption rate of course keeping a safe margin for unforeseen interruptions in the supply.

EVALUATION OF SUPPLIERS

Having finalized the product specification and the quantity to be procured, next step is to locate the likely sources of supply. An efficient purchase department normally maintains a comprehensive register of the suppliers of the range of products which are of interest to the company. For traditional items, locating sources of supply is no problem because a panel of approved suppliers is maintained based on past experience. The problems arise only when the traditional sources cannot meet the requirement and new sources are to be established. In such cases the purchase enquiries are generally sent to the firms listed in trade directories for the range of products under procurement. Normally quotations from a number of suppliers may be received in response to the purchase enquiries. Selection of the supplier on the basis of quotation is not as simple as it may look. On account of increasing complexity of the products and stringent specification requirements, the selection can no longer be made on the basis of lowest quotation alone. Low price is meaningless, if the supplier is unable to achieve the desired quality or maintain specified delivery schedule. The vendor may not have the equipment or the expertise to meet the specification requirements. The situation becomes worse if the vendor in turn depends upon purchased components or material, quality of which cannot be vouchsafed.

Selection of viable sources of supply requires proper evaluation of suppliers with respect to their ability to maintain the quality of the product at the desired level, as well as their production capacity. Some of the data required for this evaluation may be already available with the quality control organisation if the firm being considered had already supplied the store in the past. Evaluation of the firm being considered for the first time requires their capacity verification to be carried out by the quality engineers of the purchasing organisation. Final consideration, for placement of order should be limited to only those firms who have the proved capacity to supply the product of required quality and quantity. The choice can then be made on economic considerations.

CAPACITY VERIFICATION

Capacity verification of prospective suppliers is one of the important functions of Quality Control Organisation, which is essential for exercising control over the quality of the purchased product. Capacity verification generally takes the form of survey of vendor's production resources and his ability for their proper utilisation.

Before the quality engineers of the purchasing organisation visit the vendor's works, he may be asked to furnish the necessary data. A form given in annexure to this Chapter can be used to elicit necessary information from the firm. Preliminary study of the data furnished by the vendor may itself indicate that the firm is not capable of executing the order and thus rule out further consideration of the firm. However, if the firm looks promising, the detailed study of the firm's capacity may be carried out by the quality engineers. From the above it should not be assumed that the capacity verification of the vendor is the exclusive preserve of the Quality Department. For accurate assessment of vendor's capability, special expertise wherever available should be utilised. For example, if the manufacture by the vendor involves specialised technology such as chemical processing, heat treatment or vacuum deposition, an expert in the field from the Process Engineering Department may also be included in the capacity verification team. Similarly, if the financial standing of the vendor is in question an expert from Finance Department may also form part of the study team. At the same time precaution should be taken that the capacity verification is not overdone. Considerable tact will be required to elicit necessary information. Any form of criticism of the company should be strictly forbidden. The investigators should confine themselves to only those areas which directly reflect the vendor's ability to execute the order in question. Some companies have got standard questionnaire which the investigators are required to fill. Important aspects to be covered in the questionnaire are given below:-

1. Does the vendor have adequate plant and machinery to ensure required production rate?
2. Do the machines have desired capability to maintain the important quality parameters within acceptable limits?
3. Does the firm have a well-staffed Quality Organisation and a working quality control programme? (This may be evident from the quality control techniques being used for process control).
4. Does the company use considerable number of components purchased from trade or manufactured by subcontractors? If so how does the company exercise quality control on the purchased product?
5. What are the sources of raw materials required by the company? Does the company maintain adequate reserve stock to insulate itself against interruptions in supply of materials? How is the quality of raw materials assured?
6. Does the company have complete testing facilities for the product in question? If not, what alternative arrangements can be made if preshipment inspection is to be carried out?
7. Has the firm executed an order of a product similar to the one being considered? If so details of this order must be obtained.
8. Financial standing of the company.

9. Any other relevant details which reflect the ability of the firm to successfully execute the order in question.
10. Finally, the general attitude of the management of the vendor company towards the quality of their products and their own appreciation of their ability to execute the order are significant pointers which should be noted.

DEVELOPMENT OF SOURCES OF PRODUCTION

In the above discussion it was assumed that the product required was already being manufactured by a number of vendors and it was merely a question of choosing the most suitable supplier amongst them. This by no means is the normal situation at least in the developing countries like India. Quite often the sources of production have to be developed. In this case also capacity verification of potential suppliers who show interest in the product is carried out. However main thing to be looked for in such case is, whether the firm has the minimum essential plant equipment and skilled manpower? Once these basic resources are available, manufacturing capacity can be built up with help of technical guidance from the purchasing organisation. Process engineers of the purchasing company can impart the manufacturing know how to the staff of vendor company and the quality engineers can set up necessary controls to ensure that the quality of the product can be maintained at the acceptable level.

PLACEMENT OF ORDER

After analysis of the quotations and appraisal of the vendors, the purchase department places the order on the vendor who offers the most advantageous terms. While the terms of contract are being negotiated all the requirements of the product and conditions of supply must be put-down in writing and clearly explained to the vendor. A common complaint often heard when the supply is rejected is "This is unfair, we were not told of this requirement when the order was placed." Certain things such as submission of pre-production sample or a particular type of the packaging may be obviously implied by the purchaser, but these may not be so obvious to the supplier. Therefore, attention to details at the time of drafting of supply order saves many an embarrassing and costly situations later when supplies start arriving. Some of the things which are likely to be missed at the time of placing supply order are given below:-

1. If the manufacturing drawing or the product specification makes a reference to the institutional, national or international standard specification it should be clearly mentioned whether the specification issued in a particular year or the latest specification will apply.

2. Where materials are of critical importance it should be clearly laid down whether the materials are to be approved by the purchaser before they are taken into use. In the case of castings the procedure of taking test pieces should be spelt out in detail if these are required by the purchaser's quality department.
3. If pre-production sample is required, the size of the sample, mode of despatch, and the tests to be conducted on the sample should be made known to the vendor.
4. The procedure for sanctioning of deviations from the drawings and specifications, or concessions on certain quality requirements for the manufactured product should be clearly defined. The impression should not be created in the mind of the vendor that if there are minor departures from the drawings or specification, the product will be accepted. In practice it is very difficult to draw a line between minor and major departures from the drawings. Therefore, it should be impressed upon the vendor that he should stick to the drawings and the specification.
5. Place and method of acceptance inspection should be clearly explained to the vendor. If sampling inspection is to be instituted, details of sampling plans to be adopted should be indicated and agreed upon, (Sampling inspection is further discussed in Chapter 27). The procedure for disposal of rejected product and resubmission of rectified lots should also be decided before-hand.
6. Marking of the product with the nomenclature, part number and other details should be made known to the vendor.
7. Warranty clauses and procedure of preferring claims should be defined in detail to avoid different interpretations.

ESTABLISHMENT OF PRODUCTION BY THE VENDOR

After the order is placed with the vendor company, it should not be assumed that the purchaser has nothing further to do with the vendor until the store starts arriving. In the initial stages when the manufacture of the product is being established for the first time, the vendor may require lot of clarifications about the drawings and the specification. In some cases he may request for minor changes in the design to facilitate bulk production in his plant. In other cases he may request permission for use of alternative material due to non availability of specified material. To clarify all these points, quality control organisation of purchasing company would have to study their effect on the quality of the end product. They may have to take the advice of the design or process engineering department regarding design changes before agreeing to the suppliers request. Such requests for changes in design should not be viewed as criticism of the original design. It should be taken as constructive suggestions to facilitate production, and in some cases it may even result in improvement of the quality of the end product.

After initial problems are overcome the vendor should be asked to submit pre-production samples, where provided in the supply order. These samples should be carefully examined in accordance with store specification. Where the pre-production sample are not found acceptable detailed report of the defects should be made available to the vendor. If required, quality engineers or process engineers of the purchasing company may advise the vendor how to prevent the defects and improve the quality of the product. In such cases fresh pre-production samples will be called for and clearance of bulk production should be given only after these sample units are found satisfactory.

INSPECTION OF BULK SUPPLY

While the sources of supply of the product are being investigated, the quality control organisation of the purchasing company would have formulated an inspection plan for the product and set up necessary test facilities. In the initial stages of bulk supply the inspection is generally more rigid. Even where sampling inspection is provided in the contract, first few lots are subjected to 100% inspection. This is done mainly to establish the quality level of the vendor's production. If the quality level of the product is found acceptable, sampling inspection may be introduced. If the quality level is not up to the required standard, the vendor should be informed of the result of 100% inspection and asked to improve the quality of the product. In such cases further inspection may be stopped until the quality of the product is improved. On the other hand if the vendor is able to maintain the quality of the submitted lots at well above the acceptable level, quantum of inspection may be reduced. At a later stage if the quality level constantly remains good, the inspection may be dispensed with altogether and material accepted on the quality certificate of the vendor. However, an occasional sample should still be inspected to maintain some check on vendor's quality control organisation.

QUALITY RECORD OF PURCHASED MATERIAL

Proper record of the quality of material received from various vendors should be kept in a manner that it can be referred when required in future. Normally, a separate card or folder is maintained for each material or part in which details of lots submitted by each vendor and their inspection results are noted. The quality problems experienced with the product and how they were overcome should also be recorded. This data can then form the basis for the review of specification, and inspection methods at the time of subsequent purchases. In addition to the product wise records, separate vendor performance folder should also be maintained, where the resume of the performance of the vendor is recorded. This will be useful in assessment of the vendor's capability to execute future orders.

Annexure

VENDOR REGISTRATION APPLICATION FORM

(Information furnished in this form will be treated confidential)

PART - I – GENERAL

1. Name of the vendor :
2. Registered office address :
3. Factory address :
4. Telex no. :
5. Telephone/Fax/e-mail :
   Office :
   Factory :
6. Nature of the company : Manufacture/Sole Selling Agent/Dealer
7. Nature of the company : Proprietary/Partnership/Private Limited/Public Limited
   (a) In case of a proprietary co. name, address and telephone number of the proprietor :
   (b) In case of partnership co., names and address of the partners, with telephone numbers :
   (c) In case of public/ private limited co. name, address and telephone nos. of the Chief Executive :
8. Total area of the factory :
   Covered :
   Uncovered :
9. Employees:
   (a) (i) Number of technical persons
   (ii) Out of the above, number of personnel employed for QC activities.

(b) Are the minimum requirements experience and qualification laid down for Production Manager and supervisory staff?

(c) Are the minimum requirements experience and qualification laid down for Quality Control Manager & Inspection Staff?

10. Year of commencement of manufacture
11. Annual turnover during last 3 years (The company financial year may be indicated and estimated value given for current year) :
12. Whether adequate facilities are available for
    (a) Water supply :
    (b) Fire fighting :
    (c) Security :

PART - II – TECHNICAL

1. Products for which registration is sought :
2. Manufacturing capacity
3. Brief details of products manufactured
   SL. No. Type Description Annual Production for preceding three years
4. Have your products been tested by any agency? If yes, indicate details. (Copies of Qualification Approval/ Test Certificates/Test Reports may be enclosed)
5. Foreign collaboration, if any
   Production Name & Address of the collaborator Year of collaboration
6. Details of plant and machinery (only major equipment to be listed)
7. Details of laboratory and R&D facilities:
8. Inward Goods Inspection and Quality Control of raw-materials/ bought out items:
   (a) Available test equipments and facilities in the factory.
   (b) Assistance from external agencies :
   (Description of the Test, Name of the Agency carrying out the test)
9. Inspection and Quality Control of finished products:
   (a) Available test equipment and facilities in the factory:
   (b) Assistance from external agencies:
10. Principal customers:
    Name & address of the customer product supplied
    Value of supply (Rs)
    Year of supply

4

Quality Control of Manufacturing Processes

QUALITY PLANNING FOR MANUFACTURE

The quality of a product is initially created during design in the form of design particulars. However, this creation is only on paper, in the form of manufacturing drawings and specifications. Quality is actually built into the product during its manufacture. The manufacture of a product requires a host of activities involving different departments and sections of the manufacturing organisation, having the common aim of achieving the required quality and quantity targets. Planning for manufacture includes the following activities, all of which contribute towards the achievement of quality targets.

1. Selection of processes, machines and tools.
2. Process planning.
3. Design and procurement of jigs, tools and measuring instruments.
4. Planning of process quality controls.
5. Planning the quality control in incoming materials.
6. Planning of the quality appraisal of the final product.

Of these, the activities 1 to 3 are normally carried out by the Process Engineering and 4 to 6 by the Quality Engineering departments. Even though there is a broad division of responsibility, all the above planning jobs will require close consultation between these two departments. For some of the activities, such as process selection and controls, the Production department and other sections concerned will also have to be consulted while formulating the plan. It may again be emphasised, that the quality of the product is not the sole responsibility of the quality department alone. It is the concerted effort of all sections involved in the manufacture, which determines the quality or the final product. Therefore, quality considerations have to be kept in view while planning any manufacturing activity, irrespective of who does the planning. Some of these considerations are discussed in the following paragraphs.

PROCESS CAPABILITY

There has been phenomenal progress in production technology during recent years, to meet the demands of ever increasing variety and quality of the products. In addition to the introduction of new processes, even the traditional metal-forming processes such as turning, boring and milling have undergone vast changes with the introduction of high speed complex equipment such as Numerical Control and other computerised machines. With such a multiplicity of processes available for a job, the selection of an appropriate process is not an easy matter. Choosing a process with over-capability is as bad as choosing one with under capability, because an over-capable process will generally be more expensive and will needlessly increase the production cost. On the other hand, a process with less than required capability will not meet the quality requirement and may lead to excessive rejection and rework, which again will attract additional cost. Therefore, from the economic considerations, we must select a process whose capability matches the quality requirements of the job.

Generally, the approximate characteristics and capabilities of various machines are known in the shop. For example, it will be generally known to the shop foreman that machine 'X' has an accuracy of 0.01 mm, and is suitable for accurate turning jobs. Machine 'Y' gives a pitch error up to a 0.08 mm and is not suitable for fine pitch screw threads. This knowledge of the general characteristics is however, not sufficient for the selection of a machine for a high quality job, because these so-called general characteristics are subject to appreciable variations, by factors such as type of raw material, tools and fixtures and finally, the skill of the operator. At best, this knowledge of general characteristics may be used for rough selection and to narrow down the choice of machines or processes.

It is well known that no machine or process, however accurate and well programmed, can produce identical parts or jobs. Every machine or process has got its own inherent variability which cannot be avoided. It is this variability which determines, the capability of the process or machine. Preliminary assessment of process capability can be carried out by studying the variations in the quality characteristic of a certain number of jobs manufactured by the process under normal operating conditions. The range of variation in the quality characteristic gives the process capability. For example, if steel pins turned on the same setting on a particular machine show a difference in their diameter to the extent of 0.05 mm, we can say that the process capability of the particular machine for steel turning jobs is 0.05 mm. If a component drawing specifies a total tolerance of 0.03 mm in the diameter, the above mentioned machine will not be able to meet this quality requirement and hence is not suitable for the particular component. However, accurate study of process capability can be carried out only when the process is under statistical control. Process capability is discussed in Chapter 25.

PROCESS SELECTION

Once the process capabilities of available processes are known, the process selection is then just a question of matching the process capability with the tolerance specified for the job. As a result of the process capability analysis of available processes, it may be revealed that more than one process is capable of meeting the quality requirements of the product. In such cases further selection will depend upon other factors such as economics of production and availability of the machines or processes. On the other hand, it may also happen that none of the available machines may be able to meet the required tolerances. In that eventuality, a decision is required to be taken at the appropriate level, whether to install a new machine capable of the meeting the quality requirements, or utilise the existing machine, even though some of the products manufactured on the machine are not likely to meet the quality standards and will have to be scrapped. In latter case, 100% sorting inspection will be required to separate the defective parts, so that the quality of the outgoing stores can be maintained at an acceptable level. Although it is not an entirely satisfactory quality situation, as some of the defective products may still slip through inspection and result in customer complaints, it may have to be accepted, particularly if the proposed new machine is too expensive or the batch size is relatively small. To safeguard against shipment of defective product to the customers, arrangements must be made for a thorough preshipment inspection.

PROCESS CONTROL

As processes are subject to various influences such as mechanical, electrical and environmental changes, which tend to deviate the process from its initial setting, the process control aims to regulate the process to counteract these changes, so that the process quality remains within acceptable limits. Process control has assumed greater importance, not only due to increasing emphasis on precision, but because of the fact that the modern high speed processes are simply not economical, unless they remain under control. A process going out of control may result in the production of a large number of defective pieces before it is detected, which may result in considerable loss, besides upsetting the production schedule. Therefore, it is imperative that effective control systems be devised, which are able to detect the deviation in the process at the earliest possible moment, so that corrective measures can be applied before an appreciable quantity of defective work is produced. The ability to control a process requires:-

(a) Knowledge of what is required to be achieved by the process.

(b) Means of knowing what is actually being achieved.

(c) Means of regulating the process.

A process control, to be fully effective must be like a closed loop servo system (shown in Fig.1) which involves detection, analysis, correction feed back and corrective action.

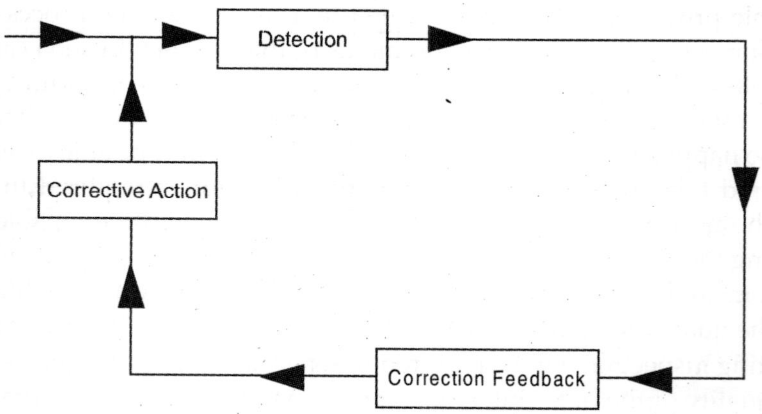

Fig. 1

A typical industrial process control would consist of:

1. Inspection of the product to determine the deviation of the process (detection).
2. Analysis of the inspection result to determine the causes of deviation and correction measures required (Analysis).
3. Transmission of corrective measures to the process operator (correction feedback).
4. Application of corrective measures (corrective action).

The effectiveness of a process control system depends upon the accuracy and speed with which the various elements of control functions are carried out. An indication of the effectiveness of a control system is provided by its reaction time, *i.e.* the time interval between the occurrence of a deviation and the application of corrective action. The reaction time of a process control system can be reduced by employing efficient detection and analysis techniques and by keeping the feed back loop as short as possible. This can be achieved by installing the inspection or other process monitoring systems at the production point itself. This concept is used in modern process controls. It has not only the advantage of short reaction time, but also of generating quality awareness in the production operators, who see for themselves, the results of process changes. However, such controls are not always possible, especially, where the inspection requires extensive test equipment and there are a number of production points. Nevertheless, efforts should be made during the planning of process controls, to keep the process inspection points as near as possible to the production points.

PROCESS CONTROL TECHNIQUES

Over the years various types of control techniques have been evolved to meet the needs of different processes. Some of these are briefly discussed below:

SELF CHECK

This is the simplest of control techniques and has been in use since the dawn of civilisation. As any job or the operation is completed, the operator himself carries out the check of important quality parameters. The check may be visual, or with the aid of simple gauges or instrument. A mason checking the face of a wall with a plumb-line or a carpenter checking the joinery pieces with a carpenter's rule are examples of this control technique. Even with the advancement of technology these simple control techniques have not lost their utility. This can still be effectively employed in relatively simple and low production rate processes, such as those used in cottage industries. Its main advantages are simplicity and short reaction time. Further, it does not need additional staff for inspection jobs. This technique however cannot be employed where inspection needs considerable time or specialised skill.

SPOT CHECK

This is another of the simpler techniques, where rather than checking every piece, a few pieces are checked occasionally to ensure that the product conforms to the specified quality. The spot check may be carried out by shop supervisor or roving inspectors. This control technique is generally used for non-precision processes giving relatively low variability such as press work, stamping and die-casting.

STAGE INSPECTION

Stage or in-process inspection involves inspection of the product after every operation or group of operations where important quality characteristics are developed. This ensures that the defective product is revealed at the earliest stage, thereby avoiding in fructuous expenditure on the further processing of defective components. Stage inspection points are located on the shop-floor itself, where the semi finished components are tendered to the inspection staff after every important stage of processing. During stage inspection, the relevant features of the product are inspected as per drawing specification and only acceptable pieces are released for further processing. Those jobs which are not found acceptable, are returned for rectification if they are rectifiable otherwise they are scrapped. Stage inspection is used for critical items or for those processes where the inherent variability is relatively high and the production of a certain percentage of defective jobs cannot be avoided. However, this method of process control is rather expensive and time consuming and is definitely not suitable for the processes with a high production rate. Further, this method of process quality control is not conducive to generating quality awareness in the production staff. It tends to give the impression that the responsibility of quality is mainly that of the inspection staff and the operator is only responsible for achieving production targets.

STATISTICAL PROCESS CONTROL TECHNIQUES

Statistical method of process control have been developed only in last few decades to meet the needs of complex mass-production processes. The statistical process control techniques are based on the principle that all processes have their inherent variability. If the pattern of this process variability can be established, the trend of the pattern can be used to predict the process quality and apply the necessary correction to keep the process under control. The two main advantages of statistical process control methods are:-

(a) They provide the information about the likelihood of a defective job before it is actually produced.

(b) It does not require physical inspection of each and every piece to maintain a high quality level.

The above characteristics make-statistical process controls ideal for high-volume production processes. Some of the widely used process control techniques are enumerated below:

- Frequency distribution
- Control charts
- Pre-control

The theory and application of these techniques is discussed in Part-III of the book.

MANUFACTURING QUALITY CONTROL

The quality of a product is actually inbuilt during its manufacture, hence manufacturing is the most crucial stage for product quality. Various process control techniques have been discussed in Part-III of the book. The actual planning of a control system and its practical application is discussed below:

A manufacturing control system essentially consists of three elements, namely:

(a) Set-up approval
(b) Process control
(c) Control through final inspection.

The above elements are found in almost every process although one or other element may be predominant, depending on the nature of the process and volume of production.

SET-UP APPROVAL

Set-up when applied to a manufacturing process, refers to the setting up of the process, such as machines, tools, jigs and fixture, temperature, pressure or any other conditions which are essential for correct running of the process. The set-up aims to create proper initial conditions for the manufacture of a product of requisite quality. The setting of a drilling jig for drilling precision holes, or the temperature setting of a furnace for heat treatment is a case in point. Control on set-up is particularly important for processes such as drilling, presswork, broaching, casting, heat sealing, printing, photographic reproduction etc., which although inherently stable, are heavily dependent on the quality of the initial set-up. Set-up control is also important for short run jobs, where the quantity involved is not sufficient to establish statistical control. The effectiveness of a set-up can be checked only by the quality of the manufactured product. The following procedure is generally adopted for approval of a set-up:

First Piece Inspection

The first piece manufactured with the set-up is critically examined for conformance with the drawings and specifications. If certain characteristics do not conform, the set-up is corrected or modified until the manufactured piece fully conforms to the quality requirements.

Pilot Production

The first piece of satisfactory quality merely indicates that it is possible to manufacture the article with the particular set-up; it does not repeal any possible variation from piece to piece. To get this information, a number of pieces manufactured with the set-up have to be checked. Therefore, it is usual to produce a small pilot batch. The pieces of pilot batch are critically examined and the frequency distribution of the important quality characteristics is studied as discussed in Chapter-22. If the frequency distribution shows that the product is within tolerance limits, the set-up is approved for bulk production. If, however, some pieces are found to be beyond tolerance limits, the set-up needs further adjustment.

PROCESS CONTROL

Approval of the set-up only ensures that proper initial conditions for the process have been achieved. It is well established that the initial conditions of the process can change during production run, which may affect the quality of the product. Therefore, it is necessary to monitor the process to detect significant changes, so that necessary corrective measures can be applied, before defective articles are produced. For the purpose of control, the processes can be considered under two broad categories, viz., machine-dominant processes and operator-dominant processes, which are discussed below:

MACHINE-DOMINANT PROCESSES

Under this category are processes such as automatic machining, screw cutting, filling and continuous flow chemical processes, where the machine or plant has the dominant influence over the product quality. Control on these processes can be exercised by the use of techniques such as $\bar{x}$ and R control charts, Pre-control and Process Sampling, which have been discussed in earlier chapters.

OPERATOR-DOMINANT PROCESSES

These are the processes which have not been fully engineered and to a large extent depend upon the skill and alertness of the operator. These include processes such as painting, arc welding, soldering, assembly, adjusting and testing operations. Since the faults in such operations are generally caused by human failings, they occur in a random manner and do not follow any set pattern. However, over a period of time every operator acquires a relatively stable "error rate" (the average number of faults for a particular quantity of products manufactured). The error rate of different operators varies considerably depending upon their skill and attitude towards quality. The probability of occurrence of defects can be related to the error rate of the operator which can be used as a basis for control. Suitable techniques for the control of such processes are 'P' charts and 'C' charts as discussed earlier. The control charts of various operators should be prominently displayed near their places of work to induce them to better their performance by reducing their error rate. Improvement in the process will also require training and motivation of operators.

CONTROL THROUGH FINAL INSPECTION

Ideally, when well-planned process controls are installed, there may be no need for any final inspection. But in reality it is seen that the process controls are not foolproof. A number of things may affect the process control; for instance, calibration of test equipment may go wrong, there may be an error in calculation, or some other unforeseen factor may crop up, resulting in the production of defective product. Further process controls are generally installed only for important stages of the process and may not cover all quality characteristics. Therefore, it is a sound practice to have some kind of final inspection, to verity the quality of the end-product. It also serves as a monitoring device to check the effectiveness of process controls. Final inspection need not be 100% inspection for the entire product. Except in the case of major equipment such as vehicles or weapon systems, it is generally based on sampling plans. Which provide an adequate check. The results of final inspection, particularly the defects found in the rejected items, should be analysed to determine the operations responsible for the defects. This data should then be fed to the production shop for suitable remedial measures. The shop foreman may caution the concerned personnel and ask them to pay more attention to the particular operation, or the process engineer may design a foolproof jig to avoid recurrence of similar defects, Thus, final inspection, besides providing assurance of outgoing quality, serves an important purpose in improving and controlling the process.

PLANNING PROCESS CONTROL NETWORK

The process controls discussed so far, mainly pertain to the activities which are required to be carried out at any particular stage of the process. Often, the final product will comprise of a number of components and assemblies, some of which may be purchased items and others may be processed in the same plant where the final product is assembled. To ensure the satisfactory quality of the end product, quality control should cover the various stages of manufacture of all components and assemblies which are processed in the plant. In addition, it should also cover the quality assurance of all incoming materials and components. This will require a network of control stations located at strategic points in the plant. At each control stations, the quality characteristics to be controlled, should be clearly defined, and adequate test equipment and trained staff should be provided to carry out this function. Detailed instructions covering the integrated quality control network have to be issued to ensure the smooth working and success of the quality control programme. These instructions should include:-

(a) Quality characteristics to be controlled.
(b) Delegation of responsibility for the control station.
(c) Procedure for the drawing of samples test pieces and methods of checking/testing of the quality parameters.
(d) Procedure for the analysis of inspection data including criteria for taking decisions regarding, acceptance of process/product quality.
(e) Procedure for transmission of information about the process quality to the production point and responsibility for carrying out process adjustment.
(f) Procedure for the feedback of information to the process planning and quality planning departments.

To plan a process control network, it is first necessary to have a flow process chart for all the components and assemblies. From this chart, a note is made of critical points where important quality characteristics are generated. Then, depending upon the nature of the process and the quality characteristic of the product, a decision is taken, regarding the control technique to be employed at each of the critical points. The exact location of the control station will depend upon the control technique, location of production points and availability of the test equipment. For example, if a particular quality parameter can be easily checked without elaborate test equipment it may be decided to use control chart mounted on the processing equipment itself and the operator himself or his supervisor may be asked to take measurements and maintain the control chart. On the other hand, the inspection of a component may require considerable time and expensive test equipment and there may be a number of machines producing the same component. In such a case one control station, located at a convenient place, may be established, where components produced by all the machines may be brought for post-process inspection. To economise on the deployment of quality control staff, common control stations may be established for controlling the quality of a number of components. Alternatively, one quality inspector may be made responsible for a more than one control station and thus act as a roving quality controller. Control stations should be so organised that they fall in the normal flow of the process and require a minimum of handling and movement of stores. Particular care should be taken to see that the control stations do not create bottlenecks in the process and the capacity of an inspection station is commensurate with the production rate of the process. A process control network is illustrated in Fig. 2.

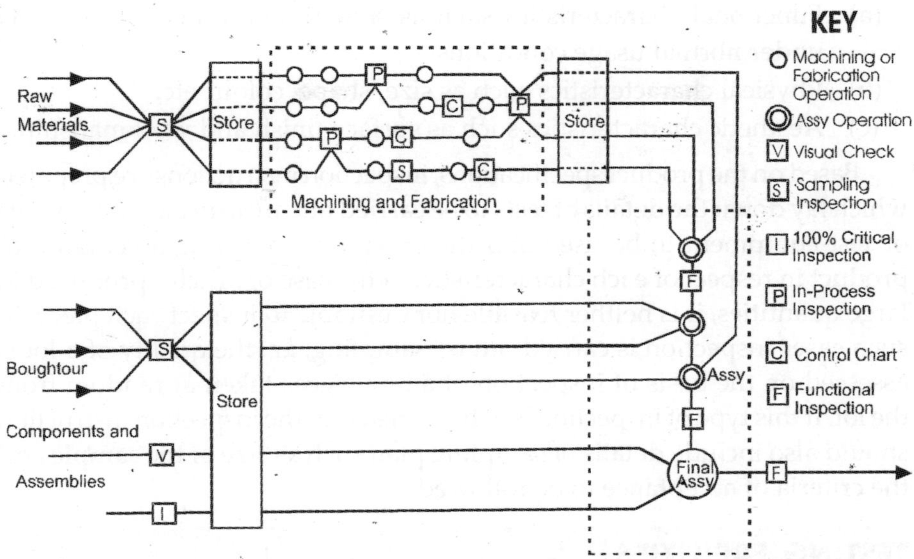

Fig. 2: Process Control Network

FINAL INSPECTION

In an ideal situation, when the manufacturing operations including process controls are carefully planned, and supervised, there may be no necessity for final inspection. But such a situation hardly exists in practice, because men are fallible, machines can be erratic and process controls can never be fool proof. Therefore, it is a sound practice to have some means of appraisal of the out going product to safeguard the quality reputation of the company. Final inspection in addition to being an appraisal function, includes a decision on the acceptance of the product, which involves:

(a) Interpretation of the specification.

(b) Testing or measurement of the product.

(c) Arriving at a decision about acceptance of the product by comparison of (a) and (b).

(d) Disposal of the acceptable and non acceptable products.

Planning and conduct of inspection is discussed below:

INSPECTION PLANNING

Inspection planning can start after the product specification is finalised. First job in the inspection planning is to identify the characteristics which are to be checked in the final inspection. These will include

(a) Functional characteristics such as smooth and efficient operation under normal usage conditions.
(b) Physical characteristics such as size, shape, colour etc.
(c) Aesthetic characteristics such as surface finish and workmanship.

Based on the product specifications, inspection instructions are prepared which lay down the details of tests to be carried out, measuring instruments or test equipment to be used and the criteria for deciding acceptance of product in respect of each characteristic. In the case of articles produced in large quantities, it is neither feasible nor desirable to inspect each piece. In such cases inspection is carried out by sampling, *i.e.* the quality of a lot is assessed on the basis of inspection of a few pieces taken at random from the lot. If this type of inspection is to be carried out, the inspection instruction should also include details of sampling plan such as size of the sample and the criteria of acceptance to be followed.

TESTING FACILITIES

During planning of inspection, consideration should also be given to the flow of product through the inspection station. The inspection station or stations should be so planned that they are in the normal route of the product so that additional movement and handling of the product is avoided. In case the inspection does not involve elaborate test equipment, mobile inspection stations may be organised, so that these can be installed where required. As far as possible the inspector should move to the product rather than vice versa. In addition to inspection stations where the product may be inspected visually or with the help of simple instruments, there is often a need to have separate Test Laboratory, where exhaustive tests can be carried out. The equipment required in the test laboratory will depend upon the type of products and the size of the company. For instance a large company producing automobile parts may need a laboratory having metallurgical testing facilities as well as metrology instruments for precision measurements.

A company making radio communication equipment will need considerable electronic test equipment and environmental testing facilities, to enable testing of equipment under simulated environmental conditions. Whatever test equipment is installed, it is essential that it should be maintained in such a condition that test results can be relied upon. For this purpose there should be a proper system of periodic calibration, so that accuracy of each instrument is verified at regular intervals. Sometimes the volume of production of a company does not warrant having its own test laboratory. In such cases it is cheaper to utilize the services of a competent Government laboratory or a private test house by payment of normal charges for each test.

CONTROL OF PRODUCT DURING INSPECTION

Inspection of product takes time, which may extend from a few hours to a number of days, depending upon the nature of the product. It is necessary to exercise suitable control on the movement of the product through the inspection area to avoid mix-up of accepted and rejected stores which in some cases (like pharmaceutical products) could be catastrophic. Preservation of components during this phase of activity needs appropriate attention. Some of the measures adopted for this purpose are given below:

(a) Inspection area should be secure. If possible it should have locking arrangement to prevent unauthorised entry and removal of stores.

(b) All stores coming in or going out of inspection area should carry written authorisation from the Inspection section.

(c) Clear labels (preferably having different colours) should be provided for the following types of stores, while they are in inspection area.

   (i) Stores awaiting inspection.

   (ii) Stores under inspection.

   (iii) Accepted stores.

   (iv) Rejected stores.

(d) Where possible different areas or compartments should be arranged for keeping various categories of stores.

(e) Where more than one batch is under inspection at a time, the identity of different batches should be maintained by allotting suitable batch numbers.

(f) After inspection and award of sentence, acceptable and rejected products should be properly segregated.

(g) Acceptable product should be stamped with acceptance mark. In case of major products where each piece is identified by a manufacturer's registered number, acceptance mark may be stamped on the inspection card or slip attached to it. For items of very small size, the acceptance mark may be affixed on the box or carton in which the product is kept. Whatever method of stamping or labeling is employed, it should be ensured that it is not easily erased or detached from the product, at least up to the time the product is finally packed and shipped.

DISPOSAL OF REJECTED PRODUCT

The product which is rejected in final inspection represents a direct loss to the manufacturer. Therefore most companies have a system of review of the rejected product. This review is generally carried out by a committee, comprising representatives of Production and Quality departments, which takes decisions on the following issues.

(a) Quantity of stores to be accepted for sale as 'second quality'.
(b) Quantity of stores to be salvaged by rectification or repair.
(c) Stores to be finally scrapped.

Once the decisions are taken, different categories of stores should be suitably marked and removed from the inspection area as soon as possible to avoid their mix up with other stores.

DEFECT INVESTIGATION

With the best of process planning and control certain defect may still be revealed during assembly or in final inspection. In that situation proper investigation must be carried out jointly by the quality engineers and the process planners to identify the causative factors. It is not enough to locate the component or material which is causing the defect. The study should be continued until the basic cause is traced, which in most cases would point to the lapse or shortcoming on some one's part. The designer may have laid down incompatible assembly and component tolerances. The jig provided by the process planner may not be suitable or a die might have worn out. A process control equipment may be out of calibration, or simply the operator may not be able to understand the drawing. Whatever is the cause, effective remedial measures must be taken to avoid reoccurrence of the defects.

QUALITY AUDIT

Quality audit is an appraisal of the whole quality control system. It is not so much concerned with the quality of the product, as with the adequacy and effectiveness of the quality control system. Quality audit may be conducted periodically, or only when occasion demands, due to existence of quality problems. Quality audit includes the examination of the following aspects:

(a) Completeness and clarity of the manufacturing drawings and specifications and procedure for their updating.
(b) Process capability of manufacturing equipment and adequacy of process controls.
(c) Quality control of incoming materials and procedure of vendor's capacity verification.
(d) Adequacy and accuracy of gauges and test equipment and procedure for their calibration.
(e) Quality organisation and quality control procedures.
(f) Reject rate of the product as revealed by in-process and final inspection results.

In addition to the above, samples of the important products may be taken for critical inspection in the laboratory. The number and type of defects in the samples will provide an index of the effectiveness of the control system. To be effective, audit must be independent of the established inspection and process controls. Audit results should be properly documented and forwarded to the Quality Manager as well as to the concerned divisions and the sections of the company. Any discrepancies revealed in the audit should be rectified within a reasonable period. Follow-up action can be progressed by the Quality Manager under whose aegis quality audit is normally carried out. A word of caution here is, that quality audit should be regarded as a tool to help in improving the quality of a product and not for witch-hunting and punitive action. Quality audit requires the active cooperation of all departments and sections concerned with the quality of the product. This cooperation may not be forthcoming if there is fear front quality audit.

5

Sales and Product Quality

QUALITY MAKES SALES

The two main factors which influence purchasing decisions are the price and the quality of a product. However, a customer considers the product quality first (to see that it meets his purpose) and enquires about the price later. It is well known that in a competitive market, the sale of a product may suffer if it is priced too high. What is not so well appreciated is, that a product can also be driven out of market on account of its poor quality. To quote J.M. Juran, an authority on quality control, "It is possible to fail in business even though the quality of the product is good. However, it is not possible to stay in business if the quality is poor, unless one has a monopoly." It is therefore essential, that the importance of product quality in creating and maintaining sales is realised by everyone in the company, and conscious efforts are made to achieve a high standard of quality to enhance the sales appeal of a product.

QUALITY AS AN AID IN COMPETITION

Quality is a potent weapon-in competition, sometimes even more effective than price. For instance, a particular line of a company may be losing sales to a competing product being sold at a lower price. The company may not be able to reduce the price of its product due to factors such as higher cost of labour, or unfavourable location of the plant. In such a situation, it could mount an attack on the quality front. By improving the quality of its product, it may take it out of the competing product's class. For the success of this strategy, there should be a distinct improvement in quality, so that the product is visibly superior to the competing brand and can justify a higher price. The use of quality as a weapon may take other forms, such as better 'after-sales service' and longer guarantee periods. However, this should be backed by improved quality and reliability, otherwise the company may lose on excessive claims, which can also deal a serious blow to the company's quality reputation.

DEVELOPMENT AT QUALITY REPUTATION

Any salesman will tell you, that the quality reputation of a company is a great asset which makes selling very much easier. It also helps in growth and diversification. Let us say, a company making kitchen appliances has been able to establish a good reputation for the quality of its products. It will be easy for the company to enter the field of other consumer goods. A customer who has had a happy experience with the cooking range manufactured by the company, would not require much convincing to purchase vacuum cleaners marketed by the same company.

How is the quality reputation established? One obvious answer may be high-powered advertisement. No doubt, a quality image can initially be created by a well-directed sales promotion campaign, but the image will not endure, unless the words are matched by deeds. A lasting quality image can be created only if everyone in the company, right from the chairman downwards, makes it his business to please the customer. A satisfied customer is the best advertisement for the quality image of any company. There arc too may companies who pay lip service to quality because it is an 'in' thing, but have no qualms while passing shoddy goods to the customer. It may appear to be good business for a short while, but in the long run, it can do irreparable damage to company's quality reputation, with disastrous consequences.

A company's concern about quality should be reflected in the policy statement outlining company objectives. Once it is known that the top management is serious about maintaining the quality of its products, it will create the right climate for the quality assurance and every one in the company will strive for the achievement of this objective. Specific means of establishing a quality reputation are:

(a) Ensuring that the only those products are sold, which fully meet the customer's needs.

(b) Arranging the prompt and courteous adjustment of warranty claims, should the product fail.

(c) Providing efficient after-sales service.

Of the above, the first depends upon the quality of design and manufacture, which has already been discussed in preceding chapters. The other two fall within the responsibility of the sales organisation are discussed below:

AFTER-SALES SERVICE

We have seen in earlier chapters that reliability and maintainability are important quality parameters for certain types of products. It should be realised that however good a product may be when it is new, it is of little use if it cannot be easily maintained in a serviceable condition during its intended life. In addition to the inherent quality of a product, effective after-sales service is an important element in ensuring reliability and maintainability. Therefore, customers are increasingly becoming aware of the need for efficient after-sales service and this, factor exerts considerable influence in purchasing decisions. The need for after-sales service varies from product to product. The minor products for one-time use needs practically no service. On the other hand major mechanical and electrical products, such as automobiles, major domestic appliances, and industrial machinery require considerable service facilities to maintain them in an operational condition.

After-sales service does not consist only of maintenance and repair facilities. It covers all post-sale efforts aimed at ensuring maximum user satisfaction. The need for these services is felt because of the fact that even with the most effective, quality control measures, the product may still not meet the expectation of the user. This may not necessarily be due to the poor quality of the product. It can be due to various other reasons, such as the ignorance of the customer regarding product capability, incorrect usage, or maintenance, unduly harsh environmental conditions etc. Whatever be the reason for the product not meeting expectations, the user will tend to put the blame on the quality of the product, unless the real cause is explained to him. An unsatisfied customer is not a very desirable advertisement for the company and therefore, in its own interest, the company should take pains to ensure that the customer is satisfied as far as possible, in any case, it should be realised that in all fairness a customer who had paid for the product, should get this money's worth in the form of product service. Unfortunately, in India and other developing countries, most companies, due to their shortsighted policies, do not pay adequate attention to this aspect of marketing and still manage to remain in business. This is due to the peculiar market conditions prevailing today, such as shortage of goods, absence of competition, and the unquestioning customer. However, these conditions will not remain for long and those companies which do not change their attitude towards the customers will be forced out of business.

For the orientation of quality policies and attitude towards the customer, we have a model in M/s Sears Roebuck of the USA, who have gone to extraordinary lengths in an attempt to ensure total customer satisfaction. In their early years of business, their customers mainly consisted of fanning community. Their policies earned them the well-deserved sobriquet, 'Sears, the fanners friend'. Their attitude to the customers helped them to achieve a phenomenal rate of growth. The emulation of their example will pay rich dividends in the long run, to a company in any field of business.

PLANNING AFTER-SALES SERVICES

Important elements in after-sales service are,

(a) Education of the customer.
(b) Maintenance and repairs where required.
(c) Looking into customer complaints.

Each of these elements require careful planning, organisation and coordination, which is discussed in the following paragraphs.

EDUCATING THE CUSTOMER

Educating the customer is one of the normal jobs of sales personnel. Before a customer buys anything, he must know about the characteristics and the capabilities and the product, to enable him to decide whether it will meet his requirement. Advertising and other sales promotion programs, such as demonstration of the product and the issue of free samples, partly fulfils this need. However, in the case of major equipment and machinery the education of the customer does not end with this perfunctory introduction. It may require the issue of brochures, booklets or technical manuals, giving complete information about the product, its characteristics and capabilities, as well as instructions for installation, operation and maintenance. These documents should be written in a language which the prospective customer can understand. Further, it may call for the organised training of the customer or his representatives in operation and maintenance, so that maximum benefit can be obtained from the purchased equipment. This activity is normally coordinated by the marketing division, although the technical publications are generally prepared by the design department in consultation with the quality engineering department. Personnel from other technical departments may also be drawn for organising the demonstration of the equipment and training of the customer's staff.

MAINTENANCE AND REPAIR

Most of the machines and pieces of major equipment, however, well designed and manufactured, still require some attention in the form of preventive maintenance and occasional repairs, to be able to perform their intended function for any length of time. When a customer buys a piece of equipment or machinery, he expects the supplier to provide maintenance, advice, and servicing and repair facilities, as and when required. Most of such machinery is normally covered by a warranty, whereby the supplier is legally bound to provide these services up to a stipulated period. The efficient provision of these services will require the following:

(a) ***Creation of a Service Organisation:*** Normally, the service organisation is a branch of the sales department and is manned by technical staff which has an intimate knowledge of the subject machines or equipment, so as to be able to provide technical advice regarding installation, operation, maintenance and repair.

(b) ***Setting up of Repair Facilities:*** Servicing and repair centres may be set up and managed by the company itself, or it may issue licences to other repair agencies to provide these services on its behalf. In either case, it will be the company's responsibility to provide repair manuals, the training of the repair agency staff, special tools, equipment, spare parts and other accessories required efficient maintenance and repair. The company should also arrange for periodic quality audits of the repair agencies to assure itself that the quality of repair is of the required standard.

(c) ***Feedback on Repair Problems:*** Quality engineers of the company should maintain close liaison with the repair agencies, because many inadequacies in the quality of the product, are brought out only during repair. The repair agency should be encouraged to report all unusual defects which could possibly be attributable to faulty design or defective manufacture, or where the rectification of defects is difficult. The analysis of these defect reports could result in improvement in design, process of manufacture or repair techniques.

GUARANTEE OF QUALITY

The guarantee of quality is primarily meant to protect the customer, should the product purchased by him turn out to be defective. This often takes the form of an undertaking by the selling company, that it will replace the article free of charge or refund the money if the product is found to have any defect attributable to improper materials or faulty manufacture. Producers often use guarantees to convince customers about the quality of their products. This is particularly useful when a new product is marketed.

The guarantee is a powerful sales tool if used properly, but like all powerful weapons, it can cause considerable harm if misused. There may be the temptation to use it only as a sales gimmick and the company may not have any serious intention to honour its guarantees. (Technical excuses for disowning the claim, can always be found). However, in such cases, sales boost will be short-lived, and it may do more harm than good, because dissatisfied and cheated customers are the worst advertisement a company can have. Even if the company is honest and means to honour the guarantees, the desired results may still not be achieved, unless care is taken to attain and maintain specified quality levels. Otherwise, extravagant guarantees may pile up quality claim from customers, which if fulfilled, may turn any possible profit into loss. Further, even though financial loss to the customers may be prevented by the company by providing guarantees, product failures do cause annoyance and inconvenience, which affect the quality reputation of the company. Therefore, guarantees which are to be offered for a product, must be carefully considered in relation to the quality inputs, such as design efforts, process planning and control, and quality-appraisal activities. Some of the considerations for planning quality guarantees, are given below:

FIELD SERVICE DATA

Guarantees should be based on field service and/or extensive laboratory test data. For instance, if it is found that the normal life of a product ranges from 500 to 1000 hours, it should be unwise to guarantee it for much more than 500 hours, even though the average life may be nearer 800 hours. When a product is guaranteed for a certain period, the customer expects it to function perfectly during its guaranteed life. If the product fails earlier, he feels that it is substandard, apart from which, any failure within the guarantee period is a direct loss to the company, since free repair/replacement has to be provided.

IDENTIFICATION OF PARTS TO BE COVERED

In the case of major equipment, it is not necessary that every single part of the equipment should be guaranteed by the company. If certain standard bought out parts are used in the equipment, which are guaranteed by their respective manufacturers, these could be excluded from the guarantee of the company manufacturing the main equipment. For instance, the tyres fitted on cars are covered by the guarantee of the tyre manufacturer and not that of the car makers. Certain other items of a brittle nature, which can easily be damaged by mishandling may also be excluded from the guarantee, because it is difficult to say whether any particular damage has occurred due to a manufacturing defect or mishandling. This practice is followed by the manufacturers of electrical appliances whose guarantee does not cover glass, porcelain and Bakelite parts.

Terms of Guarantee

The terms of the guarantee should be clear and unambiguous, leaving no scope for misunderstanding or conflicting interpretation. A guarantee card should include the following informations:

(a) Period of validity

(b) Liability of the manufacturer

If it is free repair or replacement it must be stated as to who will have the option. Generally it is the manufacturer who decides whether an article is to be repaired or replaced.

(c) Procedure of submitting guarantee claims

This should include the responsibility for the dispatch of a defective article if it is to be sent to the company or their accredited service station.

(d) Conditions which make the guarantee invalid

Such conditions may include accidents, mishandling, improper use, or repair by an unauthorised agency.

ORGANISATION FOR EVALUATION OF CLAIMS

The adjustment of guarantee claims is generally the responsibility of the sales department. Since the investigation of complaints involves thorough technical knowledge of the product, this task may be entrusted to the service engineers who form part of the sales department. Alternatively, guarantee claims may be investigated by the quality control department. The latter has better know-how and testing facilities for proper analysis, but being centralised, if may take longer for the claims to be finalised, causing further annoyance to the customers. Often a compromise is found, the minor claims being settled by the regional service centers, and major ones being referred to the central quality department. Whatever procedure is adopted, it should be simple and should ensure that the claims are speedily decided. Nothing is more frustrating to a customer than a protracted correspondence about the adjustment of a guarantee claim.

ADVERTISEMENT OF QUALITY

So far, the advertisers have been mainly playing up the design features of the product. Quality of conformance has hardly figured in any advertisement, yet it can be powerful plank for any sales promotion campaign. Quality control activities during the manufacture of a product has great potential for advertisement, which can be exploited particularly for the well-informed market of industrial goods. It may however be mentioned, that the advertisement of quality of conformance must be based on facts and not merely the imagination of a creative artist. Lasting sales cannot be built on words alone. In the ultimate analysis there is no substitute for the genuine quality of the product which alone can sustain sales. Advertisement merely helps in the full exploitation of quality where it has been achieved.

QUALITY IMPROVEMENT THROUGH CUSTOMER FEEDBACK

The raison detre of all business is the customer. All functions such as design, production and distribution, aim to secure his pleasure (of course at a cost), by the satisfaction of his needs. Therefore, his reaction to any product plays a vital part in moulding the quality of a product. The sales organisation plays an important role in improving the quality of a produce by providing a feedback of the customer's needs and preferences. It is generally the customer's need, which starts the life cycle of a product. Sometimes, a product appears first and the customer's need is generated afterwards. Even in such cases, there is the necessity of obtaining a consumer reaction before the product is produced on a mass scale. Prospective customers may like the general idea of a new product, but may not like it in the form in which it has been presented, or certain additional features may be required to make it more useful.

Since sales personnel are in direct touch with the customer, they are in the best position to advise about his requirements and expectations. Customer reaction on specific products or ideas is normally obtained by a market survey, which is generally conducted through the sales organisation, although some companies may have special staff for this purpose. Quality improvement does not finish when bulk production has been established. It is a continuing process. Therefore, the sales organisation should ensure that there is a continuous feedback of the customer's needs (which may keep on changing) and his problems with the company's products. It is this feedback which stimulates ideas for the newer models of the product that are offered for the greater satisfaction of the consumer, which in turn help the sales to grow.

6

Organising Effective Quality Management

THE NATURE OF ORGANISATION

Organisation is one of the most important elements of management in any field of human activity. Essentially it is a concept, the application of which enables work to be done efficiently. No person, however brilliant, energetic or versatile, is capable of being a 'master of all trades'. There are always jobs which one can do better than others. Organisation makes use of specialization, by allocating specific jobs to those who are considered most suitable for the subject jobs. Secondly, it enables the establishment of effective communication between workers and supervisors. Finally, it establishes relationships between different groups engaged in similar or different jobs so that the efforts of all the groups can be integrated for the achievement of common objectives. According to Luis A. Alien, "organisation is the process of identifying and grouping the work to be performed, defining and delegating authority and establishing relationships for the purpose of enabling people to work most effectively together in accomplishing objectives."

WHY DO WE NEED ORGANISATION?

By organisation here is meant, formal organisation. For a very small establishment comprising of only a few persons, there may be no need for any formal organisational structure. This may be so, because everyone fully understands everyone else and they know their limits of responsibility and authority. In any case, even if anyone oversteps or neglects his position, the person in charge is immediately available to correct, the erring employee.

On the other hand, in a relatively large company the benefit of the close proximity of the boss is absent. Therefore, the rules of the game of business have to be formally laid down, so that everyone knows exactly what he is required to do, and what the limits of his authority are. Thus, it makes for harmonious human relations and reduces the chances of misunderstanding and error. The other advantages are:-

(a) It provides for the optimum use of resources.

(b) It stimulates creativity by removing routine burdens from those who are supposed to do creative thinking.

(c) It aids in the correct evaluation of individual contributions.

In short, it facilitates effective management.

ORGANISATION FOR QUALITY MANAGEMENT

For the management of any activity, there is no single system or set of systems of organisation which can be adopted. Organisational structures are as varied as there are businesses of functions and the men who manage them. For designing the organisation structure for the management of quality, we must know the factors that influence this activity. The rational consideration of these factors will give us a clue to the type of organisation which will be most suitable for a particular business. These factors are briefly discussed in the following paragraphs:

COMPANY POLICIES AND OBJECTIVES

Any organisation exists for the purpose of achieving certain stipulated objectives, and therefore every component of the organisation should strive towards their achievement. Any element or component which does not contribute towards this end, is redundant and has no place in the organisation. When related to quality management, the philosophy and attitude of a company has a marked influence on the organisation. How important is quality to them? How much emphasis is to be laid on quality? A particular management may feel that their products do not require elaborate quality programme. The market conditions may be such that almost anything will sell. Therefore, to maximize profits they may utilize the opportunity to go full steam towards the production of greater numbers without much regard to the quality of the product. In any case, they may feel, the inspection department is there to remove exceptionally bad jobs. On the other hand, another company may take a longterm view and may make quality as one of the major company objectives with a view to winning the confidence of customers and establishing a positive quality reputation, which will help them in further growth and the securing of a sizeable share of the market. Also, this stance towards quality management may be due to a desire to gain an edge over competitors by making higher quality a major plank of their sales promotion campaign. This may require the establishment of elaborate organisation for quality engineering and control, so that the resultant product justified the quality claims made by the firm.

TYPE OF BUSINESS

All business can be broadly categorized into two classes:

(a) Traditional business, with fixed methods of manufacture, and specific customers. The safes are generally assured by long-term contracts or through an established sales agency.

(b) Diversified business covering many product types, and requiring flexibility and constant innovations to meet changing market conditions.

In the former case, the products are well established and few quality problems are likely to arise. Hence a comparatively small quality organisation can meet the requirements. On the other hand, a company of the latter type has to make considerable effort towards new design and development, and consequently a considerable number of problems relating to quality can be expected to arise. Therefore, in this case, a specialised and sizeable quality organisation will be required.

TYPE OF PRODUCTS

Quality requirements and parameters vary widely with different products. Precision machine tools, automobile components and sophisticated electronic equipments to name a few, may require elaborate measures such as design evaluation, process controls and after-sales services to ensure that the product meets the customer's requirements. On the other hand, brick kilns and timber industries need only a little care on the part of the workers and the supervisors. Thus, quality organisation will depend upon the nature and needs of the industry.

COMPANY SIZE AND ORGANISATION

It should be clearly understood that the quality management is a staff and service function and exists for the sake of providing service to the other sections of a company. It has no independent existence for its own sake. Therefore, it has to mould itself to suit the organization of the company. The restructuring of the company organisation to fit a specific type of quality organisation is analogous to "the tail wagging dog." If it is a small company employing only a few persons, the various essential quality functions may have to be amalgamated in a single position held by one individual. In case the company cannot afford even this, quality management tasks may be allocated to an individual dealing with production or sales, as an additional responsibility. On the other hand in large corporations with plants in widely separated areas, the quality organisation has to be such that quality services are available to all the components of the corporation, which need them. To work out the actual organisation, a decision has to be taken, as to which elements of quality management function should be centralised for economy and effectiveness, and which should be delegated to individual plants or divisions. This in turn depends upon the degree of centralisation in other functions like design and engineering. The organisational pattern should be such that expert advice on all matters relating to quality is available to the higher management and at the same time, specialised quality services are provided with ease, down to the shop floor level in various plants.

The organisational structure of the company itself suggests the type of quality organisation that may be required. In a functionally organised company, most of the quality functions will be centrally directed by the Quality Manager, whereas in a divisional type of company structure, the bulk of the quality functions may be delegated to the various divisions. Only those services may be centrally retained, as are necessary for providing advice to the management, or because their economics prevent their being divided. At the same time, the effective channels of communication should be established, to ensure that specialised quality services can be available at whatever point in the company organisation, they are needed.

MARKET AND CUSTOMERS

As already mentioned, the circle of quality begins and ends with the customer. It starts with the assessments of his requirements and ends when these requirements have been met. Therefore, it is necessary that he and his needs should have a marked influence on the quality organisation. As the goods of better quality are being offered due to advances in technology the customers are also becoming well informed and more demanding due to social progress. Major customers are increasingly becoming aware of the precise quality level they require and have developed means of ensuring that the products they receive, meet these requirements.

Product specifications are getting more comprehensive and stringent and Acceptable Quality Levels (AQL) pertaining to all important parameters are being laid down by customers in precise terms. Therefore, the manufacturers have to tailor their quality program and organisations to meet these requirements. To ensure the implementation of proper quality programs, some purchasers, particularly the Defence Services, include a Clause in the contracts whereby the quality program of the manufacturing firm is auditable by the purchasers representative.

Added to these, are the market conditions such as intense competition. If a company cannot compete in terms of selling prices because of certain unavoidable reasons, it may seek to improve the quality of its products to obtain an edge over its competitors. This in turn will need the creation of a special organisation to achieve the desired results.

DESIGN OF AN ORGANISATION

Designing any organisation essentially consists of three basic steps.

(a) ***Identification and Grouping of Jobs:*** As a first step, various tasks that have to be carried out for the achievement of objectives must be identified. These tasks should then be grouped into sets of similar jobs that can be carried out by one or more individuals having similar training and skills. Further these individual sets should be grouped so that a number of allied sets can be placed under one component of the organisation for effective supervision.

(b) ***Allocation of Authority and Responsibility:*** The next step is to allocate specific sets of jobs to the charge of individuals whose authority and responsibility are clearly defined. Also, an effective method for the passage of instructions and advice from the management and feedback from the lower ranges of the organisation should be devised.

(c) ***Establishment of Cooperative Relationships:*** In any company or enterprise, different groups perform various jobs according to their responsibilities, yet the work of each and every group contributes towards the attainment of common objectives. To ensure that various groups work as a team and their work is complimentary, cooperative relationships should be established between various individuals and groups. This aspect is of great importance in quality managements because the quality cannot be built into the product by the quality organisation alone. It requires the joint efforts of all segments of the company organisation. Thus 'quality is everyone's business'. Here there is a pitfall; just because quality is everyone's business, in practice it may become nobody's business. Therefore a specific quality organisation is required to ensure that everyone concerned with quality plays his part, and activities of various groups are coordinated and integrated into a unified quality programme.

QUALITY FUNCTIONS

The main quality functions can be considered in two distinct groups, namely **Quality Engineering and Quality Control.**

Quality Engineering

This comprises of specialist staff functions as well as activities connected with the development, defining, and planning of quality during the pre-production stage. Its main work elements are given below :-

(a) Advice to the management on the quality policy of the company and laying down realistic quality objectives.

(b) The analysis of the customers quality requirements and the formulation of design specifications.

(c) The review and evaluation of product design with a view to improving quality and reducing quality costs.

(d) Defining quality standards and preparation of product specifications.

(e) Planning process controls and formulation of procedures to ensure quality conformance.

(f) Development of quality control techniques and inspection methods including the design of special test equipment.

(g) Conducting process-capability studies.

(h) Analysis of quality costs.

(i) Planning and organising quality control for incoming stores and materials including the capacity verification of the vendors.

(j) Quality audit of the company.

(k) Organising training in quality programme.

Quality Control

It is concerned with the interpretation and implementation of quality plans. It comprises of in-process and post product on testing, which are aimed at ensuring the quality conformance of products. The main work elements are enumerated below:-

(a) Assistance in establishing quality controls at various points of the manufacturing process.

(b) Maintenance and calibration of process control equipment.

(c) Investigation of defects and assistance in solving quality problems during production.

(d) Implementation of quality control measures for incoming materials and stores.

(e) Running a test laboratory for carrying out necessary test and analysis.

(f) Organising stage or interstage inspection or spot checks whenever required.

(g) Arranging final inspection to assess the quality of the end-product and the effectiveness of quality control measures.

(h) Checking the quality of the packaging to ensure that the product is able to withstand transportation hazards.

(i) Conducting tests for the measurement and analysis of goods on which customer complaints have been received.

(j) Feedback of defect data and customer complaints to the Quality Engineering Section.

DECENTRALIZATION OF QUALITY FUNCTIONS

It is not essential for all the above work elements to be performed directly by the Quality Department. All that is required is, that these tasks be performed by the most appropriate individual or group to ensure effective quality management. Based on the overall company policy, the Quality Manager may recommend to the management, the allocation of various quality tasks to the department or sections which can perform these with maximum efficiency and economy. Some sub-functions like the operation of process controls, stage and interstage inspection may be delegated to the production shops, if this measure helps in the smooth flow of production. Similarly some work elements in inward material control, except actual inspection and testing may be transferred to the purchasing department if technically competent persons are available.

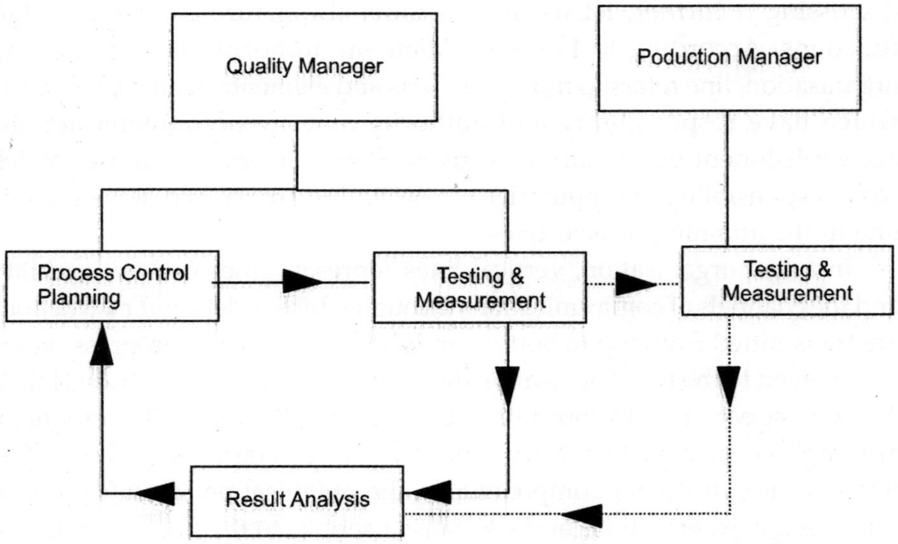

Fig. 1

There are advantages as well as disadvantages resulting from the decentralisation of quality functions. The main benefit is the smooth flow of production and less interdepartmental friction. On the other hand, the longer feedback loop (refer Fig. 1) results in slower reactions, which means that, should any defects arise in the product, a relatively longer time is taken before corrective measures are applied and thus a substantial number of defective products may be produced in the meantime. Moreover, production shops in a rush to meet the targets, may overlook the tell-tale signs indicating unsatisfactory state of the process until it actually goes out of control and has to be shut down. These risks should not be taken lightly in complex high-speed production lines. Decentralisation on a large scale, should be attempted only in plants with well-established quality control programmes of proven effectiveness, and relatively fixed lines of production.

While delegating specific responsibilities, the quality component, which is ultimately responsible for quality management, should device adequate control mechanisms by which it can monitor the effectiveness of delegated functions, so that suitable corrective measures can be applied before quality is substantially affected.

QUALITY—A STAFF FUNCTION

Considerable confusion exists, regarding the status of the quality component in the overall organisational structure of the company. Before discussing it further, let us first consider the nature of line and staff functions. According to Louis A. Alien, an authority on management organisation, line refers to those positions and elements of an organization which have responsibility and authority and are accountable for the accomplishment of primary objectives. Staff elements are those, which have responsibility and authority for providing advice and service to the line in the attaining of objectives.

In a line organisation, vertical lines represent lines of accountability and the channels of communications through which orders and instructions are transmitted from top to bottom and the compliance or progress report is conveyed to the top. The relationship between positions at various levels is that of superior and subordinate. On the other hand a staff component, although connected to its principal by a line relationship, is in staff relationship with other components in the organisation. A staff position can provide expert advice and specialised service to the line components, but it has no direct authority over them, even though the line components may be at a relatively lower level. Similarly no line component has authority over a staff element. The relationship between line and staff elements is that of cooperation and mutual respect, in which the staff elements provide advice and service to assist the line element to perform its functions better.

The line chief is obliged to give serious consideration to the advice given by the staff department, although he can over rule such advice, but only when there are sound operational reasons for doing so. Normally, the staff members, because of the position as advisors and assistants to the principal, are delegated the authority of issuing certain types of instruction on behalf of the chief. In such cases, instructions issued by the staff should be treated in the same way as instructions from the principal. In case such instructions cannot be complied with due to any reason, the recipient is expected to inform the staff or the principal regarding this fact, and have the instructions modified or cancelled.

In the light of the above, the detailed analysis of the work elements of Quality Management would show that it is essentially an advisory and service function. This component by itself cannot build quality into any product. It can only advise and assist other departments in attaining quality objectives. However, important its role may be for a company, it still remains a specialised staff and service function.

DESIGNING ORGANISATION FOR QUALITY MANAGEMENT

Having seen that quality management is basically a staff function, the design of its organisational structure should start from the top downwards. It is the responsibility of the Quality Manager to provide the necessary staff advice and service to the company. Therefore, his first decision will be whether or not he will be able to perform this function by himself? If not, what additional human help he will require? This he can do by deciding about the portion of responsibility that he will keep for himself, and the portion that he will delegate to his subordinates. Further, the number of subordinates will depend upon the grouping of the work elements, the quantity of work, and the areas of deployment. For instance, a company having a single product line may have two plants at different locations. To provide efficient quality services, the Quality Manager may have one quality engineering group, but will have to organise his Quality Control Wing into two parts and locate one at each plant. The same process of delegation should continue downwards, until the lowest operating level has been reached.

The internal structure of the quality component is generally a line organisation, because quality is its prime function. However, specialised staff positions may also be present, as seen in the organisation given in Fig. 2.

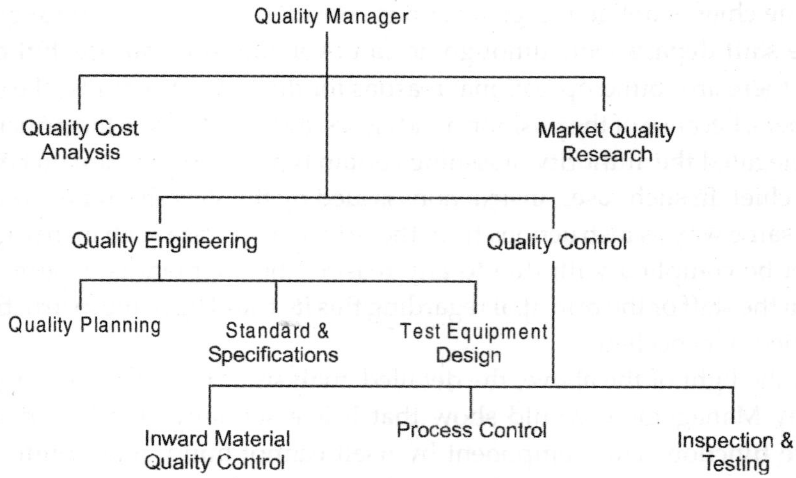

Fig. 2

Here Quality Engineering and Quality Control, along with their subgroups, are connected to the Quality Manager by a line relationship, because the accountability of the objectives of the function is carried to the lowest operating level. On the other hand, Quality Cost Analysis and Market Quality Research provide advice and service to the two main line groups and as such, are staff to these quality components. While delegating responsibility to various subordinate positions, it should be ensured that their responsibilities and authority are clearly defined. Although the overlapping of responsibilities and functions cannot be altogether avoided, it should certainly be minimized. Further, the delegation of authority should be commensurate with the responsibility.

FITTING THE QUALITY COMPONENT IN A COMPANY ORGANISATION

Having decided on the internal structure of the quality component, the next step is to establish proper relationships with other departments. This is done by locating the quality component or its sub-divisions at those places in the company organisation where they can perform their tasks and achieve the desired results with maximum effectiveness, economy and minimum of friction. This will further depend upon various factors considered earlier in this chapter.

TYPICAL QUALITY ORGANISATIONS

Having discussed the general considerations governing quality organisation, we shall now study certain typical cases to illustrate the organizing principles. The following situations will be considered:-

1. Single product line at the one location (mediumsized company).
2. Multi-product company at one location (medium-sized company).
3. Single-product, multi-plant situation.
4. Large divisionalised corporation with different product divisions.
5. A jobbing factory, manufacturing according to customers' designs and specifications.
6. Cottage industry.

SINGLE PRODUCT LINE AT ONE LOCATION

In this case, a medium-sized company is having one basic product line of compressors for industrial use. All company operations including design and manufacture, are carried out at one location. Although manufacturing involves various specialised technologies, it is not generally advisable to split the quality engineering element. A suitable quality organisation for this situation is shown in Fig. 3.

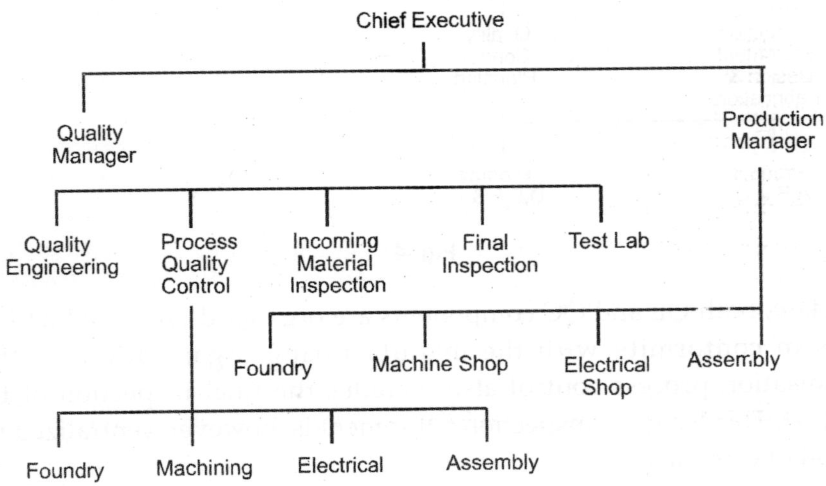

Fig. 3

A single product oriented quality engineering group will be more effective and economical. However, a separate process control element is provided for every manufacturing shop. Inward material control, final inspection, and the test laboratory are centralized for economy and effective control.

MULTI-PRODUCT COMPANY AT A SINGLE LOCATION

In this case, the manufacturing operations of the company are organised on the product line system, rather than on a functional basis. Products of a similar nature are grouped in production shops, so that the same plant may be utilized for different products, according to product demand, by suitable adjustment of the process. Only the Foundry serves all the shops. A possible quality organisation in this company is shown in Fig. 4.

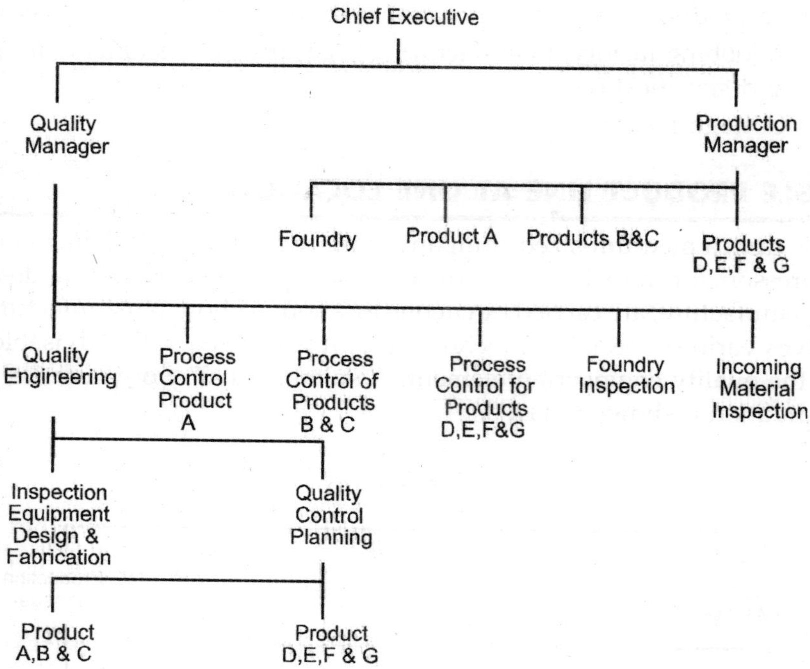

Fig. 4

Here, both QE and QC components are organised on a product-line basis in conformity with the manufacturing organisation. In this organisation process control also includes the final inspection of the product. The design of inspection equipment is, however, centralized for reason of economy.

A SINGLE PRODUCT-MULTIPLANT SITUATION

Figure 5 shows the quality organisation in a relatively large company with more than one manufacturing plant for the same product. It is possible that the machinery and equipment in the various plants may not be exactly similar, since the number of plants would have increased as the company grew and therefore, the plants established later are likely to have newer and more automated equipment. Thus, although design, sales and other functions that are independents of production techniques have been centralised, engineering is decentralised and placed under the respective plant managers.

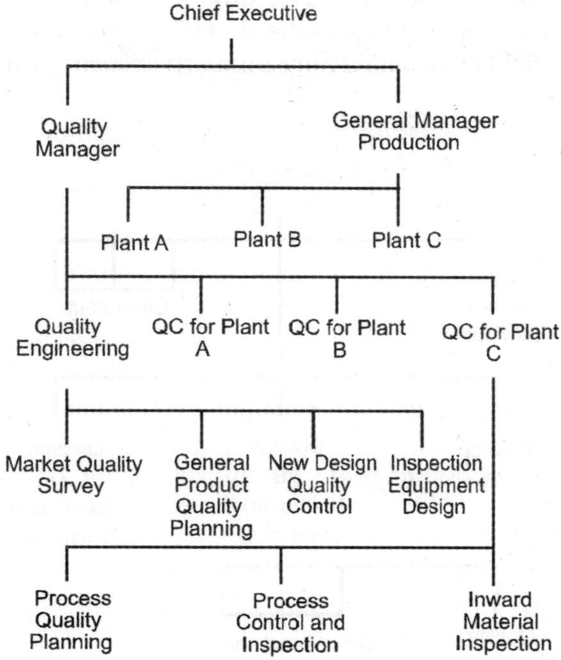

Fig. 5

To provide effective quality management in this case, quality engineering minus process quality planning, has been retained centrally, whereas quality control, including process quality planning has been divided on a plant basis, with the Quality Controllers of the plants directly reporting to the company Quality Manager. As an alternative, quality control could be decentralized and the plant quality controllers could report to the plant managers. The question of the preferable alternative depends upon various factors like company policy, personality of plant managers and types of quality problems normally faced. If the second alternative is adopted, the quality audit element should be established in the quality engineering component to constantly check the effectiveness of quality programs in individual plants.

A LARGE DIVISIONALISED CORPORATION

As companies grow and diversify their products, a stage comes, when they have to change from a functional to a divisional organisation. In the latter organisation, separate divisions for individual products or groups of similar products are established, which are self-reliant, integrated units and have semi-autonomous status within the overall company organisation. The divisions work almost like independent companies and have an organisation incorporating all the necessary line and staff components, which report directly to the Divisional General Manager. The top management also has small-specialised staff components to advise it in their respective fields. The quality organisation in such a company is shown in Fig. 6.

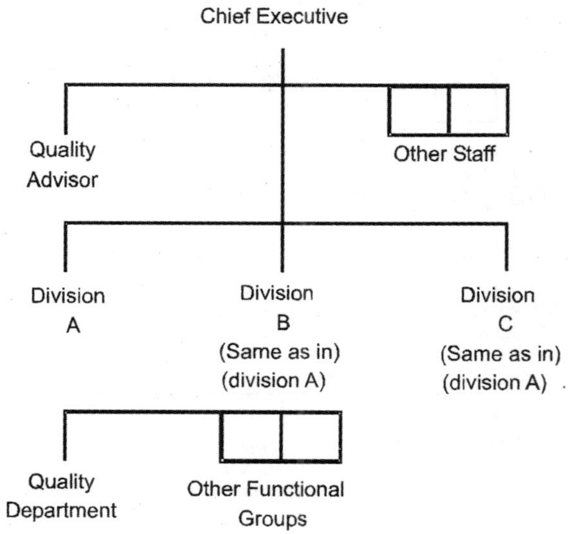

Fig. 6

In this situation, every division has its own quality management organisation, which works directly under the General Manager of the division. The Chief Executive also has a Quality Advisor to advise him in quality matters, and to ensure that standardised quality practice is followed in the divisions, in accordance with company policy. For this purpose, close liaison is maintained between the Quality Advisor and the quality management element in the various divisions. This also facilitates coordination and the rendering of inter-divisional quality assistance.

A JOBBING COMPANY

The main characteristic of a jobbing company is, that it has no specific line of production. It has the facilities of various specialised technologies, and is capable of undertaking any job within the capacity of the facilities available. The jobs undertaken are according to the customers' designs and specification. Because of the wide variety of jobs, it may require a considerable amount of process engineering effort. Such a company will be organised on functional lines, according to the specialised technology available. The volume of orders for each item in such a company, is likely to be rather small. Because of the variety and non-repetitive nature of the job, there are bound to be a large number of quality problems. The production runs will be practically of the same nature as pilot runs. Therefore, greater reliance will have to be placed on pre-production quality control measures and less on process controls, which require a considerable initial run before they are finally adjusted and can be effectively employed. For instance, jigs and fixtures should be critically examined before they are actually put to use, so that very first job is within acceptable limits. The quality organisation in such a company is illustrated in Figs. 6 and 7.

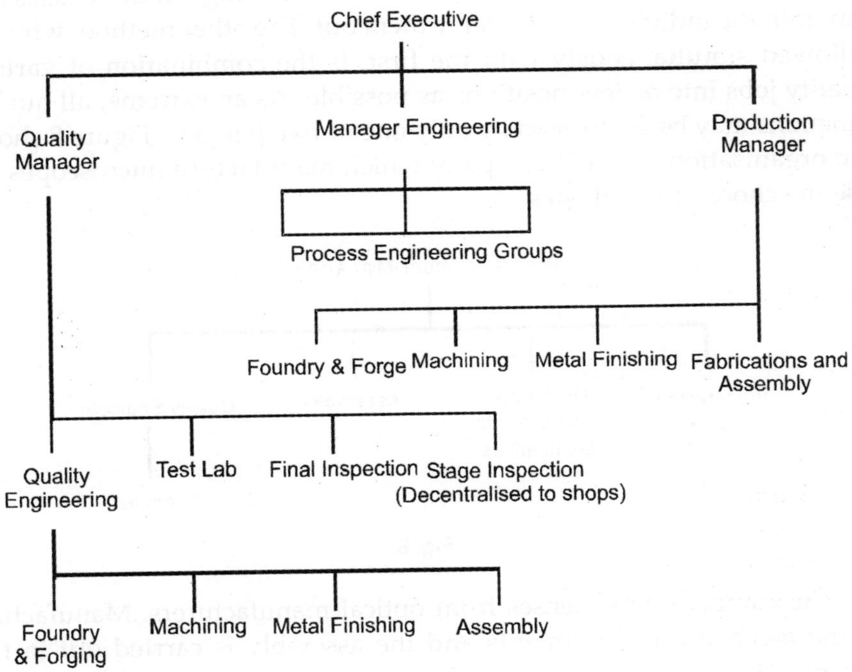

Fig. 7

There is a well-staffed QE element organised according to specialised technologies which will be required to work in close cooperation with the process engineering department, so that control can be exercised on the tools of production before they are actually put to use. Process control essentially consists of stage inspection which may be decentralised to the shops for smooth functioning. Final inspection however will have to be directly controlled by the Quality Manager to ensure the quality of the outgoing product.

A Small Company Working as a Cottage Industry

The size of a company often dictates the size and organisation of its quality component. A small company neither needs nor can afford a large staff employed exclusively on quality control jobs. However, certain quality tasks have to be performed if the quality of the final product is to be assured. How can the two conflicting requirements be resolved? This problem can be tackled in two ways. Firstly, by delegating some of the quality jobs to the operating staff estate inspection in an electrical switch manufacturing concern may be delegated to the shop supervisor. Inward material inspection in a furniture factory could be delegated to the godown keeper. All this is only possible if there is a specialised quality element which can lay down detailed instructions for carrying out these tasks and can train the individuals who carry them out. The other method, which is followed simultaneously with the first, is the combination of various quality jobs into as few positions as possible. As an extreme, all quality functions may be performed by only one or two persons. Figure 8 shows the organisation of small company which manufacture microscopes for use in schools and colleges.

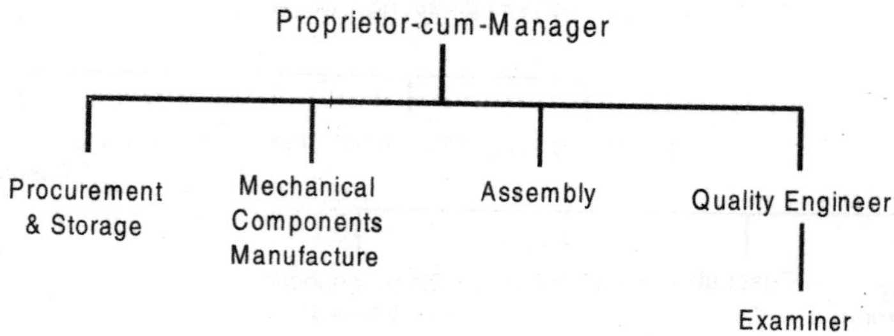

Fig. 8

The company buys lenses from optical manufacturers. Manufacture of the mechanical components and the assembly is carried out in the factory. The Quality Organisation consists of a quality engineer and an examiner. The quality engineer lays down the specifications and other quality instructions to be followed during manufacture. The mechanical components are inspected by the examiner. The quality control of purchased materials is delegated to the procurement section which has been advised to buy tested materials as far as possible. The inspection of the lenses and the assembled microscopes is carried out by the quality engineer himself. Thus even with only two such positions a high standard of product quality can be maintained.

7

Economics of Quality

Economics is the driving force for any industrial enterprise. One of the main aims of an industry is to secure economic gains in the form of profit. There may be other social objectives, the attainment of which may be highly desirable for the public good, but in the final analysis, the soundness of an industry is judged by its financial viability. Therefore, the desirability of any function or activity is generally assessed by the economic yardstick *i.e.* the extent to which it helps in the attainment of economic objectives. Although quality is a laudable objective in itself, it is subject to the same economic constraints as other activities. Quality improvement can be pursued only up to the extent to which it helps sales, and long term profitability, as such, any quality programme must be justified by the returns it brings to the company.

GENERAL PERCEPTION ABOUT QUALITY COST RELATIONSHIP

In spite of advancement of quality management concepts and tools, adequate attention has not been given to study the direct impact of quality on the bottom line of a company. That is why a number of misconceptions about quality persist among the business managers at various levels. This is one of the main reasons that quality is not a major issue for the top management of the companies. These misconceptions are discussed as follows.

(i) ***Higher Quality Costs More:*** This is the most widely held misconception about quality. However, new insights into the mechanism of quality building and manufacturing processes have shown that high quality does not necessarily cost more. In exceptional cases when superior quality may cost more, its return will compensate for more than the extra cost involved. It is important to understand how quality is built into a product in modern production processes. Quality is first defined on paper in the form of a design drawn up on the basis of market needs. The design is then translated into an actual product by appropriate manufacturing processes. The investment of more resources in Research and Development (R &D) can result in a marked improvement in product quality. Simultaneously, refining the manufacturing processes can lead to substantial reductions in over all production cost. This has been amply demonstrated both in Japan and the West across the gamut of manufactured goods. Computers, consumer electronics and household appliances are particularly good examples. Throughout the last two decades, the quality of these items has progressively improved, while their cost in real terms has dropped.

(ii) ***Emphasis on Quality Leads to Reduced Productivity:*** There is a widespread notion among production managers that quality can be achieved only at the cost of quantity. This view is a legacy of the period when quality control considered of largely physical inspection of the end products. In that situation, more stringent inspection requirements generally resulted in the rejection of a greater proportion of the output, thus reducing the acceptable quantity. However, quality control has since become far more sophisticated. The emphasis has now shifted to preventive activities during design and manufacture, so that defective articles are not produced in the first instance. Many studies have shown that application of modern quality management tools increases productivity in addition to improvement of quality. Thus, quality improvement efforts have a multiplier effect on productivity rather than acting as an impediment.

(iii) ***Poor Quality is caused by Carelessness of Workers:*** Manufacturers in developing countries often blame the low quality of their products on the lack of quality consciousness of their workers. A deeper analysis of this issue shows that workers can be held responsible only if management has thoroughly trained the operators, given them detailed instructions on what to do and provided the means for regulating the process equipment if results are found to be unsatisfactory. An honest appraisal of many manufacturing units in developing countries is likely to show that management often fails to provide these vital inputs at most workstations. Rather than

finding scapegoats, companies need to examine the weaknesses in their management systems.

(iv) ***Quality Improvement Requires Large Investment:*** There is a widely held notion that an organised quality programme needs heavy investment in new plant and equipment. However, this is not necessarily true. Plant and equipment constitutes only one component of a total quality system. By themselves, it is not sufficient to assure high quality. A number of companies in India have plant and machinery similar to those used in Europe and North America, but the quality of their products is significantly lower. By contrast, some companies even in the small scale sector are using indigenous equipment by which they are able to manufacture products and export these to Europe and Japan. In most cases, quality can be significantly improved by creating awareness among personnel about understanding customer requirements, standardising processes, proper training of operators and enforcing technical discipline. These activities do not require a heavy financial requirement, but only a deep commitment to quality and intolerance of deviations on the part of management.

COST OF QUALITY MANAGEMENT

Like all business functions, quality management have also cost associated with it. Various terms have been used to designate costs associated with quality (or non quality). Imagine a perfect automatic process which produces 100% fault free and reliable products fully conforming to the specification. Further let us also assume that suppliers provide all inputs which fully meet the specifications. In such a situation there would not be any need for inspection of input materials, semi processed component or the finished products. Further since the products have high reliability there would be no requirement for sending service personnel for attending to the faults in the product during its usage with the customer. In such a situation there would be no quality costs. However, such a situation does not exist in reality. Products and processes designed and operated by humans would have possibility of defects and failures. Therefore, certain activities would be required to prevent the occurrence of defects and failures. Further, since all processes are subject to variations certain measures would be required to keep them under control. Additionally, the end product would need to be checked for quality before despatch, to ensure that customer gets a fully serviceable product. Finally in spite of best efforts to prevent the occurrence of defects, some products will fail during service with the user which would need to be serviced. Thus in real life situation a number of activities are undertaken with specific purpose of maintenance of quality. All these activities involve certain costs to be incurred. Thus Quality Costs are the total costs incurred on activities to prevent nonconformity in product, appraise the product for conformance and dealing with situation when the product fails to meet the requirement. For the purpose of management of quality costs, these are classified in following categories:

PREVENTION COSTS

The costs associated with activities undertaken to prevent generation of poor quality or occurrence of non-conformity in products or services. These could be activities such as design review quality planning, process capability evaluation, vendor assessment, process controls, quality education and training and quality improvement projects.

APPRAISAL COSTS

The costs relating to measurement and testing of products or evaluation of service for conformity to quality standards. These could be cost of inspection/verification of purchased materials, inspection/testing of in-process material and final inspection/performance check of the final product. This also includes costs associated with audit of quality management system and calibration of testing and measuring instruments.

FAILURE COSTS

These are costs incurred when product or service does not meet the quality standards or customer requirements. For proper evaluation, these costs are divided into internal and external failure costs as described below.

(a) ***Internal failure costs:*** There are costs incurred when the products fail within the factory. It includes costs of scrap, rectification, re-inspection or testing, downgrading of products to be sold as seconds, re-handling, enhanced work in progress, etc.

(b) ***External failure costs:*** It is those costs, which are incurred, when non-conformity of product is noticed after it is delivered to the customer. It may include cost of processing customer complaints, repair and replacement cost and even penalty and legal costs when non-conformity issue gets into litigation.

Quality costs discussed above are direct cost which are related to production or delivery of a particular product or service. Since this book is about Total Quality Management, we should also consider quality cost not related to production or service delivery, but due to poor quality of performance of other functional departments. In fact these indirect or hidden quality costs are much higher in magnitude than product related costs. In fact product related quality cost which are visible represent only the tip of an ice berg. Much bigger costs are hidden, as these cannot be easily determined by traditional accounting system. Some of the hidden costs are shown in Fig. 1.

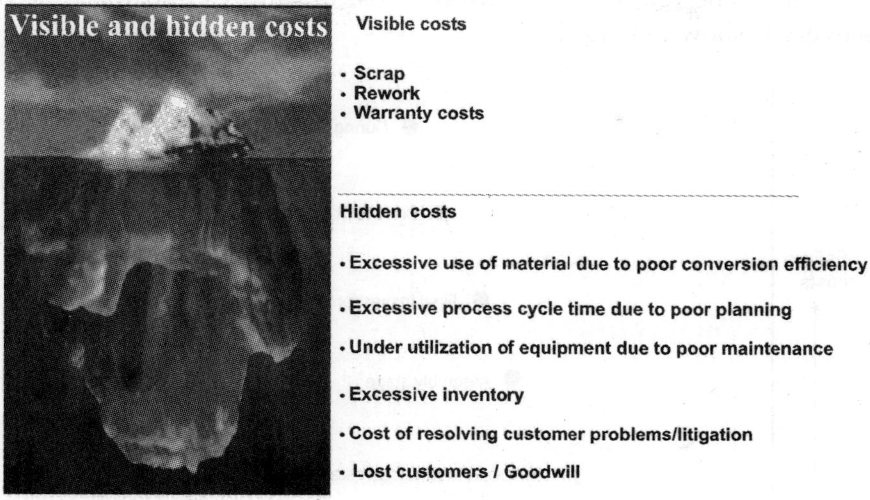

Fig. 1

MEASUREMENT OF DIRECT QUALITY COSTS

We have already seen that total direct quality cost has three main elements, *i.e.* prevention, appraisal and failure. No comprehensive study has been carried on quality costs for Indian industries. However, on empirical basis typical elements of quality cost would be of the order shown in Fig. 2.

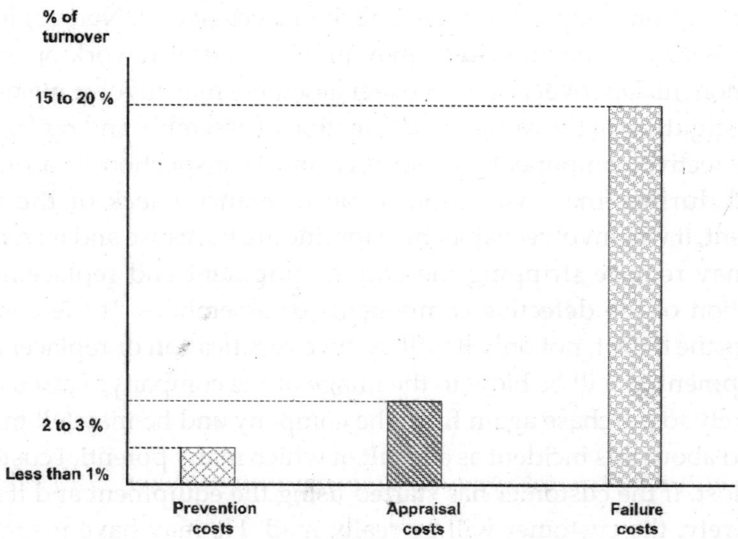

Fig. 2: Categories of Quality Costs

There is a potential for major saving in costs by reduction of failures. For this we need to understand the type of failures and when these are discovered. The relationship between cost of failures and the time of discovery is shown in Fig. 3.

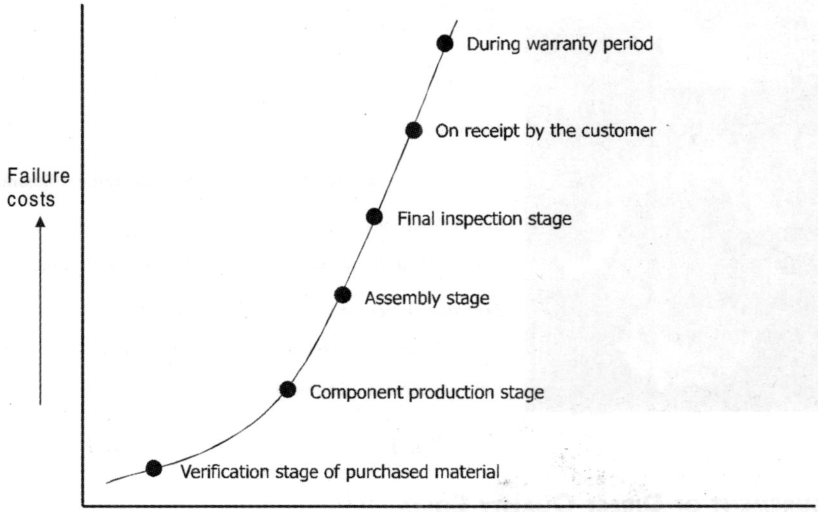

Fig. 3: Stages of Discovery

It will be seen that earlier the defect or failure is detected lower is the quality cost. For instance if non conformity is discovered at the verification of input material stage the quality cost is only on the paper work for seeking replacement from supplier and possible re-inspection cost. Non-conformity at component manufacture stage may involve cost of rework or scrap of the component. Discovery of defect after assembly may involve major work for investigation of the cause of malfunction of assembly and replacement of the defective component, reassembly and re-inspection. If a defect is detected during final inspection or performance check of the whole equipment, it will involve major effort for finding the cause and its removal, which may require stripping the entire equipment and replacement or rectification of the defective components or assemblies. If the customer discovers the defect, not only it will involve rectification or replacement of the equipment, it will be blow to the image of the company. The customer is not likely to purchase again from the company and he may tell many of his friend about this incident as a result of which many potential customers may be lost. If the customer has started using the equipment and if it fails prematurely, the customer will be really mad. He may have made some investment in installation of the subject equipment along with other associated equipment and services. In this situation he may demand not only replacement of equipment but also reimbursement of other costs incurred by him. If the customer uses the equipment for commercial purposes he may sue the company not only for the cost of the equipment but also for loss of business due to failure of the equipment. Considering all these costs the company will need to undertake all measures necessary to prevent failures. At the same time it should strengthen the quality appraisal system to ensure that if a defect occurs it is caught at the earliest stage. Some quality zealots in their effort to reduce quality cost may recommend reduction of inspection and testing activities, as these do not add any value as far as customer is concerned. While theoretically it seems to be true, but until the company has significantly improved the process capability, the appraisal activities and failure costs will have to be increased in the early stages of quality journey to ensure that non conformities are detected at the earliest stage as discussed above. It is only at a stage of quality programme when there is a major improvement in process capability and various mistake-proofing measures have been adopted which make occurrence of defect unlikely that the company can consider reduction of appraisal costs. General trend of quality costs during a well-run quality programme is shown in Fig. 4.

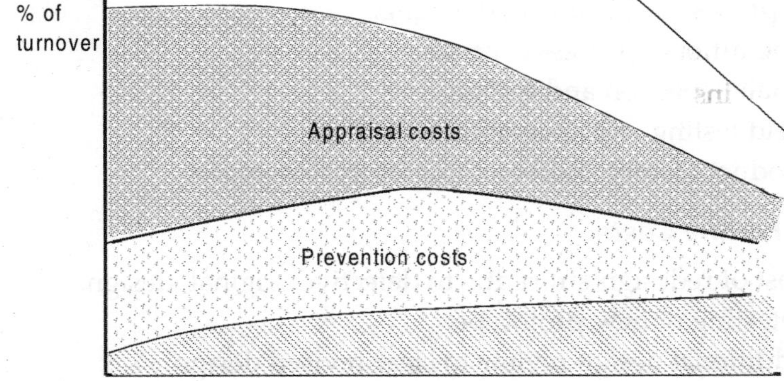

Fig. 4: General Trend of Quality During Quality Program

MANAGEMENT OF QUALITY COSTS

The aim of quality cost management program is to reduce Total Quality costs. Here we are talking about only the direct quality costs, such as cost of prevention, appraisal and failures as discussed above. There is an old saying that you cannot improve any thing, which you cannot measure. Therefore the first step in quality cost management programme is to measure costs being incurred now. Typical quality cost items under various categories of quality costs are given below.

Prevention Costs

1. Market research to identify customer needs.
2. Customer survey to ascertain desirable quality characteristics.
3. Development of proto type for customer review.
4. Review of specifications to ascertain that it meets user requirements.
5. Design review by a multi-disciplinary team from ease of production point of view.
6. Training for quality.
7. Development of quality assurance criteria.
8. Process capability study and development of process quality controls.
9. Capability verification of vendors.
10. Salaries and other expenses of staff of quality department.

Appraisal Costs

1. Inspection/testing of purchased product.
2. Verification/validation of production and testing facilities.
3. Calibration of measuring and test equipment.
4. In process inspection and testing.
5. Operation of process controls.
6. Final inspection and testing.
7. Field testing and evaluation.
8. Product quality audit and quality system audit.

Internal Failure Costs

1. Cost of redesign effort due to defective original design.
2. Retesting of new prototype.
3. Additional design review to clear revised design.
4. Products wasted due to design changes.
5. Analysis of defects found in purchased product.
6. Cost of rectification/replacement of defective product.
7. Re-inspection/retest of rectified/replace product.
8. Cost of process hold up due to defective purchased product.

External Failure Costs

1. Cost of processing customer complaints.
2. Cost of rectification of product on site.
3. Cost of arranging replacement of defective product.
4. Warranty claims.
5. Cost of litigation and liability claims.
6. Penalty cost as per contract if applicable.
7. Cost of lost goodwill and lost market share due to quality problem.

We have been able to identify various activities, which involve quality costs. But finding actual cost is not easy as you are not likely to find all costs being incurred now from the present accounting system. Therefore you may have to estimate some of the cost items from other technical data available in the quality records. Another point to be noted is that we are looking for only major cost items which will give us a fair estimate of quality costs. Some guidance on obtaining various quality cost items are given in the following paragraphs:

PREVENTIVE QUALITY COSTS

Data on preventive costs on market research would be readily available with the marketing department. Cost of prototype and design can be estimated from the data with R & D department. Remaining preventive quality cost would have to be provided by Quality Department itself which is planning quality cost management programme.

APPRAISAL COSTS

Estimation of appraisal costs are relatively easy. This relates to activities being carried out by the quality department or at the test laboratory. Since very small time of quality department is spent on preventive activities, it would be fair to allocate 90% cost of quality department and 100% cost of test laboratories as appraisal costs.

INTERNAL FAILURE COSTS

Quality costs due to design defects would have to be estimated from the redesign effort. Cost of products which became unusable due to design changes should be available from the parts usage data. Cost of defective purchased product will have to be estimated on the basis of extra effort spent by the material procurement department and quality department. Production hold up costs if any can be obtained from the production department. As far as internal failure cost in production is concerned, data on rejection and rework would normally be available in the production department which can form the basis of estimating their quality costs.

EXTERNAL FAILURE COST

The cost of processing customer complaints can be readily determined as entire customer care department is most engaged in resolution of customer complaints. Data on rectification and replacement of sold should also be readily available in the sales department. However, care should be taken to collect also the indirect cost of repair and replacement. In addition to cost of components and equipment replaced, other associated costs such as travel expenses of servicing personnel and their time spent should also be taken into account. Penalty and litigation costs will be readily available from accounts. However, intangible costs of lost good will and its impact on market share will require thought and considerable consultation with the marketing and sales.

OVERALL QUALITY COSTS

Quality costs discussed above are only direct quality cost of producing product or service. Total cost of non-quality incurred in the company would also include cost of failures or poor efficiency in other departments. Some of the non-value added costs incurred in other functional areas are:

- Excess inventory due to poor material management
- Low equipment availability due to poor maintenance
- Avoidable movement of personnel and material due to poor layout
- Excess production due to over ambitious sales forecast.

For this, more advanced like process mapping, process flow analysis and Activity Based Costing would need to be employed to assess the cost of non-value added activities carried out in all departments of the company. These are discussed in chapter-14.

ECONOMICS OF QUALITY FROM THE CUSTOMER'S VIEW POINT

So far, we have discussed the economics of quality in relation to the producer. It will be of interest to know how the customer sees the quality of the product. A customer is not concerned with the cost of manufacture or the various elements of the quality costs. To him, what matters is the cost which he has to pay for obtaining a service or the fulfilment of a need. This cost does not mean only the purchase price or the acquisition cost of the product. In addition, it may also include operating the maintenance cost, which are equally important for the customer. For instance, while purchasing a car in addition to the price tag, we also consider the fuel consumption which is indicative of running costs.

During recent years it has been realised that for long life products, particularly for commercial and industrial use, the operating and maintenance costs during the life of the product often exceed its purchase price. This has led to a new approach called 'life cycle costing' for comparative evaluation of competing products. Life cycle costs generally include:-

(a) Purchase price
(b) Transport and installation charges
(c) Total operating costs during the useful life of a product such as fuel or power charges.
(d) Maintenance costs, such as servicing and repair charges including inventory cost of the spares.
(e) Non-availability cost. This represents the losses, which are suffered due to non-availability of the equipment when it is under maintenance or awaiting repairs. These losses may be in the form of idle booking of labour, rental for the equipment hired for temporary use, or loss of revenue, which normally accrues from the equipment.

The costs shown in (a) to (c) above can be computed without much difficulty. But computation of costs shown in (d) and (e) requires data on reliability and maintainability of the equipment (discussed in chapters 20, and 21). If the manufacturer provides this data, a reasonable estimate of these costs can also be worked out. Importance of non-availability costs should not be underestimated. For instance, if a load-carrying vehicle remains under maintenance for two days, the repair charges may be only Rs. 500, but the loss of freight may be as much as Rs. 5000/- per day. Since the quality of the product is dictated by the user's requirements, it is essential that the Designers and Production Engineers appreciate the user's economics and try to optimise the life cycle cost for better acceptance of their products.

PLANNING OF QUALITY COST REDUCTION PROGRAMMES

The importance of preventive quality control programmes for reducing quality costs needs no emphasis. However, these programmes themselves cost money and the resources at the disposal of a Quality Manager are often limited. Therefore, these should be utilised in such a manner as to yield maximum results. Only such quality programmes should be undertaken which can quickly show results and prove their effectiveness in cost reduction. This will win the confidence of the company management and generate enthusiasm for quality programmes. A preliminary survey, to detect weak spots in a process can be made by monitoring the frequency of failures in the process which result in the production of defective jobs. In a multi product manufacturing company, it could begin with the isolation of the product having a high rate of rejection. Let us say the number of rejects in the various products over a certain period is plotted as shown in Fig. 5.

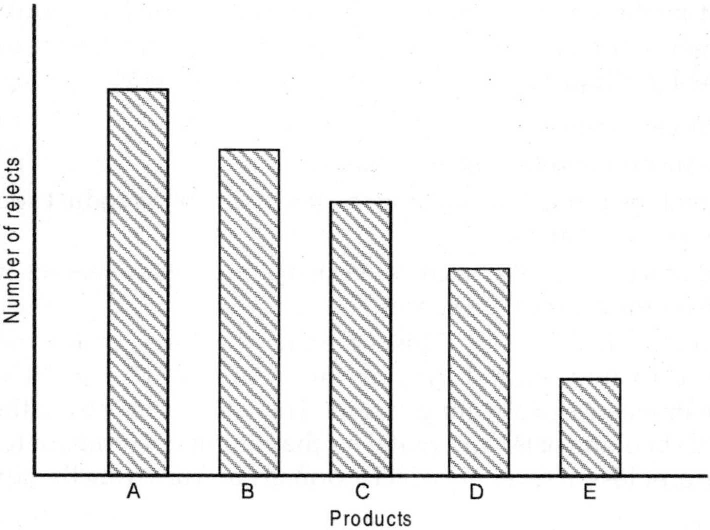

Fig. 5

Looking at the histogram, one might feel that product A is most suitable for the application of preventive quality programmes, but it may not be necessarily so. Since we are aiming at cost reduction, we must analyse the cost of rejects or failures. It is possible, that even though the number of failures of product A is more, each failure may be costing very little and the total failure cost may be much less than that of product B. On the basis of the cost of failures of products, the graph may appear something like Fig. 6.

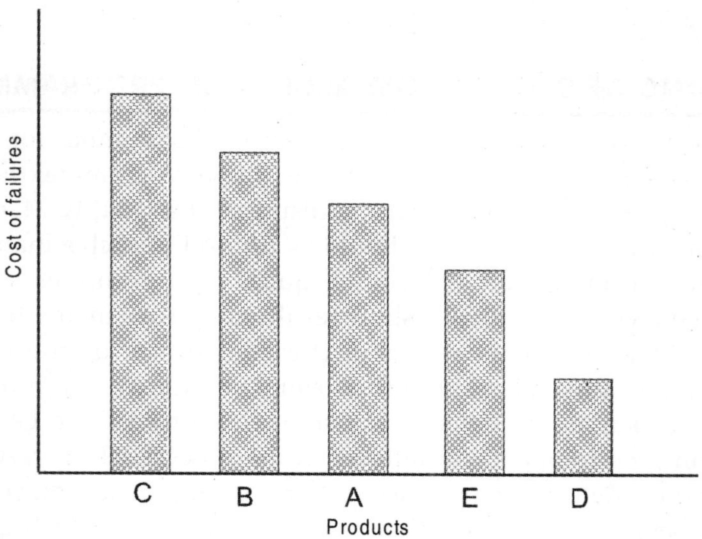

Fig. 6

It can be seen that product C, and not A is the economic weak spot and is therefore more suitable for the application of quality programme. In a complex process involving many technologies, the preliminary survey could start from the frequency of different types of defects and their causes. The cost of failure due to each major cause should be estimated and tabulated. The cause showing the highest failure cost deserves first attention. While evaluating the savings resulting from the quality programmes, it should be clearly understood that it is not necessary for every quality programme to show immediate results in the form of cost reduction. A quality study may reveal a design weakness or unsuitability of a particular equipment or machine. The immediate expenses on some quality programmes may appear infractuous, but if they have been selected and planned properly, these are often more than justified in terms of long term gains, especially in the case of continuous or repeated production process.

8

The Human Factor in Quality

Most quality initiatives are based on systems and techniques with the aim of improving quality and productivity. Often, a newly developed technique such as ISO-9000, Process Reengineering, and Six-Sigma etc. become the focus of the quality program. It is assumed that once the system and procedures for the selected technique are in place, the desired results will follow. What is not realized is that of the systems and procedures are implemented by people, and the effectiveness of the program therefore is largely dependent on the capability and motivation of these individuals. Furthermore, since all quality programs, at some level, stress continuous improvement, it is also the 'openness' of the organization to ideas from all levels that is equally key to success.

Unless the capabilities and motivation of the employees in the organization are aligned with the new quality management systems, even brilliantly planned quality initiative are likely to fail. Equally, no matter the quality management system used, an organization that is not open to ideas from all levels of its workforce is unlikely to improve.

Unlike the very objective and deterministic nature of systems, humans, as individuals and as organizations are much too subjective and non-deterministic. For instance, it is very difficult to predict, how an individual would react to a new situation. Some would be cautious on one circumstance, and reckless in another. Individuals are both emotional and yet exhibit rational behaviour, curious to try new things yet resist change.

Given this complexity, it is surprising that most TQM plans do not give adequate consideration to human factors of implementing TQM. Instead, implementations generally concentrate on training programmes to make employees aware of TQM concepts and their roles in the implementation. However, the knowledge of TQM and various processes provide the capability but not necessarily the commitment. Furthermore, neither is the organization's openness to change and new ideas affected to a great extent.

As an amusing side note, Brian Thomas, the author of the book "Human Dimension of Quality" has developed an equation for effectiveness of an individual as given below. Effectiveness (E)= Motivation (M) × Capability (C) × Control (C). *i.e.* $E= MC^2$ (Similarity to Einstein's equation unintended). Here control implies the extent to which an individual feels empowered to contribute his ideas to his job.

From this equation it will be clear that effectives of a person is the product of three variables mentioned above. Capability and motivation can be developed by HRD programmes. But these only develop the potential of an individual. To harness this potential a person needs to be given proper degree of control over his actions. To understand this concept let us consider the CEO. He has full authority to take whatever actions he desires (within reason). If he has capability and commitment for a cause he can be fully effective. On the other hand a shop floor worker in spite being capable and highly motivated may not be able to seize the opportunities for improving his process unless he has control over his operation, *i.e.* he is empowered to make changes in his operations to achieve better quality or improve productivity which are the parameters for measuring the success of TQM. This third element for effectiveness solely depends on the management, which has the major responsibility for the success (or failure) of TQM initiative. Therefore, before discussing building capability among personnel we discuss the role of the management for developing human resource.

ROLE OF MANAGEMENT

The management of most companies in India have not realized the true potential of quality management. To most of them it is just a fancy name of inspection which can be carried out by a handful of inspectors. However, to appear modern in their management approach, the name of the erstwhile Inspection department is usually changed to Quality Management department headed by the Quality Manager. Some companies have even upgraded this department to TQM Division or Organizational Excellence Division headed by a high ranking official such as Vice President or Technical Director. However, if we examine jobs on which the personnel of this division are employed, we will see that almost all of them are employed on some kind of inspection or verification activity. Some may be carrying out inwards goods inspections, others may be testing in process products, and still others may be employed in final inspection or in the test laboratories. You will hardly find some one studying how can a particular product fail in service, and how its quality can be improved.

When a process is functioning satisfactorily, it is rare that some one in the Quality Department would be thinking about the situations when the process could malfunction and considering measures for preventing defective product. The real purpose of Quality department is preventing defects in products or errors in service. But in actual practice personnel of Quality Department are in busy in fire fighting and solving quality problems which have already occurred either in the production or with the users. Thus, there is very little change in the way quality is assured.

Second issue is that other departments such as Production, Material Management or R&D feel that they know their job and there is no need for Quality personnel to meddle in their affairs. Due to this attitude, the departmental heads resent intrusion by Quality department for collecting data or for assisting in solving their problems. Therefore, there is a need for a strong message to go that quality is a company and not the responsibility of only the Quality department. There should be a system of constituting multidisciplinary committees to address various quality issues. The emphasis should be on prevention of defects and errors rather than appraisal and solving post production quality problems.

In most TQM initiative the training programmes on concepts and tools are mainly focussed on higher and middle management. This is based on the assumption that organization survival and growth mainly depends on their ability. While this may be valid as a general concept, but tends to ignore the contribution of employees. All new management initiatives aim to bring about various business processes with a view to improve the quality and quantity of outputs. It should be realised that the person operating these processes have intimate knowledge of the process and known to the weakness and problems as well as possible solution to bring about improvement.

It is a different question that they do not share this knowledge with their superiors for fear of giving an impression that they have difficulty in carrying out their operations, or worse still they will be beamed for the problems. In any case most of the managers are so pre occupied with their jobs that they do not have time to listen to anything, which is not of immediate concern for production. Those who have studied the quality movement in Japan would know that they had launched massive programme for training workers on quality tools and techniques. Because of this knowledge workers are able to suggestion for improvement should go to workers; they have formed quality circles (discussed in chapter-37) through which they discuss ways and means to improve their process in their own time outside the working hours.

If a company wants high level of commitment and enthusiasm for quality from the staff, the management must treat them as stakeholders in the enterprise rather than a resource to be optimally exploited. CEOs are often heard saying, "Employees are our most valuable asset." One may ask them if they have time and system to appreciate their values?

One way of valuing employees is to consider them as agents of:

- Revenue increase – This is particularly true for product designers and salespeople.
- Capacity increase – Line employees that increase your capacity to produce, or deliver service.
- Efficiency increase – Line employees and managers who cause efficiency improvement in revenue acquisition or enhancing capacity by a variety of means, such as, by improving utilization, by enthusing their staff or their peers, by reducing waste, by being passionate about improving products or processes or about quality.

We must take employee valuation seriously and systematically. We should not merely focus on their formal input. We should also look at their intangible inputs, whether it takes the form of enthusiasm, passion or conflict-resolution. Unless we do that, we will not be appreciating their full contribution to the organization.

The single most important means of rewarding employee value is through money, while effective for some employees, is not the prime motivator of high performance. Instead, managers need to structure reward based on individual needs. The possible choices in addition to cash are:

- Exposure/Rotation – Exposure to a different function, leading to professional development.
- Information Access – Access to information, the fact is that 'being in the know' is perhaps the 'cheapest' form of compensation a manager can provide and one of the most valued.
- Public/Praise – Promotion or a title change.
- Care/Respect – This is quite simply an acknowledgement of the employee's existence! The most extreme case, which we see virtually everywhere, is that we can pass lower-level employees without acknowledging their presence. It is small talk or a kind word about his job, his family, and his problems that can be all the reward that an employee needs!

Another measure of generating enthusiasm for quality is to eliminate fear of criticism and create an environment of openness where personnel at any level can meet the senior functionaries and share their concerns about processes and activities in their area of operations. The frontline employees should be encouraged to look for opportunities for improvement in their process. They must be empowered to take appropriate action to control the process and bring any abnormalities to the notice of their superiors.

CO-OPERATION OF OTHER FUNCTIONAL GROUPS

Mere acceptance of quality program by the top management cannot automatically assure its successful implementation. Other company personnel may pay lip service to the quality program, but unless their whole-hearted cooperation can be secured, the chances of success of the program are rather slim. The first factor in this respect to be considered is the normal human reaction to any change. Machiavelli once said, "There is nothing more difficult of success nor more dangerous to handle than to initiate a new order of things." Resistance to the introduction of the quality control program may be aggravated by the fear of loss of one's standing, and authority or suspicion of it causing redundancy, or simple stubbornness. Another factor which acts as an impediment to quality control is the production-oriented attitude. With the advent of mass production technology, maximizing production has become the sole aim of the production engineers and managers. In the process, quality has suffered. This attitude is based on the mistaken belief that accent on quality tends to reduce productivity, or that quality can be achieved only at the cost of quantity. Production staff have to be educated to remove this misconception. Actually, a well planned quality program generally results in increased production due to reduced scrap and rework and longer production runs due to a known rate of process drift.

As the implementation of the quality programme requires the active cooperation of other functional groups, they should be involved at the planning stage itself. All affected groups and departments should be consulted during the formulation of the quality programme and they should be encouraged to put forward their points of view and suggestions, which should be given due weightage while finalising the programme. This can be achieved by adopting a committee approach for the management of widespread quality activities. Various committees comprising of executives from all the concerned departments could be formed for the planning and coordination of specific quality activities such as,

- New product planning and design review,
- Quality planning and process control,
- Defect investigation, and analysis of customer complaints,
- Quality motivation.

The aim should be to secure the genuine participation and involvement of other functional groups, so that they feel, it is their own programme and not something which has been forced on them by an outside agency. Under such circumstances, the programme will have a much better chance of success.

TRAINING

We have discussed above the management role in developing motivation among employees and creating proper control environments which encourage employee to take quality initiatives in their area of activity. These two elements are only facilitators provided the employee has the requisite competence and knowledge about the process and quality improvement tools. This capability can only be built through training. Although general need of training is well accepted by all but it is treated as one of the minor issues. Generally the responsibility for this is given to HRD Department. This department tries to interact with other departments and works out a yearly training plan and projects a certain budget. Once the training budget is approved training events are organized in house or some personnel are deputed to various training institutions for the specified courses. The metric for assessing effectiveness of HRD is the number of personnel, trained and the expenditure incurred. Whenever there is a major problem with quality of a product or service which is traced to inadequacy of technical competence and skill of operating personnel the blame game starts. Operations blame the HRD for poor training and skill building. HRD defends by saying the subject training need was not identified by operations people. Real cause is lack of proper training management system. It should be realized that training is not an end in itself. It is only a tool which if properly used can improve the quality of processes, products and services. Training can be classified into two broad categories:

(a) ***Technical training:*** This is aimed at developing basic knowledge and skills required for the job for which a person is employed. This can be refresher training to have a person's skills or training on new technology and systems introduced in the organization. All this training equips a person to give consistent performance in the assigned job.

(b) ***Quality related training:*** This is aimed at developing a capability to improve the current level of activity with a view to improving quality of product/service for achieving greater customer satisfaction. This could also be for improving productivity and cost reduction to enhance cost competitiveness. This would include training on quality management concepts/system and quality improvement tools.

Both categories of training is necessary for introducing TQM in an organization.

PLANNING OF TRAINING

For planning any training program, you need to be clear about the aim or objective of the training. The objective could be to train personnel for manufacture of a new product or launch of a new service. If a company is receiving complaints about a product or service, the objective could be improvement of product quality or delivery process for achieving greater customer satisfaction. Important considerations for developing a training plan are given below:

1. The exact need of the training should be identified. This would include the level of personnel to be trained, the scope of the training by way of subjects to be covered and the duration of training.
2. Once the training needs are identified, suitable method of training needs to be decided. It could be by participation in open seminars and training programs or by organization of in house program. The number of persons to be trained and cost of training would determine the mode of training.
3. Training is provided to personnel so that they can apply the knowledge gained during training. Therefore, opportunities should be provided to the trained personnel to apply their knowledge for the benefit of the organization. Training which is not applied in time is a wasted asset. It also has a demoralising effect on the employees who will not take training seriously in future.
4. If training was provided for a specific need, fulfilment of that need must be assessed. Application of training must be evaluated whether it has achieved the specified objectives.
5. Results of evaluation should be thoroughly examined and shortcomings of the training should be identified. Based on this analysis, changes may be made in the content of the training or methodology of conduct of training. While redesigning training packages, you must build on the strengths and overcome the problem faced. The concept of PDCA can be used for continuous improvement in training for competence building of employees.

ATTITUDE OF WORKERS

If we were asked to name one individual who contributes the maximum to the quality of product, the answer undoubtedly will point to the operator. It is he who actually builds quality into the product. His attitude to work is a decisive factor in determining the quality of the product. Unfortunately, the obsession of modern managers for higher production (or productivity) has affected the attitude of the operator to the detriment of quality. In this context, Frank Nixon, the well known quality engineer rightly says, "The apostles of F.W. Taylor for instance, lesser men on the whole than the master, have concentrated so much upon output and its increase that they have succeeded in so modifying the operative's outlook and that of many a manager too, that he has come to identify work with quantity. What they forgot was that it was 'good pieces that were required, not just more of them. And they succeeded in large measure in destroying the operator's identity with and pride in his work." There is a need to redefine productivity so that it includes quality of the product also in addition to its quantity. Due recognition of quality will re-awaken the spirit of craftsmanship and pride in the quality of work.

WORKERS' RESPONSIBILITY FOR QUALITY

It will be interesting to ask the questions, as to who is ultimately responsible for the quality, the management or the operator? The answer will generally depend upon the quality situation of the company. If the company is able to maintain good quality of their product, the management may take the credit for it. On the other hand if the quality of their product is rather poor, they will generally blame the worker, and bemoan his lack of interest and loss in the pride of workmanship. Let us analyse the extent of the worker's responsibility in the non-conformance of quality. Quality conformance can be achieved only if the process is kept under a slate of control. It is the management's responsibility to provide the operator with the necessary means by which he can exercise effective control over the process. This involves the following:-

(a) The operator must know what he is supposed to do.
(b) He should have adequate facilities and empowerment to perform.
(c) He must have means by which he can know the results of his action.
(d) He must be able to regulate the process, should the results be unsatisfactory.

Once the above means have been provided to the operator, it now depends upon the ability and the will of the operator. If he is still not able to achieve the quality the cause must lie with him. Here again, merely pinning the responsibility on the worker does not solve the problem. The causes of his inability to meet the quality targets must be investigated to find suitable remedial measures.

CAUSES OF OPERATOR'S ERRORS

Operator's errors result from three main causative factors, namely,

(a) Incompetence
(b) Lack of awareness
(c) Carelessness and lack of interest.

INCOMPETENCE

Operator can be expected to achieve quality conformance only if he has the necessary skill. Some operators may be able to achieve the quality targets consistently, while others may not be able to maintain the required quality level in spite of their best efforts. The difference may be in the skill. Once this deficiency has been identified the remedy lies in training the operators to enable them to acquire necessary proficiency in their job.

LACK OF AWARENESS

There are some errors which are made by the operators without their being aware of it. Such errors can be minimised by making the process as fool-proof as possible. Use of fixtures which automatically ensure that the job is correctly positioned for the operation, or an assembly design where the product cannot be assembled the wrong way are some of the examples of fool-proofing. In addition, certain devices may be incorporated in the process, which provide a visual or sonic alarm when an error is made, so that the operator is alerted in time. Other measures to reduce such errors are proper lighting, clean working conditions and avoiding undue fatigue and long working hours.

CARELESSNESS AND LACK OF INTEREST

The majority of the operator's errors are caused by this factor. How has this situation been brought about, where the operator or worker is apparently not interested in the product he manufactures? The main cause of his disinterest is the lack of knowledge about the product. Seeming indifference on the part of operators to the quality of the product is not due to the fact that they want to produce bad jobs. It is mainly due to ignorance and lack of understanding of the implications of poor quality. The old craftsmen made all the components of a product themselves, and saw the result of their labour in the final product. Thereby they were aware of the flaws if any in the finished product, and took pains to improve the quality by eliminating the flaws in the next piece.

In the modern mass production technology, the product has been broken down into small discrete elements, and a worker may be producing thousands of small parts every day, without knowing where they fit, what is their function and what may happen if they are not made exactly according to the specification. Under these circumstances he cannot be blamed if he is not very much concerned about its quality.

MOTIVATION OF WORKERS

What makes people work? This is a complex question which has not yet been fully answered. The situation is further complicated when a worker is required simultaneously to attain two or more targets seemingly aimed in different directions. Should he meet the production target or should he concentrate on quality. To him quantitative output is more important because it is this which often determines the size of his wage packet. Why should he then bother about quality? However, the situation is not so hopeless as it appears. We have already seen that there is no basic conflict between quality and quantity. They are in fact complementary, but this has to be explained to the worker and his misconception removed. He must be convinced that it is in his as well as the company's interest that he should attain the required quality level in addition to meeting the quantity targets. Some of the measure aim in this direction are discussed below:

FINANCIAL INCENTIVES

In most industries, the financial incentives are based on piece rate system, which are output oriented. Though a worker generally does not get paid for a job which gets rejected due to bad workmanship (if detected in time), the form of incentive makes him strive for minimal quality which will just pass inspection. Whatever idealists may say, financial incentive is a major motivating factor which makes the operators work. As long as financial incentives are linked with quantitative output only, the worker cannot be expected to make a serious effort for quality improvement. Some form of financial incentive linked with quality of the product such as quality bonus or merit payment will provide a strong motivation for the operator to improve the quality of his work. For quality incentives to be effective, the quality of the product must be measurable in quantitative terms, so that there is no dispute about quality assessment and the workers know exactly what is required of them.

WORKER'S INVOLVEMENT IN QUALITY IMPROVEMENT

The most effective means of stimulating interest in quality and creating pride in workmanship is by direct involvement of the workers in the quality improvement programmes. Genuine participation can be expected only if operatives are given full opportunity to express constructive criticism and suggest methods of improvement. Suggestions of the workers should be given serious consideration, and if found practicable, should be straightway implemented, and the author of the suggestion should receive due recognition and public appreciation. If the suggestion is not found useful, its drawbacks should be discussed with the workers and the difficulties in its implementation should be explained to them. It is possible that the author or some other worker may come up with new ideas for overcoming the problem. In no case should any suggestion be just brushed aside, because it apparently looks absurd. In fact they should be encouraged to offer any solution which comes to their mind without fear of being ridiculed. This approach can be given practical shape by constituting shop quality committees, which could meet periodically and review the working of quality programmes. These meetings, if properly conducted will draw upon the experience and ideas of the actual operatives, which will be invaluable in highlighting the weak spots so that suitable corrective measures could be taken. This climate of joint consultation will give the workers a sense of participation and involvement and generate enthusiasm for the quality programmes. In the recent years, a number of formalised motivation techniques aimed at securing workers participation have been developed. The notable among these are Zero Defect campaign in USA, and QC Circle movement in JAPAN.

9

Management of Service Quality

What is a service quality?

ISO 9000:2005 defines quality as:

"Degree to which a set of inherent characteristics fulfill requirements."

This definition of quality is equally applicable in services sector. The difference is in identifying the "features" mentioned in the above definition. In a physical product, the features could be the look and feel of the product, its functional performance in meeting customer requirements, reliability, and ease of maintenance etc. On the other hand, in service industry the major deliverable is the service though it may contain a certain amount of physical product also. For example, banking, insurance, travel, security and sanitation sectors provide only services, whereas hospitability, healthcare may contain some physical element such as food and medicines. For products, the quality can be measured in quantitative terms, but in services quality evaluation is largely subjective. A workable definition of quality for service sector is given by the equation.

$$\text{Quality (Q)} = \frac{\text{Performance (P)}}{\text{Expectation (E)}}$$

Thus closer the service performance is to the expectation of the customer higher is the quality.

ATTRIBUTES OF SERVICE QUALITY

While detailed elements influencing quality in different service sectors may vary considerably, these in general can be categorized under the following attributes:

1. **Reliability**: Ability to provide the promised service dependably timely and accurately.
2. **Safety and security**: Ability to ensure safety of the customer and his assets as well as security of environment and information relating to the customer.
3. **Assurance**: The competence of personnel and the system and their ability to convey trust and confidence.
4. **Tangibles**: Building and infrastructure of the service facility, equipment, communication, materials and appearance of personnel.
5. **Responsiveness and empathy**: Ease of access, care taken to understand customer needs, providing prompt and courteous service.

Major difference in specifying quality for products and services is that unlike products you cannot define characteristics which are measurable in quantitative terms. That is not to say that service quality cannot be evaluated. The service can be measured by independent observation and through feedback of customers both of which have some degree of subjectivity. The second difference is that while product quality can be measured in absolute terms, in service quality customers may give different weightage to various quality attributes as such the perception of overall service quality may differ from customer to customer. For example, reliability is the most important attribute in financial and travel services. On the other hand customers in Government services and food service industry give more importance to responsiveness and in lodging and recreation sector tangibles get higher weightage.

CUSTOMERS' VIEW OF SERVICE QUALITY

Another way of looking at service quality is through the wish list of customers. Some service organizations have codified service quality in terms of customers bill of rights. Communication of bill of rights to the customers is the true test of management in their belief in service quality. To illustrate defining quality which customers can demand, the customers bill of rights in Air Canada and Toyota service centers is given below:

CUSTOMERS BILL OF RIGHTS IN AIR CANADA

Accurate information, courtesy, comfort and punctuality are some of the basic rights to which every Air Canada customer is entitled. And no one is more qualified than you to see to it that these rights are protected.

- The customer has the right to get through to reservations without waiting and to receive prompt, friendly, courteous service and accurate information.
- The customer has the right to cheerful and efficient service at the sales offices, cargo terminals, airport checkins, and departure gates.
- The customer has the right to a hassle-free flight, a comfortable seat, a good meal, friendly service, and an entertainment system that works.
- The customer has the right to be serviced in the official language of his or her choice.
- The customer has the right to depart and arrive on time.
- The customer has the right to receive his or her baggage and/or cargo promptly and in good condition.
- The customer has the right to be kept informed when there are delays or when things to wrong, and to be treated with extra care in these circumstances.
- The customer has the right to receive prompt decisions concerning compensation.
- The customer has the right to be treated with care and compassion.

CUSTOMERS BILL OF RIGHTS IN TOYOTA

- The right to a clear explanation of the reasons for all recommended repairs and adjustments.
- The right to know in advance of the cost of repairs to your car.
- The right to approve any work done on your car beforehand.
- The right to a clear-cut, understandable schedule of charges.
- The right to quality repairs.
- The right to the lowest cost repairs with good quality, safety of operation, and compliance with emission control and safety legislation.
- The right to delivery of your car when promised.
- The right to deal with courteous and concerned people.

CREATING ENVIRONMENT FOR QUALITY IMPROVEMENT

It should be remembered that man is the dominant element in service delivery. It is the personnel of marketing or sales which make the first contact with the customers. They are the ones who understand the requirements of the customer and initiate internal processes to provide the service. Next come the operations people who interact with the customer at various stages of service delivery including settlement of bills. Each one of the contact points can be a **Moment of Truth** when the customer judges the service quality and forms an opinion. Thus quality can be improved by having documented standards for various activities. Though standards help, it is the actual conduct of the company person interacting with the customer which determines the quality as perceived by the customer. In short, it is the motivation and enthusiasm of customer facing employees to please the customer which will carry the day. This attitude does not come just by sending employees for training on customer satisfaction, though it is certainly helpful in building competence. The key to the motivation is with the top management. The CEO and senior members of the management have to be drivers. For this CEO and top functionaries have to get out of offices and meet the frontline staff. They have to ask questions about their job and their problems with the customers as well as their bosses. They should get the real picture whether they have right facilities and set up. Do the staff feel they have adequate authority or they have to defer decisions to the senior bosses? What kind of authority would enable them to provide prompt and superior service? Once they have understood the problems at the front line, they must take actions to address various issues brought out by the employees. Otherwise an impression will be created among employees that management does not care what they have said and next time they will not open up when someone asks about their job.

The CEO has to show by his actions that he really cares for customers. These actions could be CEO or senior official ringing up some customers who have been provided a service as to whether they are satisfied and how the service could be improved. Occasionally CEO can even walk up to the place the service is provided and chat with customers on various service matters. In addition to the impact on the customers with whom CEO interacted, a strong message would go to the employees that boss really cares about customers, and would not tolerate any action by the employees which causes customer dissatisfaction. This concept of customer care and empowerment of employees can be given institutional shape by redesigning the organizational structure.

Normal organizations such as shown in Fig.1 are based on control. Here manager at higher level controls those below for proper functioning and performance. Customers actually come at the bottom of the pyramid. In this organizational structure, persons at various levels try to please their immediate bosses and control those below. To the frontline worker, his superior is more important than the customer which he is serving. In case his superior calls him, he would have no hesitation in requesting customer to wait while he attends to urgent call by his boss. Truly customer driven organization should follow an inverted pyramid structure which is a support model as shown in Fig. 2.

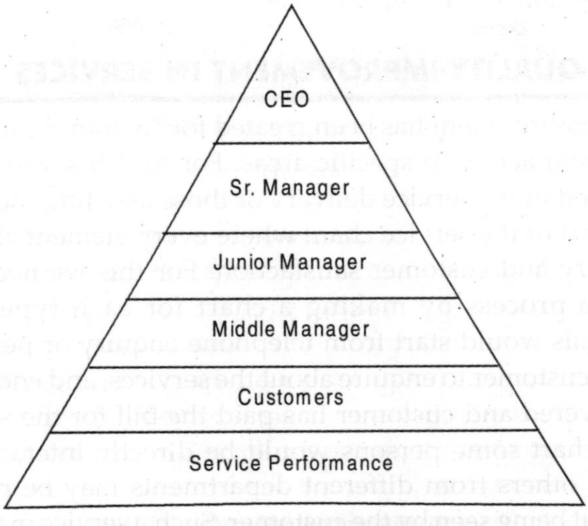

Fig.1 Control Model Organization

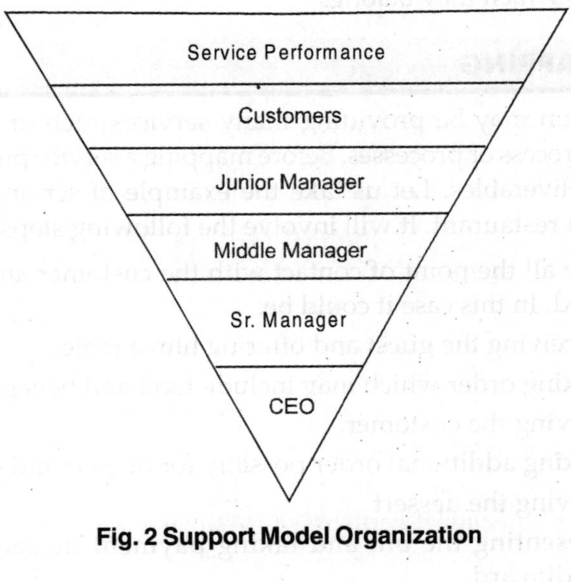

Fig. 2 Support Model Organization

In the second model, the CEO and higher management support and empower the junior management and staff in serving the customer better. The control function of course will remain, but the focus will be on support facilitation of lower levels to serve the customer better. In this organizational model, a clear message goes that customer is really the boss of every one including the CEO. Various measures to develop customer focus has been discussed at length in chapter-12, which are applicable both in manufacturing and service sector.

PLANNING QUALITY IMPROVEMENT IN SERVICES

Once proper environment has been created for customer care, we can take up improvement action in specific areas. For this, first we need to make people involved in the service delivery or those assisting them realize that they are all part of the service chain where every element affects the total service delivery and customer satisfaction. For this we need to map the entire service process by making a chart for each type of customer transaction. This would start from telephone enquiry or personal contact by a potential customer to enquire about the services, and end when service has been delivered and customer has paid the bill for the service. In this service flow chart some persons would be directly interacting with the customer and others from different departments may be processing the service without being seen by the customer. Such a service map help people involved in the service see the total service delivery process and their own part in it. This enables them to function as a team irrespective of the department to which they belong.

PROCESS MAPPING

An organization may be providing many services each of which would have its own process or processes. Before mapping a service process, identify the service deliverables. Let us take the example of serving meal to the customers in a restaurant. It will involve the following steps:

1. Identify all the point of contact with the customer and the process involved. In this case it could be:
   - (a) Receiving the guest and offering him a table.
   - (b) Taking order which may include food and beverages.
   - (c) Serving the customer.
   - (d) Taking additional order possibly for dessert and coffee.
   - (e) Serving the dessert
   - (f) Presenting the bill and taking payment in cash or through credit card.
2. Identify supporting processes

Some of the above customer service processes may have support processes which in this example could be:

   - (a) Communication of customer order details to the kitchen and bar.

(b) Preparation of dishes and drinks by the respective sections.
(c) Delivery of dishes and drinks to the waiter.
(d) Computation for preparing bills by respective sections.
(e) Accepting the payment through credit card transaction process.

EXAMINATION OF PROCESSES

To identify opportunities for improvement, examine all processes by asking questions which bring clarity in the process and whether it is aimed at providing full satisfaction to the customers. Some typical questions are given below:

(a) Who is responsible for the process?
(b) Does he have requisite competence?
(c) Has the customer been explained all the choices and time implications? This will help the customer to make a choice taking into consideration time available.
(d) Does the serving person ask the customer about his special requirement such as spices or other contents of the meal, or the size of the portion to be served?
(e) How does the serving person ensure that he has correctly understood the customers' requirements? He could repeat the order to the customer to get his confirmation.
(f) How is it ensured that the customers' order has been correctly conveyed to the kitchen, particularly the special requirements?
(g) Does the waiter get the feedback when first course of the meal is served? This will help in making adjustment in the other courses. If a customer does not like any dish is there a system to offer replacement or another dish without any extra charge?

Thus process mapping and its examination is a powerful tool for identifying improvement opportunities.

QUALITY IMPROVEMENT IN FINANCIAL SERVICES

To illustrate the quality improvement methodology we will now take the case of financial services which is the largest growing segment in the service sector. This sector has been chosen because there are major differences in this sector as compared to other sectors. These are briefly described below:

(a) *The customers are buyers as well as suppliers:* The customers supply information which forms the basis for the service to be provided by the bank. It could be withdrawal of cash transfer of funds to some other account, making a change in the nomination for an insurance policy or converting an individual account into a joint account. Based on these requests these are processed and changes are made and communicated to the customer. Thus customer also plays a part in the quality of service provided.

(*b*) In some areas customers have limited understanding of what they are purchasing. Thus they may not be able to specify their requirements. For example buying an insurance policy it is not only the total amount of coverage and rate of premium. There are various options and terms of the policy which a customer has to choose. Unless the customer is explained the implication of all the terms he cannot make an informed choice which may lead to his dissatisfaction when his claim is processed.

(*c*) *Cooperation with competitors:* In some areas of provision of service the companies may cooperate with competitors for money transactions or agreeing on insurance claims.

(*d*) *Application of statistical techniques:* These service organizations cannot apply statistical process control techniques in financial transactional process; unlike products and other service these do not have tolerance limits. If Rs.10,000 is to be transferred even Rs. 99,999 which represents an error of 0.001% is not acceptable. Thus zero error in financial transaction is a must, as such non-statistical controls have to be applied to ensure accurate service. However, statistical techniques can still be applied in cases such as delays in transactions.

SPECIAL QUALITY ATTRIBUTES

While service quality attributes discussed earlier in the chapter are applicable to financial sector also, but there are a few other attributes mentioned below have a major influence on quality in this sector.

(*a*) *Cost of services:* While cost does figure in purchase decision of any product it is not considered a quality attribute. Here the product itself is related to money. As the financial product becomes commodity, cost reduction has a major effect on making the product attributive, thus it becomes a quality parameter.

(*b*) *100% accuracy:* In financial services there is no margin of any error. The basic element of banking is trust, which will be eroded if there are significant errors.

(*c*) *Speed and timeliness:* The nature of banking service is such that time is literally money as the amount of interest earned is based on time. If the process of remittance from a source takes one week to get credited in the customers' account, he will lose that weeks interest. Thus speed of financial transaction is a major quality parameter. In addition to loss of interest, delay in crediting of the amount in the account may result in bouncing of a cheque issued from that account causing major embarrassment and loss of reputation or even in a loss of a business proposition.

(*d*) *Measurement of service parameters:* Quality improvement in any financial service organization needs proper measurement of delivered service quality. In financial services, it is comparatively easy to measure the service quality. The errors in financial transactions are detected by internal controls and in statutory audits. Even errors made by the operating personnel and later corrected when detected can be tracked because the incorrect entries would be reversed in the computer system. In addition, customers are also alert about the bringing the errors in their accounts to the notice of the bank. Analysis of these errors and their causative factors help in deciding quality improvement measures. Measurements discussed above mainly pertain to financial errors which is only one source of customer dissatisfaction. Other attributes of service quality, such as lack of promptness, courtesy and difficulty due to physical environment can also be the cause of dissatisfaction and loss of customers. The status of these attributes can be determined through process mapping as discussed in the example of food service process. In financial services the process mapping will start from the time the customer makes the first contact with an employee or agent of the financial service institution. It will track all subsequent processes till the customer completes the financial transaction with a bank. In the case of insurance service, mapping should also include processing of claims from its submission to its final settlement. Critical examination of various customer contact points in the process map may reveal the weaknesses and generate ideas for improvement.

SOURCES FOR IDENTIFYING IMPROVEMENT OPPORTUNITIES

Feedback From Customers

In addition to clues from the process mapping, customers' feedback is also an important source for getting ideas for quality improvement. While examining the feedback and complaints from the customers, the data pertaining to the subject process should be analyzed to study the weaknesses in the service processes and how these could be improved.

Suggestions From Employees

Employees involved in the service delivery have pretty good idea abut the service quality. In addition to formal feedback, they can assess from the body language of the customer whether they have liked the service or the aspect with which they are not satisfied. They can offer suggestions for improvement which if implemented are likely to work because the employees would take the ownership of improved processes.

IMPLEMENTATION OF IMPROVEMENTS

All improvements identified as a result of examination of processes or by analysis of customer feedback and employee suggestions need to be examined by a multi-disciplinary committee to assess their feasibility and financial impact. These need to be prioritized on the basis of their impact on customer satisfaction and ease of implementation. In the first phase the suggestions involving procedural change and development of skills can be implemented, as these are relatively easy to implement. Once these process improvements have been made, their impact on the customer satisfaction needs to be assessed objectively. Positive impact should be communicated to employees through various channels and the contribution of quality improvement teams and authors of suggestions should be publicly recognized. This will encourage other employees to think about improvement in their areas of responsibility.

Once the beneficial effects of improvement made in the first phase has been validated, the management can take up improvements such as upgradation of facilities, infrastructure and communication system which may involve considerable investment. If improvements have been identified through proper analysis of their impact on customer satisfaction, the investment made would be recovered in a short time and improved service would enhance market share and profitability. It should also be recognized that improvement of service quality is not a onetime exercise. With intensifying competition and rising demands of the customer, service quality has to be continuously improved if the organization has to survive and retain its market share.

PART-II

10

Concept and Philosophy

In Part-1 of the Book we have discussed the basic concept of product quality and how it is built through the activities of various departments of an organization. The technical functions we have discussed in last few chapters contribute the basic structure of quality management system. However, quality management is a much more complex issue and involves soft issues like leadership, culture of the organization, attitude towards customers, motivation of employees and finally the contribution of quality in the profitability of an organization which is the prime objective of any business organization. To manage all these issues, a broader concept of quality has been evolved which deals with not only the quality of products and services but the performance of organization as a whole in its journey towards excellence. This concept is known as Total Quality Management.

CONCEPT OF TQM

TQM is a philosophy for the optimal utilization of resources for the maximum benefits of all stakeholders of the organization, including society at large. The International organization for standardization (ISO) defines TQM as follows:

> *"Total Quality Management is the management approach of an organization, centered on quality, based on the participation of all its members and aiming at long-term success through customer satisfaction, and with benefits to all members of the organization and to society."*

Some other organizations have elaborated on this definition for greater clarity. According to the Total Quality Forum of the USA, TQM is defined as follows:

> *"TQM is a people-focused management system that aims at continual increase in customer satisfaction at continually lower cost. TQM is a total system approach (not a separate area or program) and an integral part of high-level strategy. It works horizontally across functions and departments, involving all employees, top to bottom, and extends backward and forward to include the supply chain and the customer chain."*

TQM has three basic tenets:

- It is TOTAL involving all departments/groups in an organization at all levels.
- It relates to QUALITY in the broader sense of organizational excellence, and does not just refer to product quality.
- It is a MANAGEMENT function and is not just confined to a technical discipline.

New management and quality tools and techniques may evolve and some current tools may become obsolete. However, because of the universal nature the above three tenets of the basic concept of TQM will always remain relevant to the pursuit of excellence.

WHY DO WE NEED TQM?

Ideally, everyone in the organization should be committed to TQM. However, according to Deming's research, some 94% of the problems related to quality are caused by management and the system they create. Product and service quality and its cost have always been important factors for securing a higher share of business. However with the globalization of the economy in the wake of the WTO regime, competition has intensified and organizations providing higher quality at lower costs are immediately rewarded and can take the market share of the poor performers. Thus the management of companies around the world have started paying serious attention to quality. This is illustrated by the following view of John Young, former President of Hewlett-Packard, a leading global company.

> *"In order to compete in a global economy, our products, systems and services must be of a higher quality than our competition. Increasing Total Quality is our number one priority here at Hewlett-Packard."*

TQM PHILOSOPHY

No management concept has contributed as much to the phenomenal industrial progress in the 20th century as the TQM. This century has produced a number of illustrious management thinkers whose impact on industry and services for the benefit of society could justly be compared with that of the famous classical Greek Philosophers on their abstract thought. The world is lucky to have received the combined wisdom of Eastern as well as Western quality experts in this regard, since both Japan and the West were contributors to the body of knowledge on quality management. The TQM movement has been influenced largely by the following seven 'quality gurus' - four from the USA and three from Japan. The essence of their philosophy for implementing TQM is discussed in the following paragraphs.

W. EDWARDS DEMING

Dr. W. Edwards Deming was born in 1900. He obtained a doctorate in mathematical physics and subsequently worked for the US Government, where he applied Shewhart's statistical process control to his work at the National Bureau of the Census. He is famous for his work in Japan as General MacArthur's Advisor, where he helped with the industrial reconstruction of Japan after the Second World War. Japanese industrial leaders applied his teachings on quality management, which was probably one of the factors that helped them to capture substantial share in US markets over the next few decades – in that sense he was probably more honoured in Japan than in his own country. In his honour the Japanese Union of Scientists and Engineers (JUSE) has instituted the Deming Award for excellence in Quality. He advocated the 14-point approach given below for managerial transformation, which in turn could lead to effective implementation of quality management. <<Are you sure the Deming phraseology is correct – may want to check it exactly – some of the phrases in italics below have incorrect grammar or don't make sense>>.

1. *Create constancy of purpose for improvement of products? and services?* Dr. Deming suggests a radical new definition of a company's role. A better way to make money is to stay in business and provide jobs through innovation, research, constant improvement and maintenance. I would not agree with this interpretation – it seems to me that the phrase is more restricted in its scope – it simply seems to suggest that companies innovate as a series of plateaus, *i.e.,* they develop some product and then continue to sell it until it is clearly obsolete and then try to make a new one. He seems to suggest that innovation should be both continuous and endless. Nothing about staying in business or creating jobs.
2. *Adopt the new philosophy*. For the new economic age, management needs to take leadership for change into a 'learning organization'. Furthermore, we need a new belief system in the company, in which mistakes and negativism are unacceptable.
3. *Cease dependence on mass inspection*. Eliminate the need for mass inspection by building quality into the product.

4. *End awarding business on price.* Instead, aim at minimum total cost and move towards single suppliers and forge long-term relationship.
5. *Improve constantly and forever the system of production and service.* Improvement is not a one-time effort. Management is obligated to continually look for ways to reduce cost and improve quality. This is the same as point #1, but applied to production rather than innovation.
6. *Institute training.* Too often, workers have learned their job from other workers who have themselves never been trained properly. They are forced to follow unintelligible instructions. They can't do their jobs well because no one tells them how to do so.
7. *Institute leadership.* The job of a supervisor is not to tell people what to do, nor to punish them for errors, but to lead. Leading consists of helping people to do a better job and to learn by objective methods.
8. *Drive out fear.* Many employees are afraid to ask questions or to take a controversial position, even when they do not understand what their job is or what is right or wrong. Instead, they may continue to do things the wrong way, or not do them at all. The economic losses resulting from fear can be both appalling and invisible. To assure better quality and productivity, it is necessary that people feel secure.
9. *Break down barriers between departments.* Often a company's departments or units are competing with each other or have goals that conflict. They do not work as a team and therefore, they cannot solve or foresee problems.
10. *Eliminate slogans, exhortations and numerical targets for the workforce.* These never help anybody do a good job. Let workers formulate their own slogans. Then they will be committed to the contents.
11. *Eliminate numerical quotas or work standards.* Quotas take into account only numbers, not quality or methods. They are usually a guarantee of inefficiency and high cost. A person, in order to hold a job, will try to meet a quota at any cost, including doing damage to his company.
12. *Remove barriers to taking pride in workmanship.* People are eager to do a good job and distressed when they cannot. Too often, misguided supervisors, faulty equipment and defective materials stand in the way of good performance. These barriers must be removed.
13. *Institute a vigorous program of education.* Both management and the workforce will have to be educated in the new knowledge and understanding associated with this program, including teamwork and statistical techniques.
14. *Take action to accomplish the transformation.* It will require a special management team with a concrete plan of action to carry out the quality mission. Workers cannot do it on their own, nor can managers. A critical mass of people in the company must understand the 14 points.

In late eighties Deming promoted the concept of Management by positive co-operation which consists of three elements:

- Joy in work.
- Innovation, and
- Co-operation.

To implement this concept he proposed creation of a 'Win-Win' environment as opposed to the adversarial climate of 'I- Win- You- Lose' engrained by increasing competition. This is particularly applicable to establishing long-term customer – supplier relationships.

PLAN-DO-CHECK-ACT (PDCA) CYCLE

One of the most important contributions of Deming is the Plan-Do-Check-Act (PDCA) cycle. These are the four fundamental steps for any corrective or quality improvement activity. The PDCA cycle is illustrated in the figure below:

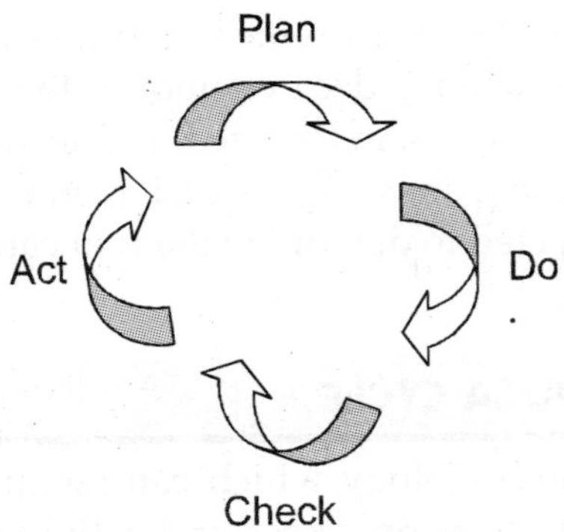

Fig. 1

This cycle is an important tool for taking corrective action to bring a process into control. For this activity, Dr. Deming advises that we should concentrate on the removal of assignable causes of problems to bring a process under control. The PDCA cycle can also be used for an organized quality improvement effort. The activities involved in the four PDCA steps are briefly explained below:

PLAN

This is the most crucial step in the PDCA cycle. It is in this step that a plan is created for corrective activities. This involves diagnosis of the problem to determine root causes. A number of statistical and non-statistical tools are available for this diagnosis, which are discussed in part II of this book. When the PDCA cycle is to be used for quality improvement, we need to first define the objective of this improvement. Once the objective is defined, the strategy and tools to achieve the objective can be decided upon, and a plan prepared.

Do

This is the phase when the plan is implemented. For this it is necessary to communicate the plan to the persons who will be involved in implementation. It is important that they fully understand the Plan and have the required skills to implement it. In addition, management has to provide the necessary resources for implementation of the plan.

Check

In this phase the performance after implementation of the plan is measured and analyzed to assess the extent to which the desired results have been achieved. If expected results are not achieved, the analysis may also help to pinpoint the cause of failure.

Act

Based on the results of the measurement and analysis during the Check stage, the next course of action is decided upon. If the results are satisfactory then the changed process is standardized and incorporated into regular procedures or work instructions. However, if results are not satisfactory, a further search is conducted to determine the root causes - which forms the basis of new plan cycle.

APPLICATION OF PDCA CYCLE

PDCA is a generic methodology which can be applied to bring about improvement in all kinds of processes and activities. Dr. Juran, another renowned quality expert has added a third dimension to the PDCA cycle. He advises that the cycle should not be viewed as flat; rather it should be viewed as an ever-rising spiral as shown in Figure-2. At the end of one cycle, the next planning activity should be for a higher level of quality. This quest for successively higher quality levels should go on, as this is an endless journey.

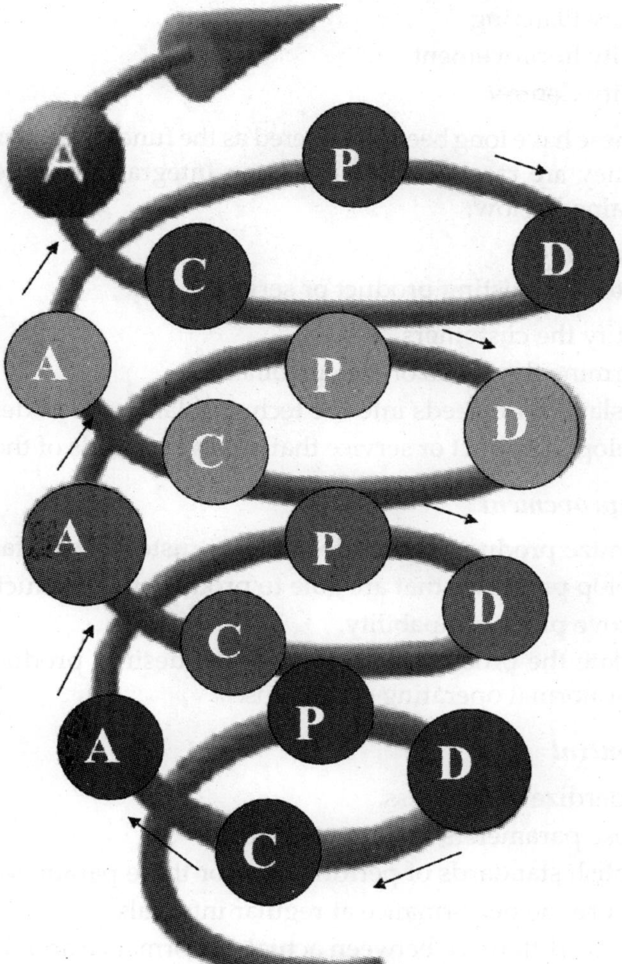

Fig. 2

JOSEPH M. JURAN

He is a contemporary of Deming. Born in 1904, he started his career as an engineer in 1924. He became internationally famous with publication of his first Quality Control Handbook in 1951. He was also invited to Japan in 1954 where he conducted a number of seminars for Japanese managers. His message to them was that quality control should be organized as an integral part of management.

His unique contribution is the idea of the Quality Trilogy, with the following three elements:

- Quality Planning
- Quality Improvement
- Quality Control

While these have long been considered as the fundamental management functions, they are rarely considered in an integrated manner. They are briefly explained below:

Quality Planning

In the context of existing product or services:

- Identify the customers.
- Determine the needs of the customers.
- Translate those needs into the technical language of designers.
- Develop a product or service that meets the needs of the customers.

Quality Improvement

- Optimize product features to enhance customer satisfaction.
- Develop processes that are able to produce the product or service.
- Improve process capability.
- Validate the process(es) to achieve the desired product or service under normal operating conditions.

Quality Control

- Standardize the process.
- Choose parameters to be controlled.
- Establish standards of performance for these parameters.
- Measure the performance at regular intervals.
- Note the difference between actual performance and the standard.
- Take action to close the performance gap.
- Check whether corrective action has been effective.
- Continue this performance according to the standard.

To achieve Quality Improvement, Juran has suggested a 10-step approach, as given outlined below:

1. Build awareness of opportunities to improve.
2. Set goals for improvement.
3. Organize to reach goals.
4. Provide training.
5. Carry out projects to solve problems.
6. Report progress.
7. Provide recognition.
8. Communicate results.

9. Keep score.
10. Maintain momentum.

Juran was the first quality expert who stressed the fact that we should not concentrate solely on the end-customer. According to him, internal customers are equally important for ensuring the quality of the end-product. Each internal process has its own customer, and we must understand the requirements of internal customers. It must be ensured that products or services delivered to internal customers in the intermediate stages of production/operation are "fit for use." The entire customer supplier chain within the company must be strong if we are to fully satisfy our ultimate customer.

PHILIP CROSBY

He was born in 1926 and started his career as a reliability engineer. He was later part of Martin Company's missile program, which started the "Zero Defect" movement. He exposed the weakness of traditional quality control methods as practiced in most manufacturing companies at the time. The then-prevailing concept of Acceptable Quality Limits (AQL) and concessions for out-of-tolerance jobs or waivers of substandard products offered a false sense of quality assurance. Actually it represented a failure of quality control, since authority for the acceptance of 'minor' non-conformance to specifications gradually led to increasing tolerance for substandard products under pressure of targets and deliveries. Unfortunately this situation still prevails in industries in many developing countries, and is the main reason why their products are not able to achieve international standards of quality.

Crosby promoted the concepts of "Do it Right First Time" and advocated four absolutes of Quality Management, as outlined below.

1. Quality is defined as conformance to requirements, not as 'goodness' or 'elegance.'
2. The system for causing quality is prevention, not appraisal.
3. The performance standard must be zero defects, not "that's close enough."
4. The measurement of quality is the price of non-conformance, not indices.

Phillip Crosby did not confine himself solely to the philosophy of quality management - he also suggested a concrete plan of action for implementing TQM.

CROSBY'S 14- STEP PROGRAM

STEP 1

Management Commitment

Top management must become convinced of the need for quality improvement and must make its commitment clear to the entire company.

STEP 2

Quality Improvement Team

Management must form a team of departmental heads to oversee quality improvement. The team's role is to see that needed actions take place in its departments and in the company as a whole.

STEP 3

Quality Measurement

Quality measures that are appropriate to every activity must be established to identify areas needing improvement.

STEP 4

Cost of Quality Evaluation

The controller's office should make an estimate of the costs of quality to identify areas where quality improvements would be profitable.

STEP 5

Quality Awareness

Quality awareness must be raised among employees. They must understand the importance of product conformance and the costs of non-conformance.

STEP 6

Corrective Action

Opportunities for correction are generated by Steps 3 and 4, as well as by discussions among employees. These ideas should be brought to the supervisory level and resolved there, if possible, or pushed higher for necessary action.

STEP 7

Zero-Defects Planning

An *ad hoc* defects committee should be formed from members of the quality improvement team. This committee should start planning a zero- defects program appropriate to the company and its culture.

STEP 8

Supervisory Training

Early in the process, all levels of management must be trained to implement their part of the quality improvement program.

STEP 9

Zero-Defects Day

A zero-defects day should be scheduled to signal to employees that the company has new performance standards.

STEP 10

Goal Setting

To turn commitments into action, individuals must establish improvement goals for themselves and their groups.

STEP 11

Errors Cause Removal

Employees should be encouraged to report to the management about any problems that prevent them from performing error-free work. Reported problems must then be acknowledged by management within 24 hours.

STEP 12

Recognition

Public, non-financial appreciation must be given to those who meet their quality goals or perform outstandingly.

STEP 13

Quality Councils

Quality professionals and team chairpersons should meet regularly to share experiences, problems and ideas.

STEP 14

Do it All Over Again

To emphasize the never-ending process of quality, the program (steps 1-13) must be repeated. This renews the commitment of old employees and brings new ones into the process. It also creates a no- nonsense environment that reinforces again and again, one basic theme: zero-defect management is possible.

In his Book "Quality Without Tears", Crosby says,

"The main problem of quality as a management concern is that it is not taught in management schools. It is not considered to be a management function, but rather a technical one. However, with the pressure on quality erupting worldwide and the difficulty in getting senior management to do something about it, it becomes apparent that a new management is needed for quality".

TOM PETERS

Tom Peters is one of the most famous 'Management Gurus' of the 1990s. His philosophy is that the quality improvement process will be successful if it is driven by the company's leadership, and he has prescribed twelve elements which can usher in a quality revolution. These are:

1. Management obsession with quality
2. Passion (and champions)
3. Measurement of quality
4. Quality is rewarded
5. Every one is trained for quality
6. Multi-function teams
7. Small is beautiful
8. Create endless Hathorne effect
9. Parallel organizational structure devoted to quality improvement
10. Every one is involved
11. When quality goes up, costs go down.
12. Quality improvement is a never-ending journey.

KAORU ISHIKAWA

Professor Ishikawa is a famous quality expert from Japan. He was born in 1915, he obtained a degree in engineering in 1939 and subsequently was a professor at Tokyo university. He was awarded the Deming prize and an industrial standardization prize for his writings on Quality Control. He was also given the Grant Award by the American Society for Quality (ASQ) for his education program on Quality Control.

His biggest contribution to Quality Management is simplifying statistical techniques for quality control in industry. His famous cause–and – effect diagram also provides a powerful tool for problem- solving and quality improvement. This is discussed in chapter-33. He is also the pioneer of the Quality Circle movement in Japan, which is now being practiced in other countries including India to involve workers in the quality improvement efforts. The methodology of this concept is discussed in chapter-37.

In addition to the promotion of statistical tools for quality control and improvement, Prof. Ishikawa is also associated with the Company – Wide Quality Control (CWQC) movement which started in Japan in the 1950s. CWQC implies that quality control efforts are not confined only to the quality of products and production processes. They are equally applicable to other functions in the company such as Design, Materials Management, Marketing and after- sales service. Proper application of CWQC results in:

- Reduction of defects and improvement in product quality and reliability.
- Reduction in wasteful work and rework.
- Improvement in productivity and reduction in product cost.
- Better relationships between departments.
- More rational maintenance of equipment.
- Improvement in human relations.

In fact CWQC served as a basis for the further development of TQM concepts.

SHIGEO SHINGO

Mr. Shigeo Shingo was another prominent Japanese quality expert. He was born im 1909 and had an industrial engineering background. He emphasized the idea that once it was noticed that a defect has occurred during any process, the process should not be allowed to continue. It should be stopped to define the cause and prevent the recurring source of the defect. For this purpose he allowed the workers to stop a production line if they noticed a defect. Although this appears to be a drastic action, it brought home the importance of fault-free jobs to workers in the assembly line. They realized that if they allowed defective work to leave their work- station, they would then have to bear the responsibility of any subsequent line stoppage. Therefore, they were doubly careful to ensure that they performed their work perfectly. Shingo is famous for his non-statistical innovations for reducing defects – for instance he developed the concept of 'Poka–Yoke' or mistake-proofing. He introduced simple mechanical devices into assembly operations which prevented parts from being assembled incorrectly and signaled when a worker had forgotten one of these parts. These simple mistake- proofing methods resulted in a drastic reduction of defects.

His other work involved a major reduction of production and assembly time by streamlining the processes to reduce delays and bottlenecks. He developed 'Single Minute Exchange of Dies' (SMED) and the Just – in – Time System at Toyota, Japan. In this production system, input materials are delivered to production process just as they are needed. This led to a drastic reduction of inventories, leading to large savings of storage space, manpower and inventory carrying costs. His famous book on the Toyota Production System has been translated into many languages and has propounded new concepts in production management, with worldwide influence.

GENICHI TAGUCHI

Genichi Taguchi was born in 1924. He attended Kiryu Technical College where he studied textile engineering. He is best known for his innovative application of statistical theory to manufacturing problems. His major contributions are "Loss Function", 'off line' and 'on line' quality control. To explain the wider implications of quality assurance, he enunciates:

1. Quality is the loss imparted to the society from the time a product is shipped.
2. In a comparative economy, continuous quality improvement and cost reduction are necessary for staying in business.
3. A continuous quality improvement program includes incessant reduction in the variation of product performance characteristics approximating to their target value. *Six Sigma* is the practical application of this strategy.
4. The customer's loss due to a product's performance variation is often approximately proportional to the square of the deviation of the performance characteristic from its target value. *This is popularly known as 'Quality Loss Function'.*
5. The final quality and cost of a manufactured article are determined to a large extent by the engineering design of the product and the process of its manufacture.
6. The performance variation of product or process can be reduced by exploiting the nonlinear effects of the product and process parameters on the performance characteristics.
7. Statistically planned experiments can be used to determine the settings of product and process parameters that makes it robust to withstand environments encountered to reduce performance variation.

The concept of orthogonal arrays was contributed by Dr. C.R. Rao. Dr. Gaguchi introduced linear grahs. This made it easy and user friendly to formulate optimal design for experiment to develop robust product and process parameters that saved time and allied resources and yet assured valid conclusions. He has authored books on:

- Quality Engineering in Production Systems
- Introduction to Quality Engineering, Designing Quality into Product and Processes
- On-line Quality Control During Production, and
- Introduction to off-line Quality Control

STANDARDIZED QUALITY PRINCIPLES

All these quality experts have approached quality management from their own perspectives and experience. The guidelines and advice given by them is very useful, but it may leave the average quality practitioners confused as to which methodology of quality management to follow. Thus there was a need to build a universal consensus on a methodology for effective management of quality in any company. To meet this need, the International Organization for Standardization has developed a standard known as ISO-9000:2000 for Quality Management Systems. This standard recommends the application of the eight quality management principles given below:

1. Customer- focused organization
2. Leadership
3. Involvement of people
4. Process orientation
5. Systems approach to management
6. Continuous improvement
7. Factual approach to decision making
8. Mutually- beneficial supplier relationships

These principles are discussed in detail in chapter 11 which deals with the ISO-9000 standard.

11

ISO-9000 STANDARDS

WHAT IS ISO?

The International Organization for Standardization, also called ISO, is a federation of national standards organizations in the worldwide*[1]. It was founded in 1946 with the aim of developing a uniform set of international quality standards. At present, it has 158 members representing different countries. As on 1 January 2007, it has developed over 15,000 international standards for products, test methods and systems.

WHAT ARE ISO-9000 STANDARDS?

ISO-9000 is a family of standards which defines a quality management

---

***[1] Why this abbreviation?**

Readers may wonder why the organization is known by the term ISO and not 'IOS' which would be the normal acronym. The reason is that ISO is a multi-lingual organization with its documents published in at least three languages *viz.*, English, French and Spanish, and consequently it might be inappropriate to assume primacy for the sequence of words as they appear in English. Instead, ISO is rooted in 'ISOS', a Greek word, which means 'equal'. For instance 'iso' is also a common English prefix which denotes equality or uniformity, as in isotherm (equal temperature) or isobar (equal pressure), etc. Since standards aim to achieve uniformity regardless of language or national location, the term ISO has been chosen to represent the International Organization for Standardization worldwide.

system that can assist organizations in enhancing customer satisfaction and provide confidence to their customers that the products supplied by them will meet the customer-specified requirements. A Quality Management System (QMS) based on these standards can serve as a framework for establishing and institutionalizing quality management in an organization. Quality management systems based on these standards are designed to continuously improve the performance of the organization while addressing the needs of its customers and all its stakeholders. ISO-9000 series of standards were first published in 1987. Originally these standards were designed for application in manufacturing sector. On seeing overwhelming response from industries all around the world, these standards were revised and made generic in nature so that these could be applied to any organization. As on 1 January 2007, main standards in ISO-9000 series are:

- ISO-9000, which describes the fundamentals of quality management systems and specifies the terminology for them.
- ISO- 9001, which specifies requirements for a quality management system where an organization needs to demonstrate its ability to produce products that fulfill customer and applicable regulatory requirements and aims to enhance customer satisfaction.
- ISO-9004, which provides guidelines that consider both the effectiveness and the efficiency of the quality management system. The aim of this standard is improvement of the performance of the organization and satisfaction of customers and other interested parties.

Complete list of ISO-9000 related standards published so far is given below:

LIST OF PUBLISHED STANDARDS OF ISO/TC 176

ISO 10002:2004

Quality management — Customer satisfaction — Guidelines for complaints handling in organizations

ISO 10005:2005

Quality management systems — Guidelines for quality plans

ISO 10006:2003

Quality management systems — Guidelines for quality management in projects

ISO 10007:2003

Quality management systems — Guidelines for configuration management

ISO 10012:2003

Measurement management systems — Requirements for measurement processes and measuring equipment

ISO/TR 10013:2001

Guidelines for quality management system documentation

ISO 10014:2006
Quality management — Guidelines for realizing financial and economic benefits (available in English only)
ISO 10015:1999
Quality management — Guidelines for training
ISO/TR 10017:2003
Guidance on statistical techniques for ISO 9001:2000 (available in English only)
ISO 10019:2005
Guidelines for the selection of quality management system consultants and use of their services
ISO/TS 16949:2002
Quality management systems – particular requirements for the application of ISO 9001:2000 for automotive production and relevant service part organizations
ISO 19011:2002
Guidelines for quality and/or environmental management systems auditing

NEED FOR ISO-9000 STANDARDS

We have seen in the previous Chapter that various quality gurus have prescribed their respective methodologies for managing quality in an organization. With so many models for quality management, a quality manager may be confused as to which model to follow. The result is that he may create his own recipe for quality management, based on his own understanding and the preference of his superiors in the organization. However, this state of affairs is unsatisfactory, as shown by the following reasoning:

- The quality of a product is a major factor in any purchase decision. Before placing an order, the purchasing organization likes to know whether the supplier is capable of supplying products that will meet all its requirements. Traditionally, the purchaser calls for samples from potential suppliers and inspects them to determine whether the samples conform to specifications. Nonetheless, actual shipments may contain nonconforming products even when the prior samples have passed all tests. Consequently major buyers generally send their technical experts to assess the quality control systems of suppliers to assure themselves that these suppliers will be able to supply products of consistent quality, and that high-quality samples are not just a one-off phenomenon.
- The assessment of quality control systems is subjective in nature. Experts from different purchasing organizations, drawing on their companies' own experiences, may have different perceptions of an

effective quality control system. As a result, a supplier may receive varying assessment reports from different purchasers for comparable products and production systems.

- Thus there arises an urgent need for standardization of quality management methodologies or in other words, a system that can serve as a benchmark or reference standard for the assessment of any suppliers' quality system.
- Such a system could also be useful for third-party assessments, reducing the need for purchasers to carry out individual evaluations and sparing suppliers the burden of multiple assessments.

It is for these reasons that the International Organization for Standardization has issued the ISO-9000 series of standards for quality assurance systems.

THIRD PARTY CERTIFICATION

Generally, quality management is a fuzzy concept and as such, it is difficult to assess the degree of implementation and effectiveness of quality management. The ISO-9000 standards are designed so that the degree of implementation of a quality management system can be assessed systematically. ISO-9001 lays down well-defined requirements in the form of a specification. Thus a trained assessor can objectively assess whether the organization has fully implemented a quality management system or not. This has enabled third- party assessment and certification of the companies that claim to have implemented the ISO-9001 standard. For this purpose, an appropriate institutional structure for the accreditation of certification bodies has been put in place.

To accomplish this, almost all major countries have established National Accreditation Boards for the accreditation of Quality Management System certification bodies. Furthermore, in order to bring harmony to the accreditation methodology, an International Accreditors Forum (IAF) has been established, which is an association of Accreditation Boards. IAF has issued guidelines to regulate the functioning of Accredition Boards and criteria for the accreditation of certification bodies to inspire confidence among the customers. The certifiability of the ISO-9001 standard has been the major reason for its rapid adoption by a large number of companies around the world. As on 1 January 2007, over 400,000 companies around the world have been certified against this standard.

QUALITY MANAGEMENT PRINCIPLES

At the core of ISO-9000 are eight Quality Management Principles which lay down the basis for a quality management system. These principles have been derived from the teachings of various quality gurus and were standardized based on extensive discussions within the ISO Technical Committee 176, which has developed the original ISO-9000 standards. These Quality Management Principles are described in the following paragraphs.

Principle # 1 – Customer Focus

The sole reason for the existence of a company is to serve its customers. It is they who finance its operations. Therefore, organizations should understand current and future customer needs, should meet customer requirements and strive to exceed customer expectations.

Application of this principle involves:

- Understanding customer needs and expectations.
- Ensuring that the objectives of the organization are linked to customer needs and expectations.
- Communicating customer needs and expectations throughout the organization.
- Measuring customer satisfaction and acting on the results.
- Managing customer relationships.
- Ensuring a balanced approach between satisfying customers and other stakeholders.

Principle # 2 – Leadership

The top management of a company establishes the vision and mission for the company. They should create and maintain the internal environment in which employees can be motivated to achieve the organization's objectives.

Application of this principle involves:

- Defining the vision and mission for the company considering the needs of all stakeholders including customers, owners, employees, suppliers, investors/stockholders, local communities and society as a whole.
- Developing a strategy for the organization that tries to fulfill this vision and mission, and setting challenging goals and targets.
- Creating and sustaining shared values, fairness and ethical role models at all levels of the organization.
- Establishing trust and eliminating fear.
- Providing people with the required resources, training, work environment and freedom to act with responsibility as well as accountability.
- Inspiring, encouraging and recognizing people's contributions.

Principle # 3 – Involvement of People

People at all levels are the essence of an organization and their full involvement enables their abilities to be used for the organization's benefit.

Application of this principle involves making people:

- Understand the importance of their contribution and role in the organization.
- Identify constraints on their performance.
- Accept ownership of processes and problems as well as their responsibility for solving them.
- Evaluate their performance against their personal goals and objectives.
- Actively seek opportunities to enhance their competence, knowledge and experience.
- Freely share knowledge and experience.
- Openly discuss problems and issues.

Principle # 4 – Process Approach

A desired result is achieved more efficiently when activities and related resources are managed as a process.

Application of this principle involves:

- Systematically defining the activities necessary to obtain a desired result.
- Establishing clear responsibility and accountability for managing key activities.
- Analyzing and measuring the capability of key activities.
- Identifying the interfaces between key activities within and across the functions of the organization.
- Focusing on the factors - such as resources, methods, and materials that will improve key activities of the organization.
- Evaluating the risks and consequences of activities on customers, suppliers and other affected parties.

Principle # 5 – System Approach to Management

Identifying, understanding and managing inter-related processes as a system contributes to the organization's effectiveness and efficiency in achieving its objectives.

Application of this principle involves:

- Creating and operating a system to achieve the organization's objectives in the most effective and efficient way.
- Understanding the inter-dependencies between the processes of the system.

- Using structured approaches that harmonize and integrate processes.
- Providing a better understanding of the roles and responsibilities necessary for achieving common objectives and thereby reducing cross-functional barriers.
- Understanding organizational capabilities and establishing resource constraints prior to action.
- Targeting and defining how specific activities within a system should operate.
- Continually improving the system through measurement and evaluation.

PRINCIPLE # 6 – CONTINUAL IMPROVEMENT

Continual improvement of the organization's overall performance should be a permanent objective of the organization.

Application of this principle involves:

- Defining the metrics/axes that collectively define the organization's performance.
- Employing a consistent organization-wide approach to continual improvement of the organization's performance.
- Providing people with training in the methods and tools of continual improvement.
- Making continual improvement of products, processes and systems an objective for every individual in the organization.
- Establishing goals to guide, and measures to track continual improvement.
- Recognizing and acknowledging improvements.

PRINCIPLE # 7– FACTUAL APPROACH TO DECISION-MAKING

Effective decisions are based on the analysis of factual information.

Application of this principle involves:

- Ensuring that incoming data are based on the observation of facts, and are sufficiently accurate and reliable.
- Making data accessible to those who need it.
- Analyzing data using valid methods.
- Making decisions and taking action based on actual analysis, balanced with experience and intuition.

PRINCIPLE # 8 – MUTUALLY BENEFICIAL SUPPLIER RELATIONSHIPS

An organization and its suppliers are inter-dependent and a mutually beneficial relationship enhances the ability of both to create value.

Application of this principle involves:

- Establishing relationships that balance short-term gains with long-term considerations.
- Pooling of expertise and resources with partners.
- Identifying and selecting key suppliers.
- Clear and open communication with them.
- Sharing information and future plans with them.
- Establishing joint development and improvement activities with them.
- Inspiring, encouraging and recognizing improvements and achievements by them.

REQUIREMENTS OF ISO-9001

The latest edition of ISO-9000 standards was issued in 2000. The requirements to be met by an organization implementing the ISO-9001-2000 standard are contained in clauses 4 to 8 of the standard. Key requirements are briefly outlined in the paragraphs below:

Clause 4 : Quality Management System

Establish, document, implement, maintain and continually improve the effectiveness of the QMS. This would involve:

(a) Identification of processes needed for the QMS, and their interaction.

(b) Implementation of actions necessary to achieve planned results and continual improvement.

(c) Documentation must include.
- Quality manual including policy.
- Procedures and work instructions.
- Quality records.

Recognizing that paperwork can be onerous, ISO-9000: 2000 version has tried to reduce the need for documentation. It now requires only six mandatory operating procedures. However, most of the companies normally have more procedures to bring clarity to their quality management system. ISO-9001:2000 standard emphasises on evidence of an effective QMS. For this purpose a company is required to maintain at least 18 records of ISO-9000 related activities to demonstrate the functioning of QMS.

Clause 5 : Management Responsibility

Top management should demonstrate its commitment to the establishment and maintenance of a QMS and to continually improving its effectiveness. In order to achieve this, top management should undertake the following activities:

- Define a quality policy with particular emphasis on meeting customer as well as regulatory requirements, and communicate it to the organization.

- Establish verifiable quality objectives and direct the relevant departments to plan for their achievement.
- Ensure that responsibility and authority for the Quality Management System are defined and understood by all the concerned employees.
- Ensure that customer requirements are determined and the organization takes measures to meet these requirements and enhance customer satisfaction.
- Appoint a Management Representative (MR) who will be responsible for coordination and effective implementation of the Quality Management System.
- Carry out a periodic review of the organization's Quality Management System to ensure its effectiveness and assess opportunities for improvement.

CLAUSE 6 : RESOURCE MANAGEMENT

The organization shall determine and provide the resources required to effectively implement the Quality Management System and its continual improvement to enhance customer satisfaction. This would require the following activities:

- Determine the competence of personnel required to perform various tasks, arrange suitable training for them, and ensure that they have acquired the requisite skills.
- Determine and provide adequate infrastructure such as buildings, process equipment and supporting services.
- Ensure that the work environment needed to achieve conformity to product requirements is maintained.

CLAUSE 7 : PRODUCT REALIZATION

This is the most important clause of the standard; it contains requirements relating to the determination of customer needs, design and development of the product, purchasing, production processes and control of measuring devices. Key requirements under this Clause are provided below:

- Determination of customer requirements for the product, its delivery and servicing, as well as statutory and regulatory requirements.
- Reviews to ensure that product requirements are clearly defined, contractual requirements are mutually agreed to and the organization has the ability to meet these defined requirements.
- Establishment of customer communication regarding product information, contract- related enquiries and customer feedback.

- Planning and control of design and development of the product. This would include design inputs, design outputs as well as review of the design and its validation.
- Ensuring that the purchased product conforms to the specified requirements. For this the organization should have a system for the evaluation and selection of vendors, and for verification of the conformity of purchased products.
- Ensuring that the organization has a plan for the production of products or provision of services, and ensuring that processes are carried out under controlled conditions. This would include availability of suitable equipment, work instructions and facilities for measurement and monitoring of processes. In cases where the output of the processes cannot be verified after production, the production processes should be validated to demonstrate the required capability. In cases where traceability is a requirement, devising a suitable system to track the unique identity of each product, for instance, a batch of drug or a consumer durable product.
- Where some customers' property is utilized for product realization, it should be ensuring that proper care is taken of that property.
- Establishment of a system for carrying out measurement and monitoring of processes. This would involve suitable testing and measuring equipment and their proper calibration to ensure valid results.

Clause 8 : Measurement, Analysis and Improvement

The organization shall:

- Apply preventive quality control by monitoring and measurement of processes to ensure that these processes are capable of achieving planned results.
- Establish a system for monitoring and measurement of product characteristics to ensure the product meets all its specified requirements.
- Establish a proper system of identification and control of non-conforming products to prevent their unintended use or delivery. Such non-conforming products must be rectified to eliminate the defect or non-conformity. In case of minor defects, the product may be accepted under a concession, approved by the designated authority.
- Collect data about customer satisfaction and product conformity and analyze it to observe trends and opportunities for preventive action.
- Take steps to continually improve the effectiveness of the QMS

using quality data analysis, internal audit results and management review.

- Establish and implement a documented procedure for corrective action to eliminate the causes of non-conformities and address customer complaints.
- Determine various actions required to eliminate causes of potential non-conformities and maintain records of actions taken and results achieved.

THE PROCESS APPROACH

The ISO-9000 standard strongly advocates the adoption of a process approach. Although companies are vertically organized and may be based on functional departments for proper control, the fact is that product realization activity moves horizontally across processes within a department and across different departments. Often, the output of one process becomes the input for the next process. The systematic identification and management of the processes employed within an organization and particularly the interactions between such processes, is referred to as a "process approach."

The process based quality management system described in ISO-9000 family of standards is illustrated in Figure-1. This illustration shows that customers and other interested parties provide valuable inputs. Based on these inputs, management of the organization designs the products/services and plans product realization processes. The organization needs to manage its resources for operating various product realization processes.

The resultant product is then supplied to the customers after internal measurement/verification. Feedback on perception of customers about quality of product/service gives indication of the extent to which their needs and expectations have been met. In addition, compliance to the documented quality management system is checked through internal audits. This data about product conformity and effectiveness of QMS is analyzed for improvement. This analysis is reviewed by the management for taking measures to improve the quality management system. This model of a process-based quality management system resembles the Plan-Do-Check-Act cycle of Deming as given below:

Plan	Product planning and provision of resources.
Do	Product realization through various processes.
Check	Measurement and analysis of products and system.
Act	Management review for approval of improvement measures.

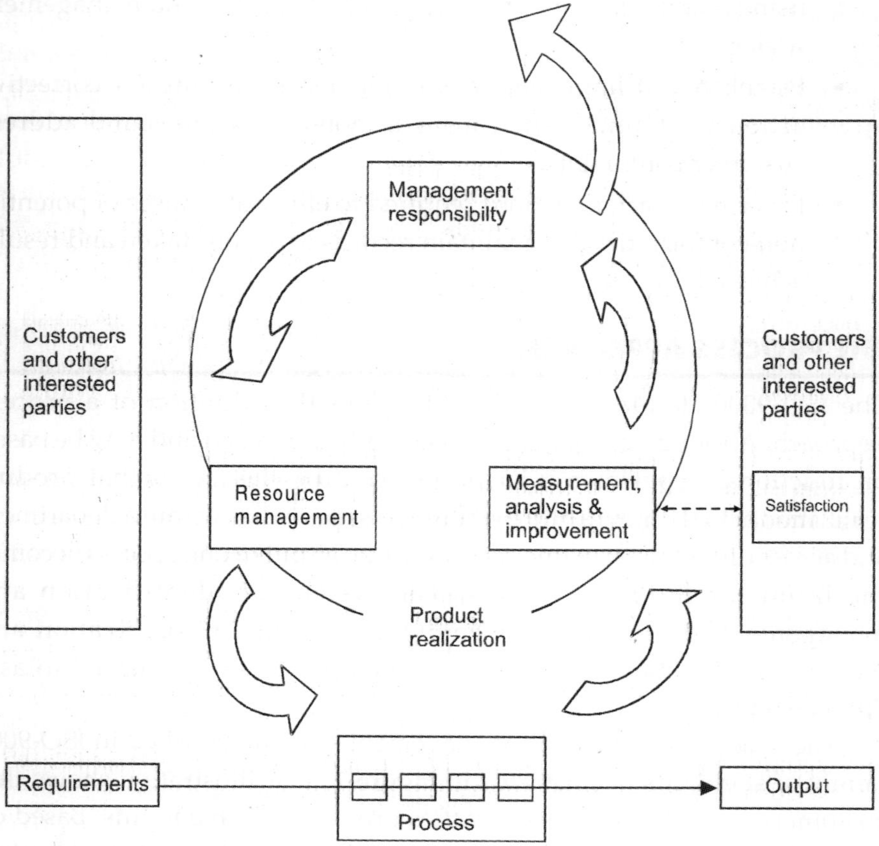

Fig. 1: Continual Improvement of the Quality Management System

IMPORTANCE OF ISO-9000 FOR DEVELOPING COUNTRIES

The ISO-9000 standards are particularly useful for developing countries. Most developing countries historically had controlled economies, and there was very little competition. The imports were highly restricted and as such, manufacturing companies had captive markets. Under these conditions the major emphasis was on maximizing production to increase profits. In this environment, quality was the major casualty. Some companies in developing countries had surplus production capacity and could compete on the basis of price, on account of the indigenous availability of raw materials and low labour costs. However, these companies could not export their products because of poor quality. ISO-9000 standards can serve as a good framework for organized quality improvements in companies located in developing countries. Further, with the certification of their Quality Management Systems against ISO-9000 by internationally accredited certification bodies, these companies can change their poor-quality-supplier image. ISO-9000 certification can provide confidence to the domestic and as well as foreign customers that the company will be able to ensure consistent quality and meet the product requirements. Governments of developing countries have also realized the importance of ISO-9000 standards in their export efforts, and are strongly promoting these standards through awareness seminars and other financial incentives such as subsidizing certification expenses. However, while companies have benefited from ISO-9000 certification, there is a tendency - particularly among small and medium companies - to somehow get and then use ISO-9000 certification primarily as a marketing tool. These companies develop documentation with the help of consultants, make just enough compliance efforts to obtain certification, without making any serious effort to use the standards for their intended purpose – the improvement of product quality. These companies do not realize that they may be able to get their first order on the strength of ISO-9000 certification, but that repeat orders will come only if the customers are satisfied with the supplied products or services. Thus, properly used, ISO-9000 is an important tool which can be used as a centerpiece for national quality campaigns in developing countries, and as a means for their companies to make real and lasting market-share gains.

IMPLEMENTATION OF ISO-9001

Establishment and maintenance of a quality management system compliant to ISO-9001 requires the involvement of management and staff of all departments in the organization. The main elements for effective implementation of a quality management system are briefly provided in the following paragraphs:

ROLE OF MANAGEMENT

Success in implementing ISO-9001 largely depends upon the leadership and involvement of the top management. One way of demonstrating the commitment of top management is for the CEO to chair the Quality Committee or ISO-9000 steering committee, in order to oversee the establishment of a quality management system, its maintenance and the continuous improvement of its effectiveness. Some of the other responsibilities of top management are:

- Promotion of the quality policy and related objectives in the organization.
- Provision of necessary resources.
- Establishment of customer focus in the organization in order to ensure that all activities are carried out keeping customers' interest in view.

- Resolution of inter-departmental problems in the maintenance of the quality management system.
- Periodic review of the quality management system and taking decisions for achievement of quality objectives and improving the effectiveness of the quality management system.

DOCUMENTATION

Documentation helps in the standardization of quality- related activities for consistent conformity with customer requirements, establishment of traceability and providing evidence for evaluation of the quality management system. Quality system documentation should include the following documents:

- Quality manual containing quality policy and definition of quality system.
- Quality systems procedures and work instructions, which are essential for the proper maintenance of the quality management system. According to ISO-9001, the procedures mentioned below, have to be maintained: (List of mandatory procedures is given in Annexure-I of this Chapter). In addition, procedures and instructions should be documented if their non- observance can cause a risk of non-conformity in products and services.
- A quality record of important activities should be maintained to provide objective evidence for evaluation of the QMS, during internal audits and assessments by the certification body. The list of quality records to be maintained is given in the Annexure-II to this Chapter.

EVALUATION OF QUALITY MANAGEMENT SYSTEM

Any system has a natural tendency to degrade over time. People may take some things for granted and assume that activities are being carried out as prescribed. Certain steps or processes may be skipped or short- cuts taken under the pressure of delivery to customers. Again, due to pressure from senior management to meet the targets, certain concessions/deviations may be accepted or processes may be continued even though certain specified conditions cannot be met.

The effectiveness of any quality management system need to be evaluated periodically to ensure that it is being properly implemented and complies with ISO-9001 requirements. For this purpose ISO-9001 provides for the institutionalized audit of any QMS. This could be by internal auditors of the organization, via a second-party audit conducted by the customers of the organization or via a third-party audit by an accredited certification body. Auditing is a structured exercise by trained auditors who carry them out on check sheets developed for each specific audit. ISO-19011 provides detailed guidance for conducting audits of quality management systems. Auditors specifically look for the following:

- Whether concerned staff is aware of the documented process instructions and have the requisite skills?
- Are the procedures being implemented properly?
- Are the processes effective in achieving desired results?

CONTINUAL IMPROVEMENT

ISO-9001 lays great stress on continual improvement. That is why it requires that the organization lays down quantifiable quality objectives which can be measured to assess the degree of achievement obtained. The aim of continual improvement is to enhance the satisfaction of customers and other stakeholders. To comply with this requirement of ISO-9001, the organization needs to take the following steps:

- Study of the present situation and identification of areas for improvement.
- Establishing clear targets for improvement.
- Use of various quality improvement tools to analyze the situation and development of solutions for achieving improvement.
- Trial implementation of solutions and evaluating the results towards the achievement of objectives.
- Institutionalization of required changes in the QMS for sustained implementation of the solutions.

ISO-9004:2000

ISO-9001:2000 and ISO-9004:2000 are a consistent pair of standards which complement each other but can also be used independently. Where ISO-9001 is used for certification and contractual purposes, ISO-9004 provides guidelines for organizations which want to go beyond the requirements of ISO-9001 towards further organizational excellence, profitability and growth. Another difference is that while ISO-9001 primarily focuses on compliance of the product requirements and customer satisfaction, ISO-9004 has a broader scope of meeting the needs and expectations of other affected parties, such as employees, owners, suppliers and society.

This standard can be compared with criteria of National Quality Awards such as Baldridge Quality Award of USA and Rajiv Gandhi National Quality Award of India. This standard addresses the following issues:

- Customer loyalty, repeat business and referral.
- Cost management, financial results and market share.

- Motivation of people for achievement or organizational objectives.
- Interests of other stakeholders of the organization.
- Corporate social responsibility.

The main focus of ISO-9004 is the relentless pursuit of improvement in all aspects of the organization through the direct application of quality management principles.

ISO-9000 AND TQM

There is a lot of confusion about the relevance of ISO-9000 in the implementation of a TQM philosophy. Some ISO-9000 zealots promote the idea that ISO-9000 is a better alternative to the outdated concept of TQM. The author has been deeply involved in the development of ISO-9000:2000 the Leader of the Indian Delegation to ISO-TC-176 and considers ISO-9000 to be a powerful concept for quality management in an organization. However, it also needs to be understood that this standard does not directly addresses all aspects of excellence. For instance, it does directly cover productivity, cost competitiveness and business results. It also does not address employee satisfaction, and corporate social responsibility. Thus TQM will always remain the overall philosophy for wider aspects of quality management and organizational excellence. The three basic elements of TQM are:

- Pursuit of quality in the broader sense of organizational excellence.
- Its application to the total organization covering all departments and all levels.
- It being a management function and thus driven by the top management.

These three elements are so universal that they will be applicable to any organizational initiative for improvement. New tools and techniques may be introduced but the basic philosophy of TQM will always remain relevant to the organization in its journey toward excellence.

Thus ISO-9000 is not an alternative to TQM, but a very important tool for embedding TQM in an organization. ISO-9000 helps in standardizing the best practices in an organization. It institutionalizes the role of various employees and their knowledge of various processes in the organization. It enables proper evaluation of the work of staff for taking measures to enhance their competence. It also ensures that when an employee leaves the organization, the relevant process knowledge is not lost and the new employees can be more easily trained. The Quality Management System helps in consolidating and maintaining the gains of any quality improvement effort. This is illustrated in the Figure-2.

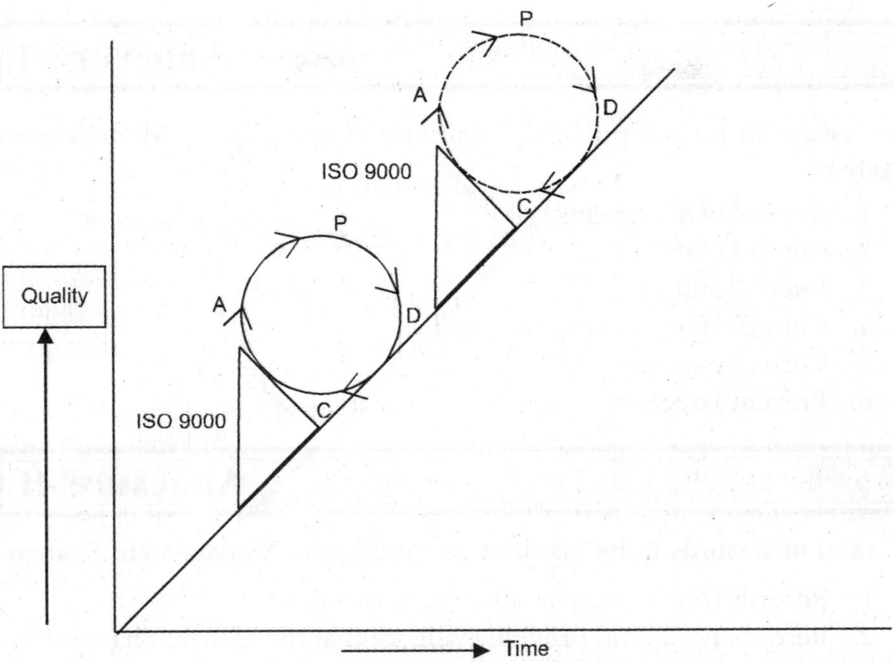

Fig. 2

As quality improvement projects are implemented through PDCA cycles and a certain amount of improvement is achieved, the changed process conditions are incorporated in the quality system documentation. Thus ISO-9000 acts as a 'wedge' which prevents slippage in quality improvement. Then the PDCA cycle is rolled further to achieve successively higher levels of improvement. In this way, new process conditions are institutionalized in the QMS which ensures that the improved state of the relevant process is maintained.

Another very important contribution of ISO-9000 in TQM is that it makes it difficult for anyone to take shortcuts or take liberties with the quality of products or services. For instance in an ISO-9000- based quality management system, it is stipulated that only designated officials should be authorized to approve deviations or concessions and these should be in writing. This strengthens the position of quality professionals as well as operational staff and discourages senior manager from issuing verbal instructions for the acceptance of deviations/concessions or operating processes when they are out of control.

Annexure -I

Procedure to be compulsorily maintained for Quality Management System:

1. Control of documents
2. Control of records
3. Internal audit
4. Control of non-conformity product
5. Corrective action
6. Preventive action.

Annexure -II

List of Records to be maintained for Quality Management System

1. Records from management reviews (5.6.1)
2. Records needed to provide evidence that the realization processes and resulting products meet requirements (this may include a number of records for different processes) (7.1)
3. Records of the results of the review and actions arising from the review (7.2.2)
4. Product requirements for design inputs (7.3.2)
5. Results of reviews (7.3.4)
6. Results of the verification and any necessary actions to be maintained (7.3.5)
7. Results of validation and any necessary actions (7.3.6)
8. Results of the review of changes and any necessary actions (7.3.7)
9. Results of evaluations and any necessary actions arising from the evaluation (7.4.1)
10. Validation of processes for production and service provision (7.5.2)
11. Unique identification of the product where required (7.5.3)
12. Reports of customer property lost, damaged or otherwise found to be unsuitable for use and records maintained (7.5.4)
13. Calibration or verification of monitoring or measuring devices (7.6)
14. Result and follow up action of internal audits (8.2.2)
15. Person(s) authorizing release of products (8.2.4)
16. Nature of nonconformities and any subsequent actions taken (8.3)
17. Records of the results of corrective action taken (8.5.2)
18. Records of results of preventive action taken (8.5.3)

12

The Customer-focused Organization

The customer is the raison-de-etre for any business organization. Quality begins with understanding customer needs and ends when the customer is satisfied with the resulting product or service. That is why customer focus is the first quality principle of the ISO-9000 standard. Its importance in quality management can be judged by the fact that all major Quality Awards in the world allocate maximum marks to customer satisfaction. To develop a customer- focused company, management should begin by looking at quality from the customers' point of view. It should be realized that a customer is not really interested in the internal processes, or sophisticated process controls and quality management systems of any company from which he acquires a product or service. The bottom-line for him is whether the relevant product or service meets his/her requirements and whether he considers it as good value for money.

WHO IS A CUSTOMER?

Before discussing customer focus, we need to clearly understand who a customer is. A customer is a person, group or an organization which receives a product or service from another person, group or an organization, with the latter being considered the supplier. The ultimate customer who receives a product or service is referred to as the **external customer**. It is he who defines the requirement of a product or service to meet his/her needs. These requirements serve as the basis for design of product or service and formulation of specification by the supplier which contain quality parameters. In addition, he also decides the price he is willing to pay and the manner of delivery, which he requires. Finally he is the one who is the final arbiter of the quality delivered to him. That is why any business organization has to make all efforts to satisfy the external customer to stay in business.

INTERNAL CUSTOMERS

When we talk of customers, we generally think of people or entities to whom we sell our product or service in other words we think of external customers as the only form of customer. However, the basic definition of a customer is "a person or a group which receives a product or service." Going by this definition, various departments and functional units within a company can also be considered as customers because each one of them receives some product, service or information from someone else in the company. The famous Quality Guru Ishikawa introduced the concept that in any multi-department organization, the 'next' operation is the customer for the group responsible for the 'previous' operation. No department can function alone. For example, the Design department is provided information by the Marketing about the requirements and preferences of the customers based on which a design is created. Design for its part, develops product designs and process plans and provides them to the Production department. Thus R&D is a customer as well as a supplier. Similarly, the Production department is also a customer of the Material Management and Maintenance departments as they supply input material and maintenance services respectively, and the quality of these inputs has a direct impact on the quality of production. In this way there is a whole chain of internal customers and suppliers, who progressively add value to the relevant products and services before these are delivered to the external customers. Since internal customer departments are part of the organization, they may not forcefully project their requirements or articulate dissatisfaction with inputs supplied by other departments for fear of annoying their colleagues and the senior management. This attitude militates against the basic principle of customer satisfaction. It does not require much imagination to understand that the external customers cannot be satisfied unless all the internal customers are satisfied.

Merely using terms like "best- quality product" or "customer satisfaction guarantee" has no meaning unless the company specifies what the satisfaction threshold is, and what it would do if this threshold is not met. For instance Pizza Hut may offer its pizza free if the order is not ready within 5 minutes. Some companies may give the customer a certain cash amount in case of a specific service shortfall. For instance, Delta Dental Plans of Massachusetts give you the customer a cheque for $ 50 if he is transferred from phone to phone during an insurance enquiry.

This concept of taking a customer seriously is also being adopted by some of the Indian companies. For instance Bharati Telecom, the telephone service provider, guarantees that if a landline telephone fault is not rectified within 4 hours, it will credit Rs. 100 in the next month's bill to the subscriber.

Backing a service guarantee with a specific penalty ensures that employees understand the value of service delivery on a personal basis. It also assures the customers that the company is serious about quality. For example poor quality of tools and equipment, incomplete work instructions, delayed material inputs, defective materials inputs from the previous operation etc. will definitely affect the quality and delivery of the products going to external customers. Thus a conscious effort is required to understand the needs of internal customers so that there is a smooth flow of added value from department to department, leading to products and services, which satisfy the external customers.

Accordingly, companies that are serious about a customer focus, need to take the following steps to improve internal processes:

Interfaces within the company need to be analyzed *i.e.*, internal providers and receivers of products/ services need to be identified.

Each internal customer must establish his product or service requirements and discuss these with the relevant provider for clear understanding. If a particular characteristic of a product or service cannot be provided, the two parties must agree on an alternative solution without sacrificing the quality of the ultimate product or service. This discussion should result in the preparation of documents which are referred to as "Quality Level Agreements" or "Internal Service Agreements." This could be treated as an informal contract which must be taken seriously.

For smooth functioning, the internal customer should inform his supplier if there is any change in the product/service or its delivery schedule. Similarly the supplier should inform the customer in time if they are not able to meet a requirement and should reach an agreement on changes either in the product or its delivery schedule.

There should be frequent meetings between suppliers and internal customers to resolve problems if any, and to develop a team approach.

DEVELOPING CUSTOMER FOCUS

A company is sustained by the revenue received from its external customers. It is the customer who ultimately provides the salary and perks of all employees from the CEO down to the lowest most junior trainee. Thus the organization needs to focus significant efforts to satisfy the customers in order to maintain the organization's revenue stream. The customer focus should start from the marketing department. Over the last few decades, marketing and sales have become key function in an organization because it is they who bring in customers. Traditionally, marketing tried to operate 'mass' campaigns to reach the maximum number of customers, with the implicit assumption that all customers had the same needs. They focused only on building the image of the product with the customers.

The first shift began in the 1960s, when 'Direct Marketing' was introduced. This involved communicating with customers through promotional mailings and response requests. This was the first organized/ systematic attempt at getting customers' views about the products (as opposed to product requirements). As more data became available from customers, it became possible to analyze the customer preferences which enabled segmentation of customers based on their specific needs. This in turn led to the concept of 'target marketing' where the products were promoted to customer/prospect subsets based on segmentation of perceived customer needs (*e.g.*, male and female babies might need differently shaped diapers). However the focus was still on internally-conceived products, and with the aim of selling to the maximum possible number of units.

It was only in 1990 that the marketing departments embraced the strategy popularized by Regis McKenna. This was first shift of focus toward using customer inputs in the design of the product itself. In this approach marketing departments made an effort to determine customer requirements and preferences, which were good inputs for developing new products. This also offered the opportunity to cross- sell existing products. While this no doubt helped companies in getting more customers, the next question that arose was – would these customers stay with the company? was would they stay with them?

It is important for any company to address this question since it is well known that it requires much more effort to get a new customer than to retain an existing one. An often-quoted statement in marketing is that it costs a company five to seven times more to sell a product to a new customer than to an existing one. This alone should be a sufficient reason to do everything possible to retain existing customers. Retention however, requires a conscious effort on the part of every one in the organization to fully satisfy existing customers by marking their every interaction with the company a pleasant experience. Companies, which are trying to develop a customer focus must ensure that their marketing campaigns must not simply highlight the merits of their products – they must also explain in clear terms what any customer can expect from a product or service. No tall claims and no instant gratification

- customers do not like promises, which are not kept. It is important to maintain the credibility of your organization if you expect customer loyalty.

CREATING A CUSTOMER-CENTRIC CULTURE

Customer focus cannot be developed in an organization merely by having systems and procedures specifying the responsibilities of various departments and functional groups. You need to create organizational culture of sensitivity and empathy with respect to the customer. A culture of customer focus can be developed only through the total commitment of top management, which should be reflected both in a formal Quality Policy and in concrete action by the management. This involves the following action plan:

1. Before top management assumes responsibility for creating an environment conducive to customer focus, it needs to be convinced that such an action makes economic sense. This would require the establishment of a clear linkage between customer satisfaction and the profitability of the organization. For this, data needs to be generated about (a) the loss of customers and its impact on sales and profitability, (b) the differential between the cost of retaining existing customers and acquiring new ones and (c) profitability of different segments of customers. This subject is discussed in detail in the chapter on CRM.
2. Communicate the customer-focus philosophy and the policy of the top management to the entire organization. This communication should highlight the importance of customers to the company's profitability and growth. It should be explained that the main purpose of everyone in the organization is to attract customers, satisfy their needs and secure their loyalty. The total satisfaction of customers should be the objective of the company. Studies have shown that whereas a satisfied customer may share his experience with two or three persons, a dissatisfied person may influence 7 to 10 other potential customers.
3. Every department or group in the company should identify its internal customers. It should take pains to understand and define the requirements of their internal customers so that every one in the group is aware of the customers' expectation. There should be frequent interaction with internal customers to understand their issues, as discussed in earlier sections. They should proactively obtain feedback from their internal customers so that corrective action can be taken when their internal customers find some deficiency in the product or service. This step can be taken further by establishing interdepartmental teams to assure better coordination and problem resolution.

4. It should be realized that customer expectations always keep on rising. In an environment of intense domestic and international competition, companies have to continuously improve the quality of their products and services to enhance customer satisfaction. For this, the best approach is to appoint an inter-disciplinary team to take input from the market and from existing customers, for the development of improved products and services.
5. Customer- facing personnel in any company have a particularly important role in providing customer satisfaction. Studies have shown that 40-50 % of dissatisfaction with products is not due to the product itself, but with the way it is delivered and serviced. Thus it is important to train the front-line staff to develop a customer- friendly attitude. Generally there are posters and the like in marketing and sales offices, saying, "The Customer is the King." Often of course, that is true only until he has made a purchase and paid for it. Subsequently if he has a question or complaint, he is often asked to wait until the sales persons can spare some time between dealing with new-customer issues. When the customer finally gets a chance to explain his problem, the sales staff forget the maxim that the customer in always right–they adopt a defensive posture and try to prove that the customer is wrong. They may try arguments to show that problem was caused by improper product usage or the customer's lack of clarity, not following instructions, not providing proper direction, and so on. This make a mockery of the 'customer focus' that may be professed by the organization. On the face of it, sales personnel may be trying to save company the cost of repair or replacement. However, they do not realize that not only they are losing further sales from this customer but by making him angry, they are increasing the chance that he will tell 10 other potential customers about his better experience. Therefore staff must be provided with sufficient and appropriate training on proper interaction with the customers, and the 'big picture' of customer retention as opposed to the narrow approach of immediate cost savings. In case of errors or some deficiencies in service, the staff should not get into arguments about the cause of problem - instead they should empathize with the customer and should be empowered to pacify the angry customers (within reason) by offering free service or some other compensation so that the customer is not lost.
6. Provide easy accessibility for the customer by extended hours of service and easy telephonic access. Often the first customer contact with any company is through the telephone. Automated customer response systems may be economical for the company, but they need

to be managed in such a way that the customer can speak to the desired person without having to wait for eternity listening to music and the bland message "you are very important to us. Our customer service representatives will attend to you shortly." Long wait times can put off any customer. If you must use these mechanisms, it would be much better to provide an indication of wait time up front – so the customer is not wondering if they will be on hold for 15 seconds or 15 minutes. To facilitate customer access, some companies have dedicated customer service representatives for major clients. These clients can approach their relationship executive at any time through his or her mobile phone. This goes a long way in assuring the client that the company really cares about them.

7. Promote customer focus in the organization by publicizing notable successes in achieving customer satisfaction. Reward individuals and teams for outstanding performance in handling difficult customer situations or for getting special appreciation from customers.
8. Monitoring the progress of the company towards a customer- driven organization. Devise schemes for conducting customer satisfaction surveys, and encouraging customers to provide feedback on products or services. In service organizations some companies employ decoy customers to get independent inputs about the treatment given to a normal customer. Take appropriate measure to improve the weaknesses found by the monitoring process.

MEASURING CUSTOMER SATISFACTION

One of the characteristics of a customer-focused organization is that it strives to continuously improve customer satisfaction. There is an old adage - you cannot improve any entity if you can't measure it. Thus measurement of customer satisfaction is essential if you want to improve the experience of customers while dealing with the company and secure customer loyalty. A company needs to develop formal plans for measuring customer satisfaction. For this it needs to decide what to measure, how to measure it and how to make use of measurement results. One or more of the following methods can be used for measuring customer satisfaction:

(a) *Customer feedback after delivery of product or service*: This is one of the simplest, fastest and the most effective methods of measuring customer satisfaction. Shortly after a new product/service has gone into use, the customer should be immediately asked to evaluate the product or service and comment upon areas of satisfaction and dissatisfaction.

(b) *Customer complaints and suggestions:* The organization must have a formalized system of recording all customer complaints and as well as the methods of their disposal. Customer complaints must be taken very positively as valuable inputs by the organization and should immediately trigger the improvement activities as relevant.

(c) *Customer surveys:* If a company decides to carry out a customer survey, it would need to design a suitable questionnaire to obtain maximum information. It should also decide the scope of survey, that is to how many customers are to be covered by the survey. The basic rule of sample selection is that it should represent a cross section of all the relevant customers of the company. For example, if the customer database consists of large, medium and small organizations, the sample must represent the same distribution of customer size. Another segmentation (say for domestic appliances) could be individual users who buy for their own consumption vs. institutional buyers who use the product for providing services to others. The survey should be comprehensive enough so that the company can obtain a response with a sufficient sample size from which meaningful deductions can be made. Some methods of conducting customer surveys are as follows:

i. *Mail survey:* This is the most common method of customer surveys. To improve the response rate, the survey questionnaire should be accompanied by a well-written covering letter signed by the CEO. As far as possible the letter should be addressed to the person or department in the customer company, which is responsible for assessing the quality of product or service. In addition, non-respondents should be contacted by phone and their inputs requested. (a) this assumes that the customers are other companies and not individual consumers, and (b) one needs to be careful not to 'hound' non-respondents since they sometimes simply don't want to respond or just don't care enough to respond.

ii. *Telephone surveys:* Companies also often use telephonic surveys as an alternative or supplement to mail surveys. The survey personnel can call the decision makers or the influencers at the customer company assuming it is a company and not an individual consumer to identify their requirements and obtain their perceptions about company's products and services. Telephone surveys generally achieve higher response rates and provide quicker results, but are often more expensive to administer and run the risk of alienating customers if improperly done.

iii. *Website/e-mail survey:* This is also another quick and very low- cost method for obtaining customer feedback. To improve the response rate, the company might offer some incentives to the respondents such as a prize in a draw or discount coupons. It should however be made clear that the survey is for customers only, otherwise company may be swamped with responses from the general public. It may be noted that customer incentives are not only restricted to website/e-mail surveys – they can also be offered with mail surveys.

iv. Another alternative is to get customer surveys (or focus groups) organized through a market research organization. Although it may be somewhat more expensive, they may also do a more professional job, since this is their core competence.

Whatever method is adopted for obtaining customer feedback, it is important that responses received from the customers be properly analyzed and improvement actions be initiated where adverse comments have been received.

13

Leadership and Team Building

LEADERSHIP ROLE OF MANAGEMENT

It is difficult to separate the role of leadership from that of management. According to Dr. Deming, "the job of management is not supervision, but leadership." Embedding TQM in an organization involves culture change to a new set of beliefs, values and behaviour patterns. Therefore, leadership at all levels is crucial for the success of TQM. Top management should provide leadership by defining the vision and mission of the organization, by setting objectives and providing resources. However, this level of support, though essential, is not sufficient. Unless top management provides guidance and drives the TQM movement, it will not be taken seriously at lower levels. Middle management also has important role to play in providing leadership by developing strategies and plans for achieving objectives and by empowering front-line executives to introduce a TQM approach in various business processes and customer interactions. The actual task of TQM implementation will be carried out by teams which will be driven by team leaders. Leaders assess the progress of every stage through a proper monitoring mechanism, and make adjustments where required. They make their employees feel that the goals of the organization are their personal objectives, which must be achieved. It should be clearly understood that this level of interest cannot be created by issuing directives or orders. The person concerned needs to genuinely feel that the required effort is in their interest and they should own the processes. This can only be achieved by strong leadership.

CHARACTERISTICS OF A LEADER

A manager in an organization may be able to get certain jobs done by his subordinates by virtue of his position and authority. However if he exhibits leadership qualities he will be able to achieve much more. The mantle of leadership is not assumed by a person or granted by his superiors - it has to be earned. A person will be perceived as a leader by his subordinates, peers and superiors, only if he is able to demonstrate some of the following characteristics:

(a) **Vision and Mission:** The leader should be able to conceive a future state and articulate how it can be achieved. He needs to have a clear image of the desired results and behaviours. He should also be able to communicate his vision convincingly to his subordinates as well as superiors. A leader at middle/ junior level should ensure that his vision and mission is in alignment with the organization's overall vision.

(b) **Self-confidence:** He should have confidence in himself and his ability to achieve the desired objectives in spite of obstacles that may come in his way. He should be resolute and have the inner strength to face the challenges. He should also have trust and faith that his team will support him in his endeavour.

(c) **Decision Making:** It is a well established that whenever there is a tricky problem, it invariably lands in the lap of the leader. He should be able to take the right decision, even if it may not be liked by some team members. In this he should be willing to take risks. In case of unexpected results due to his decision, he should have the courage to accept the responsibility and not look for alibis or scapegoats.

(d) **Social Skills:** He should be a good communicator. He should be cooperative and willing to collaborate even if someone else takes the lead, as long as efforts are towards the achievement of common organizational objectives. He should be able to build teams, develop their capabilities and assign responsibilities as well as give team members credit for their work. He should be a mentor to his team and be a role model if he is to earn their respect. Another important characteristic of a leader is his ability to resolve conflicts which are bound to occur in any team effort. He should be fair in his approach so that all team members feel that the leader will take care of their interests.

MANAGEMENT FUNCTIONS

In any organization there is a well-defined management structure with well-defined responsibilities for managers at various levels. These managers display their leadership qualities to achieve superior results. Total Quality Management philosophy does not expect managers to be or do anything different. It only enables them to institutionalise quality in all their processes and build a sound foundation for the long-term growth of the organization. The basic functions of the manager remain the same, and they are briefly mentioned below:

Planning

- Defining objectives of the department or group under the charge of the manager.
- Mapping processes and interfaces with other related departments/ functions.
- Establishing performance standards for all subordinates.

Organising

- Arranging resources for the performance of activities of the organisation or the group.
- Establishing an organizational structure for managing the processes.
- Developing or adopting systems and procedures for the performance of activities.

Staffing

- Selecting personnel with requisite knowledge and expertise.
- Arranging for specialised training and competence building.
- Motivating personnel to build a cohesive team for achieving planned objectives.

Controlling

- Monitoring performance against the planned targets.
- Taking corrective action where required.
- Encouraging staff to identify opportunities for continual improvement and providing facilities for improved performance.

In any organization there are always some people who are not content with the routine jobs given to them. They have fire and passion in them to do something extraordinary, and to take on challenging tasks. It is job of leaders to find such people and groom them as champions of the TQM movement. They can motivate others with their enthusiasm and can form spirited teams to spread a TQM culture in the organization.

HOW CAN LEADERS INTRODUCE TQM CULTURE?

TQM culture in an organization is highly visible. One can see it in the general ambience and the conduct of people performing even routine jobs. Even during a casual or unannounced visit one may observe a high level of order and neatness, the way one is received at the gate, the way one is conducted through the facility, etc. You may well find professional yet courteous behaviour. You are unlikely to find people lounging about. Everyone will be busy in his or her assigned task. You will not have to ask many questions when you want to meet someone or visit a particular location. Once the purpose of your visit is known by the reception personnel they will make all the arrangement, with a minimum of delay or the filling of unnecessary forms which do not add any value for you or the company. If you are a customer contacting a company on the phone for information or any other purpose you will be straightaway put in touch with the concerned person. Even if the person required is not available at that time someone else will be able to respond to your query. How does such an environment come about? Not by accident. It is created through a powerful leadership.

Where does the leader start when introducing a new culture? He should have a dream and vision of how the organization can be taken forward on its TQM journey. For this, he must accurately know the current state of affairs in the organization. If you want to go somewhere, you obviously need to know your starting point, otherwise you may not end up at your intended destination. Thus, it is extremely important that the leader should know how things stand at present in the organization. One of the important principles of TQM is management by factual data. This is easier said than done. The way many companies are managed, the top leaders are shielded by a number of layers of managers. The information reaching the top is coloured by the perception of the second and third rung of managers. There is a well- entrenched (and understandable) mechanism which prevents the truth reaching the top. The data may be filtered, modified or distorted to present a good picture to the boss. This is so because many employees feel threatened and insecure. They feel that if an unpleasant picture reaches the top boss, they will be the first victims of his ire, even though the person conveying the information may have no role in creation of the unpleasant situation. One of Deming's important principles is "Drive out fear from the organization." Unfortunately, most organizations are driven by fear. There may be a number of advisors and managers assisting the CEO in running the organization. But because of the fear factor, they try to keep him in the dark about the unpleasant facts as long as possible, until a crisis develops which cannot be kept under wraps. If the symptoms of any problem are exposed as early as possible, the problem may also be addressed as early as possible, and prevented from developing into a crisis. To remove the fear factor among employees, a good leader should encourage and reward employees who provide information about any non- conformity or any other symptom which could lead to quality problems. It is of the utmost importance that the leader have accurate information on a day-to-day basis.

According to Max De Pree, "The first responsibility of a leader is to define reality." This cannot be determined by remaining in a plush office and relying on information conveyed by subordinates. The Japanese lay great stress on being involved with the work place. The Japanese word for work place is "Gemba." Masaki Imai, the author of the famous book "Kaizen" strongly advises that leaders at all levels must leave their offices as often as possible and visit Gemba and retain control of work place where the actual action of building quality takes place. Masaki Imai has developed a quality improvement tool called "Gemba Kaizen." Lots of ideas can arise by different persons looking at the Gemba and questioning the way things are being done.

Once the current situation is fully understood by a leader, the next step activity is to set goals for moving toward the vision. Obviously one cannot hope to achieve the vision in one leap. The journey has to be carefully planned by setting goals or milestones at every stage. Generally, managers set modest goals to insure against failure and consequently criticism for non-achievement. It should be clearly understood that in the TQM journey, goals exist to challenge people, says Nemoto of Toyota. TQM is not the art of achieving so- called realistic or feasible goals. It is about achieving extraordinary results. The confidence to take on challenging goals comes from a deep understanding of the potential of the PDCA cycle and freedom from the fear of failure. The leadership should create such a supportive environment.

Another problem which must be appreciated by the leader is that when TQM is introduced, problems that management is unaware of, are bound to occur. If the leadership gets angry and begins to allocate blame, the organization is not ready for TQM. The leaders must value people as they are and not blame them for the problems of the company. One of the major elements in the success of TQM is how the company leadership appreciates and acknowledges the work done towards implementing TQM. In fact, most Quality Awards require evidence of how leaders recognize and appreciate people's achievements on the TQM journey. The most critical task of leaders for introducing TQM is to enable others to act. One way to institutionalise TQM is for an organization to build spirited teams which can take up the job of bringing about visible improvement in processes which add value. It could be reducing defects or mistakes, compressing cycle time or using lesser resources for the job without affecting quality. The success of the teams creates an environment for other people the company to start looking for opportunities of improvement in their areas of work too.

TEAM BUILDING

Teams are an integral component of TQM process, because teams are the vehicles to achieve the goals established by the company. TQM champions discussed in the previous section, provide leadership to the teams. The formation of teams demonstrates management commitment to TQM through the dedication of resources and the establishment of an institutional structure to begin and sustain a continual improvement process. There are various kinds of teams depending upon the tasks and the problems they are required to address. A few examples are given below:

(a) ***Process improvement teams:*** They focus on developing or improving a specific business process. Such teams try to achieve breakthrough level improvement in this improved or new process. Each such team has a well-defined project plan which is agreed upon at the beginning. Such teams would normally have a management sponsor who provides resources and organizational support.

(b) ***Cross-functional teams:*** These are multi- disciplinary teams that address organization- wide issues such as the general look and maintenance of their facility, or improvements in training and competence development.

(c) ***Special project teams:*** Such teams are constituted for long- duration dedicated project to develop a new product system or a process. Some examples are:
   - Re-engineering an entire process.
   - Introduction of new system such as ERP or CRM.
   - Preparing for a National Quality award.

SELECTION OF TEAMS

In any organization there are always some people who are not content with the routine jobs given to them. They have the fire and passion to take on challenging tasks - to do something extraordinary. It is the job of the leaders to identify such people and groom them as champions of the TQM movement. They in turn can motivate others. They can form the nucleus of spirited teams to spread TQM culture throughout the organization. Before forming a team, the management must define the tasks and the goal of the team. The actual selection of team members should be left to team leaders. However, there should be a structured methodology for constituting the teams. Keeping in view the task given to the team, the leader must identify all the competences required for the team members. Competence is a composite capability which depends upon following five factors:

Knowledge

Formal education, professional courses undertaken and self-study achievements.

Skills

Specialised skills acquired through training courses and certificates obtained to demonstrate proficiency in the use of tools and techniques.

Experience

Period spent on the application of knowledge in different functional areas or organizations, and positions held.

Aptitude

Natural talent and innate qualities for particular activities.

Attitude

Frame of mind and emotional temperament for interacting with people and reacting to situations.

In addition to the personal attributes of team members, the team leaders should also consider the problem of cooperation with the supervisors of the selected members, who may not be part of the team. Such a supervisor may have offered the team member's services to the team, but the member's involvement in their 'regular' job may not leave much time for team activities. It must be ensured that the activities of the teams in no way affect the relationship between the team members and their superiors. There should be no pressures for people to join the TQM team. They must be keen to take up TQM-related activities with the full support and encouragement of their bosses.

DEVELOPMENT OF TEAMS

Constituting the team is the first step and is relatively easy. However it has to go through various stages of development before it can deliver results. There are four main stages of development which are briefly discussed below:

1. **Forming**

   When team members come together for the first time, they bring with them their own identities and values which are shaped by their respective backgrounds and experiences. There may be uncertainty about their role and apprehensive about whether they will be able to perform well. At this stage, the leader clarifies the purpose of the team and explains the goal and roles for each member. He also defines the rules of behaviour. At this stage he also seeks acceptance and commitment from members for achieving the team goals.

2. **Storming**

   In this phase members try to impress other members about their capabilities and achievements. Inter-personal conflicts and attempts by some members to dominate may also surface. It is for the leader of the team to resolve these issues and assert his authority without appearing to be domineering and autocratic.

3. **Norming**

   Here efforts are made to persuade team members to shift their focus from personal concerns to meeting the collective challenges of the team before open communications have been established, and spirit of cooperation and mutual respect have developed. At the end of this phase, inter-personal conflicts are reduced and the team starts to work in a collaborative manner.

4. **Performing**

   At this stage the team starts working cohesively. Team members are supportive of each other's efforts in achieving the collective mission. A certain amount of pride in being part of the team may have developed, and the team starts making progress towards achieving its goals.

TEAM PROCESSES

There are two types of processes involved in the teamwork. The first is related to the task and achieving the objectives of the team. The second relates to maintaining the capability of the team by building the morale of team members and maintaining good relationships between team members.

TASK-RELATED FUNCTIONS

The first meeting of the team to discuss the task is very important for the success of its mission. Therefore, it should be well planned. Attention should be given to the following points for a good start:

- Where possible, the CEO or another senior manager sponsoring the project should participate in the meeting.
- The sponsor should explain the importance of the project within the overall context of the company's goals.
- The leader should clearly explain the contours of the project and team's objectives.
- Members' roles should be clarified.
- The technical process of improvement/problem solving and the resources being deployed, should be defined.

- The project plan with associated milestones, schedule and review procedures should be explained.

MAINTENANCE-RELATED FUNCTIONS

These are soft functions which are nonetheless very important for the effective functioning of the team. Attention to the following points helps in maintaining cohesiveness and smooth team functioning:

- Fixing meetings in consultation with the members. If all members cannot attend a particular meeting, ensure that four to five key members are able to participate.
- Ensure that members are punctual so that they do not waste the time of others.
- Maintain proper communication discipline. Allow everyone to project his or her viewpoint concisely. If anyone tries to monopolise the conversation or forces their views on others, they should be politely but firmly dealt with by the leader.
- Personal criticism of any team member, his value and his actions should be strictly prohibited.
- Evaluation of viewpoints or suggestions should only begin after all members of the team have had their say.
- The leader and other members should focus on establishing common ground and reconcile intra-team differences.

PITFALLS IN TEAMS

Teamwork is a powerful concept as it brings different perspectives and skills to bear on the problems being addressed. However, there are a number of instances where teams may fail to deliver. Management and team leaders should be aware of the following pitfalls and problems:

- Not selecting a strong leader.
- Improper selection of team members and heavy proportion of incompetent or undisinterested members.
- Team members with no personal stake in a positive outcome. Members will generally take their work more seriously as if their personal interest is involved.
- Not having regular meetings of the team.
- Not holding team members accountable for their assignments.
- Selecting a desired solution before a detailed study of the process.
- Inadequate support and interest of the top management.

14

Lean Production System

The phrase "Lean Production System" (LPS) means a manufacturing system which consumes less human and material resources for producing and delivering quality product to the customer in much less time that is taken in a traditional manufacturing practices. The concept of Lean manufacturing originated in Toyota Motors in Japan in 1950s and 1960s. It was on the basis of this innovative manufacturing system, an unknown motor car company was able to market their cars in highly competitive markets of USA. They had inherent disadvantage of having to transport their car half way round the world and competing in a saturated market. Yet they were not only able to establish their presence in USA but posed serious competition to the big giants like General Motors and Ford. This manufacturing system largely remained a secret with Toyota and some other Japanese companies. It was only in eighties, seeing the Japanese miracle in car manufacturing that a research team of MIT, USA undertook the International Motor Vehicle study project. The research team studied the auto production in 14 countries over a five year period. The finding of the study were published in the form of the famous book "Machine that changed the World", authored by James Womach, Denial Jones and Daniel Roose. The Book describes the characteristics of Lean production as "It uses less of everything compared to mass production, half the human effort in the factory, half the manufacturing space, half the investment in tool and half the engineering hours to develop a new product in half the time. Also it requires keeping less than half the inventory need on site and results in fewer defects."

TRADITIONAL MANUFACTURING SYSTEM

Before discussing the Lean Production System, let us analyze the traditional manufacturing system. The basic philosophy in the traditional management system is to maximize quantitative production and then have aggressive marketing to sell the product. Main steps in traditional system of manufacture are given below:

Production cycle starts in the factory

⇩

- Production plan based on demand forecast.
- Material procurement to meet production plan.
- Material receipt and inspection.
- Storage of materials and components till required for processing.
- Actual production in various process stations with stress on maximizing production.
- Storage of components required for assembly.
- Assembly, final inspection and packaging.
- Storage of finished goods in company go-downs and zonal depots.
- On the shelf in retail outlets.

⇩

Ends with the customer.

Since the production is pushed from factory, this is also known as PUSH system.

CHANGING DYNAMICS IN THE MARKET

Liberalization of economy and globalization of markets has brought major challenges for Indian industry. With elimination of import hurdles and drastic reduction of custom duty under the aegis of WTO regime, global competition has come right at our doorsteps. A number of well-established companies which were doing well during controlled economy era have failed because they could not face competition. Other companies are also under great strain. It is paradoxical that companies in the organized sector having same plant and equipment as used by European or South East Asian countries are not able to compete in quality and even price in spite of advantages of indigenous availability of raw material and much lower cost of labour. Main reason for this could be that most Indian companies have not appreciated the new economics in the market. Companies in India are sill following traditional method of fixing sale price of products based on the equation.

COST + PROFIT MARGIN = SALE PRICES

The cost of product is determined by the standard cost accounting methods of material cost, labour cost and fixed overhead for infrastructure, marketing and services. The company management then decides the profit margin it should have. Based on this, sale price is fixed. With increasing competition and globalization of markets, this system no longer works. Prices in most of the industries are falling. Companies using different sales channels are competing for the share of customers' wallet. Customer has access to all the information about the product and has multiple choices. This has made customer more powerful. He now demands high quality at reasonable prices. In this environment it is the customer who determines the price (based on the market competition). The new price and profit equation is:

PRICE (DICTATED BY MARKET) - COST = PROFIT

Thus the only way to improve profit is by reducing cost without affecting product quality. But the cost has to be reduced intelligently and not by arbitrary cost cutting such as down sizing, reducing training budget or cannibalizing the maintenance budget. Such measures weaken the company in the long run. Thus there is a need to adopt a new approach to cope with changing dynamics in the market.

WEAKNESS IN THE TRADITIONAL SYSTEM

This system has the following inherent weaknesses:

- Risk related to forecasts.
- Long overall business process cycle.
- Good comfort level at various stages leading to slack in the system.
- It hides the problems, waste and obstacles in the business process flow.
- Encourages departmental focus, as their efficiency is judged on the basis of output. *(departmental enterprise)*

This also pushes up costs and affects competitiveness.

The traditional system may have worked in the past, but it is not sustainable in the new market environment. The critical factor which is responsible for inefficiency in the traditional system is the waste embedded deep in the system of which management is not aware of. Therefore, there is need to discuss in detail various types of wastes which in Japanese language is called 'Muda'.

WHAT IS MUDA?

'Muda' is a Japanese word which means waste. Muda is defined as an organizational activity which consumes resources but does not create any value in the product or service for which customer is willing to pay. Experts of Lean Production System have classified eight types of Muda which are briefly described below:

MOTION

Motion is an entity which does not add any value. Some motion of man, machine or tool is necessary for performance of work. But there is lot of motion which is not an essential element for well planned work. For example poor ergonomic design of work place affects productivity, quality and even safety. A worker may have to walk, or bend to pick up the job and load in the machine. It may involve twisting or over-stretching in performance of work. In fact, poor ergonomics is a major factor in fatigue and safety hazards at the work place. Other examples of unnecessary motion could be when the worker is looking around for tools or some parts which are stored haphazardly.

DELAY

Delay is probably the largest factor of work. If you look around at any time in a factory or a construction work site, there is 60% chance that you will see at some work places, workers waiting for material, tools, machines, drawing, work instruction or someone to check that the job done by them is right. The actual process time is usually a small fraction of overall time taken to complete the job. 50% or even more may be accounted for as delay due to one reason or other.

TRANSPORTATION

It is waste due to inefficient plant layout, overly large equipment as in traditional batch production, where large batches of work in progress may have to be moved from process to process. Improper location of work in progress store, packaging and storage of finished goods can also lead to unnecessary waste due to transportation.

RECTIFICATION/REJECTION

This is an obvious waste. If a product is manufactured which does not meet the specified requirements, it obviously cannot be sold. In such cases first effort will be made to rectify the defects. All efforts made in the rectification *viz.*, additional material, labour and re-checking is a waste. In case the product cannot be rectified, it is scrapped in which case all material, labour, machine, time, energy and other resources is a total waste.

OVER-PROCESSING

There may be cases where certain processes are carried out to provide additional features or finish to the product which are not really required by the customer nor he will pay for the extra effort. Some of the over-zealous companies taking pride in their technological excellence may over-engineer the product, but customers may not be willing to pay additional price for such products. Thus this is also a subtle form of waste.

INVENTORY

Material cost is normally the major component of total product cost. Waste in inventory relates to keeping much more stock of materials, parts and semi-finished products than are necessary for immediate production. There is a tendency to keep excess stock to ensure against material shortages leading to stoppage of production. But planners do not often realize the cost of this insurance. Secondly, a set production is scheduled every month to meet the production target. This is continued even when there are fewer requirements of downstream processes. Thus inventory provides a major scope for reduction of Muda and reducing costs.

OVER-PRODUCTION

This is considered to be a major waste when production is carried out based on projected demand. This often leads to excess production which needs warehouses, maintenance of stock, interest loss on locked up capital and losses due to obsolescence of some products. Over-production also needs maintenance of higher inventory further adding to the cost of waste.

WHAT IS LEAN PRODUCTION SYSTEM (LPS)?

Lean Production System is systematic approach to identifying and eliminating waste (non-value added activities) through continuous improvement by flowing the product only when the customer needs it in pursuit of perfection. Lean Production System is systematic approach to identifying and eliminating waste (non-value added activities) through continuous improvement by producing the product only when the customer needs it in pursuit of perfection. This is also called pull system as opposed to push system followed by traditional system. LPS is a production management system which aims to provide the customers:

- What they want
- How they want
- Where they want
- At a competitive price

- In the quantities and varieties they want, and
- Always of expected quality

LEAN PRODUCTION (LPS) PHILOSOPHY

LPS is a manufacturing philosophy that shortens time between the customer order and shipment by eliminating waste. It is based on the following five principles:

1. Specify value
2. Identify **value stream**
3. Make the value **flow** by eliminating waste and obstruction.
4. Create **pull** according to customer demand
5. Attain **perfection** in every business activity.

To apply the above principles, a management needs to:

- Manage the business from the customer definition of value
- Create perfect business process which can deliver value with minimum wasted resources, efforts and time
- Build a lean management system to develop, sustain, and improve these processes over time
- Be clear about customer purpose, before designing the processes and then developing the human resource.

WHAT IS VALUE?

Value is a capability provided to a customer at the right time, and at an appropriate price as defined by the customer. Value is created by the producer which is the raison-de-etra of his existence. In the context of a product, it is its inherent worth as judged by the customer and reflected in selling price and market demand.

WHAT IS VALUE STREAM?

Value stream is the all set of activities required to bring a specific product or service in to being. This is achieved by the following management tasks:

- Problem solving task
- Information management task
- Physical transformation task

These tasks are briefly described in the following paragraphs.

PROBLEM SOLVING TASK

This task starts with defining value based on the requirements of the customer. It involves use of intellectual inputs for activities such as:

- Development of product design.
- Validation of design through collective review by all functional groups concerned with marketing, production and after-sales services.
- Engineering of the processes for production and quality assurance.
- Solving problems during various production processes.
- Analysis of customer complaints and planning remedial measures.

INFORMATION MANAGEMENT TASK

This concerns processing of information at various stages such as:

- Acquisition of orders
- Production, planning and scheduling
- Production and quality monitoring
- Dispatch information
- Selling related information
- Feedback information management

PHYSICAL TRANSFORMATION TASK

This deals with processes related to transformation raw materials to the finished products including verification processes till the product is delivered to the customer. These include:

- Physical transformation processes of components, assemblies and finishing operations
- Verification and testing
- Packaging
- Installation where required

VALUE FLOW

Value flows in the system from suppliers of materials till the product or service is delivered to the customer. Collectively it is called value stream. In a traditional system, value is pushed from the manufacturer to the customer. In this system value flow may be obstructed due to obstacles in the way with the result that value flow is uneven resulting in slack and all kinds of waste. On the other hand in LPS value is pulled by the customer, which removes the slack in the system due to which all the obstacles in the flow are revealed so that appropriate remedial actions can be taken. Traditional 'Push system' is analogous to deepwater stream in which boulders and other obstacles causing turbulence are hidden. On the other hand 'pull system' in LPS is like a shallow stream where even small pebble and other obstructions in the flow are visible. These are like various types of muda (waste) which now being visible, measures can be taken to reduce these bottle necks and obstacles for smooth flow of value.

LEAN TOOLS

It may be mentioned here that Lean Production System was not a one-time discovery or inspiration. It evolved over the years, and in the process several tools/techniques were developed to implement the concept of LPS. Major tools used in implementing LPS are:

- 5'S (which includes visual controls)
- TPM
- Just in Time, and
- Poka Yoke

Of these, the first tool *i.e.*, **5'S** creates standard work environment for implementing LPS. This is a powerful tool which creates proper environment for quality work and facilitates use of other quality tools. Therefore, this tool has been discussed in detail in Chapter-36.

The second tool *i.e.*, **TPM** is a technique to maintain equipment health and provide maximum availability of plant and equipment for maximizing productivity. This again can be used by itself and has been covered in Chapter-15. The two other tools are discussed in the following paragraphs.

JUST IN TIME (JIT)

JIT is a system of manufacture, based on planned elimination of all wastes and continuous improvement of productivity. It is an approach with the objective of producing the right part in the right place at the right time. Hence the phrase "just in time" – JIT production follows four basic rules:

- Do not produce something unless the customer (including downstream process) asks for it.
- Level demand to ensure even flow of work throughout the plant.
- Link all processes with the customer demand through simple visual tools.
- Maximize flexibility of people and machinery.

WHY IS JIT NECESSARY?

Industrial managers are always apprehensive that some problem may occur in product or supply chain due to which production may have to be stopped. Such situation invariability attracts wrath of top management, because in their mind, an indication of good health of the company is that production continues. The first question which CEO asks on coming to the factory is, how much was yesterday's production. To safeguard against interruption in production flow, material planners and production managers build a cushion of inventory of purchased materials and work in process at various stages. This ensures that even if there are any problem in supply from the vendor or at some stages of production, there is adequate stock in the inventory at various stages that downstream production can continue. This way no one would know about the problems and production managers would get time to solve the problems. But the organizations have to pay a heavy price for keeping this cushion. Excess inventory means locked up capital and additional space for storage. It also needs transportation and handling and possibility of degradation or obsolescence of material during the period in storage. It also fosters a feeling of smugness among production staff, who do not feel a sense of urgency in preventing and solving production problems. Even if some defective pieces are produced, they have enough reserve stock to feed the downstream processes, while they rectify the defective components or produce new parts to make up the buffer. All this mean additional cost which is loaded on the product. Thus there is a need for a mechanism to reduce all this waste and non-value adding activities with a view to making the companies cost competitive. JIT is a powerful tool to implement LPS to achieve the above objective.

PRE-CONDITIONS OF APPLICATION OF JIT

JIT is not a wonder tool which can be applied in any production unit. Before considering applying JIT, the organization must fulfill certain requirements as given below:

1. *Information about customers' requirements*
   (a) There should be reliable information about quantities of various products including different models which are required to be produced. This means that production should not be planned on the basis of sales forecast. Instead it should be based on the firm orders of the customers.
   (b) If a company is to start production on receipt of order from the customer, it has to drastically reduce the product cycle. It should be realized that once a customer has placed an order, he is not going to wait for months or weeks to receive the supplies. It means that production cycle time has to be in hours and at best in days in the case of major equipment. Thus all processes have to be optimized to achieve short cycle time to enable meet delivery commitment.
2. *Quick machine set up mechanism:* If a company has to produce in small batch, it needs to streamline the machine set up system; when a new product is to be manufactured on the machine which was set up for

another product, lot of time is lost on changing the set up. It may involve change of tools and dies in addition to other adjustment in speed and certain other parameters. To meet this requirement, lot of technological innovations were developed by auto industry in Japan, the most famous being Single digit Minutes Exchange of Dies (SMED), which reduced the time of die change for different models of cars from days to less than ten minutes. Classical example of this approach for quick set up can be found in car racing. NASCAR pit crew can change all four tyres and refuel the car in just 20 seconds using specified equipment and high degree of coordination. Other ways to ensure quick machine set up is to tooling and fixtures which are quick to install and cannot be fitted wrongly.

3. *Reliable vendors:* JIT can be applied only if there is high degree of confidence that promised delivery of bought out materials will arrive on time. In addition the vendor would have carried out thorough inspection of the shipped material so that it can be straightaway sent to the process station or assembly line without any check or inspection about their conformity to the specification. This also applies to the in-house processes which should ensure that processed components are thoroughly checked for conformity before sending these to downstream processes.
4. *Good preventive maintenance:* The idle time of machines and workers should be used for preventive maintenance. It should be ensured that at the end of every shift, the machines are properly cleaned and maintained so that these can be used in the next shift without any loss of time.
5. *Flexible workforce:* The workers should be capable of doing multi tasks. They should be able to operate several machines, carry out maintenance tasks and perform quality inspections. JIT needs teams of competent and empowered employees who take responsibility for the work assigned to them.

PRODUCTION CONTROL SYSTEM FOR JIT DEPLOYMENT

Implementation of JIT depends upon developing a production system which responds to the pull of the customer. Toyota had developed an ingenious mechanism for production control called *'Kan Ban'*. It uses simple visual signals to control the movement of materials from the stores and between work centers to replenish those sent to downstream work center. *'Kan Ban'* is a card attached to a storage or transport container. The *'Kan Ban'* gives the part number and container capacity. It also contains other information such as:

- The supplier of the products
- The customer

- Where the product is to be stored
- Method of conveyance or transport.

In Toyota two types of *'Kan Bans'* are used. These are:

1. Production *'Kan Ban'* which signals the need to produce more parts.
2. Withdrawal *'Kan Ban'*. This indicates the need to withdraw the parts from one work center and deliver it to the next work center.

It can be seen that *'Kan Ban'* gives a practical shape to the pull system and removes the slack. It ensures that no part or equipment is made unless these are required by the downstream processes or the customer. This does not allow build up of inventory at any stage and thereby reduces waste and non-value adding activities.

POKA-YOKE

Poka-Yoke term was coined in Japan in 1960s by Shigeo Shingo, an industrial engineer, at Toyota. Poka-Yoke in English would mean mistake proofing. Poka-Yoke refers to techniques which make it virtually impossible to make mistakes or errors. It was realized that defects in the products do not happen by chance. All defects are caused by errors in the equipment or mistakes made by the people, by not carrying out activities in the specified manner. Thus key to eliminate defects in the production system is preventing errors or mistakes.

Poka-Yoke refers to a device or a mechanism which either prevents a mistake from being made or alerts the worker about the error before it becomes a defect. There are various types of errors which can occur in a production process as given below:

1. *Equipment errors*

- Loose parts causing vibrations
- Improper environmental conditions
- Out of calibration measuring instruments in the equipment

2. *Set up errors*

- Using wrong or worn out tooling
- Incorrect machine adjustment

3. *Missing or improper parts*

- Certain parts missed in assembly
- Wrong parts used in the process
- Loose or improperly fitted parts

4. ***Operation errors***
   - Errors in measurement of items
   - Errors in machine adjustment.

In any well-organized company, some organized process control mechanism would be in place. They usually take the form of periodic monitoring of the process or use of statistical process controls. Since these checks are made periodically, corrective action based on these periodic checks takes time. During this period a number of defective products would have been manufactured. Poka-yoke relies more on self-check by operators before starting the operation to see proper conditions of equipment and tooling. In addition he must also be able to check the product immediately after production so that any abnormality is brought out at the earliest stage before significant number of defective product is produced.

POKA-YOKE DEVICES

Poka-Yoke devices could be in the form of:

1. Limit switches which prevent overrun of machines.
2. Cut off switches to stop the machine if it is not running properly, or there is a possibility of defects occurring.
3. Design of parts which cannot be assembled in the wrong way.
4. Light or alarm signal alerting the operator where any parameter of the process is out of control.
5. Check sheet for the operator to carry out pre-checks of the equipment and tooling before starting the process.
6. Simple devices like assembly operator having a small tray in which he places all the screws, washers and nuts which are to be used in assembly. This way, if any part is left in the tray after assembly, he would know that he has missed fitting this part. Thus it would alert him before he passes on the defective assembly.

Application of Poka-Yoke in a Manufacturing Unit

1. Study the process and identify critical processes based on Pareto principle.
2. Analyze how the defects can occur in the process, or how the process can fail.
3. Decide suitable Poka-Yoke devices such as:
   - A shut off device for preventing errors being made.
   - Attention type of devices which alerts through a visual or audio signal that an error is likely to be made.

- Design of parts which cannot be assembled the wrong way.
- Self check sheets for the operator before starting the process.
- Devices or check sheet for quick self inspection of products after manufacture.

4. Trial of Poka-Yoke methods to see if it works.
5. Training the operators and study success of the devices.
6. Provide incentives for continuous initiatives for eliminating defectives in the production system.

DEPLOYMENT OF LEAN PRODUCTION SYSTEM

Any new management initiative can succeed only if it is driven by the top management. LPS is one of the many tools available to a company to improve its operational performance and competitiveness. LPS mainly focuses on waste elimination and reduction of production cost. If a company feels that they have a good product, but are not able to get significant share of the market, because of their higher prices as compared to their competitors, then this is the appropriate tool to be employed. LPS is able to achieve major cost reduction while maintaining or even improving quality and reliability of their products. Implementation of LPS involves the following steps:

1. *Awareness training*: Awareness programs need to be organized to explain the concept of LPS and its benefits. Top management team itself needs to be exposed to the salient features of LPS and how it impacts on the bottom line. They also need to be made aware of its implementation methodology. Once they are convinced about its efficacy, this awareness training should cover all executives. It is not an engineering tool. It is rather a management approach which can improve all business processes which are directly or indirectly related to the production. This training will help in securing cooperation of executives from all departments, which is essential for success of LPS.
2. *Creation of a Lean Steering Committee*: It may be mentioned here that LPS is a project based tool. The company may deploy LPS first in one or two production lines which has maximum waste in the form of inventory and long production cycle. On seeing the success of lean deployment, it can be extended to other production lines. LPS will impact work of many departments. Therefore, it is advisable to constitute a Lean Steering Committee under the chairmanship of a senior member of the management team.

The Steering Committee would have the following roles and responsibilities:

- Selection of LPS consultant
- Approval of projects

- Provide resources to the project teams
- Monitor and review the progress
- Standardize the new processes and issue suitable documentations.
- Recognition and reward to the project teams and individuals.

3. *Selection and Training of LPS Core Group*: LPS implementation requires persons with process knowledge and innovative mind. To start with company management could select a small core group comprising of ten to twelve managers and engineers from different departments. This core group should be given extensive training in identifying various types of wastes and tools/techniques used in LPS.
4. *Business Process Waste Diagnosis*: Once the core team has been trained, a two or three day's diagnostic workshop should be organized under the guidance of a consultant. In this workshop company personnel will be able to identify the waste and evaluate its economic impact on the bottom line. Based on the diagnostic data, lean projects teams can be constituted for undertaking lean projects.
5. *Value Stream Mapping*: It is a tool to see and analyze the network of organizational processes which are creating value and generating waste during product realization and servicing processes. Through value stream mapping, current state of business processes is mapped, which are analyzed to see the wastes and identify the improvement potential. From the data of current state map a future state map is developed and action plan is made to reach to the future state.
6. *Improving Processes*

Efforts should be focused on following elements while improving processes:

- Minimize material handling. Preference should be given to low or no-cost solutions such as gravity-feed slides. Handle product once only.
- Minimize distance. Avoid walking, carrying, etc., by creating cells, combining operations within a work center, better planning, and so on.
- Minimize strain. Work centers should be ergonomically designed to avoid back and other muscle strains.
- Minimize clutter. Everything should have a home, from parts and tools at a workstation, to equipment and product within designated floor spaces.
- Minimize storage. If you have the space, it will surely get filled. Thus, continuously minimize your storage space for raw material, WIP, finished goods and spare parts throughout the supply chain.
- Maximize utilization. Make optimal use of people, space, and equipment to improve the return on investment.

- Maximize flexibility. The key to lean is creating a layout that can adapt quickly to changes in product, equipment, personnel, or material.
- Maximize smooth flow. Continuously determine and eliminate the bottlenecks, then –rebalance the line.
- Maximize visibility. To quickly spot problems, maintain a clear line of vision to anywhere, from anywhere.
- Maximize communication. Lean requires constant training on tools available to meet goals and objectives, and feedback on how well things are going.

7. *Performance Evaluation and Standardization*: After successful implementation of improvement plan and lean transformation, performance is evaluated to ensure that targets are achieved. To hold the gains, improved methodology, process activities, and steps are standardized, documented and project is closed. Completion of every lean project enhances problem-solving capability of the organization and improves the financial results. After completion of each project, new projects are taken up on continual basis to achieve the ultimate objective of world class manufacturing.

LEAN MANAGEMENT IN SERVICE ORGANIZATION

Although lean system were originally developed for manufacturing organization, the concept is equally applicable to service organizations. In fact the quantum of waste and non-value activities is more in service organizations. This has now been recognized by management experts and a number of services organizations have taken up lean management initiatives.

15

Total Productive Maintenance (TPM)

Equipment health is of vital importance for ensuring quality of manufactured products. Keeping plant and machinery in operational state is the responsibility of Maintenance Department in any organization. Unfortunately, in Indian industrial culture, maintenance function ranks quite low in the organizational hierarchy. Marketing, Finance and Production are the prime departments which have got glamour and are much sought after. Maintenance is considered as a drab function where it is felt that persons cannot show their merit. That is why very few executives volunteer to be in the maintenance department. Managements also consider that maintenance can be handled by any manager. One often hears of cases where if a technical manager who is not dynamic and is not able to show results in Production group is shunted to maintenance, which is pity. It is now realized that when such a manager is in Production group, it will have limited negative impact localized in that group. Where if he is in the Maintenance Department, it will have adverse impact on the equipment health of the whole plant. That is why Japanese companies attach great importance to maintenance engineers who are responsible for ensuring high equipment availability.

Maintenance is a well-established function in any organization particularly if it is a manufacturing enterprise. Well-organized companies have procedures for breakdown maintenance and preventive maintenance schedules. However, in actual practice, the production groups are under constant pressure to meet ever-increasing targets. Therefore, they are quite often not able to spare equipment for planned preventive maintenance. The result is high incidence of breakdowns. To prevent this fire-fighting approach the concept of Total Productive Maintenance was evolved by Toyota Company as a part of Lean Manufacturing System. TPM is a system of maintenance covering the entire life of equipments installed throughout the organization. It includes not only production equipment but also equipments used for various services. TPM is a proactive maintenance system which includes Preventive and Predictive Maintenance with total involvement of maintenance, process, design and operational personnel.

PRINCIPLES OF TPM

TPM is based on following three principles:

(a) *Maintenance of normal conditions* : Any machine or equipment has a tendency to degrade or deteriorate overtime. The operators should carry out cleaning, oiling, tightening and checking of the equipment on daily basis to prevent deterioration and maintain normal operating condition.

(b) *Early discovery of defects and abnormalities* : The operators should be on the lookout for any defects or abnormal conditions through visual observation and periodic check with the help of instruments.

(c) *Prompt corrective action :* The operators and maintenance staff should take immediate action to correct the defect or abnormality.

TPM OBJECTIVE

TPM aims to achieve zero breakdowns and zero defects. If you want zero of anything, then you must take actions to prevent the thing happening even once. Thus TPM emphasizes preventive approach to maintenance.

WHY IS TPM NECESSARY?

TPM is particularly important for India because poor machine utilization is one of the factors for losing out our competitiveness.

There is a general sense of complacency about plant utilization. If a company is able to achieve plant utilization of 70%, it is considered quite good according to general standard in Indian industry. It is not realized that all plant and machinery has certain cost associated with it, irrespective of the fact whether it is used or not. This cost is like a taxi meter which keeps running 24 hours a day. If we are using the plant only for 70% of the time, it means 30% of equipment cost is going down the drain. Unfortunately this avoidable cost does not figure in the account books of the company. Thus higher management is not aware of the avoidable losses being incurred by the company due to down time of equipment. As complex and expensive equipments are introduced, companies would like to use it to the maximum period of the day to recover high cost of acquisition. There are a number of manufacturing companies with three shifts a day. Some of the equipment like computers providing services to banking, airlines, hotels, etc., run 24 hours all over the world.

This would not be possible without TPM. Implementation of TPM has become inescapable for companies to remain competitive in global markets due to the following reasons:

- Manufacturing processes are becoming more synchronized as we drive work-in-progress out of our "Lean" Production Processes.
- Processes in the total production system are now dependent upon each other.
- Equipment available time or up-time is critical as inventory levels and production lead times continue to be reduced.
- New technology and equipment requires significant investment and therefore the related return on investment must be maximized.
- Equipment Life Cycle Costs need to be reduced to maintain competitiveness in the market.
- TPM allows for the more effective use of human resources, supports personal growth and manufacturing flexibility objectives.

LOSSES DUE TO EQUIPMENT CONDITION

Most people are generally not aware that equipment related expenses can account upto 30% of total manufacturing cost. There is a considerable scope for saving by preventing avoidable losses. These losses can be grouped into six types as given below:

1. Sudden or unexpected breakdown which results in loss of productivity. Such breakdown could be due to electrical system failure, drive failure or structural fatigue.
2. Time taken in set up of the machine, adjusting dies, tools and jigs, as well as adjustment of testing system.
3. Quality defects due to malfunctioning of equipment or tooling which may require rectification or cause rejection of the manufactured product.
4. Reduction in yield due to difference between the actual processing speed and the standard processing speed of the equipment.
5. Down time of the machine and defective product which occurs when one product ends and the equipment is prepared for the next product.
6. Idling of the machine or minor stoppages.

All these losses can be greatly reduced by implementing TPM.

AUTONOMOUS MAINTENANCE

Autonomous Maintenance is a phrase coined by Japan Institute of Plant Maintenance (JIPM). This represents the shift towards machine operators maintaining their own equipment.

Autonomous maintenance involve following activities:

- General cleaning of the equipment.
- Identify and reduce causes of dust and dirt.
- Lubrication of equipment and cleaning of filter and tightening of nuts and bolts.
- Inspection of the equipment by the operator.
- Detailed check of the equipment by maintenance department.
- Preventive maintenance by maintenance personnel.
- Adhering to work place standards and maintenance schedules.

Major Activities of TPM

1. First essential requirement of TPM is that proper machine-wise data should be maintained on the operational time of equipment defects (minor or major) observed by the operator and maintenance personnel, nature of rectification or repair carried out and efficiency (speed and process capability) of the machines.
2. The data on machines should be studied to monitor Meantime between Failure (MTBF) and Meantime to Repair (MTTR). Based on this analysis maintenance, overhaul and replacement of equipment should be planned.
3. Detailed analysis of the major problems should be carried to find the root causes. This could be done by joint teams of operating and maintenance departments, which should be tasked to suggest improvements in equipment efficiency.
4. Preventive engineering should be carried by the engineering department to simplify loading and job setting as well as improve maintainability of the equipment.
5. Product design should make efforts to design easy to manufacture products based on the analysis of manufacturing problems faced by the production department.
6. Training programs should be organized on TPM both for operating and maintenance personnel. A few selected persons for Design and Engineering should also be exposed to TPM concepts.
7. For effective implementation of TPM, role of operators and maintenance should be clearly defined.

THE OPERATORS' TPM ROLE

The operator is the principal actor in implementing TPM in an organization. He has the following role:

- Perform basic equipment maintenance, Cleaning of machine
- Cleaning and replacement of filters
- Lubrication
- Checking basic machine and safety device functions
- Maintain proper condition of machines
- Diagnose and perform minor repairs for which operators must be trained.
- Operators should have basic skills for monitoring and maintaining critical process parameters
- Perform changeover and set-up
- Record/Collect data to track equipment performance
- Maintain production control chart
- Have capability to initiate work order for maintenance/repair.

THE MANAGEMENT'S ROLE IN TPM

TPM cannot be implemented by Maintenance department alone. It requires major support by Production and Engineering departments. Typical activities required for implementing TPM are:

- Provide technical support and training for autonomous maintenance done by operators.
- Restore deteriorated equipment through Improvement-Related Maintenance.
- Identify design weaknesses and improve the equipment to error-free function.
- Improve technical maintenance skills of all maintenance personnel through systemic training and work assignments.
- Implement planned or periodic maintenance system based upon data from equipment manufacturers and operators.
- Through data analysis and periodic diagnostic tests, perform appropriate predictive maintenance to avoid equipment failure.
- Maintain work order system to provide data for above – calculate MTBF and MTTR.
- Ensure that the maintenance function is treating the root cause – not just the symptom.
- Understand the manufacturing process to successfully achieve the above.
- Maintenance personnel should have the capability to operate all the equipment.

It can be seen from the above that effective implementation of TPM requires cooperation of all technical departments. TPM is an essential element in managements' effort for quality improvement and cost competitiveness through Lean Production System. Therefore, top management of the company would have to drive this program to achieve success.

PRODUCTIVE MAINTENANCE EXCELLENCE AWARD

Well-planned TPM activities have been one of the major factors in phenomenal success of Japanese industry. Considering importance of TPM activities for manufacturing organizations, Japanese Institute of Plant Engineers (JIPE) have instituted Productive Maintenance Excellence award to recognize outstanding achievements in the area of TPM in Japan. The criteria for assessment for the award are based on the following ten points:

1. Policy and objectives
2. Organization and operation
3. Small group activities and autonomous maintenance
4. Training
5. Equipment maintenance
6. Planning and management
7. Equipment investment plan and maintenance planning
8. Production volume, scheduling and cost
9. Safety, sanitation and environment conservation
10. Results and assessments.

Large number of organizations in Japan and other developed countries have started giving importance to maintenance of equipment because of its influence on quality and cost competitiveness, which have become essential to survive in the environment of intense competition due to globalization of markets.

16

Customer Relationship Management (CRM)

There is an old saying about business which is still true:

- You don't need money to be in business;
- You don't need a factory or shop to be in business;
- You don't need personnel to be in business;
- You don't even need a product or service to be in business;
- But you are not in business, if you don't have a customer.

Thus the CUSTOMER is the one essential element of business.

This is not easy. A company may be able to acquire customers through high- powered marketing campaigns, but the harder part is to retain their loyalty. This task has become more difficult by the globalization of markets, advances in production technologies and easy access to the markets through multi-channel communication made possible by phenomenal progress in information technology. We need to undertstand the impact of these developments to come up with a suitable strategy for maintaining and enhancing the market share.

NEW CHALLENGES IN BUSINESS

The last two or three decades have seen a major change in the market environment, which poses challenges to the business organizations in retaining the customers. These are described as follows:

Increasing competition: With deregulation of economies, privatization of government monopolies and globalization of trade through the WTO regime, greater supply capacity is chasing every unit of purchasing power.

Smaller margins: With increased competition, margins between production costs and customer value are being reduced. Companies can no longer afford the luxury of large marketing budgets and inefficient sales methods.

Less differentiation among competitors: With technological advancement in production processes and automation of some service functions, there is a less differentiation among competing products. Thus customer interaction and service assume greater importance for gaining and maintaining a competitive edge.

Multiple channels of communication with customers: With the great strides that have occurred in communication technology, there is a reduced opportunity for face-to-face interaction with the customers. This makes it difficult to gauge immediate customer reaction and to adjust further interactions with the customer to ensure a positive experience.

To meet these challenges companies need to better understand the needs and expectations of customers and continually improve the design of their products and services to meet these needs. They must improve efficiencies, not only of production and delivery processes but also of marketing, sales and service processes. To retain the customers, they must provide greater value for money and enhance customer experience in all transactions with the customers. In short, every activity that is undertaken, should keep the customer's interest in mind. To gain a competitive edge, companies must concentrate on developing ongoing relationships with the customers rather than making individual quick sales. This has given birth to the concept of CUSTOMER RELATIONSHIP MANAGEMENT (CRM).

ORIGIN OF CRM

Customer Relationship Management is not really a new subject. Since the 1960s, management gurus like Peter Drucker and Theodore Levitt have been propagating a gospel which can be summarized in one sentence:

"The true business of every company is to make customers, keep customers and maximize customer profitability."

This remained a theoretical concept taught at business schools, due to the lack of tools to manage information about the vast large number of often widely distributed customers and customer transactions that most enterprises had. However, rapid advances in information technology in recent years have made it possible to acquire and analyse customer data lying in files and in the minds of personnel of the customer-facing departments of any company. On the basis of the analysis of this customer data, companies can adopt better strategies for developing long-term relationship with the customers.

WHAT IS CRM?

Customer Relationship Management (CRM) came into the business lexicon in the late 1990s and is one of the newer management mantras that include ISO 9000, TQM, Six Sigma, Business Process Reeingineering etc. With CRM 'hype' coming mainly from CRM software vendors, CRM is often confused with the technology used for its implementation. It should be realized that CRM is not a particular technique or set of tools that happen to be marketed with a 'CRM' nomenclature. At its core, CRM is a set of business policies and processes designed to acquire, service and retain customers. The aim of CRM is to increase customer satisfaction, revenue and business efficiency by building strong customer relationships – with the entire organization sharing and contributing to that view.

CRM DEFINITION

To understand any new concept or methodology, we need to have a clear definition for it.

Peter Keen, the author of *Shaping the Future* (1991) and *The Process Edge* (1997) defines CRM as follows:

"Customer relationship management is the commitment of the company to place the customer experience at the center of its priorities, and to ensure that incentive systems, processes and information resources leverage the relationship by enhancing the experience."

"In terms of technology, CRM is the design, communication and use of information to ensure that customers develop more and more confidence, trust and sense of personal value in their relationship with the company."

According to the CRM portal, www.CRM- Guru.com, "CRM is a business strategy to select and manage customers to optimize long term value. CRM requires a customer-centric business philosophy and culture to support effective marketing, sales and service processes."

It must be emphasized that the core of CRM is the creation of a customer focus throughout the organization. This requires the development of committed customer relationships and the development of a new work culture among people – which cannot be done by IT tools alone.

WHAT DOES CRM INVOLVE?

A company embracing the CRM paradigm must:

- Identify its most profitable customers.
- Align its strategy to acquiring and retaining these customers.

- Improve all aspects of the customer experience by ensuring that all functions, not merely customer facing ones, become customer centric – based on characteristics of the profitable customers or segments.
- Repeat the above steps periodically.

ARE ALL CUSTOMERS PROFITABLE?

A fundamental tenet of CRM is that all customers do not contribute to the profits of a company. Some may even cause a net loss. This is based on documented evidence that the bulk of the typical company's profits come from a disproportionately small number of customers. The implication is that firms should identify their profitable customers, and focus their efforts and resources on them in preference to others. Unfortunately with very few exceptions, this does not happen and all customers are given more or less the same treatment. While many firms regularly analyze their product and service offerings, and focus on the more profitable ones – most firms DO NOT regularly analyze their customers and choose to focus on or discard specific customers.

Problems with analyzing customer profitability: Most firms appear to believe that product profitability is synonymous with customer profitability. The most obvious flaw with this belief is the case of repeat customers. For example, guests who stay in at a hotel frequently and use none of the complimentary services are highly profitable customers... however, they are often not treated differently from people who stay once a year and use a lot of services. Another myth about customer profitability is that large volume customers are more profitable hence they are treated as valued customers. In actual practice, because of their financial muscle they derive hard bargains, and may leave the company very thin margins. Thus it would be incorrect to equate customer value with the corresponding sales revenue. Even if one wants to scientifically assess customer profitability, there is very little data on transactions with the customers. Other than the Sales department, no individual or functional group uses the customer as their unit of work. However, even the sales is compensated on revenues, not profits. Consequently, this leaves absolutely no one with direct responsibility for marginal profitability per customer. Even at a transactional level, customer costs vary, but transactional profitability data are rarely available. The main reason for this is that functional departments focus on, and are compensated for their respective units of work, rather than the customer – often even the identity of the customer is not captured. For instance, manufacturing focuses on batches, or volume, Accounts Receivable focuses on invoices etc. Systems serving individual departments exist in silos – making it difficult to extract a customer- based set of transactional information, which could then be used for meaningful cost allocation.

Measuring Customer Profitability: A fundamental requirement for the application of CRM is segmentation of customers on the basis of profitability, or value of customers to the company. For this we need to acquire enough information about the customers from all functional groups to KNOW what REAL resource consumption, and therefore REAL profitability is. For example, a company might need to pull details of all service calls made by a customer, the resources associated with each call, and combine them to determine the true service cost of supporting this customer. Wherever practical, the company needs to get enough information to directly attribute costs to each customer – these can include, sales costs, service costs, raw-materials costs, financing costs etc.

Aligning Strategy: Realigning the company's strategy to be customer-focused involves a lot more than simply issuing company policies or exhortations through circulars and briefing meetings. Instead the strategy must –

- Identify the customer profile that it seeks to target.
- Identify the quantifiable value proposition and customer experience goals for various customer segments.
- Mandate that all functional groups must recognize the customer as being the primary unit of work.
- Link some portion of compensation with customer satisfaction.
- Change the unit of work to be an identifiable customer.
- Analyze the effects that the function has on customer experience.
- Modify processes such that they improve the customer experience.
- Modify group performance metrics to include customer experience.

ALIGNING FUNCTIONS

Ultimately it is the functional groups which have to serve the customers. Therefore, functions have to be aligned to customers. Alignment of functional groups to the customers has four steps:

- Change unit of work to be an identifiable customer
- Analyze the effect that the function has on the customer experience.
- Modify processes to improve customer experience.
- Modify group performance metrics to include customer experience.

Aligning functions can be illustrated by considering a hotel laundry service for guest clothes.

- Unit of work

  Normally the unit of work in the laundry is washing loads. Change this to customer requests?

- Effect on customer experience
  Time taken to complete
- Modify processes
  Do guest clothes before house linen? Going one step further, do preferred guest laundry before non-preferred guest laundry?
- Modify group performance metrics.
  Bonus for on-time laundry completion for certain proportion of guests?

IMPLEMENTATION OF CRM

As explained earlier, CRM should not be confused with the CRM software being promoted by many vendors. It is essentially a strategy for building customer focus in a company. However, CRM technology acts as enabler to implement this strategy. Each implementation step has a corresponding technology as explained below:

(a) ***Measure Customer Profitability*** – requires a data warehouse that pulls costs and transactions from the systems serving each function, and integrates this information using the customer as the central attribute. For example, information needs to be pulled from sales, support, manufacturing, finance and training, as well as other functional systems. All of this information then needs to be analyzed.

(b) ***Align Strategy*** – requires the creation, measurement and dissemination of strategy metrics to all employees in the enterprise. For instance, key metrics for an insurance company might be time to issue a policy or time for settlement of a claim. It would be excellent to have the average time norms made known to all customers and on display to all employees so that they feel responsible to meet the norms.

(c) ***Align Functions*** – requires each function/department to have access to the customer information that it needs in order to be more customer-centric. For instance, if the manufacturing manager needs to customer profile as means of prioritizing jobs, he/she needs to have this information integrated into the manufacturing system.

CRM TECHNOLOGY

What software infrastructure is necessary for a company that wants to embrace the CRM paradigm? It depends upon the size of the company, the nature of its business, its level of computerization, the number of its locations and so on. It is instructive to first look at a typical technology set up that is representative of most companies in India. We will consider the case of a manufacturing company that has four functional departments, namely Sales, Support, Production and Accounting/Finance. We will further assume that this is an advanced company, in that each functional area is computerized. The typical set up may look as shown in Figure 1, where four distinct systems serve four distinct functions, and the Sales system 'feeds' the Support, Production and Accounting functions. Finally, each of these functions have their own customer- related transactions.

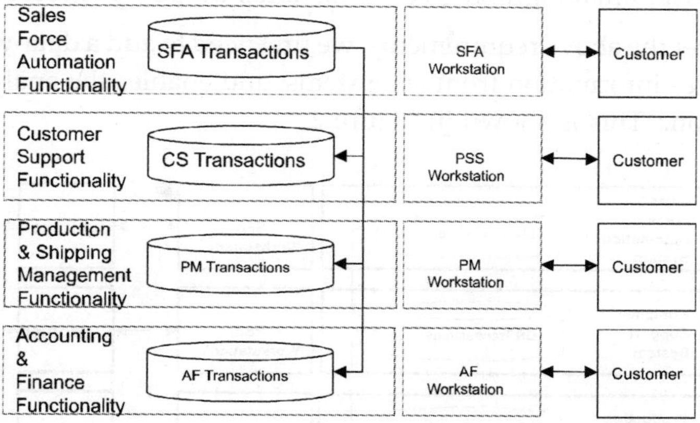

Fig. 1: Typical Technology Setup

Let us consider some of the shortcomings of this infrastructure as given below:

- Upstream systems have no input from downstream systems. For instance – a salesperson making a follow- up call has no idea whether products have been shipped, or whether there are outstanding customer- support issues. Customer support has no idea that the customer is late in paying invoices, and therefore support should be curtailed.
- There is no way the product design or product marketing or pricing functions can get one, unified view of the customer.
- The customer needs to contact, either directly or via customer support, each individual function separately to answer questions like … when can I expect my shipment? Was my cheque received?
- Clearly, this does not allow functions to make customer- centric decisions, does not support inter-function communication, and above all, does not support effective communication with the customer.

CRM INFRASTRUCTURE

A technology infrastructure that supports CRM must:

- Allow transactional information to be integrated into one view – so that the most profitable customers can be identified.
- Allow the calculation of strategic metrics.
- Give functions sufficient information to enable customer- centric decision-making, and give the customer the best possible experience.

To meet the above requirements, we first need to add a data-warehouse that sources information from all systems, and enables the analysis of the information. This is shown in Figure 2.

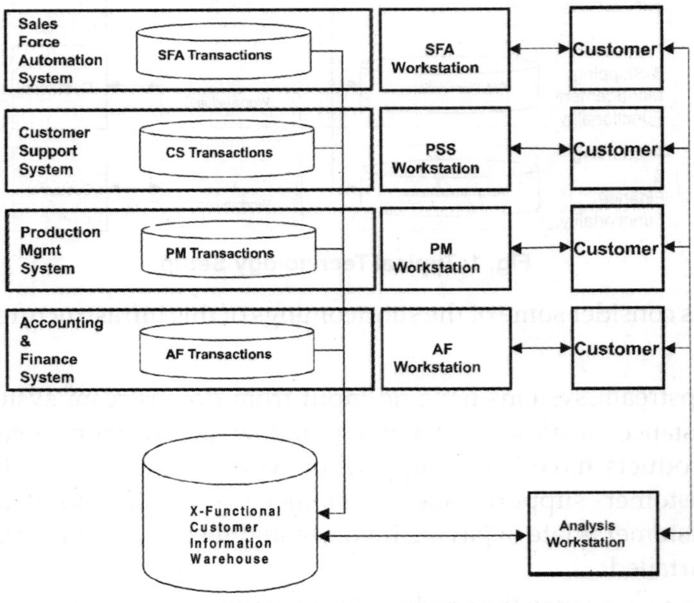

Fig. 2: CRM Infrastructure/Warehouse

In addition we need a decision- support application that shows us how to slice and dice the customer- centric database to identify:

- The most profitable customers ... for example, the customers that call support twice a year are more profitable than the ones that call over thirty times.
- Characteristics of the most profitable customers, *e.g.*, our most profitable customers are in Germany and the Netherlands.

We have also added value by the provision of the time dimension. As opposed to functional systems, which focus on work in progress, we can look at completed work over a period of time. This gives us the ability to recognize time trends. For instance, we may get information that we are getting fewer orders for Bluebirds from Germany, or that the time taken to manufacture Bluebirds is going up. We may also get information about segments of customers who take longer time to make payments against invoices.

The warehouse also allows us to calculate cross-functional metrics for evaluating the strategy. For instance:

- The average total time taken from order receipt to invoicing is 30 days. This measures transaction time in the sales, production and accounting departments.
- The average time to resolve a support call related to a late shipment is 1 day.
- The average time to resolve a support call related to an incorrect invoice is 3 days.
- The length of the average support call from Germany is twice that of any other market.

Finally, the warehouse provides inputs to each function on how to best improve the customer experience for its most profitable customers.

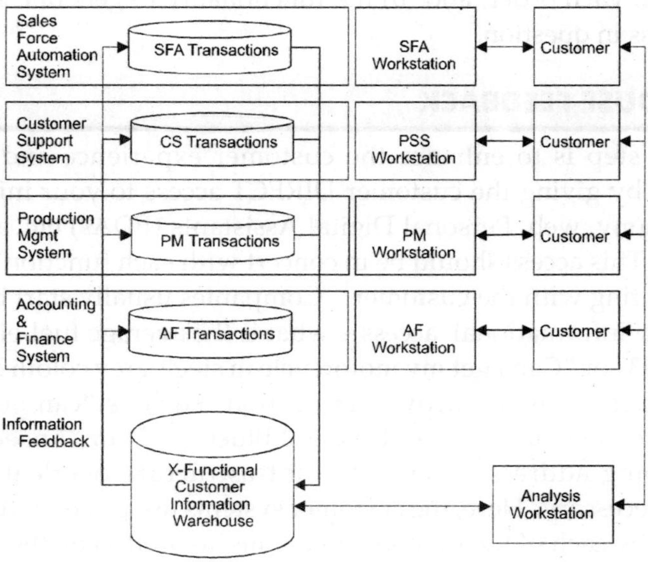

Fig. 3: CRM Infrastructure/Warehouse Feedback

- In the current example, it may be good to add more German-speaking support staff since the most profitable customers are in Germany, and since support calls from Germany take the longest to resolve ... assuming of course that the length of the call is due to language issues.

Once each function has designed a modified process that is customer-centric, we need to give each function additional information related to the customer to support the new process. We show in Figure 3 a further modification to the infrastructure where the warehouse is feeding all functional systems with additional information that is necessary under the new process.

Suppose, the sales group may be fed:

- Number of outstanding support calls and the status of each.
- Current orders in production and their expected shipping details.
- Current outstanding invoices and their status.

It should be noted that the functional system in question needs to be CRM- aware ... in that they should have the ability to integrate customer attributes and allow users of the functional workstations to use these attributes in completing transactions. For instance, if the new process calls for an e-mail to the customer when their order is shipped, the production/ shipping management system should allow – a) the import of an e-mail address for each order, and b) the functionality to generate an e-mail to the address in question.

WAREHOUSE FEEDBACK

The final step is to enhance the customer experience and functional processes by giving the customer DIRECT access to your infrastructure via telephony, web, Personal Digital Assistants (PDAs) etc. as shown in Figure-4. This access should be in concert with each function's processes for interacting with the customer. Companies usually start by allowing customers 'informational' access - 'what is the average fuel-efficiency for a Bluebird?" or "Can I get my motorcycle in steel- grey colour?" etc. Then they progress to more 'active' transactions such as "can you send me a duplicate manual?" or "can I order 2 Bluebirds?" or "I need to change my shipping address...." etc. The infrastructure overleaf shows the changes necessary. Here, the customer systems use pieces of functionality provided by each of the functional systems, as well as by the warehouse.

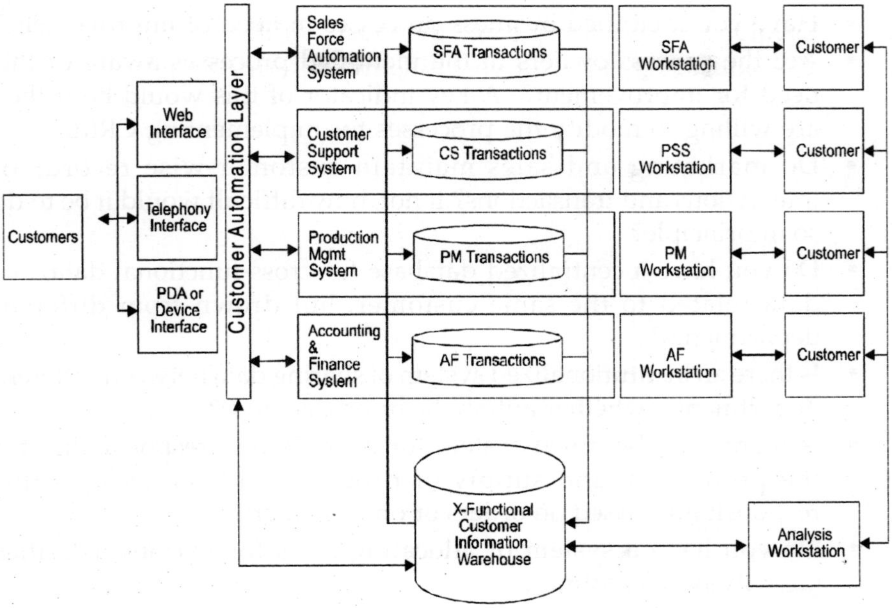

Fig. 4: CRM Infrastructure/Customer Automation

In conclusion, a CRM technology infrastructure needs to contain:

- A data-warehouse and associated analysis software.
- A feedback mechanism from the warehouse to functional systems – as well as the ability for functional systems to integrate and utilize customer information.
- An optional mechanism to automate customer interactions.

PRE-REQUISITES FOR INTRODUCTION OF CRM

At a strategic level, CRM is a customer-centered business philosophy that seeks to optimize their long-term value to the company. At an operational level it is a comprehensive set of processes and technologies for managing relationships with potential and current customers. Since CRM is data-driven, it can only be applied in companies where major business processes have been computerized and which have a strong IT infrastructure. Before starting a CRM project, it must be determined that the company is ready for CRM. A checklist of CRM pre-requisites is given as follows:

- Has management clearly understood the concept of CRM and its benefits?
- Are all existing customer-touching processes well defined, with proper process documentation and identified process owners?

- Have you identified business processes in need of improvement?
- Are the process owners in the identified processes aware of this need for improvement? A key indicator of this would be if they are willing to modify the processes for implementing CRM.
- Do marketing and sales maintain customer-wise records of interactions and transactions? If not, how difficult would it be to do so in principle?
- Do you have a centralized database for cross-functional data, *i.e.*, data related to the same customer, but drawn from different departments?
- Is there an institutionalized system of sharing data between different departments (whether automatic or on demand)?
- Is there a well-defined system for coordinating responsibility for the production and supply of products and services? Is this responsibility based on orders or on customers?
- Do you have a system of allocating costs for various activities (activity-based costing)?
- Do you determine marketing sales and service costs for different customers?
- Is management willing to undertake organizational restructuring and to empower key customer-facing staff members to take decisions based on better customer-related information and improved processes?
- Would management consider modifying compensation for employees, such that a part of the package is directly linked to customer satisfaction and retention?

ROAD MAP TO CRM

There is no single model of CRM which can be applied to all companies. Since there are likely to be wide variations in the nature of the business, the size of operation and level of automation, CRM has to be customized for every company. Nevertheless, there are certain steps for CRM implementation which are generic in nature. These steps are given below to facilitate implementation of CRM at any company.

(a) ***Preparation/ Management Education:*** The very first step in the implementation of CRM is the familiarization of top management with the concept of CRM and its benefits through an in-house seminar or training programme. If management likes the idea, it could constitute a small committee of senior executives to plan a feasibility study with the help of an inside or outside consultant. Since the study would involve most of the departments of the company, it would be advisable that senior executives of all departments must also be provided with awareness training about CRM so that they can appreciate the benefits of CRM and effectively contribute to the feasibility study.

(b) ***Preparation/ Feasibility Study I:*** The feasibility should cover the following elements:

- Assessment of the company's present competitive position in the market and identification of weaknesses in the customer relationship area which need to be corrected.
- Identification of customer-touching processes where CRM could possibly be deployed.
- Analysis of processes and definition of the scope of the CRM project.
- Determination of CRM infrastructure required.
- Cost estimates of hardware, software and associated activities (including installation, training and maintenance costs).
- Development of metrics to determine the success of the CRM project.
- Assessment of the tangible benefits within a specified time frame.
- Estimation of R.O.I.
- Identification of risk factors which could affect the success of the project.

(c) ***Corporate Approval***

- Since CRM would be a major project involving considerable investment and long- term implications, it would have to be discussed and approved by the Board of Directors of the organization.
- This could involve:
  - Presentation by the CRM committee.
  - Consideration of successful case studies from other companies and industries.
  - Visits to some companies which have undertaken CRM.
  - Formal consideration of a CRM project proposal by the Board and its approval along with the budget and financing arrangements.

(d) ***Project Steering Committee***

- A project steering committee of senior managers should be constituted to drive this process. Like all cross-functional projects, it is easy for the CRM initiative to degenerate into a 'white elephant' which never really ends and where everyone thinks someone else is responsible. To avoid this, the project team should be divided into two groups:

- A core group of (say two or three) full-time senior managers drawn from IT and the one or two most affected departments.
- A review group drawn from all affected departments that are scheduled to meet and review progress regularly, but who are not expected to work on this project on a daily basis.
- During the rollout phase of course, a much greater degree of involvement is expected from all departments, but for a large part of its lifecycle, this project does not need endless and interminable meetings where any one disgruntled department or individual can hold up the entire project.

(e) ***Design /System Specifications***

- Identification of business processes which CRM will support.
- The extent to which each process is already automated, how much remains to be automated, and how this automation may be altered by the fact that the process itself is likely to be changed.
- Design of detailed workflow maps of existing processes.
- Design of detailed workflow maps for proposed versions of existing processes.
- Approval of new workflows.
- Specification of integration with all existing computer systems that are touched by the new approved workflows.
- Development of internal system specifications for all proposed workflows that are not already automated.

(f) ***Design/Technology Selection***

- Development of a vendor map that overlays third-party offerings and strengths with the needs of this project.
- Decision on whether to use in-house IT expertise to pull all the components together, or to use an outside software contractor.
- Evaluation of third-party products and vendors and purchase of equipment and software licenses as necessary.

(g) ***Development/System Development***

- Development of a detailed hardware and software architecture based on the selected combination of third-party and in-house products. This includes:
- The database scheme.
- The user interfaces.

    - The process flow implementation.
    - The design of business rule automation and management.
    - The test suites and success metrics.
- The in-house software development as necessary.
- Development of integration suites with existing systems that need to be connected.
- Customization of third-party software products to fit into the proposed architecture.
- Prototyping and testing.

(h) ***Development /Customer focus:*** CRM is not the automation of existing customer-related processes. To derive the full benefit from technology, you must examine the value of your existing customer-touching processes as perceived by your customers. Where possible, the processes must be re-engineered to increase the speed of the activity and convenience of the customer. In addition you must build customization of processes based on past history and preferences of the customer which should be accessible in real time. All customers are not equal – the company must recognize which of its customers are disproportionately responsible for its current and future success, and treat them as such. Customer focus must be deployed at all levels in the organization by the regular monitoring of customer satisfaction and its linkage with employee compensation.

(i) ***Pilot Deployment:*** It is advisable to first deploy CRM on a pilot basis, which would involve:

- Identification of a pilot customer group. This may be customers at a specific regional office or customers of a particular type.
- Note that depending on the company, pilot customers may or may not need to be aware that they are participating in such a pilot.
- Identification of a set of pilot processes. It may not be necessary to pilot all processes that are to be covered under the CRM project – rather it is more important to pick a subset of processes that are simple enough to:
    - Be easily deployable with limited resources.
    - Where a failed or elongated pilot is not going to severely damage the company or its pilot customer prospects.
    - Which is nonetheless broad enough to give a good leading indicator of the overall success that may be expected from the full CRM deployment.

(j) ***Feedback/ Measurement:*** This may include:

- Evaluation of how well you have solved existing problems.
- Improvement in the quality of the output of business processes.
- Marginal cost reduction in processes along every dimension – how much time, how many hands, how many steps, how much money?
- Access to data for better decision-making and the ability to analyze it.
- Tangible beneficial results with respect to sales, customer retention and profitability.

BENEFITS OF IMPLEMENTING CRM

CRM is a powerful tool to implement customer focus in any organization. It institutionalizes various customer related functions under an integrated customer management system. An organization can expect following benefits from CRM.

- Provide improved customer service and promote customer loyalty.
- Evaluate customer profitability.
- Determine profitability of products and channels.
- Cross-sell and up-sell more effectively, and drive customers to more profitable channels of service.
- Decrease distribution time and maintain information for effective follow up.
- Assess the effectiveness of advertising and promotion campaigns.
- Improve the efficiency of call- center operations.
- Improve after- sales services.
- Integrate the supply chain with demand-based processes.
- Communicate and transact business over the Internet.

PITFALLS IN IMPLEMENTING CRM

Introduction of any new management concept or system has its own risk and pitfalls. The organization considering introduction of CRM should be aware of these pitfalls, so that it avoids mistakes made by some organizations which has led to failure of CRM initiative. Typical mistakes observed during implementation of CRM are given as follows:

- Poor needs assessment and a vaguely defined CRM strategy.
- Inadequate metrics and lack of undefined criteria for success.

- Inadequate involvement of top management.
- Failure to generate enthusiasm among staff across the company. IT people are usually enthusiastic about CRM projects since it means additional and interesting work for them. However, it is the operational staff to whom the idea has to be sold, to ensure the ultimate success of the project.
- Hasty selection of technology.
- Inadequate data integration.
- Inability to develop customer focus among staff to enhance customer experience during interaction.

17

Six-Sigma

Sigma (σ), is a letter in the Greek alphabet which is used by statisticians to measure the variation of any parameter. In the first half of the twentieth century, a lot of research was undertaken to study the variability of industrial processes. At that time the concept of "Standard Deviation" was introduced as a measure of the variation of data about its mean value. The standard deviation was represented by Greek letter σ (small sigma). This subject is discussed in detail in Chapter-22.

All industrial and business processes are designed to achieve a certain parameter. It may be a particular linear dimension of a component, mass of packaged material or time taken to perform a business transaction. Variation from the desired value represents the degree of performance. Lesser variation means better performance. At this stage it is sufficient to say that the performance of industrial or business processes is assessed in terms of the sigma level of the process. In the 1930s and 1940s the companies traditionally accepted variation up to three sigma as a good standard for their processes. On this basis, techniques like control charts were developed by Shewart and others as a means of Statistical Process Control and they were widely used by industry as a standard means of quality control. This technique became popular as "Statistical Quality Control" (SQC). This subject has been discussed in Chapters 25 to 30.

A 3-sigma level of process control is associated with a 99.7% Quality level, signifying three defects or errors in every 1000 measurements. With advancements in process technologies and in quality control measures initiated mainly by the Japanese, this level of quality was no longer acceptable. Now some companies in Japan started talking of defects or errors per million opportunities for making error. When considered in this context, a 3- sigma quality level represented 66807 defects per million, which was considered too low a quality level to meet the changed expectations of customers. This change of mindset is illustrated by the experience of a Japanese firm which took over a factory owned by Motorola in the United States in the 1970s. This factory produced Quasar TV sets. The new owner found the defect rate in the product to be too high. The Japanese management introduced new quality control measures which were commonly practiced in Japanese companies. With these measures they were able to bring down the defect rate to $1/20^{th}$ of the defects when the factory was under Motorola. It is worth noting that this quality improvement was achieved with the same plant, technology and the workforce. A more surprising fact was that they were able to significantly reduce the production cost at the same time.

EVOLUTION OF SIX-SIGMA STRATEGIES

Seeing the spectacular quality improvement in their TV plant under Japanese management, Motorola's management had to rethink their business strategy. In the mid- eighties Bob Galvin, the CEO of Motorola, started his company's quality journey - which became known as six-sigma – and produced astounding results. This made Motorola a business icon and quality leader. Motorola won the Baldrige Award in 1988 for their quality achievements achieved through the Six- Sigma strategy. This made Six-Sigma the new mantra for corporate success; many companies started experimenting with this strategy. General Electric under its charismatic leader Jack Welch also used the Six-Sigma approach and achieved remarkable results. Another Six-Sigma success story is that of Allied Signal. This company was on the verge of bankruptcy when its CEO Larry Bossidy decided to use the new magic mantra. The company implemented the Six-Sigma program in 1994. The cumulative impact on savings in direct costs during this period was more than US$ 2 billion and the company grew significantly. Since then there have been many organizations like Honda, Canon, Polaroid, Texas Instruments and other major companies which have adopted this strategy and joined the Six-Sigma revolution.

SIGMA LEVELS OF QUALITY

Before we discuss the Six-Sigma Strategy we need to clearly understand what it implies. The rate of defects associated with various levels of sigma are shown in Table-1.

Table-1

Quality Level	% Quality	Defective PPM (parts per million)
3 Sigma	99.73	66807
4 Sigma	99.9937	6210
5 Sigma	99.999943	233
6 Sigma	99.9999998	3.4

Now that advances in technology have made it possible to achieve very high levels of quality of conformance, customers have also started demanding products with very low defect rate. Thus the old concept of achieving 99% quality levels is no longer acceptable. On account of intense competition, companies have to strive to move to higher Sigma levels to stay in business.

WHY ADOPT SIX-SIGMA STRATEGY?

Earlier it was assumed that if you want to improve quality, you must accept higher costs of production. This took into account only the visible costs related to the costs of scrap, rework and warranties. However, this is not a complete picture. There are a number of hidden costs as discussed in Chapter-7, which in quantitative terms are much higher.

At an average Indian company, costs due to rejection and rework may be around 5%, but the total cost of poor quality ranges from 20 to 30 per cent. Unfortunately these costs are not captured in accounts book and as such are ignored. Adoption of a Six- Sigma strategy will not only improve quality of conformance but also significantly reduce all kinds of waste, resulting in lower overall costs. The cost of quality at various levels of Sigma are shown in Figure-1 below:

Sigma	Defect rate(PPM)	Cost of quality	Competitive level
6	3.4	<10%	World Class
5	233	10-15%	
4	6210	15-20%	Industry Average
3	66807	20-30%	
2	308537	30-40%	Non Competitive
1	6,90000	>40%	

Fig. 1

SIX-SIGMA PHILOSOPHY

Six-Sigma is not confined only to reducing process variability. It gives a new meaning to quality and its realization. Traditional concepts of quality focused on conformance to standards regardless of how conformance was achieved. In the Six-Sigma approach, quality is a state in which value enrichment is realized for the customer and supplier in every aspect of the business relationship.

VALUE ENRICHMENT

The term **'Value Enrichment'** for the company means that they must strive to produce the highest quality products at the lowest possible cost in order to be competitive in the global markets. For customers, the term **'Value Enrichment'** means that they have the right to purchase high-quality products/services at the lowest possible cost. To deliver value to the customers, we need to determine the characteristics of the products that are critical to the customer and keep these in view in all our business processes. At the strategic level the goal of Six-Sigma is to align an organization to its marketplace and deliver real improvements (in terms of rupees/dollars) to the bottom line. At the operational level, the Six- Sigma goal is to move the business product or service attributes within the zone of customer specifications and to significantly shrink process variation.

BASIC CONCEPT OF SIX-SIGMA

Six-Sigma is a project- based quality improvement methodology. It follows a 5-step approach of Design, Measure, Analyze, Improve and Control, which is referred by the acronym DMAIC. These steps are briefly described below:

DEFINE

The first step is to define the objective of the project. The most important input for defining the objective comes from customers. In this activity, consideration also has to be given to the strategic objectives of the company such as ROI and increased market share for growth. At an operational level, objectives may be improvement in quality of conformance to a higher Sigma level, and increase in productivity.

MEASURE

Measure the present state under the existing system. Identify parameters to be measured to monitor the progress towards achievement of the objective.

ANALYZE

Assess the gap between the present state and the desired state. Examine the data and identify ways to reduce the gap between current performance and the desired level. This analysis would require statistical tools to make inferences.

Improve

This requires creativity and an innovative approach to find new methods to make better quality products at lower costs. This would require a systems approach and the quality improvement tools discussed earlier in this book.

Control

Any new system has a tendency to slip backward if unchecked. Institutionalize the new system through revised policies, procedures, compensation and incentive schemes. The ISO-9000 Standard of Quality Management systems can be used to standardize the new system, which will help bring stability to the new system.

PREPARING FOR THE SIX-SIGMA JOURNEY

Before the launch of a Six-Sigma initiative, it must be clearly understood that Six-Sigma is not a passing fad or an activity which will be the responsibility of a few persons in certain functional areas. Six-Sigma involves a new corporate philosophy and culture. It is a long-haul process and the results will not be visible in a short period of weeks or months. In most companies, embedding Six- Sigma culture takes years. According to Jack Welch, one of the pioneers of Six- Sigma, it took GE more than five years to fully implement it and to see significant results. Six-Sigma involves the entire organization and has to be led by the top management. In Motorola, Bob Galvin, the CEO himself chaired the operating and policy committee of Six-Sigma and reviewed progress twice a quarter. Demonstration of management involvement and commitment is the most important step for ensuring the success of such an initiative.

MANAGEMENT OF SIX-SIGMA PROJECT

Although the Six- Sigma philosophy requires a culture of customer focus and intolerance of defects/errors and waste, operationally Six-Sigma is implemented through projects which are generally process- oriented, and which may be spread across different departments. Like all other projects, Six- Sigma requires a project management team. Proper selection of the team is crucial for the success of this initiative. In simple terms:

- The team must have personnel who have technical knowledge of the processes proposed to be improved.

- Any team needs a capable leader. For Six-Sigma projects the leader is an executive who is also called a champion.
- In addition to technical knowledge the team members should have other positive characteristics:
  - They should have a high -level of commitment and passion for quality.
  - They should be well respected by peers in other functional areas, because most projects are cross-functional in nature where the team has to interact with other departments.
- The team should really act as a sports team where every player has an equally important role for winning the match.
- The success of the project depends on the creativity of the team as a whole.
- The team should avoid a superior-subordinate relationship where the subordinate may not forcefully project a viewpoint for fear of challenging the opinion of the superior – this attitude may thus curb creativity.

TRAINING OF TEAM MEMBERS

The Six-Sigma strategy for achieving organizational excellence is a highly structured methodology for the execution of projects. The project personnel are required to have a well- defined body of knowledge and skills. Based on experience gained in the implementation of Six-Sigma at Motorola and General Electric, two levels of training modules were developed for training project leaders and project team members. These were formalized by the Six-Sigma academy established by Michael Harry after he left Motorola. These training programs were given the names Black Belt and Green Belt, borrowing from the Judo and Karate martial arts. Black Belt is an advanced level of program meant for leaders of the project teams. The Green Belt program is meant for project team members. Although, these programs were initially introduced by the Six-Sigma academy, a number of organizations including GE are now conducting such training courses. Of these, the training courses and certification programs of the American Society for Quality (ASQ) have worldwide acceptance. However, it is not necessary for an organization planning introduction of a Six-Sigma strategy to get training and certification from any specific organization. It has only to be ensured that the staff do obtain training and certification from a reputed organization.

BLACK BELT TRAINING AND CERTIFICATION

This program is meant for the project team leaders. The outline body of knowledge of the ASQ Black Belt program is provided below:

1. ***Organizational value of Six-Sigma:*** Six-Sigma philosophy, understanding of business systems and processes, leadership and linking projects to organizational goals.
2. ***Business Process Management:*** Process vs. functional view, voice of customer and business results.
3. ***Project Management:*** Project planning, team leadership, team dynamics, bringing in change, management and planning tools.
4. ***Six-Sigma Improvement Methodology*** covering following subjects:
   - Project scope, metrics and problem statement.
   - Process analysis, statistics, data collection, application of probability distribution, measurement systems and process capability.
   - Exploratory data analysis and hypothesis testing.
   - Design of experiments (DOE) response surface methodology and evolutionary operations.
   - Statistical process control (SPC) methods such as control charts and advanced SPC tools like cusum charts and moving average, and measurement system re-analysis.
5. ***Lean Concept and Tools:*** Theory of constraints, lean thinking, continuous flow, non-value adding activities, lean tools like 5S, Poka-Yoke, SMED and TPM.
6. ***Product Design for Six-Sigma:*** Quality Function Deployment (QFD) robust design, FMEA, and special design tools like theory of inventive problem-solving and axiomatic design.

GREEN BELT TRAINING AND CERTIFICATION

This program is meant for the members of the project team. The body of knowledge of the ASQ Green Belt program includes the following subjects:

1. ***Six-Sigma and the Organization:*** Concept of Six-Sigma, organization goals and project, lean principles in the organization and design for Six-Sigma including QFD, FMEA and road-map for Six-Sigma.
2. ***Six-Sigma – Define:*** Process management, project management, project planning tools, business results and team dynamics.
3. ***Six-Sigma – Measure:*** Process analysis and documentation, statistics, data collection, measurement system analysis and process capability assessment.
4. ***Six-Sigma – Analyze:*** Data analysis including multivariate? studies, simple correlation? and regression and hypothesis testing.
5. ***Six-Sigma – Improve and Control:*** Design of experiments, statistical process control, implementation and validation of solutions and control plan for holding the gains.

SIX-SIGMA PROJECT SELECTION

Once the management has given its approval for the adoption of a Six-Sigma strategy and a certain number of resource persons have acquired the requisite skills, the first issue is project selection. Six-Sigma is a data-driven methodology and, therefore project selection also has to be based on valid data. General impression about Six-Sigma are that it is a tool for reducing variations in the manufacturing processes with a view to achieving defect reduction. Although it is no doubt effective in improving the quality of conformance in manufacturing process, it is equally applicable to other business processes which may have a higher impact on the financial performance of the company. Therefore, before selecting a project, data should be collected about problems in all business processes. Covering manufacturing and non-manufacturing operations, particular attention should be given to the problems leading to customer dissatisfaction.

SELECTION CRITERIA

Once the measurement data on business processes is available, an initial set of projects can be selected on the basis of the following criteria:

(a) ***Process of strategic importance:*** All organizations have strategic goals and annual plans are aligned to their goals. Projects or processes that are important for achieving the strategic goals are likely to find easy acceptance by the management and functional areas.

(b) ***High cost process:*** Even a modest improvement in high cost processes through a Six-Sigma project can have significant financial impact. Processes which consume a lot of materials and labour are good candidates for Six-Sigma projects as reduction of scrap, rework and reductions in cycle time due to the project can lead to major savings.

(c) ***Processes of importance to the customers:*** Planners of Six-Sigma projects should examine the processes that are key drivers for customer satisfaction, which directly translates into higher market share. Thus organizations should focus their Six-Sigma efforts on processes which have maximum impact on customer satisfaction.

(d) ***Time required for the project:*** The initial assessment during the process of selection may provide an indication about the time required for each project. Preference should be given to projects which require less time to show tangible results. Early success will help in building confidence in the Six-Sigma initiative.

(e) ***Resources and investment required:*** Projects which do not require new technology inputs and significant capital investment should be preferred as it may be easier to get management approval for such projects.

DEVELOPMENT OF PROJECT PLANS

Once the projects have been selected, a project plan should be developed. The project plan should have the following essential elements:

- Problem to be addressed or process to be improved.
- Results expected and their financial effect (if quantified).
- Methodology to be adopted for implementation.
- Composition of project team.
- Resources required.
- Expected time period required for completion of project.

The leader of the team will need to make a presentation to the management to seek approval for the project, including authorization for necessary resources.

MONITORING OF PROJECTS

To institutionalize the implementation of the Six-Sigma strategy, a steering committee should be constituted under a senior executive such as the technical director or some member of the company's board. The steering committee should oversee the progress of the project and also resolve inter-departmental problems and other issues affecting its implementation. After completion of the project, the steering committee may appoint an audit team to assess the results as well as impact on the company's performance.

RECOGNITION OF SUCCESSFUL PROJECTS

One of the most effective means of promotion of a new initiative is dissemination of information about success. The company may celebrate a **Six-Sigma Day** during which it could present the results of successful projects and recognize the achievements of the team members through the issuance of merit certificates or financial rewards. This will go a long way in encouraging the team members to take up more projects enthusiastically. It will also enthuse other functional departments to take up Six-Sigma projects, thereby expanding the entire movement.

18

Corporate Social Responsibility

Total Quality Management, as discussed earlier, is not only about the quality of products and services, and the profitability of an organization. It has a much wider scope, because sustainable growth cannot be achieved only by addressing the concerns of customers and shareholders. A company is not an isolated entity immune to the forces of nature and society. Its performance influences and is influenced by its employees, environment, other players in the market, the Government and society at large. Thus for long- term growth the organization has to address the concerns of all its stakeholders and safeguard their interests. This realization has given birth to a new management subject which is referred to as Corporate Social Responsibility (CSR).

WHAT IS CSR?

Corporate Social Responsibility relates to a company's effect on society. It requires management of a company to consider their activities in terms of a whole social system and holds them responsible for the effects of these actions anywhere in that system.

Corporate Social Responsibility is the alignment of business operations with social values. While formulating company policies it should take in to account the interests of all stakeholders. CSR focuses on the social, environmental and financial success of a company – the so-called triple bottom line - with the aim of achieving social development while working for business success. CSR has become the new Mantra for developing a competitive edge to ensure sustainable growth. CSR has four aspects relating to the interests of different stakeholders, as outlined below.

Economic Responsibility

The company needs to ensure that it remains profitable by maximising sales and minimising costs. This pressures the company to give due importance to quality and customer satisfaction, since otherwise it might lose competitiveness and not remain profitable for long. This aspect not only addresses the concerns of shareholders but also of the employees and suppliers whose well-being depends on the financial health of the company.

Legal Responsibility

The company must obey the laws and regulations which are meant to safeguard the interests of employees, shareholders, the people at large and the environment.

Ethical Responsibility

The organization is expected to do what is morally right. It should be fair and just and exhibit a high degree of transparency about activities which affect various stakeholders.

Social Responsibility

The company should be a good corporate citizen and undertake philanthropic activities for the general social good.

With the spread of education and the exposure of all sections of society to media, people have become aware of the social obligations of business organizations. Any adverse effect of economic activity is highlighted by hyperactive media which can seriously damage the reputation of the responsible organization and even affect its performance in the stock market. Institutional investors factor company performance with respect to CSR in their investment decisions. Lastly, the deregulation of economies by national governments has placed an added responsibility on the business organizations for self-regulation and good governance. All these factors have made Corporate Social Responsibility a major issue for corporate success.

WHAT DOES CSR INVOLVE?

Business success depends on the way various stakeholders are affected by, or perceive the impact of business operations. Sustainable competitive success demands the simultaneous improvement of economic, environmental and social performance. For this the management of an organization needs to engage with internal and external stakeholders to define the scope of corporate responsibility, accountability and performance. Corporate responsibility calls for compliance of international standards, conventions and good business practices. This helps to build trust and preserve confidence in business, thereby enhancing competitiveness in the long run.

ELEMENTS OF CSR

CSR remains an amorphous concept unless it is put into practice by the concrete actions of an organization. An organization embracing CSR in addition to ensuring business profitability, should commit to the national and global standards listed below while carrying out business operations:

- Non-discrimination (UN Human Rights and local legislation)
- Equal opportunity, work environment and compensation to employees (ILO and local legislation)
- Staff development education and training (UNESCO)
- Supplier labour standards Child labour, health and safety (ILO)
- Protection and Welfare of Local Community (UNESCO, ILO)
- Fair trade practices (ETI)
- Environmental legislations.

To implement these standards the main activities which can be undertaken by business organizations are given below:

(a) Good recruitment practices of employees, including the absence of discrimination on the basis of caste, creed, gender, age and physical disability.

(b) Training and skill development of employees and managers to enhance business performance and individual employability.

(c) In addition to decent working conditions, health and safety issues along the entire supply chain need to be addressed.

(d) Air, water and other natural resources are essential for sustained business. Therefore organization should invest in eco-friendly products and processes, minimize emissions, waste and energy consumption, and help to preserve bio-diversity.

(e) Undertaking various welfare activities to improve the quality of life of the communities around company facilities, and building healthy relationships with these communities, which can add value to the organization and enhance its reputation as an employer as well as corporate citizen.

CSR AND BUSINESS COMPETITIVENESS

One of the major issues which always comes up at any CSR-related forum, is whether there is a business case for CSR. While everyone agrees that

CSR is highly desirable for society, it is not clear whether it helps in securing economic benefits to an organization considered narrowly.

For instance, this issue was discussed at length at the workshop organized in May 2003 by Forum For The Future sponsored by the Department of Trade and Industry in the UK. A number of speakers expressed the view that CSR is not necessarily a 'cost' of doing business, as there is a significant overlap between societal and environmental concerns, and what resource- based business strategy sees as the source of competitive success in business. They also suggested that a number of tools have been developed to measure business intangibles, and these tools can be applied to measure the impact on shareholder value of a company's CSR policies and performance. The result may generate evidence of the business value of corporate social responsibility.

The key conclusion of the workshop was that a business with strong CSR will often be more successful in generating economic value, for reasons that are rooted in sound business strategy. Two examples quoted in the workshop clearly illustrate the link between CSR issues and business competitiveness:

1. Marks and Spencer had historically enjoyed a competitive advantage based on its reputation with customers, its relationship with suppliers and its caring attitude towards employees, whom it supplied good meals at nominal prices. In 1990 the company shifted toward a shareholder-value driven model. It put pressure on its supply chain in order to achieve higher margins. It succeeded for a short while but then its profits fell and its share price collapsed.
2. Another classic case of the effect of reputation on competitiveness is that of the prominent accounting firm of Arthur Andersen. The company was able to charge premium fees based on its reputation for expertise and integrity. All of this advantage was lost overnight due to the Enron scandal, and the company was forced to shut down.

Corporate reputation and the importance of CSR are clearly linked, particularly when clients are in higher-income brackets. For instance, British Telecom (BT) collects attitude data every month from thousands of its UK consumers. Based on eighteen months of tracking, BT has concluded that CSR accounts for at least 25% of what drives its corporate reputation.

Engaging with local communities also gives a company an opportunity to identify new markets. Bottom-of-pyramid markets such as rural and under-developed areas, may offer collective purchasing power far in excess of 'upper' segments by virtue of sheer size. With innovative designs, marketing and financing, the needs of poor consumers can be addressed. This segment, which has largely been neglected so far, offers huge business opportunities. Thus CSR need not only be a 'cost' incurred solely to create qualitative benefits such as 'social good'. It can also enhance shareholder value by exploiting new opportunities. A classic example of this is ITC's **e-choupal** initiative, which is discussed below:

CSR SCENE IN INDIA

The concept of CSR is not new to India. The concept of entrepreneurs also being social trustees has been propounded since ancient times. It suggests that while owners of any enterprise may enjoy the wealth they create, they must also earmark a portion of it for the social good. In recent years CSR has caught the attention of progressive Indian companies.

While in general we have to rely on European examples that link CSR with business competitiveness, we do have a domestic champion in this respect - ITC. The company has created global bench by its triple bottom line initiative. Its net worth has risen eight times in the last decade 1996-2006. It has become water and carbon positive with a number of energy conservation measures and a large-scale agro-forestry program. It is rapidly moving towards zero solid waste, thus achieving success in all three critical factors of environmental sustainability. In the social dimension ITC has come up with a unique method of enmeshing social contribution into the process of generating shareholder value through its innovative ITC-**e-Choupal.** This is a powerful illustration of linking business purposes with the larger social good. It has tremendous potential to increase the income of the small farmers and engendering a rural transformation – while also greatly helping ITC itself.

The ITC **e-Choupal** leverages the power of the Internet to virtually cluster all the value chain participants, delivering the same benefits as vertical integration does in mature agricultural economies like the USA. It offers the small farmers a host of services related to agricultural know-how and best practices, timely and relevant weather information, transparent discovery of prices and so on. This digital infrastructure can also be used for channeling services related to credit, insurance, health, education and entertainment. It can also serve as a strong foundation for linking small farmers to future markets to facilitate agricultural risk management.

The ITC **e-Choupal** is not just a village digital kiosk with a human interface. Access to e-Choupals, within walking distance from individual farms, is supplemented by physical infrastructure – the ITC Choupal Saagar–which functions as a physical hub for a cluster of villages within tractorable distance. These made-to-design hubs serve as warehouses, and as rural hypermarkets for a variety of goods. In effect, the e-Choupal infrastructure is potentially an efficient delivery channel for rural development and an instrument for converting village populations into vibrant economic organizations.

ITC's initiative on CSR is not the only example of companies in India taking this subject seriously. A number of other companies have started other initiatives. A few examples are provided below:

- Whirlpool's Pondicherry Plant is managing the community development activities of the nearby village of Thirubuvanai, including education, medical care, safety and environmental services.
- TVS Electronics has partnered with the Department of Rural Development and the Sahishnata Trust to launch a 100% sanitation campaign in Tiruvidenta village in Tamil Nadu.
- Accenture has set up an internal organization called 'Service Endeavour by Volunteers of Accenture' (SEVA) and had adopted village Boganhali to improve the lot of the villagers.

The youthful workforce in these companies feels a sense of obligation to the society at large, and a variety of companies are encouraging their employees to volunteer for the community programs.

Benefits of CSR

At stated earlier, we believe that CSR is not simply a philanthropic activity- it can produce tangible benefits both in its own right and in terms of company growth and enhanced shareholder value. Some of the direct benefits are:

- Enhanced brand image and reputation which not only increases sales but also builds customer loyalty.
- It helps in development of employees' emotional quotient by encouraging their participation in social welfare activities.
- Having employees participate in the company's social welfare activities helps in team-building. It also develops a sense of loyalty and emotional bonding with the organization, which in turn increases the ability to attract and retain employees.
- Confidence in a company's social responsibility reduces regulatory oversight by Governmental organizations.
- Support of the local population facilitates various growth initiatives in the area by the company.
- Institutional investors attach great importance to a company's social responsibility rating as it is an important factor indicator of growth.

Growing interest in the impact of industrial activities on the workers and on society at large, has led to the emergence of the concept of certification of corporate social responsibility. A society called "Social Accountability International" (SAI) was established in 1997 to promote this concept for the healthy and sustained growth of industries around the world. SAI constituted an expert advisory group to develop standards for addressing workers' rights. Representatives of trade unions, human rights organizations, academia, retailers, manufacturers and contractors, as well as consulting, accounting, and certification firms, cooperated to develop the Social Accountability 8000 (SA8000) standard, published in late 1997 and revised in 2001.

SA-8000

SA-8000 is an international standard aimed at improving working conditions. Based on the principles of international human rights conventions, it is a structured document which provides guidance to apply these norms in a real-life environment in factories and other business organizations. This is the first auditable standard with a certification process which is independent of governments and is not dominated by any single interest group.

Requirements of SA-8000

Its main requirements are provided below:

Child Labour

1. The company shall not engage in or support child labour in any form.

Forced Labour

2. The company shall not engage in or support the use of forced labour, nor shall the company personnel be required to lodge deposits or identity papers on commencement of employment with the company.

Health and Safety

3. The company shall assess the health and safety hazards in its operations and provide a safe and healthy work environment. It shall take following steps to prevent accidents and injuries arising out of work at the company:

   (a) Adopt practices which minimize the hazards inherent in the work environment.

   (b) Appoint a senior management representative responsible for health and safety of all personnel and make him/her accountable for the implementation of relevant standards.

   (c) Adopt a proactive approach to health and safety, and establish a system to detect, avoid or respond to potential threats to the health and safety of personnel.

(d) Ensure that all personnel receive regular training on health and safety.

(e) Provide access to potable water and hygienic conditions for the storage and serving of food to employees.

(f) Provide clean bathrooms and good sanitation facilities to meet the basic needs of personnel.

Freedom of Association and Right to Collective Bargaining

4. The company shall respect the right of all personnel to join trade unions or associations. The company shall not subject representatives of unions or associations to any discrimination or harassment.

Discrimination

5. The company shall not practice or support discrimination in recruitment, training, promotion or compensation based on race, caste, creed, gender or disability.

Disciplinary Practices

6. The company shall not engage in or support the use of any kind of corporal punishment or physical and mental coercion or verbal abuse.

Working Hours

7. The company shall comply with applicable laws and industry standards with respect to working hours. It shall also ensure that overtime beyond specified working hours does not exceed 12 hours per week. It shall also ensure that employees shall always be remunerated for overtime at a premium rate.

Compensation

8. The company shall ensure that wages paid at least meet the legally-required or industry- minimum standards and fully comply with applicable laws.

Management Systems

9. The company shall establish and maintain a documented management system to implement the requirements of SA-8000. The management system should include the following essential elements:

(a) The company's policy for social accountability and labour conditions, with a commitment to conform to the standard and applicable laws and to continual improvement.

(b) Top management shall periodically review the suitability of the conformity and effectiveness of the system.

(c) The company shall appoint a management representative to coordinate the activities related to social accountability and ensure that the requirements of the standards are met.

(d) The company shall ensure that the requirements of this standard are understood and implemented at all levels of the organization.

(e) The company shall select suppliers based on their ability to meet the requirements of the standard and monitor their performance in relation to the standard.

(f) The company shall maintain sufficient records to demonstrate that the requirements of the standard are being met by their suppliers and sub-contractors.

(g) The company shall investigate and address the concerns or complaints of employees and other interested parties, and not take any action against persons who provide information about non-compliance with the standard. The company should also ensure that appropriate corrective action is taken in such cases, including allocation of adequate resources to fully comply with the requirements of the standard.

(h) The company shall establish procedures to regularly communicate information regarding performance against this standard to all interested parties.

(i) Where required by contract the company shall provide reasonable information and access to the interested parties to verify conformance to the requirements of the standard.

(j) The company shall keep adequate records to demonstrate that it is complying with the standard.

IMPLEMENTATION OF SA-8000

Organizations have two options to demonstrate that they are implementing SA-8000. They can either go for certification or participate in the SA-8000 corporate involvement program.

CERTIFICATION

This is similar to certification of other management systems such as ISO-9000 or ISO-14000. Here the company maintains a documented system for SA-8000 and offers itself for audit by an SAI- accredited certification body. The certification body verifies the management system of the applicant company for compliance with the requirements of SA-8000. If the certification body is satisfied about the performance of the company, it issues a certificate indicating compliance. Such companies are listed on the website of SAI.

SA-8000 Corporate Involvement Program (CIP)

CIP is a two-level self-administered program for companies in the production and distribution sectors.

SA-8000 Explorer (CIP Level-I)

In this program, companies use SA-8000 as an ethical sourcing tool by carrying out pilot audits on their own and publicly report on their implementation progress.

SA-8000 Signatory (CIP Level-II)

Here the companies implement SA-8000 as a stepwise approach in some or all of their supply chain through certification. They then communicate implementation progress to stakeholders through SAI- verified reporting.

For instance, the CIP program was launched by SAI in 1999 and large numbers of companies have joined this program since that time. (Further details of this program can be obtained from the website of SAI: www.sa-intl.org/).

19

Balanced Score Card

There has been a revolutionary transformation in the industrial scene during the past 25 years. In earlier years, companies succeeded on the basis of their ability to capture the benefits of technology and of economies of scale, and convert these into physical assets. In that period, the management of organizations was based primarily on financial control. Measures such as Return On Capital Employed (ROCE) were used to put the resources of the company to the most productive use in order to create value for the shareholders. With the emergence of the information age however, many of the assumptions of the 'classical' industrial age have become obsolete. There is a need to evolve a new management control system which takes into account intangible and intellectual assets in addition to physical assets.

PERFORMANCE MEASUREMENT IN THE INFORMATION AGE

Globalization of markets and advances in information technology have given increasing power to the customers - which poses a tremendous challenge to the companies. To meet this challenge, companies are adopting various approaches based on quality management, lean production systems, CRM, employee empowerment, re-engineering etc. Each of these has success stories, but they all suffer from one constraint – all of these initiatives are being implemented under a management system which relies on quality as well as on annual financial reports based on an accounting model that was developed centuries ago. This model may have been suitable for an environment of arms- length transactions between different entities. However it suffers from two major shortcomings:

- Firstly, it only judges past performance, which may or may not be a reliable indicator of future prospects.
- Second, it is based on the valuation of tangible physical assets and does not consider intangible or intellectual assets, such as the skills and competence of personnel, the existence of responsive and reliable internal processes and the existence of loyal customers attracted by the high quality of products and services.

For the information- age companies, these intangible assets are more critical for future success than traditional physical assets. In the current performance reporting system, there is no mechanism by which any increase in these assets can be communicated to the employees, shareholders, creditors and the community at large. Similarly these stakeholders are in the dark when these intangible assets are depleted, exposing the organization to risks and uncertainty. However it is difficult to place a reliable financial value on such intangible assets. Companies have been conducting customer perception surveys and measuring employee satisfaction indices, but there was no coherent mechanism to use these metrics for planning future operations.

VISION AND STRATEGY FOR GROWTH

All well- managed companies have a vision of their future and a strategy to achieve the same. These are prominently covered in the company's policy documents and in the Quality Manual which has to be documented by companies implementing systems such as ISO 9000 standard. The vision may be something like:

- "To be the global leader in our line of business."
- "To be the preferred supplier in the country."
- "To achieve five- folds increase in business over the next five years."
- And so on……

The problem is that visions and strategies like these often remain within the covers of policy documents that sit on the shelves of the CEO and senior managers. The major problem lies in translating such visions and strategies into operational objectives and measures to actually manage the company. Currently most companies fix financial targets based on past performance and future projection are based more on guesswork rather than on any reliable data. However, while a company's financial results may seem the result of purely internal processes, they are in fact greatly influenced by external factors such as customer perceptions, as well as internal factors such as process capabilities and personnel competence. This gives rise to the need for a new management tool which can take various internal as well as external factors into consideration when making operational plans for the future. The Balanced Score Card developed by Robert S. Kaplan and David P. Norton in the early 1990s is such a tool.

WHAT IS BALANCED SCORE CARD?

Balanced Score Card is a management system which enables an organization to assess its performance from a "360- degree" perspective and take appropriate steps to take itself on a growth path. Balanced Score Card enables organizations to clarify their vision and strategy and translate it into specific goals and activities. The Balanced Score Card (BSC) requires the management to have a 360- degree view of the organization's performance from the different perspectives illustrated in Figure-1.

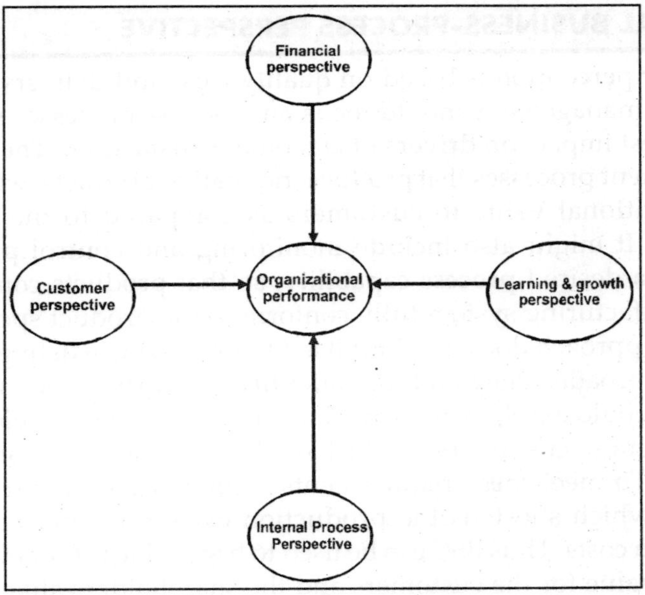

Fig.1: Balanced Score Card

Balanced Score Card assists the company in understanding and measuring how business creates value not only for the shareholders but also for other stakeholders. BSC captures critical value- creation activities, as well as the skill and motivation level of personnel, which are all value drivers for good long-term financial performance. These various perspectives are explained in the following paragraphs.

FINANCIAL PERSPECTIVE

Financial measures of performance of a company are valuable because these are easily measurable and are well understood. Measures include operating income, cash flow, sales growth, market share and return on capital employed. These metrics indicate the financial health of a company at a given point of time.

CUSTOMER PERSPECTIVE

The ccustomer perspective identifies performance in terms of customer satisfaction, acquisition of new customers and customer and profitability from different segments of customers. Other customer-related parameters include lead-time, timely delivery of orders and after-sales service. The company must develop measures for such important parameters and take appropriate steps to meet the customer expectations in order to achieve long- term growth.

INTERNAL BUSINESS-PROCESS PERSPECTIVE

Customer perception is based on quality, cost and delivery. Therefore company management should focus on business processes which have the greatest impact on drivers of customer satisfaction. These could be development processes that produce innovative products, which in turn offer additional value to customers as compared to the competing products. It might also include monitoring and control processes to maintain a desired process capability, so that products coming out of any manufacturing system fully conform to the product specifications. The BSC approach does not limit itself to improving existing processes. It takes a broader view and may identify new processes, in which the company could excel, to meet the financial and customer objectives. For example, most customers might like shorter lead times and on-time delivery. To meet these requirements a company may introduce lean systems, which shortens the production cycle time and also reduces production costs. Thus BSC can be used to trigger ideas for new processes to create value for the customers and the shareholders alike.

LEARNING AND GROWTH PERSPECTIVE

The customer and internal process perspectives help the organization with respect to critical factors for customer satisfaction and success in the market place. However, these factors are based on the current situation. With the advancements in technology and changing customer preferences, the internal processes based on existing technology may not be able to meet the requirements of the future. The learning perspective helps the organization to identify new capabilities and systems for delivering value to the customers and shareholders in order to meet the future challenges. Acquiring new technologies and management system to exploit the technologies may create the new capability. It may also involve creating new skills in the organization by training existing employees or hiring new talent. It may also point to having new information system and alignment of organization's procedures for effective implementation of any new strategy.

BSC AS A STRATEGIC MANAGEMENT SYSTEM

Balanced Score Card helps in developing metrics of performance from different perspectives, but it is not only a measurement system. It can also be used as a powerful strategic management system. It helps in translating the company's vision into strategic objectives and in the planning of activities to achieve specific targets. This is achieved through the four management processes mentioned below:

1. Translating vision and strategy
2. Communicating objectives and measures
3. Planning and setting targets
4. Feedback and learning

These processes are discussed in the following paragraphs:

TRANSLATING VISION AND STRATEGY

Most vision and mission statements declare the intentions of the top management. Statements like "best in class" or "becoming the preferred supplier" may be lofty statements, but these by themselves cannot lead to concrete action. This is a process to convert vision and strategy to well defined strategic objective and measures for each perspective as illustrated in table below.

Perspective	*Objectives*	*Measures*
Financial	• Increase shareholder value. • Growth of revenue.	• Return on investment. • Percentage increase in revenue.
Customer	• Customer retention. • Attracting new customers. • Enhancing customer satisfaction.	• % increase of repeat customers. • % increase in new customers. • Customer satisfaction rating increase.
Internal	• Reduce inventory.	• % reduction in inventory.

Contd....

processes	• Reduce development cycle time. • Improve equipment utilization.	• % reduction in cycle time. • % increase in equipment utilization.
Learning and growth	• Develop capability for implementing Lean Production System. • Introduce CRM.	• Number of persons trained in LPS. • Number of LPS projects undertaken • Number of persons trained in CRM • Number of customers whose data has been acquired.

Communicating Objectives and Measures

In most companies only top level executives have good understanding of strategy of the company. Translation of strategy into specific objectives and their measurement helps understanding of strategy by operating level managers and staff.

The objectives and their measures should be discussed with the managers and some key personnel. As a result of this, interaction of some of the objectives may be modified. This may involve some changes in the organization to align with the strategy. It also brings out the need for proper training of operational staff and the development of suitable information system. Collectively developed objectives and performance measures have a much better chance of success because participation by operating level staff brings a fuller understanding of and commitment to these measures. Once agreed upon, BSC's strategic objectives and measures should be communicated to all company personnel through the company newsletter or the use of electronic bulletin boards and groupware to distribute the Score Card through personal computers. In addition to top-down communication of BSC-related issues, there is a need for an upward communication system for the collection and aggregation of performance data. The same communication channel can be used for encouraging dialogue about measures and for making suggestions for achieving targets. Communication of Balanced Score Card helps to promote commitment and accountability for implementing the strategy of the organization.

Planning and Setting Targets

Balanced Score Card helps in planning for the deployment of strategy to achieve the specified objectives. Top management should establish targets for Score Card measures for achievement in three to five years. Targets should be ambitious, such as doubling the turn over in the next 3 years or achieving 150% increase in return on investment – in other words they should 'stretch' the organization and not simply represent a minor improvement over business as usual. Strategic initiatives are derived from Score Card measures such as drastic reduction in development cycle to bring new products to market, enhancing the capability of employees, and compressing order fulfillment time. Once the targets for customers, learning and growth have been set, managers can then develop internal processes for achieving breakthrough objectives. Management processes for planning and target setting enable an organization to:

- Clearly define long- term objectives;
- Establish quantitative targets for financial and non-financial measures on the score board;
- Devise suitable systems and procedures to achieve the targets;
- Allocate resources for achieving the desired outcomes.

Feedback and Learning

The management of any organization requires continuous feedback about the performance of various activities and the results achieved. In this context, near- term targets set for financial and non-financial measures of BSC provide a framework for getting feedback for monthly and quarterly reviews. In addition to assessing the achievement of financial targets of a business unit, the management should also examine the degree of achievement of targets for other measures *i.e.,* customer details, internal processes and innovation. Such management reviews not only assess the past performance but also preparedness for the future. However there is a limitation in the review of feedback based on the current strategy, which can be called a single- loop learning process.

Companies today have to operate in a turbulent market environment where some assumption made during the original formulation of strategy may not remain valid, because new threats and opportunities arise. This may require re-examination of the strategy itself, and its implementation methodology which is called double loop learning. In single-loop learning, the targets remain constant. If the results do not match the targets, you think of new ways to meet the targets, but you do not question the strategy itself. Double loop learning takes into account the changing market environment, new technological developments, changes in national policies impacting on the business which may provide new opportunities. That is why double loop learning is considered most innovative. It enables managers to question the assumptions based on which targets have been set. It gives free rein to their imagination to come up with new strategies to meet the challenges of the market environment. Such double- loop learning may call for intensive strategy reviews, which may make a case for a new strategy based on the knowledge about market conditions and internal capabilities. Thus feedback and learning processes can provide valuable input for developing a new vision and a new strategy.

BSC A TOOL FOR STRATEGIC MANAGEMENT

Many companies are employing the Balanced Score Card concept to improve their measurement system and hence their operational performance. The real use of this system is as the foundation for an integrated strategic management system. It enables a company to align its management processes so that the entire organization focuses its efforts on implementing long-term strategy. It provides a sound basis for periodic business reviews to assess the performance from different perspectives. Should there be a major change in the market environment, the system has a built-in capability to test a set of hypotheses about cause-and-effect relationships based on the current strategy. Thus it can give signals when the strategy itself may need to be changed, based on new threats and opportunities which may present themselves. It is this ability for the tool to continuously adjust strategy to a changing environment, which makes it so powerful tool for strategic management.

20

Quality Awards

With the liberalization of economies, reduction of tariff and non-tariff barriers under the WTO regime and rapid technical advances in communication, commercial markets have truly been globalized. You are no longer restricted by national availability of raw materials, skill or capital. Even the work space is no longer an issue. You can have corporate headquarters in one country, manufacturing facilities in another country and selling to customers in a number of other countries. Thus, materials, skills and financial resources is no longer a constraint. The only factor which has a major impact on organizational performance is the quality management. With intensifying global companies, governments and management institutions are developing new concepts and strategies to improve competitive position of their business organizations with general national wealth.

In the present world, power of a country depends upon its economic strength rather than size of the armed forces or weaponry. One of the major initiatives taken by many developed countries for improving quality of management of enterprises is institution of National Quality Awards. The lead in this case was taken by Japanese industry which was greatly influenced by Dr. Deming who initiated Quality Revolution in Japanese industry to improve quality of their products and obliterate the pre-war image of poor quality and shoddy goods. (JUSE) launched the quality prize to recognize companies which implemented companies wide quality management programs and demonstrated outstanding performance in quality of their products. To honour Dr. Deming, the architect of Quality transformation they named it the "Deming Prize." Subsequently, other countries launched their own Quality Awards, notable among these are:

- Melcom Baldrige National Quality Award of USA
- European Quality Award

Seeing need for taking concrete action for improving the quality of goods and service produced by Indian companies, Bureau of Indian Standards (BIS) established Rajiv Gandhi Quality Award in 1991. Common features of all Quality Awards are that there is well defined criteria for various aspects of management of an organization. There are detailed guides for assessors to assess the performance and award marks. Winners are decided on the basis of comparative performance. World's highest rated Quality Award is the Malcom Baldrige National Quality Award of USA. This award is administered under Baldrige National Quality Program. This Quality Award is also the one on which maximum research has been done. It has the most exhaustive criteria for performance excellence which has evolved over the years. The Baldrige Award criteria is based on the following inter-related core values and concepts:

VISIONARY LEADERSHIPS

The top management of the organization should have clear vision to meet the expectations of all the stakeholders of the organization. The leaders of the organization should develop strategies, systems and methods for achieving performance excellence. The leaders should serve as role model through their ethical behaviours and personal involvement in planning, review of performance and enhancement of the capabilities of personnel.

CUSTOMER-DRIVEN EXCELLENCE

Customers are the ultimate judge of quality and performance of the organization. Customer-driven excellence implies understanding current requirement of customers and also anticipating their future desires and market place potential. Customer satisfaction does not depend only on the quality of product. It is determined by overall experience with the organization.

ORGANIZATIONAL AND PERSONAL LEARNING

Organizational learning means continuous improvement in existing systems and methods as well as developing ability to adopt new strategy and approach to meet the changing market environment. Organizational learning also involves sharing knowledge throughout organization and developing new skills and innovative spirit in employees.

VALUING EMPLOYEES AND PARTNERS

Success of an organization largely depends on the knowledge, skills, innovative ability and motivation of its personnel. This requires:

- Managements' commitment to employees' success.
- Compensation package and recognition.
- Professional growth within the organization.
- Sharing knowledge with employees so that they can contribute better in achievement of organization's objectives.
- Creating environment freedom from fear where employees are encouraged to innovate and take risk.

The organization also needs to build partnerships with customers and suppliers. These partnerships and alliances help improving products, quality, development of new products and better supply chain management.

AGILITY

The success in increasingly competitive globalized markets with rapid changes in technology requires agility – a capacity for rapid change and flexibility. Time is the most precious commodity in today's environment. Companies have to develop innovative systems for compressing the development and production cycle time for faster introduction of new products and offer shorter delivery period. Ability also helps in building capability to provide customized products and services which can be a major competitive advantage.

FOCUS ON THE FUTURE

An organization needs clear understanding of short and long term factors for success in dynamic market environment. Therefore, company management needs strong future orientation for sustained growth and market leadership. The organization's planning should take into account technological developments, evolving e-business environments and societal expectations. The focus on future would include creating opportunities for innovation, preparing employees and suppliers for future challenges and anticipating public concerns on issues affecting business.

MANAGING FOR INNOVATION

Innovation involves making significant changes to improve products/ services and processes to create value for the organizations' stakeholders. Innovation should not be only the concern of research and development. It should be integrated in the culture of the organization at all levels so that it builds on the accumulated knowledge of the organization. Therefore, there should be organized effort to disseminate and capitalize on this knowledge to drive organizational innovation.

MANAGEMENT BY FACT

One of the basic principles of quality management is that you cannot improve anything which cannot be measured. These measurement and analysis of data is an essential part of management. Performance measurement would include product, service and customer satisfaction. Measurement is meaningful only if it is analyzed to extract measuring data and reviewing your performance and comparing it with your competitors or with best practice benchmarks for planning further improvements.

SOCIAL RESPONSIBILITY

Corporate social responsibility is coming into increasing prominence as it has been realized that industries can have a major impact on society in terms of public health, safety and environment. In addition, with the professional management of companies shareholders are at risk due to unethical management practices of company management boards. Managing social responsibility requires company leadership to take appropriate measures and demonstrate good corporate citizenship.

FOCUS ON RESULTS AND CREATING VALUE

Ultimate purpose of an organization is to create value for its stakeholders. Therefore, management needs to focus on results which demonstrate creation of tangible and intangible value. The organization should equitably balance this value between different stakeholders such as investors, employees, suppliers and customers and avoid adverse impact on any of the stakeholders.

CRITERIA FOR PERFORMANCE EXCELLENCE

Evaluation of any activity requires an assessment mechanism based on well defined criteria. Based on the core values and concepts, the Baldrige National Quality Program Committee has developed an assessment criterion. The assessment criteria have seven main elements each having two or more sub-elements. According to 2006 criteria, there are seven elements. The main elements and sub-elements along with their point values are given in the following table:

2006 Categories and Items		*Point Values*
1 Leadership		**120**
1.1 Senior Leadership	70	
1.2 Governance and Social Responsibilities	50	
2 Strategic Planning		**85**
2.1 Strategy Development	40	
2.2 Strategy Deployment	45	
3 Student, Stakeholder, and Market Focus		**85**
3.1 Student, Stakeholder, and Market Knowledge	40	
3.2 Student and Stakeholder Relationships and Satisfaction	45	
4 Measurement, Analysis, and Knowledge Management		**90**
4.1 Measurement, Analysis, and Review of Organizational Performance	45	
4.2 Information and Knowledge Management	45	
5 Faculty and Staff Focus		**85**
5.1 Work Systems	35	
5.2 Faculty and Staff Learning and Motivation	25	
5.3 Faculty and Staff Well-Being and Satisfaction	25	
6 Process Management		**85**
6.1 Learning-Centered Processes	45	
6.2 Support Processes and Operational Planning	40	
7 Results		**450**
7.1 Student Learning Outcomes	100	
7.2 Student- and Stakeholder-Focused Outcomes	70	
7.3 Budgetary, Financial, and Market Outcomes	70	
7.4 Faculty and Staff Outcomes	70	
7.5 Organizational Effectiveness Outcomes	70	
7.6 Leadership and Social Responsibility Outcomes	70	
TOTAL POINTS		**1,000**

EUROPEAN QUALITY AWARD

European Foundation for Quality Management (EFQM) has established Quality Award which is referred EFQM Award for Excellence. Criteria for this Award is also based on the concepts of Malcom Baldrige Award. The criteria for this Award has nine elements which are categorized in enablers and results as shown in Figure-1.

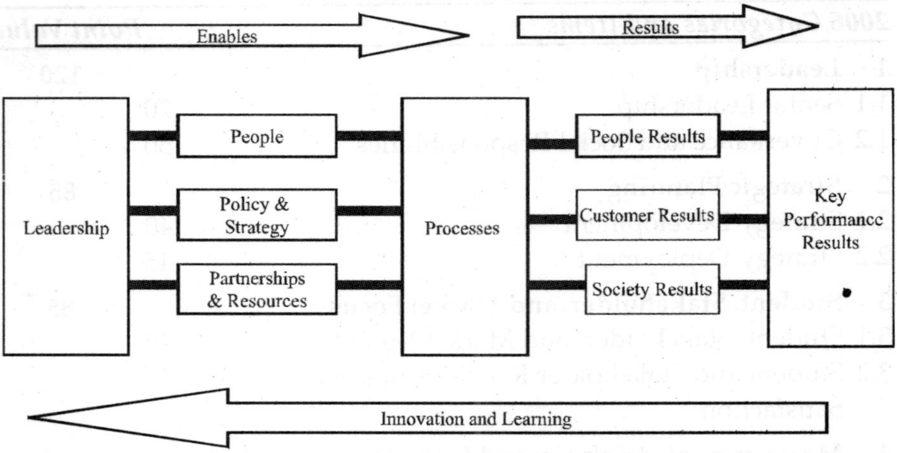

Fig.1: Model for EFQM Award for Excellence

RAJIV GANDHI NATIONAL QUALITY AWARD

Rajiv Gandhi National Quality Award was instituted by the Bureau of Indian Standards in 1991, with a view to encouraging Indian manufacturing and service organizations to strive for excellence and giving special recognition to those who are considered to be the leaders of quality movement in India. This award is intended to generate interest and involvement of Indian industry in quality programs, drive our products and services to higher levels of quality and equip our industry to meet the challenges of domestic and international markets. The award has been named after our late Prime Minister Rajiv Gandhi, recognizing the new thrust he had given to the quality movement in India so that India could move into 21st Century with pride.

There are five Awards in the following categories:

- Best large-scale manufacturing organization
- Best small-scale manufacturing organization
- Best large-scale service organization
- Best small-scale service organization
- Best of all competing companies

In addition, there are commendation certificates for companies and manufacturing and service sector.

AWARD CRITERIA

Evaluation criteria for Rajiv Gandhi Award has following nine elements:

Elements

1. Leadership
2. Policies, objectives and strategies
3. Human resource management
4. Resources
5. Processes
6. Customer focused results
7. Employee satisfaction
8. Impact on environment and society
9. Business results

Each element has a number of sub-elements. Evaluation is carried out by awarding each sub-element a score out of 100 as given in Annexure-1 to this Chapter.

Annexure -I

EVALUATION CRITERIA FOR RAJIV GANDHI AWARD

Leadership

1. Personal involvement of top management in leading quality management function
2. Demonstration by top management of consistent total quality culture
3. Involvement of top management in timely recognition and appreciation of employees' efforts
4. Identification and provision of appropriate resources
5. Involvement of top management with customers and suppliers
6. Promotion of total quality outside the organization

Policies, Objectives and Strategies

1. Reflection of the concept of total quality in organization's mission, values and vision
2. Formulation of policies and strategies on the basis of information relevant to total quality
3. Basis for business plans
4. Identification of needs and expectations of other interested parties for setting objectives
5. Key objectives. How these are derived from quality policy into measurable goals
6. Deployment of objectives to each management level
7. Communication of policies, objectives and strategies
8. Measurement! Assessment of achievement of various quality objectives and targets
9. Review and improvement of policies, objectives and strategies

Human Resource Management

1. Human resource management efforts in support of quality objectives
2. Means available to employees for effective contribution towards organization's performance and meeting quality objectives, and the evaluation of their effectiveness.

3. Preservation and development of employees' skills and capabilities through training and career development
4. Support of employee's recognition, reward, performance and feedback process to the organization's performance and quality objectives
5. Steps taken for maintaining work environment conducive to the well- being and growth of its employees
6. Measures for effective communication, both vertical and horizontal

Resources

1. Infrastructure facilities
2. Material resources
3. Technology
4. Information resources
5. Financial resources

Processes

1. Identification of key processes and their key performance indicators
2. Identification of outsourced processes and effective control thereof
3. Supply chain management
4. System for management of processes
5. Incorporation of customer/market changes in product realization processes
6. Regular process performance measurements and feedback system in relation to key performance indicators
7. Analysis of data to assess performance and identification of areas for improvement
8. Corrective action for eliminating existing causes for problems
9. Preventive action for preventing future problems/loss prevention
10. Use of improvement methods and tools for performance improvement
11. Stimulation of innovation and creativity in process improvement
12. Implementation of process changes and evaluation of benefits

Customer Focused Results

1. Identifying and meeting customers needs and expectations on a continual basis
2. Customers'/consumers' perception about the organization's capability to meet their needs and expectations.
3. Steps taken for building good relationships with customers/ consumers

4. Measurement of current levels and trends of customer/consumer satisfaction

Employees' Satisfaction

1. Assessment/measurement of current levels and trends of employees' satisfaction and steps taken to improve it
2. Employees' perception of the organization w.r.t. working conditions, health & safety, career development, job security, recognition, etc.
3. Trends and levels or other indications of employees' satisfaction and dissatisfaction

Impact on Environment and Society

1. Steps taken for environment protection and preventing harm to its neighbourhood
2. Organization's activities to assist in preservation of resources
3. Organization's activities to assist in preservation of resources
4. Additional indications of organization's impact on society

Business Results

1. Financial measures
2. Non-financial measures
3. Compliance to statutory and regulatory requirements

How Quality Awards Help Industry?

Quality award is an important tool for quality promotion through following measures:

- Recognizing the achievements of those organizations which have improved the quality of their products and services and thereby set an example for others;
- Encouraging industry to make significant improvements in quality for maximizing consumer satisfaction and for successfully facing competition in the global market as well;
- Establishing guidelines and criteria that can be used by industry in evaluating their own quality management system and identifying opportunities for improvement.
- Providing the basis for benchmarking with other organizations.
- Experience sharing by award winning companies which enable other companies embark on their quality journey to achieve organizational excellence.

21

Implementation of TQM

The introduction of any new management initiative requires careful consideration. TQM is a major initiative which will affect the entire organization. While considering the implementation of TQM, the first question which comes to mind is that the TQM concept has existed since the mid-1980s; so how is it that it has not been implemented in a large number of organizations? Although there are number of success stories where TQM has enabled a major turnaround, it is also a fact that in many organizations it has failed. The same has happened with many other management tools. For a dispassionate appraisal of TQM we need to analyze the causes of its failure in order to determine whether it was due to a weakness inherent in the TQM concept or due primarily to faulty implementation. The major causes of the failure of TQM are given below:

(a) Lack of management commitment

This is the most common reason for the failure of any TQM initiative. Commitment, by definition is an intellectual characteristic which cannot be forced on a person. Management must genuinely believe in the benefits of TQM to be committed to it. Sometimes CEOs get attracted to TQM for wrong reasons. For instance a CEO may want to impress his customers, or to use TQM as a marketing tool. Others may adopt it primarily for cost-cutting purposes. Although in the long run TQM may result in cost reduction, that is only likely to happen once TQM is fully embedded in an organization.

(b) Improper needs assessment

Any major management initiative can succeed only where there is a need for institutionalized management tools. For example, when a new company is established, there is a need to develop customer focus in order to attract customers. This can be achieved by integrating quality into the operations of the new company through the creation of an institutionalized TQM structure. However, if a young company introduces TQM just to impress the investors before going public, such an initiative is not likely to succeed because the staff at various levels does not appreciate the need for such an initiative, and they are therefore unlikely to be enthusiastic about it. Similarly, if a company has already been in existence for a long time, the forcible insertion of a TQM program into the company's culture is likely to fail since the staff in general feels "we got along fine for all this time without TQM – why do we need it now?" Unless management makes a clear and fresh case for its introduction, it is likely to fail in established companies.

(c) Inadequate preparation

TQM is not a device which can be purchased and installed. It is a structured management system and an attitudinal issue. This requires lot of preparation such as creating awareness about TQM and its benefits, and extensive training of personnel at all levels. However, since training does not offer immediate returns, companies in general provide limited budgets for such activities. Since the basic concepts of TQM are simple, senior management often does not appreciate the need for extensive training. This type of short-sighted policy does not allow TQM to take root in the organization and as such its existence is not sustained. Some companies treat TQM as a quick-fix solution to all their problems. Such companies are bound to be disappointed and give up, and blame their failures on the ineffectiveness of TQM.

(d) Reluctance to change culturally

One often hears that TQM requires a new culture. While it is true, very few companies really want to change in the first place. Traditionally, organizations are run in an authoritarian manner, and TQM requires collective management. Managers at various levels are reluctant to share power and authority by involving subordinates in decision-making and delegating authority to the persons actually creating value.

(e) Lack of short-term financial results

The operational efficiency of companies (particularly public companies) is assessed on the basis of quarterly or annual financial results. The first one or two years of a TQM initiative are spent on the training of personnel, strengthening and standardization of processes and establishment of measurement systems. Organizations looking for quick results tend to give up once they do not get significant bottom- line results in the short term.

USE OF TQM FOR ORGANIZATIONAL IMPROVEMENT

The objective of implementing TQM is to significantly improve the quality of products and services, in order to retain existing customers and acquire new ones. At the same time, improving productivity and lowering costs inherently leads to achieve higher profitability. It should be realized that TQM is not a magic wand which will remove all the problems and worries of any organization. It is only a management concept with a set of tools to achieve an organization's vision and mission. Therefore, before planning for the implementation of TQM, the organization needs to define its long-term vision. Once the organization has defined its vision and mission, it needs to assess whether its current organizational structure and management system is adequate for achieving this mission. There is a need to identify its problem areas and pain points, which are not allowing it to achieve full potential. This assessment should be a comprehensive exercise involving the study of all aspects of management. To facilitate this assessment, a detailed questionnaire is included in Annexure-I of this chapter. This questionnaire addresses the following elements, which are used by most rating organizations to assess the company's performance:

1. Leadership
2. Strategic planning
3. Information
4. Human resources
5. Customers
6. Suppliers
7. Processes
8. Impact on society
9. Business results

The questionnaire can be used to measure the effectiveness of the management on a scale of 1 to 5. To obtain an objective assessment, this questionnaire should be answered by four to five persons drawn from different departments at various levels of management. There is likely to be considerable variation in the responses of different persons. A multi-disciplinary committee of senior management (excluding the CEO) should normalize these responses. Based on this, the overall performance scores should be determined. The total score and the suggested course of action are provided as follows:

Score	Rating	Course of action
281-350	Excellent	Stay on course. Maintain effective controls to prevent slippage.
211-280	Good	You are in the best position to achieve excellence through TQM.
141-210	Average	TQM will help you to achieve quick gains in profitability by focusing on 'low- hanging fruit' first.
0-140	Below average	You need to first establish the basic institutional framework for managing quality.

CHOICE OF QUALITY MANAGEMENT CONCEPTS AND TOOLS

As explained in the beginning of the Book, a number of quality management concepts and tools are now available under the umbrella of TQM for managing quality to achieve organizational excellence. The choice of the tools depends upon the current quality status of the company, range of its operations and areas of weakness. Starting point is the quality health checks of the company based on the questionnaire given in Annexure-I. Large number of Indian companies would be in the last two grades of quality rating. Even if the company is in 'Good' grade it can still benefit by using appropriate quality management concepts and tools discussed in the Book.

Broad guidance for use of various tools are given below:

Situation	Recommended tools
1. Below average quality rating score. Ad hoc management system based on the perception of individual managers. No formal quality policy and documented operational procedures.	(a) 5'S' to create standard work environment. (b) Establishment of ISO-9000 Standard for Quality Management System (Not necessarily certification). More emphasis on internal audit of QMS, preferably by an outside auditor until capable internal auditors are developed. (c) Use of applicable quality improvement tool discussed in Part-3 of the Book.
2. Good general quality score but low rating in customer segment.	(a) Concepts discussed in chapter-12 on Customer Focused Organization.

Contd....

	(b) Establishment of CRM particularly on large-scale companies in manufacturing and service sectors.
3. Lower product/service quality as compared to the competitors.	(a) Process control tools discussed in Part III (b) Poka-yoke discussed in Chapter 14.
4. Good quality but non-competitive in prices.	(a) Lean production system (b) TPM
5. Poor score in human resource development.	(a) Develop leadership. (b) Greater focus on training of personnel on quality management.
6. Companies with good quality management system aiming for excellence.	(a) Six-Sigma (b) Balanced score card (c) Corporate social responsibility

IMPLEMENTATION METHODOLOGY OF TQM

In any new endeavour it is relatively easy to create a plan and define what to do and what competency and skills are required to carry out the stated jobs. It is also not difficult to acquire the new skills either by recruitment or by organizing the necessary training. The harder part is to show measurable results through the implementation of tools and techniques with the proper behaviour and attitude of personnel involved. Quite often excellent plans flounder during implementation. It is here that TQM can assist companies in effectively implementing their strategic and tactical plans.

TQM involves certain new concepts relating to organizational structure, policies, competence-building and cultural transformation. These are discussed below, and they can be helpful in developing a TQM implementation plan.

DIFFERENT VIEW OF COMPANY ORGANIZATION

Traditional organizations are designed on the basis of functional specialization and chain of command. This pattern of organization was developed in the late nineteenth century when there was a need to manage the newly emerging 'science' of mass production.

This pattern has certain inherent weaknesses. It does not reflect process flows or the inter-dependence of functional groups. It does not concern itself with the range of products manufactured, nor with the customers that need to be satisfied. It mainly emphasizes accountability and chain of control. This leads to a culture of departmental focus with an emphasis on achieving targets irrespective of the effect such achievement may have on other departments or on the company as a whole. A more effective view of the organization might also bring out:

- Inter-dependence of various departments
- Importance of customers and need for customer feedback
- Role of suppliers, and
- Chain of internal suppliers and customers.

This view of the organization is shown in Figure-1. In this view, you need to please the customer (internal or external) rather than your boss. Thus, employees are supposed to have a holistic organizational view rather than a narrow departmental focus. This is the actualization of Deming 9th rule... "Break down barriers between staff areas." In this concept of an organization, although various functions have their own identity, the goals of all functions are aligned to the organizational mission and objectives.

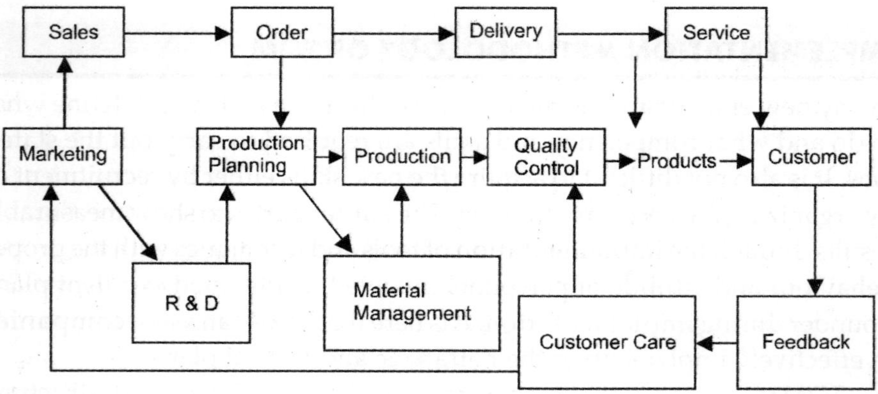

Fig. 1

INSTITUTIONAL STRUCTURE

Any major initiative or activity needs an institutional structure with well-defined authority and responsibility to manage the new initiative. Since TQM is an organization- wide initiative, the overall guidance and control should vest with the management board of the company, which should view TQM as a critical operational project. Since TQM requires cooperation and support from all departments and functional groups, a TQM steering committee should be established under the Chief Operating Officer (COO) with heads of departments as members of the executive committee.

The role of the TQM steering committee would include:

- Approval of the TQM plan
- Provision of resources

- Monitoring of progress through periodic reviews
- Resolving inter-departmental problems in TQM implementation
- Advising on corrective actions to keep the plan on track

The actual responsibility for the execution of the TQM plan should be with an inter-departmental TQM Task Force headed by a senior manager. The head of the task force should be dynamic and be passionate about quality. Much of the success of the TQM initiative will depend upon his ability to provide leadership and enthuse people.

ORGANIZED APPROACH

TQM involves the modification of operational policies, the establishment of systems, competence building and attitude alignment among personnel. Much of the TQM activities would be executed as a series of individual projects. Based on an assessment of needs, the TQM Task Force should select projects to achieve objectives related to critical business success factors. These projects should then be discussed by the TQM Steering Committee, where they be prioritized and the necessary resources authorized for them. The approved projects should then be taken up for execution.

Based on the mandate of the TQM Steering Committee, a project document should be developed with well-defined objectives, constitution of a project team including a leader in each case, a list of resources allocated and a schedule of project activities. The team leaders should then take up the projects and manage them using regular project management methods. TQM activities may involve close interaction with outside entities such as customers and suppliers, therefore, the company must share its plan for TQM and establish communication channel with concerned persons in the supplier organizations and important customers. The main effort would be required to improve internal processes. As most projects are likely to cover activities in more than one department, considerable effort may be required to establish active ties between internal customers and suppliers for smooth operation of business processes to achieve satisfaction of the ultimate customer.

POLICY DEPLOYMENT

The initial step in the implementation of TQM in an organization is to develop departmental mission statements based on organizational vision and mission and critical success factors. The aim of departmental missions is to align all major functions in each department to support company's vision, mission and values. This will assist in the implementation of TQM principles throughout the organization.

The most critical business success factor is customer satisfaction. It is well known that external customers can only be satisfied if all the internal customers are satisfied. This requires the development of specifications for all products and services flowing through the 'internal customer/ supplier' chain. These specifications will define the requirements of internal customers so that internal suppliers clearly understand the expectations of their internal customers and work towards satisfying them.

It is generally seen that internal customers are not taken as seriously as the external customers. The importance attached to the internal customer depends upon the status or the influence of head of the 'customer' department. The underlying fear is that if a powerful internal customer is not satisfied, the matter may go to the CEO, and the supplier group may be held accountable. However, at the organizational level all internal customers are equally important because dissatisfaction of any one of them can cause dissatisfaction among external customers, with all their attendant consequences.

To overcome these factors of internal politics, it is suggested that a regime of internal service agreements should be introduced. All internal suppliers and customers should enter into internal service agreements which clearly spell out the customer requirements. The internal suppliers would then take their commitments more seriously. This would also foster closer interaction between internal customers and suppliers, and any issues between them might be more easily resolved, thereby ensuring a smoother flow of value throughout the organization.

MEASUREMENT

It is well known that any thing that is not measured cannot be improved. Since TQM is all about improvement we need to develop measurements for all elements which need improvement. We have seen above that before implementing TQM the company needs to identify critical business success factors. Based on these success factors, areas of improvement in various departments need to be identified, upon which TQM efforts should focus. To plan improvements, we need to establish measures of identified elements so that progress can be assessed. The areas of improvement depend upon the type of organization and the nature of its problems. Some typical measures of different departments are provided below as an illustration, so that organizations can select their own focus areas for improvement.

Marketing

- Sales growth rate
- Accuracy of forecast assumptions.
- Number of incorrect order entries.
- Overstocked field supplies.
- Contract errors.

- Late deliveries.
- Customer complaints.
- Warranty cost as a percentage of sales.

Purchasing

- Premium freight cost/demurrage charges.
- Down-time because of parts shortages.
- Number of out of specification parts used to keep the production line going.
- Cycle time from start of purchase request until items arrive in house.
- Excess inventory.
- Percentage of purchased material rejected on receipt.

Manufacturing

- Yield per ton of raw materials.
- Percentage of parts scrapped.
- Percentage of parts reworked.
- Percentage of parts accepted on concession.
- Percentage of final product graded as seconds.
- Production per man/machine.
- Percent of production capacity in use.
- Average setup time.

Product engineering

- Number of engineering changes per document.
- Number of errors found during design review.
- Number of errors found during design evaluation testing.
- Percentage of time over-run compared to planned time for development.
- Percentage of cost over-run compared to estimated cost of development.
- Number of tooling redesigns after trial production.

Quality assurance

- Percentage of lots rejected due to errors.
- Percentage of products with defects detected by customers.
- Number of engineering changes that should have been detected during design review.
- Errors in inspection/test reports.

- Cycle time to get corrective actions.
- Percentage of appraisal cost compared to production cost.

Accounting

- Percentage of late payments.
- Time to respond to customer requests for information.
- Billing errors.
- Incorrect accounting entries.
- Payroll errors.
- Errors in cost estimates.

Financial measures

- Cost of quality as a percentage of sales
- Profit before interest and financial charges
- Profit before and after tax
- Growth in profits over last year
- Return on assets
- Return on capital employed
- Return on sales

Employee-related measures

- Employee satisfaction index
- Staff attrition rate
- Safety and performance
- Volume, nature and handling of suggestions received from employees

ROAD MAP FOR TQM

TQM is a major organization- wide program which needs careful planning and implementation. The following roadmap can be used for guidance in planning and implementation.

1. *Needs assessment*

- Carry out an assessment of the organization on the scale of excellence using a suitable variation of the questionnaire provided in Annexure-1 or any other excellence assessment model such as Malcom Baldridge, the European model for excellence, etc.
- Study the major areas of weakness in the organization and analyze its basic causes.
- Deliberate on whether TQM is the appropriate initiative to address major issues within the organization.

2. *Institutional framework and environment*

2. *Institutional framework and environment*

- Constitute a steering committee with a clear mandate for guiding implementation of TQM. The members of the Steering Committee should be trained on the basic concept and application of TQM and their role in implementation.
- Appoint multidisciplinary task force to manage TQM programs.
- Train the members of the task force on the concept and implementation methodology of TQM.
- Organize an awareness program for personnel at all levels to explain the basic need, concept and benefits of TQM.
- Take unions or staff associations into confidence and allay their fears about the adverse effects of this initiative on the job security or working conditions of employees.

3. *Establish vision, mission and objectives*

- The objectives should be based on the mission of establishing customer focus in the organization.
- The objectives should have broad applicability and should be realistic.
- The objectives should be communicated throughout the organization.

4. *Deploy policy and strategy*

- Develop goals at a functional level.
- Align functional improvement efforts with the organizational objectives.
- Translate goals into practice.

5. *Involve customers and suppliers*

- Interact with customers and understand their needs and their perceptions of the organization.
- Address customer concerns and translate them into requirements to be met by different functions.
- Understand supplier concerns, share the organization's vision and mission with them and clarify what support you need from them.
- Define specific steps which you expect from suppliers to take.

6. *Study current process*

- Study current processes.
- Document them.
- Measure performance against current standards.
- Assess performance against customer needs.
- Select processes to be improved and define improvement targets.

7. Take up improvement projects

- Constitute teams and allocate projects to them.
- Facilitate and monitor the work of these project teams.
- Measure process-improvement performance against the targets
- Evaluate the improved processes and customer satisfaction.
- Document results
- Continue improvements.

8. Identify learning needs

- Evaluate the achievement of TQM goals.
- Assess the adequacy of current knowledge and its shortfalls.
- Identify new knowledge/competency required to maintain improved performance.

9. Training and competence development

- Access training materials and resource persons.
- Identify persons to be trained.
- Address employee satisfaction and motivation issues.
- Organize training in-house or send personnel to external training institutions.
- Evaluate the effectiveness of training by studying the performance of trained persons.
- Take suitable corrective action to ensure that new skills result in improved performance of processes.
- Integrate new learning with routine jobs.

10. Assess progress

- Assess progress in the organizational performance using the same questionnaire employed for the original assessment before undertaking the TQM initiative.
- Identify weak areas of weakness.
- Analyze reasons for weakness.

11. Continue improvement

- Based on the assessment and analysis carried out in step 10, revisit the organization's mission, objectives and strategy.
- In the light of actual experience, revise the objectives and strategy if warranted.
- Repeat steps 2 to 10 and continue improvement using the PDCA cycle.

Annexure -I

QUESTIONNAIRE FOR ASSESSING BUSINESS EXCELLENCE

Leadership

1. Has the top management established vision and mission of the organization and communicated it all levels?
2. Does top management have a personal and visible involvement in all aspects of quality management?
3. Do they actively participate in creating and reinforcing customer focus throughout the organization?
4. Has the management demonstrated intolerance of poor quality products and services?
5. Does top management believe in decentralization of authority and empowering employees who actually create quality in products and services?

Note: All questions must be answered on a 1 to 5 scale.
1 is the lowest and 5 is the highest.

Strategic Planning

6. Does the company have a common vision which is truly shared by all the employees?
7. Does the company's strategic planning address realignment of work processes to improve customer focus and operational performance?
8. Are the company's strategies targeted for quantified measurable improvement in important areas and is building for future seen as more important than short term benefits?
9. Are long-term objectives taken into consideration when committing resources for new facilities, process improvements and training?
10. Do the company's long-term projections of operational performance effectively incorporate comparisons with competitors?

Note: All questions must be answered on a 1 to 5 scale.
1 is the lowest and 5 is the highest.

Information

11. Does the company have access to the latest advances in information

management/technology?

12. Do employees feel free to share information?
13. Is the company's information management system accessible to those who need it ?
14. Is the management information system regularly updated?
15. Is the information system reliable and accurate so that it may routinely be used to make decisions in time?

Note: All questions must be answered on a 1 to 5 scale.
1 is the lowest and 5 is the highest.

Human Resource Focus

16. Is there a quality culture in the organization?
17. Does the company has defined values which are consistently followed at all levels.
18. Is everyone in the organization trained to follow ethical practices?
19. Does the company have an effective system for setting both quantitative and qualitative targets?
20. Are the employees generally aware of expected performance standards and do they generally meet them?
21. Does the company make an effort to integrate employee job performance with key quality improvement targets and business results?
22. Does the company have an effective appraisal system which takes care of the career progression of all employees?
23. Does the company promote creativity and innovation, and does it encourage employees to engage in 'out of the box' thinking?
24. Is there a system for employee recognition and is good performance rewarded?
25. Is the employee motivation level high and is good performance suitably rewarded?
26. Does the company analyze reasons for employee exits and is the employee turnover ratio kept to a minimum?
27. Is everyone in the organization given training in time management and stress management so that they can carry out the company's tasks in a productive manner?
28. Does the company have a good image as an employer and is it able to attract the best talent?

Note: All questions must be answered on a 1 to 5 scale.
1 is the lowest and 5 is the highest.

Customers

29. Is the concept of satisfaction of internal customers embedded in the

organization?

30. Does the company's products enjoy a competitive edge over its nearest competitors with respect to quality?
31. Does the company promptly resolve all formal and informal customer complaints?
32. Does the company regularly determine its customers' current and expected requirements?
33. Does company involve major customers during development of new products for them?
34. Does the company have institutionalized system of Customer Relationship Management (CRM)?
35. Does the CEO or COO occasionally interact with major customers to know how the company can serve them better?
36. Does the company organize collective meetings with customers to understand their problem first-hand and take appropriate follow measures.
37. Does the company analyze and use information on customer loss/gain and product performance to develop future strategies?
38. Does the company objectively measure customer satisfaction and make effective efforts to improve it further?
39. Has there been significant improvement in customer satisfaction during last year?
40. Does the company continuously improve its system of determining customer satisfaction?

Note: All questions must be answered on a 1 to 5 scale.
1 is the lowest and 5 is the highest.

Suppliers

41. Does the company have a proper system for qualification of vendors before considering them for orders?
42. Does the company communicate its quality requirements to its suppliers?
43. Does the company evaluate supplier performance with specified requirements/parameters through mutually agreed plans?
44. Does the company organize training programs for suppliers to improve their ability to meet key requirements and response times?
45. Does the company assist suppliers in determining and improving process capability?
46. Does the company assist vendors in obtaining quality input material at competitive price?
47. Does the company have a system to generate healthy competition

among suppliers of similar items in order to improve performance?

48. Does the company provide price incentive or larger order quantity, to suppliers of higher Quality products?
49. What is the level of the company's supplier satisfaction?
50. Are the suppliers paid on time?

Note: All questions must be answered on a 1 to 5 scale.
1 is the lowest and 5 is the highest.

Processes

51. Are business processes in the company standardized and documented?
52. Does the company validate its product designs by taking into account, performance, process and supplier capabilities?
53. Does the company have system of measurement and monitoring of critical process?
54. Does the company determine the cause of product/process variations, make corrections and integrate these corrections into the relevant process?
55. Does the company regularly analyze quality costs and ensure that maximum focus is given to preventive measures?
56. Does the company regularly measure process capability of its processes and make improvement efforts?
57. Does the company use tools like TPM for proper maintenance of equipment?
58. Does the company regularly determine waste/non-value-adding activities and eliminate them to improve efficiency?
59. Does the company effectively use JIT for reducing inventory?
60. Does the company effectively deploy mistake-proofing techniques to improve its overall manufacturing processes?
61. Has the company got a well defined criteria for benchmarking and does the company make efforts to obtain information from best in the class and use this information for process improvement?
62. Does the company's work culture ensure that there is continuous search for improvement opportunities?
63. Does the company have a system of regular verification of skill and competence of personnel to operate various processes?

Note: All questions must be answered on a 1 to 5 scale.
1 is the lowest and 5 is the highest.

Impact on Society

64. Does the company comply with various regulations about safety and welfare of workers?

65. Does the company effectively evaluate the possible impact of its products and operations on society?
66. Does the company promote ethical conduct in all activities and are the company's advertising campaigns truthful and factual?
67. Does the company effectively manage energy conservation and preservation of global resources?

Note: All questions must be answered on a 1 to 5 scale.
1 is the lowest and 5 is the highest.

BUSINESS RESULTS

68. Has the company significantly improved its market share compared to the previous year?
69. Is the company's growth of revenues, profits, and ROI over the last financial year comparable with the growth in its industry sector?
70. Are the overall financial results significantly better than the previous financial year?

Note: All questions must be answered on a 1 to 5 scale.
1 is the lowest and 5 is the highest.

PART-III

PART-III

22

Frequency Distribution

PRODUCT VARIABILITY

No two articles manufactured by the same process can be exactly alike. If they appear to be similar on casual observation, it merely shows that for practical purposes, their differences are not appreciable. Had these articles been measured or tested by more accurate means, their differences would have become apparent. The variations in the manufactured products are caused by many factors such as tool wear, vibrations, non homogeneity of materials, temperature or pressure changes and, finally, the skill of the worker or the operator or the inspector. These variations have long been accepted as inevitable and, due to this reason, all manufacturing drawings and specifications show an allowed deviation range or tolerance for various quality characteristics, rather than one fixed value. For example, the diameter of a pin may be shown as 6.00 + 0.05 mm. This means that, although the nominal pin diameter is 6.00 mm, pins having diameters from 5.95 mm to 6.05 mm are considered acceptable. Although some variation in a product is allowed in the manufacturing drawings, a close watch has to be kept on industrial processes to see whether the actual variations exceed permissible limits. Most manufacturing shops use some kind of inspection to separate out-of-limit parts from those which are within limits. If there is an unusually high rejection percentage, the production manager is bound to be concerned.

However, the mere quantity or percentage of rejection is not of much help to him in deciding on the corrective action. To investigate the cause of excessive rejection, measurements of the subject quality characteristic are taken and analyzed. For proper analysis, it is necessary to understand and interpret the variation present in the data.

NATURE OF VARIATION

Two types of variation data are encountered in quality control practice, namely, discrete data and continuous data. Discrete data varies in discrete steps and cannot take any value within the range of variation. For instance, data on the number of defects in an equipment can be expressed only in integral numbers, such as 1, 2, 5, etc. There cannot be 2½ or 5¼ defects. Discrete data is illustrated by Table A. Continuous data, as the name implies, can assume any value within a specified range. For instance, the diameter of a pin mentioned in the above para may have any value between 5.95 mm and 6.05 mm. If the manufacturing process is not under control, it may even have values beyond these limits. The values need not be confined only up to 2 decimal places. If the measurements are taken with an instrument having the least count of 0.001 mm or less, the values in the third decimal place such as 5.975 mm or 6.016 mm may also occur. Typical continuous data are shown in Table B, which represent the diameter a measurement of pins having manufacturing tolerance of ±0.050 mm.

FREQUENCY DISTRIBUTION

The aim of collection of any data is that we should be able to draw some inference, which should be helpful in deciding a course of action. A glance at Tables A & B will show that it is difficult to learn much about the variation of data by a casual inspection of the mass of numbers. This data has to be presented in a more manageable form to be of practical use. One such widely used method is to present it as a FREQUENCY DISTRIBUTION. The frequency of occurrence of a value is the number of times it occurs in a data. For instance, in Table A the value "2 defects" occurs three times (against V-103, V-120 and V-135). Thus, the frequency of occurrence of "2 defects" in this data is 3. Similarly, the frequency of occurrence of other values in the data is also computed to form a frequency distribution which is given in Table C. The following inference can be quickly drawn from the frequency distribution as shown in the Table.

1. Most of the vehicles have 3 to 5 defects.
2. No. of defects vary from 1 to 10.

Table A: Final Inspection Record of Vehicles

Vehicle no.	*No. of defects*	*Vehicle no.*	*No. of defects*	*Vehicle no.*	*No. of defects*
V-101	4	V-114	7	V-127	3
V-102	6	V-115	4	V-128	4
V-103	2	V-116	5	V-129	10
V-104	8	V-117	3	V-130	5
V-105	6	V-118	6	V-131	1
V-106	5	V-119	4	V-132	3
V-107	4	V-120	2	V-133	9
V-108	3	V-121	8	V-134	7
V-109	4	V-122	3	V-135	2
V-110	6	V-123	4	V-136	3
V-111	9	V-124	4	V-137	5
V-112	4	V-125	5	V-138	5
V-113	5	V-126	7	V-139	6
				V-140	4

Table B: Measurements of Pin Diameter (in mm)

6.016	6.060	6.032
6.042	5.995	6.029
6.023	6.023	6.022
6.057	6.051	6.003
6.030	6.014	6.044
6.044	6.057	6.030
6.062	6.061	6.053
6.038	6.034	6.027
6.054	6.040	6.012
6.028	6.046	6.050
6.001	6.023	6.053
6.032	6.021	6.076
6.013	6.073	6.043
6.035	6.004	6.052
6.033	6.043	6.024
6.061	6.037	6.040
6.034	6.068	6.008

Contd....

6.040	6.041	6.039
6.014	6.019	6.012
6.018	6.025	6.028

Table C: Frequency Distribution—Discrete Data

No. of defects	*Frequency of occurrence*
1	1
2	3
3	6
4	10
5	7
6	5
7	3
8	2
9	2
10	1

For making frequency distribution of continuous data, a slightly different technique is adopted. Because of the continuous nature of data, a particular value may not occur very often. Therefore, it is necessary to group the data into a number of classes with fixed class interval, which should be preferably equal. For instance, the data in Table B could be grouped into classes having class interval of .010 mm. These classes could be 5.990-6.000, 6.000-6.010 etc. Now, all readings from 6.00 to 6.010 (excluding 6.010) could be counted and shown as frequency of occurrence against class 6.000 to 6.010. (In case the reading is 6.010 exact, it should be excluded from this class and included in the next class, *i.e.* 6.010-6.020 mm). In this manner, the frequency of occurrence of all classes should be computed as shown in Table D. Col. 1 shows the class limits or class interval, Col. 2 the mid class value and Col. 3 the frequency of occurrence. Column 4 shows the proportion of total values occurring in a class, which will be further discussed later in this chapter.

By inspection of Table D, one can quickly form an idea about the central value around which the readings vary, as well as the range of variation. The central value in this case is between 6.030 and 6.040, since the values in this class occur most frequently, and the number of readings tapers off towards lesser and greater diameter values. The spread of the readings or the range is the difference between the maximum limit of the highest class and the minimum limit of the lowest class. In this case, it is 6.080-5.990, *i.e.* 0.090 mm.

Table D: Frequency Distribution—Continuous

Class interval	*Mid class value in mm*	*No. of reading in the class*	*Proportion of total no. of readings*
(1)	**(2)**	**(3)**	**(4)**
5.990-6.000	5.995	1	1= 0.016
6.000-6.010	6.005	4	$\frac{4}{60}$ = 0.066
6.010-6.020	6.015	7	$\frac{7}{60}$ = 0.116
6.020-6.030	6.025	10	$\frac{10}{60}$ = 0.116
6.030-6.040	6.035	12	$\frac{12}{60}$ = 0.200
6.040-6.050	6.045	11	$\frac{11}{60}$ = 0.183
6.050-6.060	6.055	8	$\frac{8}{60}$ = 0.133
6.060-6.070	6.065	5	$\frac{5}{60}$ = 0.083
6.070-6.080	6.075	2	2=0.033

RELATIVE FREQUENCY DISTRIBUTION

In most problems encountered in quality control, the important characteristic is not the number of values in a particular class, but the proportion of total values which fall in that class. In these situations, it is more convenient to reduce the frequencies to the proportions, as shown in Col. 4 of Table D. Frequency distribution expressed in proportions is called RELATIVE FREQUENCY DISTRIBUTION. If two frequency distributions, based on the same varying characteristic (called variate in statistical practice) but different number of total values, are to be compared, these have to be reduced to relative frequency distribution.

GRAPHICAL REPRESENTATION OF FREQUENCY DISTRIBUTION

For visual appreciation, the frequency distributions can also be represented in graphical form. Figure 1 shows the graphical form of frequency distribution given in Table D. Such a diagram is called HISTOGRAM. Values of varying characteristics are shown on horizontal or 'X' axis, and the frequency of occurrence on vertical or 'V' axis. The width of vertical bars represents the class interval and their heights correspond to the frequency of occurrence according to a convenient scale. For instance, in Table D, there are four values in 6.000-6.010 mm class. Therefore, the top of the bar of rectangle representing this class is shown against 4 on the vertical scale. Similarly, the frequencies of other classes are plotted to get a complete frequency distribution. Another slightly different form of graphical representation is Frequency Polygon which is obtained by joining the mid points of the tops of rectangles as shown by the dotted lines in Fig. 1. Often, the frequency polygon is smoothened to form a continuous curve, which is called Frequency Distribution Curve or simply Frequency Curve.

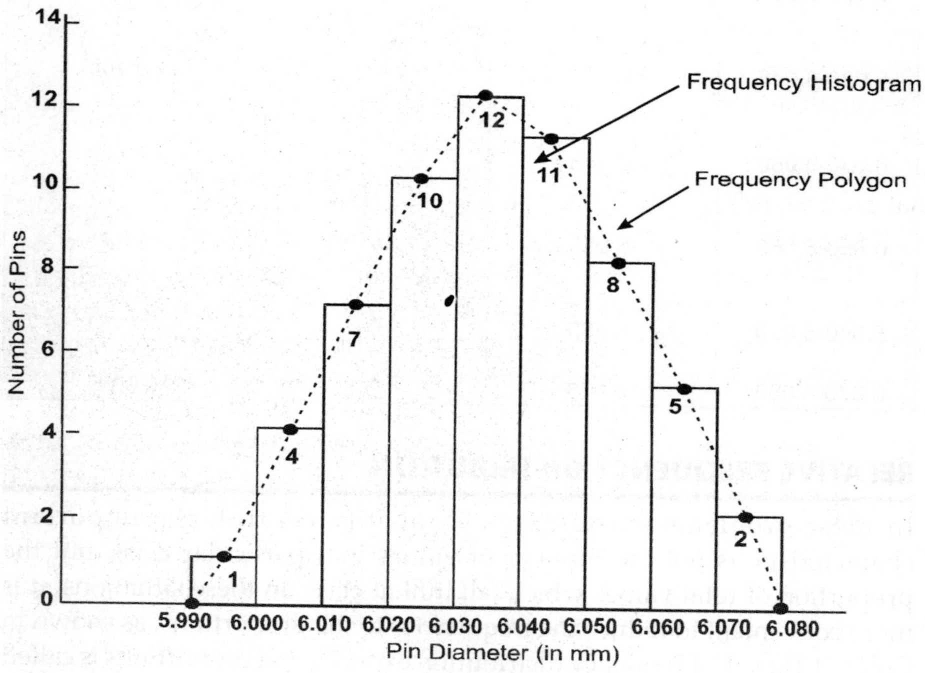

Fig. 1: Histogram

It can be seen that a graphical representation of the frequency distribution presents a much better picture of the data than the tabular form. To obtain a good visual picture of data, choice of proper class interval is important. If the class interval is too small, there will be too many classes, and we shall not get the general picture we are trying to obtain. On the other hand, if the class interval is too large, there will be too few classes, which will give a blurred picture lacking in detail. A good compromise is to choose such a class interval, which will divide the data into 8 to 15 classes.

Further, the class interval should preferably be a multiple of the measurement unit to facilitate grouping of the data. Keeping these two considerations in mind, .010 mm has been chosen as a class interval for the frequency distribution of data given in Table B. This has given 9 classes, and a reasonably good picture of the data is obtained in Fig. 1. In the same manner, the frequency distribution of discrete data can also be represented in a graphical form. In this case, each bar or rectangle of histogram will represent one particular value or a range of values, if there are a large number of different values in the data. In any case, the number of classes or bars of histogram should preferably be between 8 and 15 as for continuous data.

AREA OF FREQUENCY HISTOGRAM

We have seen that the heights of the bars or rectangles in the histogram are proportional to the frequency of occurrence. Since the width of all rectangles is the same, the area of each rectangles will be proportional to the frequency of occurrence of the readings in its respective class. Extending this argument further the area of histogram over any portion of the horizontal or 'X' axis will be proportional to the frequency or the number of readings covered in that portion. In Fig. 1, let us assume, that the class interval of 0.010 mm is represented by 1 cm on the 'X' axis, and the number of readings shown on 'Y' axis are to the scale 1 cm representing one reading. Now, the area of rectangle representing class 6.000-6.010 is 1 × 4 = 4 sq cm, which can be seen to correspond to 4 readings occurring in this class. Now let us see the area of histogram covering 3 classes, *viz.*, 5.990-6.000, 6.000-6.010 and 6.010-6.020. The area in this case is (1 × 4) + (1 × 7) + (I × 10) = 21 sq cm. It can be seen that this again corresponds to 21 readings which is the total of readings in the three classes. On the same basis, if the base covers the entire range of variation, the area of histogram will represent the total number of readings of the data. In case the distribution is in the form of Relative Frequency Distribution, the total area under the curve is taken to be 1, and the area under the curve on any portion of 'X' axis will give the fraction of total values which fall in the portion. Thus, it can be seen that the area of histogram between any two limits is proportional to the number of readings occurring between those limits. This is an important relationship and should be clearly understood. Here, we have developed this relationship for a histogram, but it is equally applicable for frequency Polygon and Frequency Curve also, which are only smoother forms of histogram.

ANALYSIS OF FREQUENCY DISTRIBUTION

Now that the data in Table B has been transformed into a visual representation, let us see what we can learn from it. The first thing which is apparent on inspection of the frequency histogram or polygon, is the central value around which most of the readings occur. This is immediately obvious from the peak of the frequency polygon. In Fig.1 the peak occurs at 6.035 mm, which can be considered as the central value. The second characteristic of the data which can quickly be obtained from the frequency polygon, is the range or spread of the values which is represented by the base of the polygon. In Fig. 1 it can be seen that the base of polygon extends from 5.990 to 6.080 mm, giving a total range of 0.090 mm. We have already seen that the two characteristics, namely, central value and range, can be easily obtained from the frequency distribution table D also. The graphical form of frequency distribution, however, makes it easier to compare these characteristics with the specifications or the drawing values. Figure 2 shows the frequency polygon and the specification limits. It can be seen that the range of variation (0.090) does not exceed the drawing tolerance of 0.100 mm (allowed). The central value is shifted towards the upper limit, which is the reason for some pins having a diameter exceeding the upper limit. This indicates either incorrect machine set-up or tool wear. Thus, the comparison of frequency distribution with specification limits enables the shop superintendent to take an appropriate corrective action. This type of application of frequency distribution, where it is treated as a simple picture to draw meaningful deductions, is very easy and effective. Since it does not involve any algebraic analysis, it can be used even by those personnel who do not possess mathematical background.

MATHEMATICAL TREATMENT OF FREQUENCY DISTRIBUTION

Whereas a general picture of frequency distribution as shown by the frequency polygon does give adequate information for simpler applications, the mathemtatical evaluation of such distribution has certain advantages, such as ease of comparison between different distributions and the ability to make inferences about the quality characteristics of a lot from its sample. We have seen that the two main characteristics of frequency distribution are central tendency and dispersion. The central tendency is generally expressed as the mean, the median or the mode. The dispersion or the spread of the distribution is expressed in terms of range or the standard deviation. Various terms for expression of the central value and the dispersion are explained in the following pages.

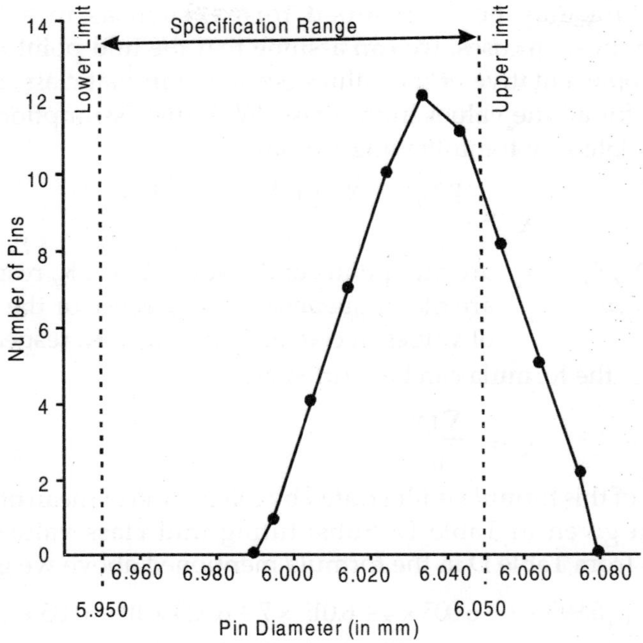

Fig. 2

CENTRAL TENDENCY

MEAN

It is the arithmetic mean or the average and is obtained by dividing the sum of all the values in a set of readings, by the number of readings in the set. Mathematically, a mean is written as:

$$\bar{X} = \frac{X_1 + X_2 + X_3 + \dots\dots\dots}{n} + X_n$$

$X_1, X_2, X_3, \dots\dots\dots\dots\dots, X_n$ are the individual values in a set.

Where $\bar{X}$ (pronounced as *x* bar) is the mean value.

n is the total number of readings in the set.

The above formula can also be written in a simplified form using the following algebraic symbols:

$$\bar{X} = \frac{1}{n}\Sigma X$$

Where ΣX (Sigma X) is a symbol of summation of all values of X from X_1 to X_n. For a set of 6 readings, 5, 9, 7, 10, 7 and 10, the mean is given by

$$\bar{X} = \frac{5+9+7+10+7+10}{6} = 8$$

Some data may be in grouped forms, such as in a frequency distribution. In such cases, we can assume that the mid point of the class interval is representative of the values occurring in that class, and can be substituted for all the values in the class. With this assumption the mean can be calculated by the following formula:

$$\bar{X} = \frac{F_1X_1 + F_2X_2 + F_3X_3 \ldots\ldots\ldots\ldots F_kX_k}{n}$$

Where $X_1, X_2, X_3 \ldots\ldots X_k$ are mid points of classes 1, 2, 3 ... K, respectively.
$F_1, F_2, F_3 \ldots\ldots F_k$ are the frequencies of occurrence or the number of values in classes 1, 2, 3 .... K, respectively.

Using Σ, the formula can be written as:

$$\bar{X} = \frac{\sum FX}{n}$$

The use of this formula is illustrated by calculation of mean of frequency distribution given in Table D. Substituting mid class values, and the frequencies from Table D in the formula mentioned above we get

$$\bar{X} = \frac{1}{n}\begin{Bmatrix} 5.995 \times 1 + 6.005 \times 4 + 6.015 \times 7 + 6.025 \times 10 + 6.035 \times 12 \\ + 6.045 \times 11 + 6.055 \times 8 + 6.065 \times 5 + 6.075 \times 2 \end{Bmatrix}$$

Since the total number of values, *i.e.* the sum of frequencies in all the classes, is 60, we can substitute 60 for n.

Thus,
$$\bar{X} = \frac{1}{60}\begin{Bmatrix} 5.995 + 24.020 + 42.105 + 60.250 + 72.420 \\ + 66.495 + 48.440 + 30.325 + 12.150 \end{Bmatrix}$$

$$= \frac{362.200}{60}$$

$$= 6.036 \text{ mm.}$$

Mean calculated in this method may be slightly different from the mean obtained directly by adding all the individual values and dividing by n. The slight error, if any, is due to the assumption made above, but usually it is negligible for all practical purposes. Since it saves labour of adding values which may be in hundreds, it is widely used in statistical practice.

MEDIAN

Another measure of central tendency, which is sometimes used is called Median. When a set of readings are arranged in the order of their magnitude, the median is the central value, which has an equal number of readings on either side. In case the set contains an odd number of values, the median is the central value. For example, in the set 7, 9, 10, 11, 12, 13, 15, the median is 11, as it has three values on either side. If there are an even number of values, the median is the average of two middle values. Thus, in a set of readings, 7, 9, 10, 11, 12, 14, 15, 16, the median is the average value of the two middle readings, *i.e.* 11 and 12 which comes to 11.5. A median differs from a mean in one important respect, i.e. it is independent of the magnitude of individual values in the data. In the example considered above, the value of the last reading could have been 50, without affecting the value of the median, which would still be 11.5. Often when a few extreme values are present in a set, the central tendency is better reflected by the median than the mean.

MEASURES OF DISPERSION OR SPREAD OF VARIATION

The range is the simplest measure of the spread of variation. In a set of readings, it is the difference between the lowest and the highest reading. Written symbolically,

$$R = X_h - X_l$$

Where R is the range.

X_h is the highest reading.

X_l is the lowest reading.

Although the range is an accepted measure of dispersion and has the advantage of being easily determined, it has certain drawbacks which detract from its usefulness, especially for data containing a larger number of readings. The foremost defect is that one or two highly exceptional and wide-of-the-mark values may unduly enlarge the range. For example, we may take a case where a set of optical glass blanks are inspected for the presence of bubbles (an objectionable characteristic). Let us say the inspection result of a sample containing ten blanks is as given in Table E:

Table E

Blank no.	*Number of bubbles present*
1	3
2	1
3	2
4	4
5	5
6	3
7	3
8	9
9	2
10	3

Lowest number of bubbles 1

Highest number of bubbles 9

Therefore Range = 9 – 1 = 8

It can be seen that the eighth reading, which is widely different from the rest, has substantially increased the range, whereas the intermediate values have had absolutely no effect. In this example, readings except 2nd and 8th may vary in any manner, so long as they remain within the two extreme values, the range will remain 8. The second defect of the range as a measure of dispersion is its marked dependence on the sample size, *i.e.* the number of readings. It tends to increase with the sample size, thus making comparison difficult. In view of these limitations, the range is not generally used as a measure of dispersion for large samples. However, on account of the ease with which it can be determined, it is widely used for small sample sizes, where it is quite a reliable index of variability.

MEAN DEVIATION

We have seen that the range takes into account only two extreme values. A more satisfactory measure of dispersion would be one where each reading in the set is given due consideration in determining dispersion. One such measure is called Mean Deviation. This is the average deviation of individual values from the mean value of the data. However, there is one difficulty in the use of mean deviation. Since the algebraic sum of all the deviations is zero, the average of these deviations must also be zero, which means the mean deviation in every case will be zero. Take, for example, the following set of readings:

2, 5, 4, 6, 8

$$\text{The mean value of these readings} = \frac{2+5+4+6+8}{5} = 5$$

The deviations of individual readings from the mean value are given in Table F:

Table F

Reading	Deviations (Reading – Mean value)
2	2 – 5 = – 3
5	5 – 5 = 0
4	4 – 5 = – 1
6	6 – 5 = + 1
8	8 – 5 = + 3

$$\text{Mean deviation} = \frac{\text{Sum of all deviations}}{\text{No. of readings}}$$

$$= \frac{-3+0-1+1+3}{5}$$

$$= 0$$

This difficulty can be overcome by ignoring the sign, and taking into account only the numerical value of each reading while calculating the mean deviation. Thus, mean deviation is defined as mean of all deviations taken as positive. Therefore, the mean deviation for the above set of readings is given by:

$$\text{Mean deviation} = \frac{3+0+1+1+3}{5} = \frac{8}{5}$$

$$7 = 1.6$$

The mean deviation calculated as above is a measure of dispersion in which every reading in the set is given due weightage. However, this mean deviation cannot be further treated mathematically, since the algebraic signs have been ignored. On account of this limitation, this expression is rarely used in quality control application.

STANDARD DEVIATION

Another measure of dispersion or variation, which takes into account all the values in a set, is Standard Deviation. This is defined as the square root of the average of the squared deviation from the mean value of the set. Sample standard deviation is generally represented by the symbol σ (small sigma) and its formula can be written as:

$$\sigma = \sqrt{\frac{(X_1 - X)^2 + (X_2 - X)^2 + (X_3 - X)^2 \ldots\ldots..(X_n - X)^2}{n}} \qquad \ldots(1)$$

where

$X_1, X_2, X_3 \ldots\ldots X_n$ are the values of individual readings in the set.

$\bar{X}$ is the mean value of all the readings in the set.

n is the number of readings in the set.

For the set of six readings, 5, 3, 5, 9, 3, 5 whose mean value is 5 the standard deviation can be obtained as follows:

$$\sigma = \sqrt{\frac{(5-5)^2 + (3-5)^2 + (5-5)^2 + (9-5)^2 + (3-5)^2 + (5-5)^2}{6}}$$

$$\sigma = \sqrt{\frac{(0)^2 + (-2)^2 + (0)^2 + (4)^2 + (-2)^2 + (0)^2}{6}}$$

$$\sigma = \sqrt{\frac{0+4+0+16+4+0}{6}}$$

$$\sigma = \sqrt{4} = 2$$

The formula for standard deviation given in (1) above can also be written as shown, which often makes calculations easier:

$$\sigma = \sqrt{\frac{\Sigma X^2}{n} - (X)^2} \quad \text{or} \quad \sqrt{\frac{1}{n}\left[\Sigma X^2 \frac{(\Sigma X)^2}{n}\right]}$$

...(2)

X represents various values of readings.

$\bar{X}$ is the mean value.

where n is the number of readings.

Σ is the symbol of summation.

Applying this formula for the set of readings given in the above example, the standard deviation is given below:

$$\sigma = \sqrt{\left(\frac{5^2 + 3^2 + 5^2 + 9^2 + 3^2 + 5^2}{6}\right) - (5)^2}$$

$$\sigma = \sqrt{\left(\frac{25 + 9 + 25 + 81 + 9 + 25}{6}\right) - 25}$$

$$\sigma = \sqrt{29 - 25}$$

$$\sigma = 2$$

This is also called sample standard deviation because this is calculated from value the sample.

If the above observations are considered a sample form a lot, then to obtain an 'unbiased' estimate of σ for the lot multiply above standard deviation by $\sqrt{\frac{n}{n-1}}$.

SIMPLIFICATION OF CALCULATIONS

Methods of calculation of standard deviation discussed above, although quite simple, are rather tedious and time-consuming, particularly where there are large numbers of readings in the data whose values contain many digits. Imagine applying the above formula to the data containing figures such as 379.65, 391.56, 403.81, etc. The squares of these values will be still larger figures and the calculations may become extremely difficult. In actual practice, special electronic calculators for quality control purposes are available. In these calculators, various statistical characteristics, such as mean, standard deviation and other parameters can be quickly determined by feeding the basic data.

23

Normal Distribution

We have seen in the last chapter that variation in industrial products is due to various causes such as machine or process characteristics, tools, materials–and, of course, the skill of the operator. When these factors are acting in a random manner, a particular frequency distribution is obtained, which is called NORMAL DISTRIBUTION. Frequency distributions approaching Normal Distribution occur most often, not only in the industrial field, but also in all other situations where chance is the sole determining factor. Much of the industrial statistics are based on this distribution. A curve signifying Normal Distribution is shown in Fig. 1. Without going into its mathematical equation, we can describe the Unimodal Normal Distribution Curve by the following general characteristics:

(a) Maximum ordinate of the frequency is at the centre of the distribution, that is, at the arithmetic mean.

(b) The distribution is symmetrical about mean and bell-shaped.

(c) Mean, Mode and Median of the distribution coincide.

(d) Points of inflection (where the curve changes from convex to concave or vice versa) are at a distance of one standard deviation from the mean.

(e) Theoretically, the curve extends to infinity in both directions, but, for practical purposes, it can be considered to join the 'X' axis at a distance of three standard deviations from the mean on both sides.

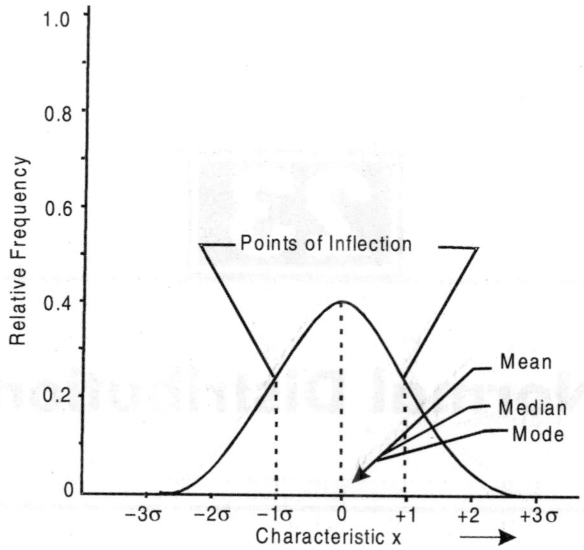

Fig. 1

'X' and 'Y' coordinates of the Normal Relative Frequency Distribution Curve are given in Table A:

Table A

X (In terms of standard deviation)	*Y (Relative frequency)*
− 3.0 σ	0.0044
− 2.5 σ	0.0175
− 2.0 σ	0.0540
− 1.5 σ	0.1295
− 1.0 σ	0.2420
− 0.5 σ	0.3521
0 (*i.e.* mean)	0.3989
+ 0.5 σ	0.3521
+ 1.0 σ	0.2420
+ 1.5 σ	0.1295
+ 2.0 σ	0.0541
+ 2.5 σ	0.0175
+ 3.0 σ	0.0044

RELATIONSHIP OF AREA AND DISPERSION OF A NORMAL CURVE

We have seen in the earlier chapter that the area under the curve between any two limits is proportional to the frequency of occurrence or relative frequency. For the normal distribution, a very important relationship exists between the spread of the distribution and the area under the curve. When the spread is expressed in terms of the standard deviation, the relationship between the spread and the area under the curve is given in Table B*. For instance, the area under the curve from the mean value up to one standard deviation as seen from Table B is 0.34134 or 0.341 approximately. This means that 0.341 or 34.1% of the total area under the entire curve falls in this region as shown in Fig. 10.2. Since the area represents the relative frequency of occurrence of values in the set, it means that 34.1% of all the readings in the data fall in this region. If the region extends 1.0 σ on both sides of the mean value, the area in the region will be 2×34.1 or 68.2% of the total area. In other words, 68.2% of all the readings will be in the region $\pm 1\sigma$ from the mean value. The remaining 31.8% readings will be spread over in two regions -1σ to -3σ and $+1\sigma$ to -3σ.

Table B: Area under Normal Curve

Distance X from the mean value in terms of standard deviation	*Area under curve from the mean up to X*
0.0 σ	0.00000
0.5 σ	0.19146
1.0 σ	0.34134
1.5 σ	0.43319
2.0 σ	0.47725
2.5 σ	0.49379
3.0 σ	0.49865

*The enlarged table of areas under the normal curve is given in Appendix 'A' of this Chapter.

It can be seen from Table B that 0.49865 or 49.865% of all the readings will fall in the region between the mean value and 3σ on one side. In other words, (2 × 0.49865) or 99.7% of all the readings will fall within $\pm 3\sigma$ from the mean value. Thus, only 0.3% or 3 readings out of 1,000 are likely to fall outside these limits. Therefore, for all practical purposes, maximum dispersion can be taken to be $\pm 3\sigma$ or a total of 6σ. Table B is extremely useful in estimating the percentage of values which are likely to fall within a particular zone of variation, when the mean value and the standard deviations are known. For example, let us suppose that the drawing limits for a particular linear dimension of a part are 55 mm and 62 mm.

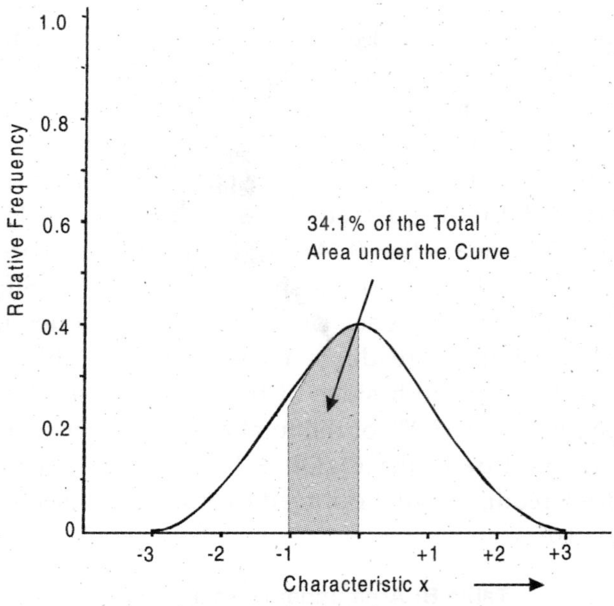

Fig. 2

The measurement of a sample of parts shows that the mean value is 58 mm, and the standard deviation of the measurement is 2 mm. Assuming that the sample represents the bulk, the percentage of the parts which are likely to be within the acceptable limits, can be estimated as follows:

The deviation of lower limit from the mean value is 58–55 = 3 mm. This deviation in terms of standard deviation (which is 2 mm) is equal to 3/2 or 1.5 σ. Assuming the distribution to be normal, the proportion of the area under the curve from the mean value up to 1.5 σ as seen from Table 8, is 0.43319 or approximately 0.433. Similarly the deviation of the upper limit from the mean value in terms of standard deviation is:

$\frac{62-58}{2} = 2\sigma$ The proportion of area under the curve from the mean up to 2 σ, as found from Table B, is 0.47725 or approximately 0.477. The proportion of the total area under the curve from 55 mm to 62 mm

= 0.433 + 0.477.

= 0.910 mm

This means that 91% of the parts are likely to be within the acceptable limits.

GRAPHICAL TREATMENT OF FREQUENCY DISTRIBUTION

So far we have learnt the mathematical analysis of frequency distribution and the determination of statistics like mean and standard deviation. Now we will see how these statistics can also be obtained by graphical methods.

To those who are not familiar with the graphs, it may take a little time to grasp the subject, but once there are understood, the application of graphical methods is extremely easy and has the advantage of avoiding tedious mathematical calculations.

CUMULATIVE FREQUENCY DISTRIBUTION

As we have seen in the previous chapter, frequency distribution is usually presented in the form of a graph where the 'X' axis represents quality characteristic and 'Y' axis represents the frequency of occurrence. Suppose the frequency distribution of inner diameter of a batch of bearings is as given in Table C. The graphical representation of this distribution is shown in Fig.3. Another graphical representation of the same data is by presenting it in a cumulative form which is best explained by an example. Using data given in Table C, cumulative frequency distribution is shown in Table D. In this table, the cumulative frequency of occurrence shown in column 3 means the cumulative number of readings which have occurred in all the previous classes.

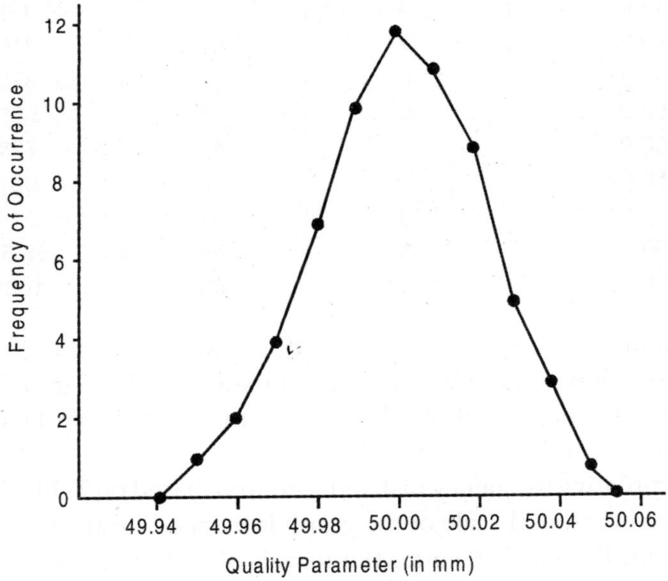

Fig. 3

Table C: Frequency Distribution

Diameter (in mm)	*Number of bearings*
49.95	1
49.96	2

Contd....

49.97	4
49.98	7
49.99	10
50.00	12
50.01	11
50.02	9
50.03	5
50.04	3
50.05	1

Table D: Cumulative Frequency Distribution

Bore dia. (in mm)	*Frequency of occurrence*	*Cumulative occurrence*	*Percentage of cumulative occurrence*
49.95	1	1	1.5%
49.96	2	3	4.5%
49.97	4	7	11.0%
49.98	7	14	21%
49.99	10	24	37%
50.00	12	36	55%
50.01	11	47	72%
50.02	9	56	86%
50.03	5	61	94%
50.04	3	64	98.5%
50.05	1	65	100%

For instance, against 49.97 mm bore diameter, the cumulative occurrence is shown as 7, which includes 1 reading of 49.95 mm, 2 readings of 49.96 and 4 readings of 49.97 mm. Column 4 in Table D shows the percentage of cumulative occurrence.

The cumulative frequency distribution curve based on Table D is shown in Fig.4. The horizontal scale of the graph is marked for the bore diameter readings from 49.94 to 50.06 mm, at intervals of 0.01 mm. The vertical scale is graduated for the cumulative percentage of readings. The percentage of readings falling up to a certain value is plotted against that value.

For example, the total number of readings from the lowest up to 49.98 mm are 14. The percentage of these readings to the total of 65 readings comes to 21. Thus over 49.98 on the horizontal scale, a point is plotted which represents 21 % on the vertical scale. Similarly, all other values of the percentage cumulative occurrence are plotted on the graph. If all these points are joined, we get an 'S' shaped curve shown in Fig.4. Any point on this curve gives the percentages of total readings which occur up to the value shown on the horizontal scale vertically below that point. This form of graphical representation is particularly useful in determining the median of a distribution. It will be recalled that the median is that value which has an equal number of readings on either side if arranged in order of their magnitude. In the cumulative distribution curve, the median can be determined from the point where the 50% cumulative occurrence line cuts the curve. The value on the horizontal scale vertically below this point represents the median of the distribution. From this curve, the median of the distribution is found to be approximately 50.00 mm.

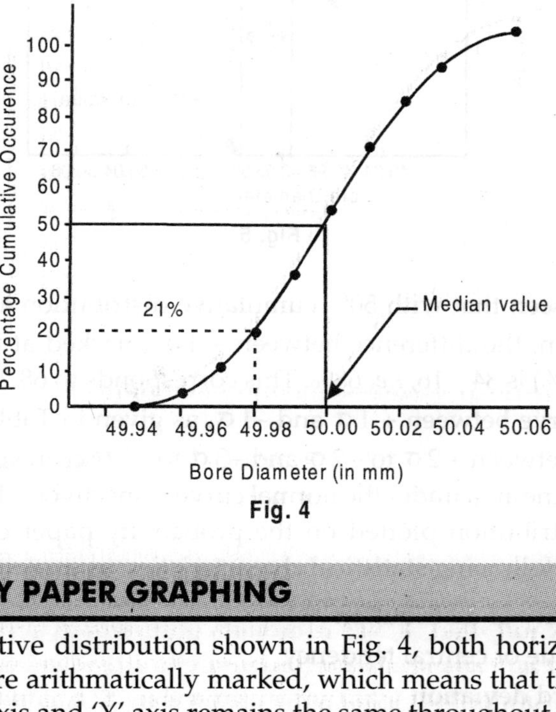

Fig. 4

PROBABILITY PAPER GRAPHING

In the cumulative distribution shown in Fig. 4, both horizontal and the vertical axes are arithmatically marked, which means that the scale of the graph for 'X' axis and 'Y' axis remains the same throughout the graph. For example, if 10 mm represents 10% frequency distribution, the distance between 10% and 20% points or 30% and 40% will be the same, *i.e.* 10 mm. A slightly different graphing technique involves use of the probability paper, where the scale representing the quality characteristic on the 'X' axis is the same as in arithmatically marked graph, but the scale representing the cumulative percentage of occurrence on the 'Y' axis is differently marked. The marking of this scale is so designed that a normal distribution will give a straight line rather than as 'S' - shaped curve. A probability paper is shown in the Fig.5 from which it will be seen that the space representing interval of 10% in the vertical scale is much less in the middle than at the top and bottom. The vertical scale of the probability paper is used to represent cumulative percentage of distribution, and the horizontal scale to represent the quality characteristic of the product. Plus one sigma (+ 1 σ) and minus one sigma (- 1 σ), the limits are also generally marked on the vertical scale.

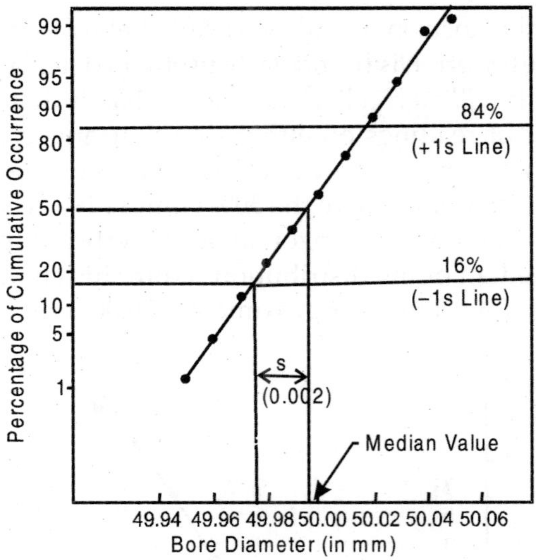

Fig. 5

It will be seen that with 50% cumulative distribution as the centre of the distribution, the difference between + 1 σ (marked at 84%) and –1 σ (marked at 16%) is 84 – 16, *i.e.* 68%. This corresponds to 68.27% area under the normal curve between + 1 σ and –1 σ, as given in Table C. Similarly, the intervals between + 2 σ to – 2 σ and +3 σ to – 3 σ correspond to 95.45% and 99.73% of the area under the normal curve respectively. The cumulative frequency distribution plotted on the probability paper can be used to determine the following statistical characteristics, as explained below:

(a) Normality of distribution
(b) The value of central tendency
(c) Standard deviation

DETERMINATION OF NORMALITY

The determination of normality of a curve is illustrated by the analysis of cumulative distribution curve based on data in Table C. Plotting the cumulative percentages from Table C on the probability paper, we get 11 points on the graphs shown in Fig.5. Now, we have to fit a curve to these points. It will be seen that the points against 4% to 98% on the vertical scale are approximately in a straight line. The criterion for normality which is generally followed in quality control applications is that if the points between 5% and 95% of the distribution are approximately in a straight line, the distribution can be considered to be normal. Based on this cirterion, the distribution given in Table C can be taken to be normal.

DETERMINATION OF MEDIAN AND MEAN

As in the case of cumulative distribution on an arithmatically marked graph, the Median can be determined from the point where the distribution curve cuts the 50% line. In case the distribution is normal, the Median will also be the Mean of the distribution. If however, the graph is substantially curved, the Mean will be different. To find the Mean in such cases, a straight line should be drawn between the points on the curve where it cuts the +1σ and –1 σ lines. The point where this straight line crosses the 5% mark corresponds to the Mean, the value of which can be read from the horizontal scale. In this case, since the graph is a straight line, both the Median and the Mean are given by point M whose value on the horizontal is 49.998 mm, or approximately 50.00 mm.

DETERMINATION OF STANDARD DEVIATION

The standard deviation of the distribution can be obtained by noting the readings on the horizontal scale between the points where the curve crosses 50% mark and +1 σ line or between 50% and –1 σ line. In this case, it is found to be approximately .02 mm. Thus, it can be seen that graphical techniques, particularly using the probability paper, provide a much simpler method of analysing frequency distribution for solution of quality problems.

OTHER FREQUENCY DISTRIBUTIONS

The discussion so far has been generally confined to the so-called normal frequency distribution. Although distributions approaching the normal curve do occur more often, the reader should not get the impression that other forms do not exist. Actually, there are a number of situations where distributions other than normal are met, and any quality engineer must know how to deal with them. We have seen earlier that the normal distribution occurs where only chance causes are acting. There are also occasions, when one or more factors predominate and influence the shape of the frequency distribution curve. Non-normal shapes of frequency distribution which are generally met in the industrial situations are shown in Fig.6 which include -

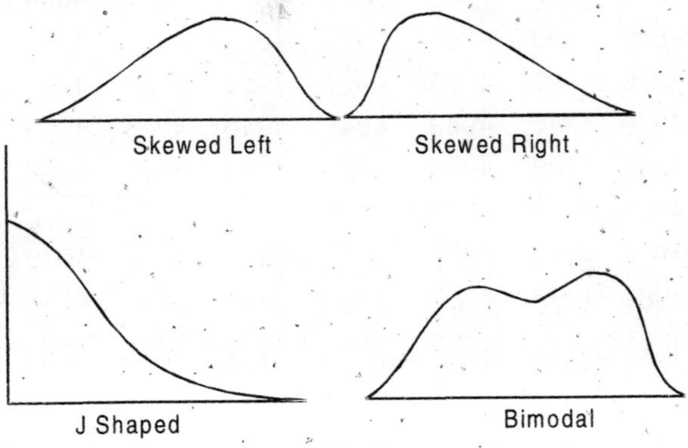

Fig. 6

APPENDIX -A

Z = DEVIATION FROM THE MEAN VALUE
EXPRESSED IN TERMS OF STANDARD DEVIATION

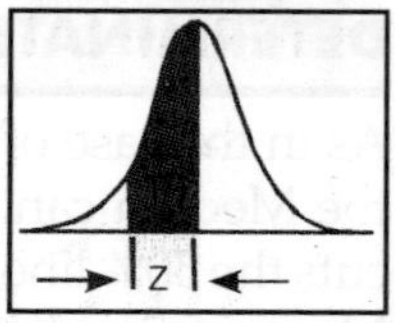

AREA UNDER NORMAL CURVE

z	.00	.01	.02	.03	.04	.05	.06	.07	.08	.09
0.0	.0000	.0040	.0080	.0120	.0160	.0199	.0239	.0279	.0319	.0359
0.1	.0398	.0438	.0478	.0517	.0557	.0596	.0636	.0675	.0714	.0753
0.2	.0793	.0832	.0871	.0910	.0948	.0987	.1026	.1064	.1103	.1140
0.3	.1179	.1217	.1255	.1293	.1331	.1368	.1406	.1443	.1480	.1517
0.4	.1554	.1591	.1628	.1664	.1700	.1736	.1772	.1808	.1844	.1879
0.5	.1915	.1950	.1985	.2019	.2054	.2088	.2123	.2157	.2190	.2224
0.6	.2257	.2291	.2324	.2357	.2389	.2422	.2454	.2486	.2517	.2549
0.7	.2580	.2611	.2642	.2673	.2704	.2734	.2764	.2794	.2823	.2852
0.8	.2881	.2910	.2939	.2967	.2995	.3023	.3051	.3078	.3106	.3133
0.9	.3159	.3186	.3212	.3238	.3264	.3289	.3315	.3340	.3365	.3389
1.0	.3413	.3438	.3461	.3485	.3508	.3531	.3554	.3577	.3599	.3621
1.1	.3643	.3665	.3686	.3708	.3729	.3749	.3770	.3790	.3810	.3830
1.2	.3849	.3869	.3888	.3907	.3925	.3944	.3962	.3980	.3997	.4015
1.3	.4032	.4049	.4066	.4082	.4099	.4115	.4131	.4147	.4162	.4177
1.4	.4192	.4207	.4222	.4236	.4251	.4265	.4279	.4292	.4306	.4319
1.5	.4332	.4345	.4357	.4370	.4382	.4394	.4406	.4418	.4429	.4441
1.6	.4452	.4463	.4474	.4484	.4495	.4505	.4515	.4525	.4535	.4545
1.7	.4555	.4564	.4573	.4582	.4591	.4599	.4608	.4616	.4625	.4633
1.8	.4641	.4649	.4656	.4664	.4671	.4678	.4686	.4693	.4699	.4706
1.9	.4713	.4719	.4729	.4732	.4738	.4744	.4750	.4756	.4761	.4767
2.0	.4772	.4778	.4783	.4788	.4793	.4798	.4803	.4808	.4812	.4817
2.1	.4821	.4826	.4830	.4834	.4838	.4842	.4846	.4850	.4854	.4857
2.2	.4861	.4864	.4868	.4871	.4875	.4878	.4881	.4884	.4887	.4890
2.3	.4893	.4896	.4898	.4901	.4904	.4906	.4909	.4911	.4913	.4916
2.4	.4918	.4920	.4922	.4925	.4927	.4929	.4931	.4932	.4934	.4936
2.5	.4938	.4940	.4941	.4943	.4945	.4946	.4948	.4949	.4951	.4952
2.6	.4953	.4955	.4956	.4957	.4959	.4960	.4961	.4962	.4963	.4964
2.7	.4965	.4966	.4967	.4968	.4969	.4970	.4971	.4972	.4973	.4974
2.8	.4974	.4975	.4976	.4977	.4977	.4978	.4979	.4979	.4980	.4981
2.9	.4981	.4982	.4982	.4983	.4984	.4984	.4985	.4986	.4986	.4986
3.0	.4987	.4987	.4987	.4988	.4988	.4989	.4989	.4989	.4990	.4990

Non-normal frequency distribution can be utilized as much for drawing meaningful deductions about the quality characteristic of the product, as normal distributions. The mathematical treatment of the distribution for calculating the mean value and standard deviation applies to all the shapes of frequency distribution. It is only the relationship of these statistical characteristics with the shape of the curve and their interpretation which is different. As already mentioned, the most widespread use of frequency distribution is as a picture of data to see the spread and the central value. For this purpose, all the shapes are equally convenient. Sometimes, non-normal distribution is caused by a factor which can be identified and eliminated. In other cases, the distorting cause cannot be detected and the distribution is accepted as the inherent feature of the process. For example, moderately skewed distribution is considered usual for powdered metal processes.

24

Theory of Probability

Probability is a term which indicates the likelihood of occurrence of an event in the future. All those who have participated in gambling or other games of chance, know that while betting they think of the odds, or their chances of winning. Although they may not be aware of it, they are, in fact, dealing with probability. Therefore, it is not surprising that the theory of probability owes a lot to the casinos of Europe for its initial development. The theory of probability is of great importance to industrial managers, as most of the statistical techniques for management decision-making and quality control are based on this theory. Therefore, clear understanding of the concept of probability is essential for the study of modern quality control methods.

Consider the simple case of the toss of a perfect coin. When a coin is tossed, there is as much a chance of a head coming up as a tail. If the coin is tossed only a few times, it is possible that the heads may occur more often than the tails, or vice versa. But if we consider a large number of tries, the incidence of occurrence of the heads will be almost equal to that of the tails. In terms of probability, the chance of getting a head or tail in any try can be expressed as having a probability of ½ or 0.5.

Probability, in general, can be considered as a measure of the likelihood of occurrence of an event and is designated by a number between 0 and 1. A probability of zero refers to that event, which cannot take place at all. For instance, in the case of the toss of a coin, we know that both a head and a tail cannot come up at the same time, for it will be either a head or a tail.

Thus, the probability of occurrence of both head and tail simultaneously can be taken to be zero. On the other hand, a probability of 1 is associated with the total certainty of occurrence of an event. The numbers between 0 and 1 indicate varying degrees of likelihood of occurrence of an event. Now, we can define the probability in general terms as given below:

If an event can occur in N mutually exclusive and equally likely ways and if M of these possesses a characteristic A, then the probability occurrence of A is the fraction $\frac{M}{N}$.

Probability given in the above definition is customarily written as,

$$P(A) = \frac{M}{N}$$

The term "mutually exclusive" in the above definition requires some explanation. Mutually exclusive means that all the N ways in which an event can occur are different from each other and the event cannot occur in more than one ways at a time. For example, in a six-sided dice marked with numbers 1 to 6, only one face can come up at a time. Thus, a dice can fall in six different ways which are mutually exclusive.

DETERMINATION OF PROBABILITY

It is clear from the definition given above that to determine the probability of a particular event, it is first necessary to know, in how many different ways the event can be possible. For example, let us take the case of a box which contains ten balls, out of which eight are white and two are red. Now, if one ball is picked up without looking in the box, what is the probability of a red ball being picked up? There are a total of ten balls, and any one of these is equally likely to be picked up. Thus, we get N = 10. Two of the ten balls have a common characteristic in the sense that they are red in colour. If any one of these two balls is picked up, we will have met our requirement of having picked up a red ball. Thus, M = 2.

According to the definition, the probability of a red ball being picked up in one try is given by

$$P(A) = \frac{M}{N}$$

$$\text{or} \quad P(\text{red}) = \frac{2}{10} = 0.02$$

Taking another example of a six-sided fair dice, any one of the six faces is equally likely to come up when it is thrown, thus N = 6. Further, as all the six faces of the dice are different, M = 1.

The probability of any particular face coming up is given by, $P = \frac{M}{N} = \frac{1}{6}$ or 0.166 (approx).

PROBABILITY AND FREQUENCY DISTRIBUTION

The definition of probability discussed above implies that, the total number of events, and those with a particular characteristic are exactly known. In actual industrial situations, this is hardly the case. Quality Control staff is often required to estimate the likelihood of occurrence of defects in an equipment or a batch of articles. In such cases, the total number of articles may be known, but the exact number of defectives are obviously not known. Otherwise, there would be no need to make an estimate. In other situations, an estimate may be required regarding the likelihood of production of defective pieces by a particular machine. Here, even the total number of pieces involved is not known, since they are still to be produced. In such situations, the definition of probability discussed above is not of much use, and a different approach is required to determine the probability. In these circumstances, we must estimate the proportion of events or objects with a particular characteristic and the total number of events or objects. This can be done by repeated trials of events or drawing random samples from the lot and ascertaining the number of pieces with the particular characteristic, whose probability is to be determined. Then, we can use the following definitions of Probability:

If an event has been tried or an object drawn n times, and in F_A of these, the event or object *A* did occur, then the probability of event A is $P(A) = \frac{F_A}{n}$.

From the above definition, it will be seen that F_A is, in fact, the frequency of occurrence and $\frac{F_A}{n}$ is a Relative Frequency. For this reason, this definition is also called Relative Frequency definition of probability. The use of this definition of probability is illustrated by the following example. The recent data on the occurrence of defects in the TV sets coming out of assembly line, based on the inspection record of the last 100 sets is given in Table A. The question of continuing 100% final inspection or to switch over to sampling inspection is under consideration. Before a decision is taken, the management requires to know the probability of getting TV sets with no defects.

Table A

Number of defects	*Frequency of occurrence*
0	62
1	27
2	6
3	3
4	1
5	1
Total	**100**

From the definition of probability discussed above, probability of occurrence of zero defects is given by

$$P_{(o)} = \frac{F_o}{n}$$

Where F_o is the frequency of occurrence of zero defects, 'n' is the number of objects (in this case TV sets).

From the data given in Table A.

$$F_o = 62$$
$$n = 100$$

Substituting values of F_o and n,

$$P_{(o)} = \frac{62}{100} = 0.62$$

Thus the probability of getting TV sets without any defect is 0.62 or 62%.

PROBABILITY OF VALUE IN A SPECIFIED RANGE

Relative frequency definition of probability can also be used for making an estimate of probability of getting a value within a specified range, in the case of continuous data. For this, we must first obtain frequency distribution of the characteristic whose probability is required, by random sampling as discussed in detail in Chapter IX. For continuous data, the definition of probability takes a slightly different form as given below:

$$Px_1 - x_2 = \frac{\text{Area between } x_1 \text{ and } x_2}{\text{Total Area under Frequency Distribution Curve.}}$$

Where $Px_1 - x_2$ is the probability of occurrence of characteristics between the range x_1, to x_2

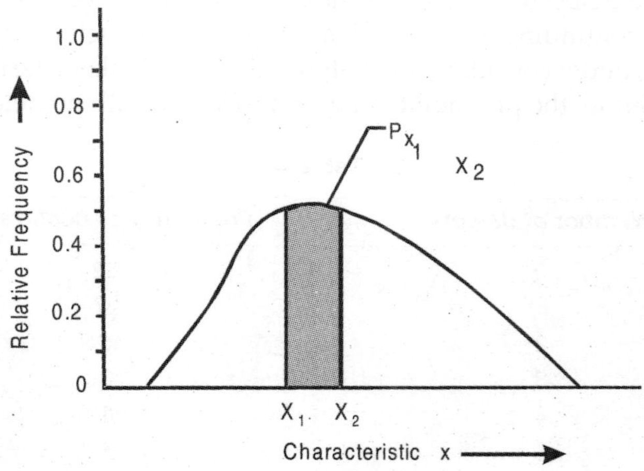

Fig. 1

We have seen in the last chapter that for Relative Frequency Distribution, the total area under the curve is always 1. Hence for Relative Frequency Distribution, probability is given by, $Px_1 - x_2$ = Fraction, of area under the curve between x_1 and x_2. This is illustrated in Fig.1. It may be noted that for probability estimates of the quality of products still to be manufactured, the above relation is valid only if the frequency distribution remains stable, *i.e.* the process conditions do not change materially. However, this relation holds good for any shape of the frequency distribution, provided it has been obtained by a fairly large sample.

PROBABILITY THEOREMS

We have so far discussed the probability of an individual event, whereas in industrial situations we are often concerned with multiple events. The probability of such events can be determined by the application of two basic theorems of probability, which are explained below:

Theorem I

Addition of Probabilities

This theorem states that if the individual probabilities of two or more mutually exclusive events are known, the probability of occurrence of any one of these is given by the sum of the individual probabilities. For instance, in the case of dice, we know that the individual probability of any of the faces is 1/6. Let us suppose that a person playing dice has bet on number 2, as well as 3, which means that he will win if either 2 or 3 comes up. To find the probability of his winning, we have to add the individual probabilities of 2 and 3.

Probability of 2 coming up, *i.e.* $P(2) = \frac{1}{6}$

Probability of 3 coming up, *i.e.* $P(3) = \frac{1}{6}$

Probability of 2 or 3 coming up

$$= P(2) + P(3) = \frac{1}{6} + \frac{1}{6} = \frac{1}{3}$$

Thus, probability of his winning = $\frac{1}{3}$ or .333 (approx.)

To illustrate its application in industrial situations, let us suppose that in the case of TV sets assembly plant discussed earlier, we want to know the probability of finding less than two defects in TV sets after assembly. This in other words, means that we have to determine the probability of occurrence of zero or one defect in TV sets. On the basis of the theorem discussed above, this is given by,

P (0 or 1) = P (0) + P (1).

From the frequency distribution given in Table A,

$$P(0) = \frac{62}{100} = 0.62$$

$$P(1) = \frac{27}{100} = 0.27$$

$$P(0 \text{ or } 1) = 0.62 + 0.27$$
$$= 0.89$$

Thus, the probability of finding less than two defects in the TV sets is 89%.

Theorem II

Multiplication of Probabilities

According to the multiplication law of probability, the probability of a joint event is given by the product of the probabilities of the individual independent elements of the joint event.

This again can be illustrated by the dice example. Let us suppose two dice are thrown simultaneously. What is the probability that the face marked 2 will come up on both the dice. We know the individual probability of occurrence of 2 in a fair dice is 1/6. The probability (P_m) of 2 occurring on both the dice is given by,

$$P_m = P(2) \times P(2) = \frac{1}{6} \times \frac{1}{6} = \frac{1}{36}$$

To take another example, let us suppose, the probability of an engine failure in a particular twin-engined aircraft, within the first 1,000 hours of the run is .02. The probability $P(f)$ of both its engines failing within the first 1,000 hours is given by,

$$P(f) = .02 \times 0.2 = 0.0004.$$

It should be noted that since the probability figures (which are always less than 1) are multiplied, the probability of a joint event is always less than the probability of an individual element of joint event.

25

Control Charts

A Control Chart is a statistical technique for controlling the quality of a product being manufactured. It was first devised by Dr. Walter A. Shewhart after whose name these charts are also called Shewhart charts. In a relatively short period, this technique of quality control has found wide acceptance, particularly in the USA and Europe. The main advantage of a control chart is that it can predict the rejects when they are likely to occur, which enables corrective action to be taken before a defective product is actually produced.

THEORY OF CONTROL CHARTS

It is recognised that certain variations in the quality of any product will always occur, however much we may try to hold the production conditions alike. As we have discussed in the earlier chapter, these variations are the result of a number of causes acting in a random manner and are an inherent feature of any process. There are other variations which result from a few (often only one or two) unusual causes which can be identified. These latter variations can be eliminated by removing the assignable causative factors. We have seen earlier that the variations due to random causes follow a set pattern given by the normal curve, whereby the behaviour of the variation can be predicted. When the variations in the quality of a product follow this pattern, the process is deemed to be under statistical control. When the pattern of variation is disturbed, it can be taken as an indication that some factor other than chance is at work. This state of process is termed as an out-of-control condition and efforts are made to identify and eliminate the assignable cause to bring the process again under control.

We have seen that for all practical purposes, the maximum variation in the quality characteristic is $\pm 3\,\sigma$, provided the distribution is normal. In other words, when the process is under control, the variation in the characteristic of a product should not exceed $\pm 3\,\sigma$ from the mean value. Let us consider a graph such as shown in Fig.1, where the vertical axis represents the variation in the quality characteristic and the horizontal axis represents the order of articles produced. Of the three horizontal lines, the middle line represents the mean value and the upper and the lower ones signify $+3\,\sigma$ and $-3\,\sigma$, respectively. Now, if the measurements of the quality characteristic of the articles produced are plotted on this graph, the upper and lower lines can be used as the limits for control. As long as the plotted points remain within the limit lines, the process can be considered under control.

If a point falls outside the limit lines, it can be taken as an indication that the process is out of control. This, in essence, is the basic principle of the control charts.

In actual practice, however, it is found that the plotting of points for individual observations does not reveal the trend of variations effectively and the chart gets cluttered. In actual control chart applications, observations or measurements are taken on samples comprising of four or five consecutively processed articles each, drawn from the production run at regular intervals. Instead of plotting a point for each observation, one point is plotted for each sample which represents the average value in the sample. The control limits are also fixed accordingly, for the sample averages. The process is deemed to be under control as long as the points representing sample averages remain within the control limits, and conform to the predicted normal pattern over time.

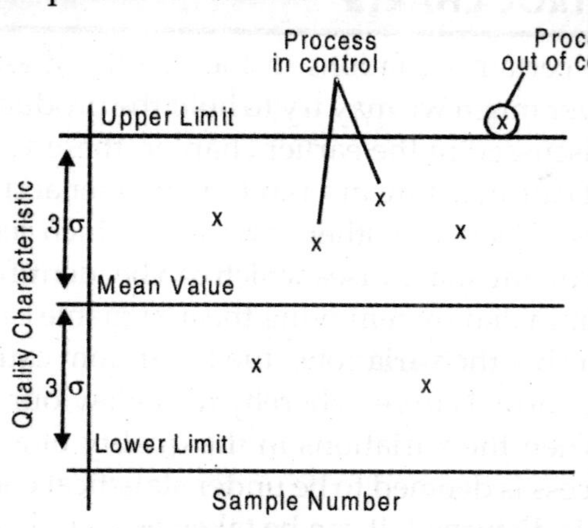

Fig. 1: Principle of Control Charts

CONTROL CHARTS FOR MEASUREMENTS

We have seen that the distribution of variable measurement data can be adequately described by two statistical characteristics, namely mean value ($\bar{X}$) and range (R). To control a process generating a particular quality characteristic, its mean value and the range must be controlled. This is achieved by $\bar{X}$ and R control charts. The construction, operation and application of these charts is discussed in this chapter.

RANGE CONTROL CHARTS

Range Control Charts (normally called R-charts) are used to control the range or dispersion of the process. On such a chart, the central line represents the mean range and the ± 3σ lines are used as control limits, which are given by the following formula:

Upper Control Limit (UCL) = $\bar{R} + 3\sigma_r$

Lower Control Limit (LCL) = $\bar{R} - 3\sigma_r$

Where $\begin{cases} \bar{R} \text{ is the mean range of the sample ranges.} \\ \sigma_r \text{ is the standard deviation of the sample ranges.} \end{cases}$

In quality control practice, standard deviation of the sample range (σ_r) is estimated from the mean Range ($\bar{R}$) by using the following relationship:

$$\sigma_r = \frac{d_3}{d_2}\bar{R}$$

Where $\begin{cases} \text{Factors } d_2 \text{ and } d_3 \text{ vary with the number of observation.} \\ \text{in the sample and can be obtained from Table A.} \end{cases}$

Thus, Upper Control Limit can be written as:

$$UCL = \bar{R} + 3\frac{d_3}{d_2}\bar{R}$$

$$= \left(1+3\frac{d_3}{d_2}\right)\bar{R}$$

For ease of calculation, if we set $D_4 = \left(1 + 3\frac{d_3}{d_2}\right)$

we can write

$$UCL- = D_4\bar{R}.$$

In the same way, Lower Control Limit can be written as:

$$LCL = \left(1-\frac{3d_3}{d_2}\right)\bar{R}$$

If $D_3 = \left(1 - \frac{3d_3}{d_2}\right)$, we can write

$$LCL = D_3 \bar{R} .$$

Factors D_3 and D_4 for various values of sample size (n) are given in the following Table A:

Table A

Number of observation in sample	*Factors for computing control limits and process limits*				
n	d_2	d_3	A_2	D_3	D_4
2	1.128	0.853	1.880	0	3.268
3	1.693	0.888	1.023	0	2.574
4	2.059	0.880	0.729	0	2.282
5	2.326	0.864	0.577	0	2.114
6	2.534	0.848	0.483	0	2.004
7	2.704	0.833	0.419	0.076	1.924
8	2.847	0.820	0.373	0.136	1.864
9	2.970	0.808	0.337	0.184	1.816
10	3.078	0.797	0.308	0.223	1.777

$\bar{X}$ Control Chart

An $\bar{x}$ control chart is used to control the central tendency of the process. On such a chart, the central line represents the grand mean ($\bar{\bar{X}}$) of the sample means ($\bar{X}$). The upper and lower control lines represent the 3σ limits for sample means which are given in the following formula:

$$\text{Upper Control Limit (UCL)} = \bar{\bar{X}} + 3\sigma_{\bar{x}}$$

$$\text{Lower Control Limit (LCL)} = \bar{\bar{X}} - 3\sigma_{\bar{x}}$$

Where $\begin{cases} \bar{\bar{X}} \text{ is the grand mean of the sample means.} \\ \sigma_x \text{ is the standard deviation of the sample means.} \end{cases}$

Here, it must be noted that the standard deviation of the sample means is not the same thing as the standard deviation of the measurements of individual pieces. Standard deviation of the sample means can be estimated from the mean Range $(\bar{R})$ by using the following relationship:

$$\sigma_x = \frac{\bar{R}}{d_2\sqrt{n}}$$

Where $\begin{cases} \text{n is the sample size, and} \\ d_2 \text{ can be obtained from Table A.} \end{cases}$

Thus, the upper and lower control limits for the $\bar{X}$ chart can be written as:

$$UCL = \bar{\bar{X}} + \frac{3\bar{R}}{d_2\sqrt{n}}$$

$$LCL = \bar{\bar{X}} - \frac{3\bar{R}}{d_2\sqrt{n}}$$

For ease of calculation, if we set:

$A_2 = \frac{3}{d_2\sqrt{n}}$, then we can write

$$UCL = \bar{\bar{X}} + A_2\bar{R}$$
$$LCL = \bar{\bar{X}} - A_2\bar{R}.$$

Where $\begin{cases} \text{Factor } A_2\text{, for various values of} \\ \text{n can also be obtained from Table A.} \end{cases}$

STANDARD AND HOMOGENEITY OF DATA

Control charts are normally designed on the basis of the observed data. It is important that the data should be homogeneous and accurate and be obtained under stable conditions. Before collecting the data, it should be ensured that the process conditions such as setting, tooling temperature and pressure conditions are standardised to the extent possible. If there are more than one production units or machines, each should be taken as independent process requiring separate control chart. Further, while discussing the general theory of control charts, it was assumed that the quality characteristic to be controlled is normally distributed. To check the validity of this assumption, frequency distribution of the subject characteristic should be analysed. Control chart should be established only if the analysis shows that the frequency distribution is, more or less, normal.

DATA COLLECTION PROCEDURE

The basic information required for construction of control charts is the central tendency or the process mean, and the sample range. To be reliable, these two statistical characteristics must be based on the observations taken on a fairly large number of samples. Although there is no hard and fast rule regarding the exact number of samples which are to be taken into consideration, it is recommended that the mean value and the range must be based on at least 25 samples. The sample size (*i.e.*, the number of observations in each sample) which is employed for control chart work is generally 4 or 5, although, occasionally, a slightly larger sample size may be used. A small sample size is generally preferred, because the range is the reliable measure of dispersion for small samples. In practice, it has been seen that few processes are within control when first investigated. Since the degree of control of the process is not known at the time of construction of the control chart, it is advisable to use a small sample size in which the effect of assignable causes is not significant. Having decided the sample size, the required number of samples should be taken at appropriate intervals. The time interval between the two consecutive observations will generally depend upon the stability of the process. More stable the process over time, the longer the interval.

CONSTRUCTION OF R-CHARTS

We have seen above that the basic data for the construction of $\bar{\square}$ —R charts is the variability of the process which is indicated by the Range. Unless the R-chart shows that the process is under control with respect to the range, no useful purpose will be served by the construction of a chart. The actual procedure for the construction of R-chart is illustrated by the following example:

Let us suppose that control charts are to be introduced for the final machining operation of pins of diameter 6.00 ± .06 mm. Measurements of 25 samples comprising five pins, each are shown in Table B.

To construct R-chart, the range of measurements for each sample should be calculated as shown in Table B.

In Table B the readings of sample no. 1 are:

5.99 mm

5.98 mm

6.01 mm

5.97 mm

6.00 mm

Range (R) = Highest reading — Lowest reading

= 6.01 – 5.97

= .04 mm

Similarly the range for all the samples can be calculated and are shown in R-column in Table B. The average or mean range ($\bar{R}$) for all the 25 samples can be obtained by adding all the sample ranges and dividing the result by the total number of samples. The sum of the samples ranges from Table B, is 0.88 mm.

$$\text{Therefore, } \bar{R} = \frac{.88}{25} = .035 \text{ mm}$$

Table B

Sample no.	Measurements of pin diameter (in mm)					Sum of diameter measurements (in mm)	Mean value of measurements	Range of variation in the sample
	1	2	3	4	5	Total	$\bar{x}$	R
1	5.99	5.98	6.01	5.97	6.00	29.95	5.990	0.04
2	6.01	6.00	5.97	5.99	6.00	29.97	5.994	0.04
3	6.00	5.99	6.00	5.99	5.98	29.96	5.992	0.02
4	5.98	5.99	6.00	5.99	6.01	29.97	5.994	0.03
5	6.02	6.01	6.01	6,00	5.99	30.03	6.006	0.03
6	5.99	6.01	6.00	6.02	6.03	30.05	6.010	0.04
7	6.00	6.01	6.02	6.01	6.03	30.07	6.014	0.03
8	6.01	6.00	6.04	6.02	6.02	30.09	6.018	0.04
9	5.99	5.98	6.00	5.97	6.01	29.95	5.990	0.04
10	6.02	6.01	6.01	6.00	6.02	30.06	6.012	0.02
11	6.01	5.99	6.02	6.00	5.98	30.00	6.000	0.04
12	5.99	5.98	5.99	6.02	6.00	29.98	5.996	0.04
13	5.97	6.02	5.98	6.00	5.99	29.96	5.992	0.05
14	5.98	6.00	6.01	5.99	6.02	30.00	6.000	0.04
15	6.01	6.03	6.00	6.02	6.01	30.02	6.014	0.03
16	6.00	6.02	6.02	6.01	6.04	10.09	6.018	0.04
17	5.98	6.00	6.01	5.99	6.01	29.99	5.998	0.03
18	6.00	6.01	6.00	6.00	6.02	6.00	6.006	0.02
19	6.02	6.01	5.99	6.01	6,02	30.05	6.010	0.03
20	6.01	6.04	6.00	6.01	5.99	30.05	6.010	0.05
21	6.00	6.01	6.03	6.04	6.01	30.09	6.018	0.04
22	6.02	5.99	6.02	6.01	6.02	30.06	6.012	0.03
23	6.01	6.03	6.02	6.04	6.03	30.13	6.026	0.03
24	6.01	6.03	6.02	6.04	6.01	30.11	6.022	0.03
25	6.04	6.01	6.03	5.99	6.02	30.09	6.018	0.05
						Total	150.160	0.88

Thus, the centre line of the R-chart is the line which represents .035 mm.

$$LCL = D_3\bar{R}$$

and $$UCL = D_4\bar{R}$$

In this case, the sample size *n* is 5. The values of D_3 and D_4 in Table A are zero and 2.114, respectively. Since $D_3 = 0$ the Lower Control Limit will also be zero. As it is not possible to get a range less than zero, it is unnecessary to refer to the Lower Control Limit in this particular case. Substituting the value of D_4, we get

$$UCL = 2.114 \times .035 = .074 \text{ mm.}$$

R-chart constructed with these preliminary limits, on which the R values for all the 25 samples have been plotted is shown in Fig.2.

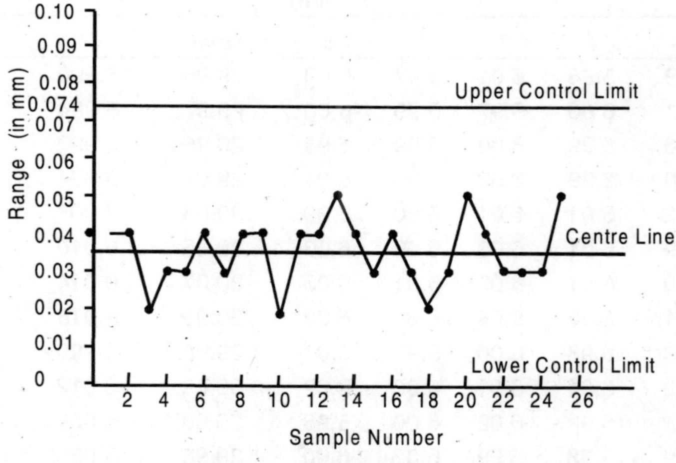

Fig. 2: R-Control Chart

ANALYSIS OF R-CHART

An examination of the R-chart in Fig.2 shows that all the points are within control limits, which indicates that the variability of the process is within control. Sometimes, it may happen that one or two points are tying outside the control limits. In such a case, efforts should be made to trace the cause of excessive variation in that particular sample. In case an assignable cause is found, it should be eliminated and these particular values may be ignored and the control limits should be recalculated. Alternatively, fresh samples may be taken for construction of control charts. Here it should be noted that it is also possible that a point may be outside the control limits even when no assignable cause is present. It will be recalled that the area under the normal curve between $\pm 3\sigma$ of the mean value is 0.997. This means that 99.7% of all the readings are likely to fall within $\pm 3\sigma$ limits or control limits. Thus, it is possible that three readings out of a thousand may fall outside the control limits even when no assignable cause is present. This small risk of occurrence of one odd point beyond the control limits due to chance causes is inherent in the control charts based on 3σ limits and should be kept in view while tracing the causes of points falling outside the control limits. However, in practice, this situation is encountered rarely and control charts with 3σ limits are found quite satisfactory for quality control.

A question may arise in the mind of a keen reader regarding the need for a lower control limit for an R-chart. In fact a lower range indicates less variability, which should be welcome. The reason for having LCL for an R-chart is that under normal conditions, chance causes can account for reduction in range only up to a certain extent, *i.e.* 3σ limits. In case there is a genuine reduction in range, it may be due to assignable cause(s) such as the use of a new material or tool. The management would like to perpetuate the reduction in range by incorporating the causative factors in the process, if economical.

CONSTRUCTION OF $\bar{X}$ CHARTS

When R-Control Chart shows that the process is under control with respect to range, we can proceed with the construction of $\bar{X}$ Control Chart. To construct $\bar{X}$ chart, the mean value ($\bar{X}$) of each sample should be calculated as shown below. The readings of the sample no. 1 shown in Table B are:

5.99 mm
5.98 mm
6.01 mm
5.97 mm
6.00 mm

The sum of these five readings is 29.95mm. The mean value $\bar{X}$ can be found by dividing the sum of the readings in the sample by the number of readings.

or $$\bar{X} = \frac{29.95}{5} = 5.99 \text{ mm.}$$

Similarly $\bar{X}$ for all samples can be calculated whose values are shown in $\bar{X}$ row of Table B. The overall mean or the grand mean ($\bar{\bar{X}}$) can be obtained by dividing the sum of all the 25 means (*i.e.* 150.160), by the number of samples.

Thus $$\bar{\bar{X}} = \frac{150.160}{25} = 6.006 \text{ mm}$$

Therefore, the centre line of the $\bar{X}$ chart is given by the line which represents 6.006 mm. We have already seen that,

$$UCL = \bar{X}+A_2\bar{R}$$

$$LCL = \bar{X}-A_2\bar{R}$$

Where $\left\{\begin{array}{l}A_2 \text{ is factor depending upon the sample} \\ \text{size and can be obtained from Table A.}\end{array}\right.$

Since the sample size *n* is 5, the value of A, from Table (A) is found to be 0.577. Substituting the values of $\bar{\bar{X}}$, A_2 and R as already determined, the following control limits are obtained:

$$UCL = 6.006 + .577 \times .035$$
$$= 6.026 \text{ mm}$$
$$CL = 6.006$$
$$LCL = 6.006 - .577 \times .035$$
$$= 5.986 \text{ mm}$$

$\bar{X}$ chart with 25 values of $\bar{X}$ plotted on it, is shown in Fig. 3.

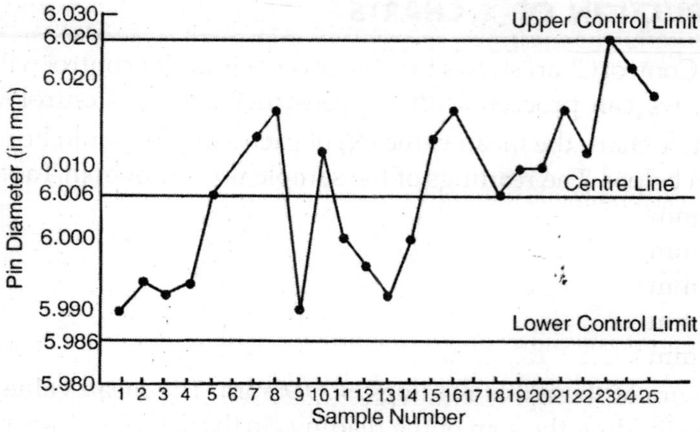

Fig. 3: Control Chart

Analysis of $\bar{X}$ Charts

The inspection of $\bar{X}$ chart in Fig. 3 shows that none of the plotted points is outside the control limits, which indicates that the process is within control even with respect to the mean value of the diameter of the pins. The examination of the control chart should not be confined to looking for the points lying outside the control limits. Even the points lying within the control limits can provide valuable information about the behaviour of the process. For example, there may be concentration of points on one side of the centre line, which indicates that the process centre has shifted. Therefore, in addition to looking for points outside the control limits, the following criteria can be used to detect out of control situation:

(a) 7 successive points lying on one side of the centre line.
(b) In any 11 consecutive points, 10 points lying on one side of the centre line.
(c) In any 14 points 11 or more points lying on one side of the centre line.
(d) Any obvious increasing or decreasing trend.

Let us apply the above criteria to control chart shown in Fig. 3. It will be seen that all the last 10 points are lying in the upper half of the control chart. Also the first 7 points and last 10 points show marked increasing trend. Thus, judged from the criteria, the process considered out of control, showing potential for improvement.

This is also borne out by the fact that sample no. 23 is just lying in the Upper Control Limit, and very soon the points may be falling outside the upper control limit. Thus, we must look for the factor which caused this condition and the process should be corrected. Reasons for trends need to be looked into. Generally it is traceable to tool wear. Either harder tool should be used or adjustments need to made more frequently.

OFF CENTERING OF THE PROCESS

In an ideal case, the process should be centred at a value midway between the tolerance limits. Sometimes, the study of the control chart of a process shows that there is a gradual shift of points towards one control limits. This indicates the process drift possibly caused by tool wear or some other such factor. In a process where this tendency is established, it may be advisable to set the process a little away from the centre in the direction opposite to the process drift, provided the variability range of the process is stable and considerably less than the tolerance range of the product. This will increase the time interval between process adjustments and thus would be more economical. In such cases, one should be careful in using the above-mentioned criteria of the process. Suppose the process has been set towards the lower control limit, then initially there is likelihood of concentration of points in the lower half of the control chart which should not cause any worry as long as the points are not falling outside the lower control limit. After some time, because of the process drift, there will be a tendency of points to fall in the upper half. Again, as long as the points are within the control limits the process should not be disturbed. It should be reset only when the points fall outside the control limits.

PROCESS CAPABILITY STUDY

Process capability is the quality performance capability of a process with respect to its variation under in-control conditions. After $\bar{X}$ and R control charts show that the process is in control, process capability study is generally undertaken to find out whether the process can meet the job tolerance limits. It will be recalled that this aspect is also checked earlier during analysis of frequency distribution before installing control charts. The purpose of this recheck is to substantiate the findings of earlier analysis. It should not be forgotten that the earlier frequency distribution was studied when the process was newly setup and it may not have settled down. Further, over a time certain factors may have altered the variability of the process. Therefore, it is always a sound practice to study process capability before commencing a long run of a product.

Mathematically, process capability is defined as 6 standard deviations.

It should be noted that this standard deviation pertains to the individual observations on items or pieces, which can be obtained from the mean range ($\bar{R}$) by using the following relationship:

$$\sigma_1 = \frac{\bar{R}}{d_2}$$

Where

$\sigma 1$ is the estimated standard deviation for individual observations.
$\bar{R}$ is the average range of sample ranges.
d_2 is a factor which varies with sample size as given in Table A.

As an illustration, let us determine the process capability from the data given in Table B, and see whether it meets the specification limits. By definition process capability = $6\sigma_1$

Since $\sigma_1 = \frac{\bar{R}}{d_2}$

Process capability $6\sigma_1 = 6\,\frac{\bar{R}}{d_2}$

$\bar{R}$ from Table B is 0.035 mm,
d_2 for sample size n = 5, from Table A is 2.326
Therefore,

$$\text{Process Capability} = 6 \times \frac{0.035}{2.326} = 0.090 \text{ mm}$$

Specification tolerance for pins is ± 0.06 mm, *i.e.* total tolerance range = 0.12 mm.

Thus, it can be seen that the process capability of the subject process is well within the tolerance range of the product, and if it is centered properly is capable of machining up to the required tolerance.

PROCESS CAPABILITY INDICES

Process capability has a major influence on the quality of the products coming out of the process. Therefore, few indices have been developed to measure the quality of processes. Commonly used indices are Cp and Cpk. These indices are explained below:

Cp INDEX

Cp is the inherent variation of the process compared to the tolerance of the parameter of the product being processed. Calculation of Cp is illustrated in the Figure as follows:

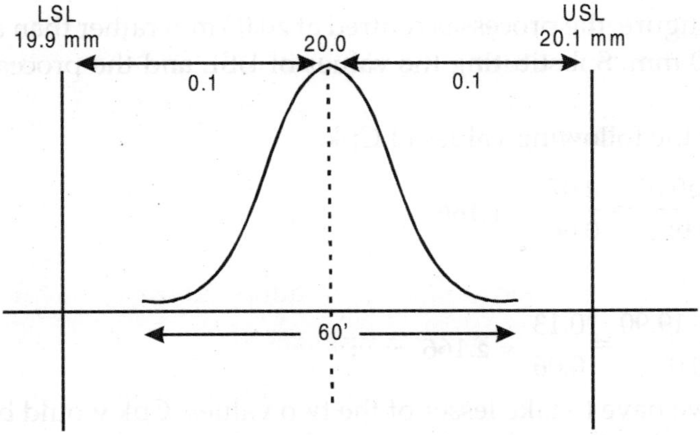

Fig. 4

Suppose a pin of diameter 20.0 ± 0.1 is being machined on a lathe whose standard deviation is 0.02 mm. Lower Specification Limit (LSL) = 19.9

Upper Specification Limit (USL) = 20.1

Total tolerance (T) = 0.2

$$Cp = \frac{T}{6\sigma} = \frac{0.2}{6 \times \sigma.02} = \frac{0.2}{0.12} = 1.66$$

In general industry practice, Cp should be equal to or more than 1.33. As such, in the above example, it is quite satisfactory.

It will be seen that in the above example, the process was centred at nominal, *i.e.*, 20.0 mm. There may be cases when the process is shifted to one side. In such cases, more reliable index of process capability is Cpk. By definition,

$$Cpk = \text{Lesser of}: \frac{USL - \bar{X}}{3\sigma} \text{ or } \frac{\bar{X} - LSL}{3\sigma}$$

This is illustrated in the figure given below:

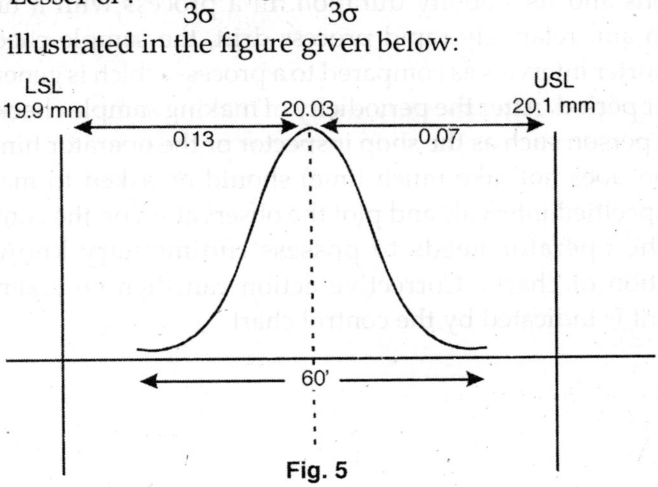

Fig. 5

In this figure, the process is centred at 20.03 mm rather than at nominal value of 20 mm. Substituting the values of USL and the process mean of 20.03 mm,

we get the following values of Cpk:

$$\frac{20.1-20.03}{3\times0.02}=\frac{0.07}{0.06}=1.166 \qquad ....(1)$$

and

$$\frac{20.03-19.90}{3\times0.02}=\frac{0.13}{0.06}=2.166 \qquad ...(2)$$

Since we have to take lesser of the two values, Cpk would be 1.166.

In general industry practice, the value of Cpk should be equal to or more than 1.33. Thus, in this case, process capability index Cpk is not acceptable. Therefore, there is a need to centre the process nearer 20.0 mm to ensure that the machined pins meet the specification tolerance.

USE OF MEASUREMENT CONTROL CHARTS IN PRODUCTION

Once the analysis of the initially constructed chart shows that the process is under a state of control both with respect to the range as well as the central value, the control charts are ready for use for controlling the quality of the process. The control charts with the centre line and control limits marked on it should be placed near the machine, the quality of whose output is to be controlled. This will enable the operator to see, for himself, the variation in the quality of components produced on that machine. This, in addition to providing the process control, will stimulate his interest in the quality of the store he is producing. The periodicity of making sample checks will depend upon the nature of the process and time required to make the observations and its stability duration. In a process with a high rate of production and relatively rapid process drift, the sample checks will be made at shorter intervals as compared to a process which is generally stable for a longer period. After the periodicity of making sample checks has been decided, a person such as the shop inspector or the operator himself (if the observation does not take much time) should be asked to make sample checks at specified intervals and plot the observation on the control charts. For this the operator needs to possess rudimentary knowledge for interpretation of charts. Corrective action can then be taken when its requirement is indicated by the control chart.

26

Control Chart of Attributes

Control charts discussed in the previous chapter involve inspection data in quantitative measurements. Sometimes, it is neither economical nor practicable to carry out actual measurements of the quality characteristics. In mass production, inspection is generally carried out by 'go' and 'not go' limit gauges, where the product is sentenced either 'acceptable' or 'not acceptable' without giving actual deviations from the tolerance limits. Further, one or more of the quality characteristics may be such that they are not easily quantified – for example, colour of a fabric, flavour of a food product or clarity of the image in an optical instrument. Also, the mere presence of an undesirable attribute or nonconformity such as a leak, or a crack irrespective of its extent, may render the product unacceptable. In all such cases, where the product is examined for the presence or the absence of certain attributes, the inspection data merely consist of the number or the quantity of the product found acceptable and that found defective or nonconforming, without giving the actual dimensions or the values of the quality characteristics. In the case of such inspection, different types of control charts, called control charts for attributes, are used.

DEFECTS AND DEFECTIVES

The term 'defect' or (nonconformity) refers to the failure of a quality characteristic to meet the specified standard. For example, a blow-hole in a casting may be one defect, which may cause its rejection. In addition, its wall thickness on one side may be less than the minimum specified which is another defect. That, by itself, may render the casting unacceptable. In this case, though there are two defects, the nonconforming unit is only one. The term 'defective' designates an item which has one or more 'defects' or 'nonconformities'.

QUALITY OF THE PRODUCT

The overall quality of a product inspected for attributes may be expressed as fraction defective or percent defective.

$$\text{Fraction defective} = \frac{\text{Number of units found defective}}{\text{Total number of units inspected}}$$

$$\text{Percent defective} = \text{Fraction defective} \times 100$$

In the case of relatively complex equipments such as engines, machine tools or TV sets, the quality may be expressed in terms of number of defects per unit or per 100 units.

$$\text{Defects per units} = \frac{\text{Total no. of defects observed}}{\text{No. of units inspected}}$$

$$\text{Defects per 100 units} = \text{Defects per unit} \times 100$$

CONTROL CHARTS FOR PERCENT DEFECTIVE

The control charts for attribute inspection data are also known as P-charts, where P stands for percent defective. Like the control charts for measurements, the samples consisting of a number of articles are inspected at periodic intervals and the percent defective for each sample is calculated and plotted on the P-control chart. The plotted points show the variation in the percent defective from the sample. Unlike the control chart for measurements, the sample size in P-charts needs to be larger and any convenient sample size can be chosen. Control limits for attribute control charts also are based on $\pm 3\sigma$ concepts. The standard deviation of P is given by,

$$\sigma_p = \sqrt{\frac{\bar{P}(100 - \bar{P})}{N}}$$

Where $\begin{cases} \bar{P} \text{ is the average percent defective.} \\ N \text{ is the sample size.} \end{cases}$

The control limits for P-charts are obtained by the following formulae:

$$\text{Upper Control Limit} = \bar{P} + 3\sqrt{\frac{\bar{P}(100-\bar{P})}{N}}$$

$$\text{Centre Line} = \bar{P}$$

$$\text{Lower Control Limit} = \bar{P} - 3\sqrt{\frac{\bar{P}(100-\bar{P})}{N}}$$

CONSTRUCTION OF P-CHARTS

The procedure for construction of P-charts is illustrated by a case study. A firm manufacturing fuel tanks for vehicles, wished to introduce P-charts to control the quality of their product. 100 tanks out of their daily production were inspected every day and the inspection record for the month of April is given in Table A.

Since the number of fuel tanks inspected every day was 100, the percent defective in the daily production was numerically equal to the daily rejection. Based on 25 days' inspection record for the month of April, the average percent defective (P) is given by,

$$\bar{P} = \frac{\text{Total no. rejected}}{\text{Total no. inspected}} \times 100$$

$$= \frac{500}{25 \times 100} \times 100$$

$$= 20\%$$

Table A

Date (April)	Number rejected	Date (April)	Number rejected
1	14	16	23
2	22	17	14
3	25	18	6
4	15	19	7
5	20	20	33
6	14	21	Holiday
7	Holiday	22	17
8	12	23	34
9	24	24	11
10	10	25	16
11	17	26	25
12	35	27	Holiday
13	36	28	Holiday
14	Holiday	29	36
15	16	30	18
		Total no. rejected	**500**

Centre Line (CL) = $\bar{p}$ = 20%.

$$\text{Upper Control Limit (UCL)} = \bar{P} + 3\sqrt{\frac{\bar{P}(100-\bar{P})}{N}}\,\%$$

$$= 20 + 3\sqrt{\frac{20\,(100-20)}{100}}\,\%$$

$$= 20 + 3\sqrt{16\%}$$

$$= 32\%$$

Lower Control Limit (LCL) =

$$\bar{P} - 3\sqrt{\frac{\bar{P}\,(100-\bar{P})}{N}} = 20 - 3\sqrt{\frac{20\,(100-20)}{100}}$$

$$= 20 - 3\sqrt{16}$$

$$= 8\%$$

P-chart based on inspection data in Table A is shown in Fig. 1. The ordinate of the chart is marked for percentages of defectives and the abscissa represents the dates on which the samples were inspected. One point is plotted for the percentage defective found in each day's production.

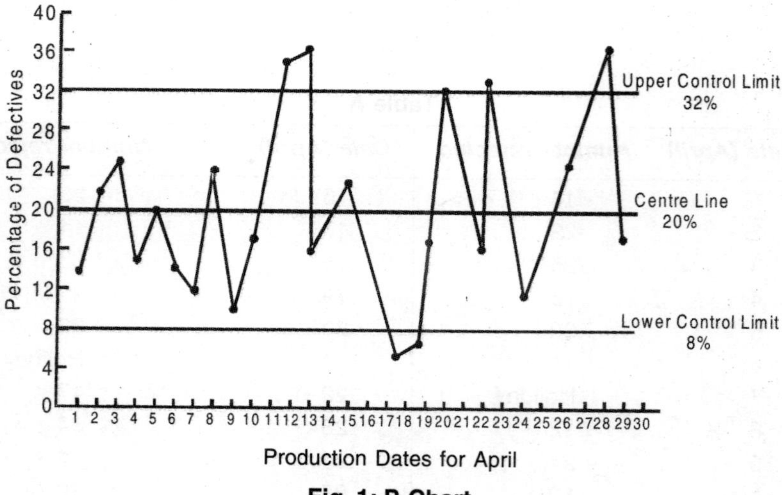

Fig. 1: P-Chart

ANALYSIS OF P-CHARTS

As in the case of measurement control charts, before the control limits are finally accepted for future control, the chart is analysed to see whether the process is within control. Looking at the chart in Fig. 1, it is clear that the process in April was running out of control. As many as 5 points are beyond the upper control limit and 2 points are below the lower control limit. Therefore, an investigation of all the out-of-control points was carried out. The investigation revealed that,

(a) One of the welding machines was not working satisfactorily on 12th and 13th April and was repaired on 14th April.

(b) On 18th and 19th April, the regular inspector was on leave and the inspection of the fuel tanks was carried out by a currently appointed junior inspector who was under study to the regular inspector.

(c) Most of the defects found in the final inspection were due to poor workmanship.

From the above observations, the excessive rejection on 12th and 13th April could be attributed to the faulty welding machine. Very low rejection on 18th and 19th April probably was not a genuine figure. It is likely that the substitute inspector was not able to detect some of the faults. No specific cause could be found for the excessive rejection on the 20th, 23rd and 29th, except the general impression of the poor skill of the workers. Besides the excessive rejection on certain dates, even the average value of the percentage defective was much too high and was not acceptable to the management.

QUALITY IMPROVEMENT BY CONTROL CHARTS

The main utility of the P-chart is that it indicates the magnitude of the quality problem and highlights the areas of weakness. A control chart, by itself, cannot improve the quality of the product. Quality improvement can result only if the follow-up action is taken to rectify the shortcomings indicated by the control chart. In the case of the study discussed above, the management launched an intensive quality improvement programme, which included training of workers, review of jigs and fixtures, process capability studies and replacement of unreliable machines. This programme took about two months, after which a significant improvement in quality was noticed. The inspection data for July based on constant sample size of 100 tanks are given in Table B.

Table B

Date	Number rejected	Date	Number rejected
1 July	2	16 July	10
2 July	5	17 July	7
3 July	9	18 July	4
4 July	12	19 July	10
5 July	5	20 July	2
6 July	4	21 July	Holiday
7 July	Holiday	22 July	8
8 July	8	23 July	4
9 July	4	24 July	13
10 July	10	25 July	Holiday
11 July	6	26 July	6
12 July	14	27 July	8
13 July	10	28 July	Holiday
14 July	Holiday	29 July	2
15 July	9	30 July	5
		Total no. rejected	**175**

To set up a control chart, revised control limits were computed from the data of Table B, as given below:

Constant sample size N = 100

No. of samples inspected = 25

Total no. of rejects = 175

$$\text{Average percentage defective } (\bar{P}) = \frac{175 \times 100}{2500} = 7\%$$

$$\text{Therefore,} \quad CL = P = 7$$

$$UCL = \bar{P} + 3\sqrt{\frac{\bar{P}(100 - \bar{P})}{N}}$$

$$= 7 + 3\sqrt{\frac{7(100-7)}{100}}$$

$$= 7 + 3 \times 2.55 = 7 + 7.65$$

$$= 14.65\%$$

$$LCL = \bar{P} - 3\sqrt{\frac{\bar{P}(100 - \bar{P})}{N}}$$

$$= 7 - 3\sqrt{\frac{7(100-7)}{100}}$$

$$= 7 - 7.65$$

$$= -.65\%$$

We see that the Lower Control Limit comes to a negative value. This is often the case in quality control situations, where the percentage defective is small. As there cannot be any value of percent defective less than zero, Lower Control Limit in such cases is taken as zero.

A control chart with the above limits based on the inspection data for July is shown in Fig. 2. It can be seen that the average value of percent defectives had come down to 7% (a marked improvement from 20% in April), and no point had fallen beyond the upper control limit. Also, no long series of points on any side of the centre line were noticed, which means that even when judged by the out-of-control criteria discussed in the previous chapter, the process was found to be within control. However, as many as 10 points fall below the center line. It means that the process is capable of producing still lower defectives. The conditions of situations on these dates should be studied which could give indications how the process can be further improved.

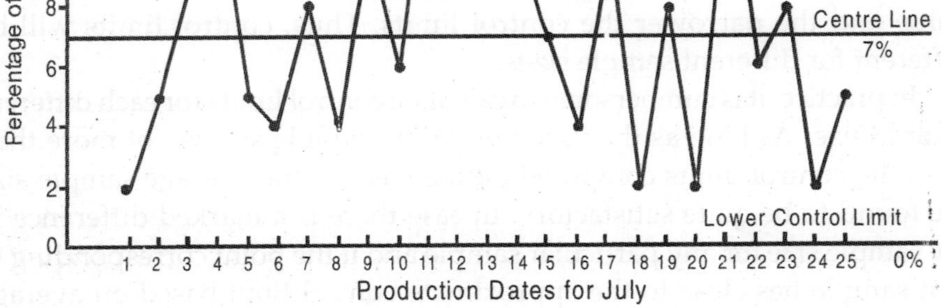

Fig. 2

UTILITY OF LOWER CONTROL LIMIT

The reader may wonder about the need for a lower control limit for a percent defective chart. In fact, the lower the value of the percent defective in a sample, the better will be its quality, which should be welcome.

We have seen earlier that when a process is operating at a particular central value, the chance causes can explain variations only up to 3σ higher and lower than the central value. If a particular point falls below the lower control limit, the first thing which should be checked is the effectiveness of inspection. Quite often, tax inspection will be found to be the cause. If however the point is genuinely found to be below the Lower Control Limit, the causative factor should be identified and efforts made to perpetuate the assignable cause which has been responsible for significant improvement in quality. Thus, it can be seen that a Lower Control Limit has an important function in the improvement of quality.

P-CHARTS WITH VARIABLE SAMPLE SIZE

In the discussion of percent defective charts so far, we have taken a constant sample size. In many cases, P charts are based on 100% inspection of the output which may be varying from day to day or week to week. We know from the previous discussion that 3σ Control Limits are,

$$\bar{P} \pm 3\sqrt{\frac{\bar{P}(100 - \bar{P})}{N}}$$

In the above relation 3σ value, *i.e.* $3\sqrt{\frac{\bar{P}(100 - \bar{P})}{N}}$ is inversely proportional to $\sqrt{N}$.

This means that the larger the sample size N, the smaller is the 3σ value and the narrower the control limits. Thus, control limits will be different for different sample sizes.

In practice, it is cumbersome to calculate control limits for each different sample size. As long as the variation in the sample size is not more than 20%, the control limits computed on the basis of the average sample size are found to be quite satisfactory. In case there is a marked difference in the sample size for any particular sample and if the point corresponding to that sample lies close to the approximate control limit based on average sample size, the exact limit for that particular sample can be calculated to ascertain whether the point lies outside the limit. This is illustrated by the following example. Fig. 3 shows a chart for a product whose average defective percentage is 6 and the average sample size is 200. Based on this, the upper and lower control limits are 11% and 1%, respectively.

Points corresponding to the 14th and 16th sample (consisting of 100 and 250 pieces) are lying close to the upper control limit.

The exact limit for 14th sample (of 100 pieces) is given by,

$$\text{UCL} = \bar{P} + 3\sqrt{\frac{\bar{P}(100-6)}{N}}$$

$$= 6 + 3\sqrt{\frac{6(100-6)}{100}}$$

$$= 13\%$$

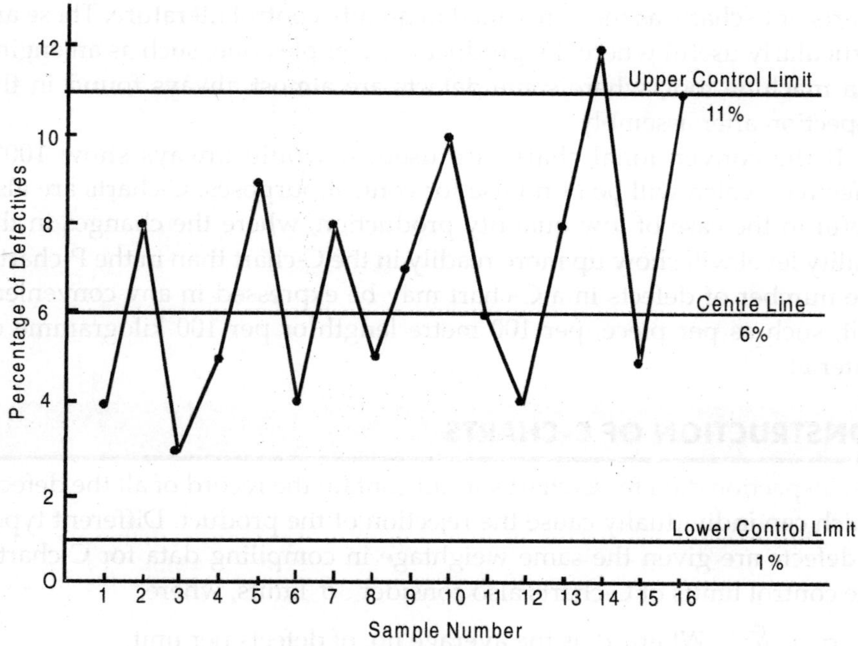

Fig. 3: P-Chart for Variable Sample Size

Thus, 14th sample, though 12% defective, is still within control because its actual upper limit is 13%.

The exact limit for the 16th sample (of 250 pieces) is given by,

$$\text{UCL} = \bar{P} + 3\sqrt{\frac{\bar{P}(100-6)}{N}}$$

$$= 6 + 3\sqrt{\frac{6(100-6)}{250}}$$

$$= 10.5\% \text{ Approx.}$$

As the 16th sample is 11% defective, it is actually out of control. Excessive variation in the sample size in this example has been shown merely to illustrate the point. In actual practice, output will rarely vary to this extent and there will seldom be any need for the calculation of exact limits for a particular sample.

NUMBER OF DEFECTS CONTROL CHARTS (C-CHARTS)

Percent defective or P-charts discussed above are useful only where the production rate is fairly large and there are a few types of defects. In some cases, it is more convenient to work with the Number of Defect Control Charts or C-charts as they are called in quality control literature. These are particularly useful where the product is a complex one, such as an engine or a machine tool, where some defects are almost always found in the inspection after assembly.

If the conventional charts are used, it would always show 100% defective, which will be of no use for control purposes. C-charts are also useful in the case of low quantity production, where the changes in the quality level will show up more readily in the C-chart than in the P-charts. The number of defects in a C-chart may be expressed in any convenient unit, such as per piece, per 100 metre length or per 100 kilogramme of material.

CONSTRUCTION OF C-CHARTS

The inspection data for C-chart should contain the record of all the defects which can individually cause the rejection of the product. Different types of defects are given the same weightage in compiling data for C-charts. The control limits of C-charts also consider 3σ limits, where,

$\sigma = \sqrt{\bar{C}}$ Where $\bar{C}$ is the average no. of defects per unit.

Centre Line = $\bar{C}$

Upper Control Limit = $\bar{C} + 3\sqrt{\bar{C}}$

Lower Control Limit = $\bar{C} - 3\sqrt{\bar{C}}$

The procedure for data collection, construction of control chart and analysis is similar to that of P-charts discussed earlier, as will be clear from the following illustration:

XY company manufacturing engine-driven compressors needed to introduce C-charts for the quality control of the compressors. Inspection data for the 20 compressors manufactured in one month is given in Table C.

Table C

Compressor no.		No. of defects	Compressor no.		No. of defects
XY	101	2	XY	111	4
XY	102	5	XY	112	4
XY	103	7	XY	113	3
XY	104	3	XY	114	7
XY	105	5	XY	115	12
XY	106	1	XY	116	2
XY	107	4	XY	117	3
XY	108	6	XY	118	1
XY	109	3	XY	119	4
XY	110	2	XY	120	2
			Total no. of defects		= 80

Control limits based on the data in Table C were calculated as follows:

No. of units inspected = 20

Total no. of defects noticed = 80

Average no. of defects per unit ($\bar{c}$) = $\frac{80}{20} = 4$

Centre Line = $\bar{c} = 4$

Upper Control Limit = $\bar{c} + 3\sqrt{\bar{c}}$

$= 4 + 3\sqrt{4} = 10$

Lower Control Unit $= \bar{c} - 3\sqrt{\bar{c}}$

$= 4 - 3\sqrt{4}$

$= 4 - 6 = -2$

Therefore, LCL can be taken to be zero. C-chart based on Table C is shown in Fig. 4.

It can be seen from this chart that the number of defects in unit no. XY 115 is more than the upper control limit, the cause of which should be investigated. Here, the centre line, *i.e.* $\bar{c}$ was arrived at from the actual performance of the last one month. Often, the standard acceptable value of $\bar{c}$ is fixed by the management from past experience and is used for the quality control of future production. This standard value of $\bar{c}$ may be reviewed periodically or when any change is made in the process.

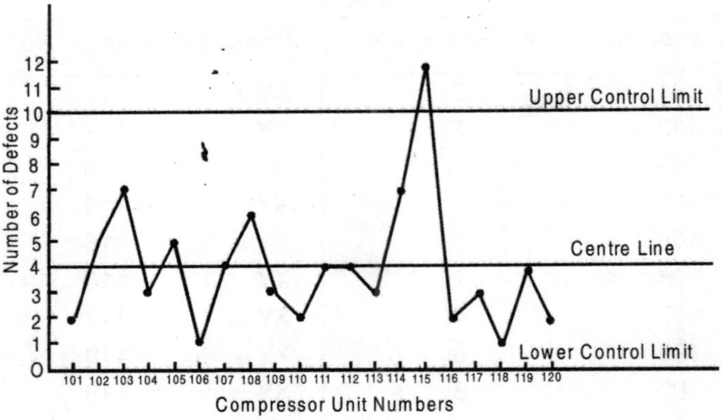

Fig.4: C-Chart

WEIGHTED DEFECT CONTROL CHARTS

The main drawback of the basic C-chart is that it treats all the defects alike. Certain defects may be of a minor nature requiring only a slight adjustment which could be carried out in a few minutes. There may be other defects requiring complete stripping and reassembly which may take many hours. An out-of-control point on the C-chart where all the defects are bulked together may cause unnecessary concern to the management when the out-of-control condition is due to a series of defects which can be quickly rectified. On the other hand, the management may have a false sense of complacency by an in-control point which may include two or three major defects. This may sound a serious limitation of C-charts, but industrial experience shows that for most purposes it is a sound practice to consider all the defects as of equal importance. For one thing, all types of defects generally require some rehandling and reinspection which forms a considerable part of the rectification effort. Secondly, all defects due to bad workmanship indicate lapses on the part of individuals, all of which must receive due attention. However, in the cases where relative seriousness of defects and consequent rectification effort does vary widely, it may be advisable to weigh the defects on the basis of their rectification cost or the likely harm these can cause to the user. This can be done by the categorisation of defects in two or more classes, such as A, B and C.

Depending upon the relative seriousness and rectification cost involved, each class of defects is given due weightage by allotting demerit points. For example, for a particular product, the relative seriousness of defects may be expressed by allotting 10, 5 and 1 demerit points for type A, B and C defects, respectively. If a unit has two type A defects, three type B defects and eight type C defects, its total demerits will be,

$$2 \times 10 + 3 \times 5 + 8 \times 1 = 20 + 15 + 8 = 43.$$

Similarly the demerit points for other units are also determined and the number of demerits per unit could be used as an index of quality. Calculation of control limits and other procedure for construction of weighted C-charts is exactly similar to the basic C-chart. The only difference is that 'C' in the formulae of control limits will represent demerit points per unit, rather than the number of defects per unit. Though a weighted C-chart or demerits control chart as it is sometimes called, involves additional computations, it will certainly reflect the process quality more accurately than the basic C-chart and may be worth the effort in certain situations.

PRE-CONTROL

One of the criticisms of control charts is that its computations are too complicated for shop personnel and it requires specially trained persons to maintain the control charts on production machines. To overcome this difficulty, several modifications and simplified versions of control charts have been tried out in the industry. One technique which has met wide acceptance is called PRE-CONTROL. This technique does not require any calculations and charting, yet it gives quick indication, when the process is going to be out of control.

We have seen earlier in this chapter that when the process is in control, the variations in the product follow the normal curve. Let us assume worst process condition which can be accepted from quality angle, *i.e.* when the process capability is just equal to the drawing tolerance allowed on the product. In such a state, the process has to be set at the centre of the tolerance range and any shift in the central tendency of the process would result in some defective work. Frequency distribution of the process variation and the drawing tolerance (T) are shown in Fig. 5. It will be recalled that the process capability or the natural tolerance (T) of the process is $\pm 3\sigma$. Now if two pre-control limit lines are drawn, so that each is ¼ T inside the drawing limit, it can be seen that the pre-control limits are at $\pm 1.5\sigma$ from the mean value. Reference to Table B in chapter 23 will show that the area under the normal curve between $\pm 1.5\ \sigma$ is 2×0.43319 or 0.86 (approximate) of the total area. This means that 86% of the jobs will be inside pre-control limits and the balance 14% will be equally distributed in the two sections between pre-control limits and the tolerance limits Fig. 5. Therefore, under normal conditions, 7%, *i.e.* one part in every 14, will occur outside a pre-control limit. Now, if two consecutive parts from the production are checked the chance of both the parts falling outside a pre-control limit (according to multiplication law of probability) is $\frac{1}{14} \times \frac{1}{14}$ or $\frac{1}{196}$.

Thus, when the process is running normally, it will be a rare chance to get two consecutive jobs outside the pre-control limits. If it does occur, there is much greater probability $\frac{(195)}{(196)}$ that the central tendency of the process has shifted. It is also equally unlikely that one part is outside higher pre-control limit and the next is outside the lower pre-control limit. If it does happen, one can conclude that the process range has been widened or process variation has increased by some external factor and very soon defective jobs are likely to be produced. From the above, it can be seen that if we have a gauge with pre-control limits and if two jobs in a row are found to be outside the gauge limits, it can be taken as an indication that the process is out of control and requires readjustment. This principle is made use of for exercising control over the process by pre-control limit gauge.

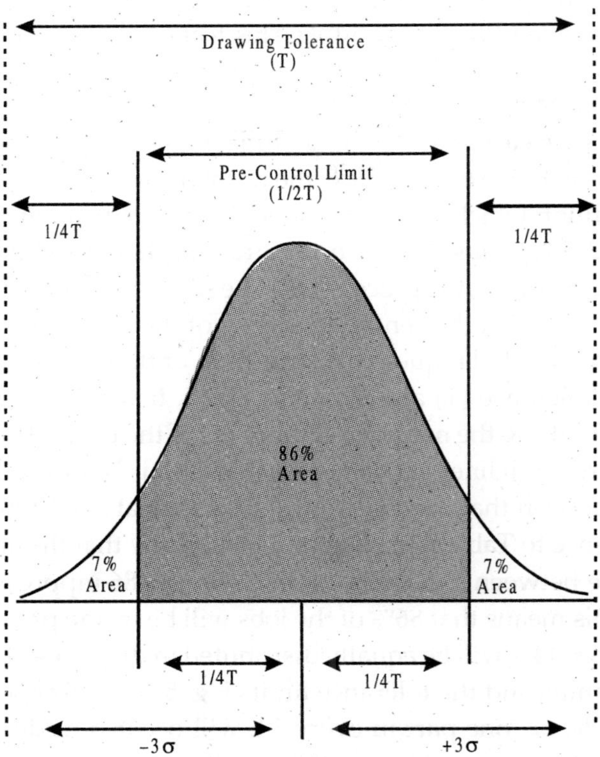

Fig. 5: Frequency Distribution and Pre-Control Limits

PROCEDURE OF PRE-CONTROL

The following rules are recommended for application of pre-control in a production process:

(a) Establish pre-control limits which are narrower than the drawing tolerance limits to the extent of ¼ tolerance from each limit as shown in Fig. 5.

(b) Provide a Go, and Not go, gauge with the above limits, or arrange a measuring instrument on which the above pre-control limits are clearly marked.

(c) Start the process and produce the first job. This job should be thoroughly inspected according to the drawing tolerances. If the job is outside the tolerance, the process should be reset, until 'within tolerance' job is produced.

(d) Check the first 'within tolerance' job with pre-control gauge, or instrument. If the job is outside pre-control limits, run the process and check the next job. If the next job is also found to be outside pre-control limits, the process should be stopped and readjusted. If the second piece is found within pre-control limits, the process should continue to run. During this stage, every piece should be checked by the pre-control gauge, and the process should be adjusted, only if two consecutive pieces are found outside pre-control limits.

(e) If out of the two successive pieces, one is outside the high pre-control limit and the other is outside the low pre-control limit, it shows that the range of variation has increased, the cause of which should be immediately looked into.

(f) When five successive pieces are found within pre-control limits, frequency gauging can be introduced. Frequency gauging is a periodic check rather than checking every piece. For instance, every fifth or ten piece may be checked by pre-control limit gauge.

(g) When frequency gauging is being carried out, continue the process, as long as the checked pieces are within pre-control limits. If any piece is found outside the limits, the very next piece should be checked. If this piece is within the limits, leave the process alone. If, however, the above-mentioned piece is also outside the pre-control limits, reset the process and proceed as in (d) above.

(h) To establish the periodicity of check in frequency gauging, it should be aimed that about 25 checks are carried out between two settings of the process. Let us say every fifth job is being checked and it is found that 50 checks are carried out *i.e.* 250 jobs are produced before the process requires resetting. In such a case the frequency of check can be reduced to half, *i.e.* every tenth job may be checked, in which case about 25 checks will be required between settings.

In the similar manner, the frequency of checking can be increased if it is found that the process requires resetting after fewer than 25 checks.

Pre-control technique is a simple control method which can be easily understood and applied by the operator or the section supervisor. It does not require any recording or calculations. It may not be as exact as the control charts, but it does sound the warning bell when the process is about to produce defective jobs.

PRACTICAL APPLICATION OF CONTROL CHARTS

Three basic control chart techniques, namely measurement control charts, P-charts and C-charts have been discussed in these two chapters. There are various other modifications and adaptations of these, which may be employed by quality engineers to suit particular situations. Notable among these is the Pre-control technique which has been discussed at some length in this chapter. While a control chart is a very effective quality control technique, its limitations should also be clearly understood. Some of the control charts, particularly of the measurement type, provide the control of only one quality characteristic of the product or the component. A product may have a number of important quality parameters which determine its overall quality. If all those parameters are to be controlled, as many control charts will be needed as there are quality parameters.

The installation of a measurement control chart does not automatically mean that conventional inspection can be dispensed with. It should be remembered that a control chart aids in bringing the process under statistical control, which means that the possibility of a few defectives appearing in the final inspection cannot be ruled out. Further, all quality characteristics may not be controlled by control charts. The main advantage of a control chart is that it gives the warning of a defective product before it is actually produced, thus saving rejection losses, which is the chief reason for its popularity.

A question may arise that, in view of the effort and expense involved in the installation of a single control chart, how widely can it be applied for a product having a large number of components and quality parameters. The answer to this can only be based on economics. The control chart should only be used where it is more economical to invest in setting up a control chart than accepting the likely rejection losses. It is generally advisable to install control charts only for those processes where important product characteristics are generated which have a marked influence on the quality of the product. The indiscriminate use of control charts by over-zealous quality control men for the sake of promoting a particular control chart technique should be discouraged. It should be borne in mind that the control chart is one of the many quality control techniques, and should be used only where the process conditions and economic considerations warrant it.

27

Theory of Sampling Inspection

Whenever any material or store is purchased, there is always the question of its quality. Does it conform to the quality requirements of the purchaser? If the quantity involved is small the purchaser may take the word of the manufacturer regarding its quality. However, when the store is purchased in bulk, the purchaser normally likes to assure himself by more positive means, that the quality of the store does conform to his requirements. It may also happen that the components or materials manufactured in one section of a factory are used for further processing or assembly in another section. Even here it is desirable to know that the components or materials conform to specifications to avoid production, difficulties in the subsequent operations. The quality appraisal of the bulk quantity may take the form of physical inspection of the entire product, or only a small part of it. When the quality of the bulk is determined on the basis of the inspection of a small portion, it is termed as 'SAMPLING INSPECTION'. Various aspects of the sampling inspection and the way it differs from 100% inspection are discussed in this part.

100% INSPECTION

Cent percent inspection means the inspection of each and every piece of store or material. This type of inspection has the obvious advantage of giving complete assurance that all the defective materials have been eliminated from the inspected lot. However, it has certain drawbacks, which makes it unsuitable for certain situations. Since each piece is to be inspected, it proves very expensive and time-consuming, particularly where large quantities are involved. In the case of stores such as ammunition where inspection takes the form of destructive tests, 100% inspection is impossible, as it would mean 100% destruction. Further, it is not generally realised that the assurance given by 100% inspection is not really complete. The risks involved in cent percent inspection arise from human errors of failing to detect defective articles due to the boredom and fatigue of repetitive inspection operations. Controlled experiments on 100% inspection have shown that the percentage error is, by no means, negligible. Another serious criticism levelled against 100% inspection is that it appears to divert the responsibility for the quality from the producer to the inspector. Once a product has been accepted after 100% inspection, the producer tends to think that his responsibility regarding its quality is over and if any defects are found in the product later on, the inspection should be answerable. It needs hardly to be said that it is the manufacturer who builds the quality (or lack of it) into the product. The inspector may fail to detect a defective (assuming it is detectable) but he certainly cannot add a defect in the product.

SAMPLING INSPECTION

Sampling inspection is a technique for assessing the quality of a lot comprising of a large number of articles, by inspecting only some of them. The group of articles chosen for inspection is called a 'SAMPLE' which may be defined as a part representing the quality of the whole. For example, if a sample of 100 articles out of a lot of 1,200 is found to have two articles defective, it is reasonable to expect that the remaining 1,100 will also contain 2% defective articles, provided all the 1,200 pieces were manufactured under similar conditions. This may be true under an ideal situation, when exactly similar manufacturing conditions can be maintained, but, in actual practice, the sample will not exactly represent the true quality of the lot and there may be some variation in the quality levels of the sample and the lots. Therefore, the acceptance of lots on the basis of sample results will involve a certain amount of risk of wrong decisions, *viz.* acceptance of some lots of lower than specified quality, and rejection of certain others of acceptable quality. The former is a risk for the consumer or purchaser and later for the producer. While considering risks in sampling inspection, it should not be forgotten that 100% inspection also involves certain errors the consequences of which, in some cases, may be even more than those arising from sampling inspection.

Another important advantage of sampling inspection is that it provides a strong incentive for the producer to improve the quality of his goods. In 100% inspection whatever be the quality of the store, the purchaser's inspectors sort out the defective articles for the producer, and he has no incentive to improve the quality of his stores. On the other hand, if the stores are accepted on the basis of sampling inspection, the producer knows that as long as the quality of the store is better than the acceptable level, most of the lots will be accepted, but if the quality deteriorates, increasing number of lots will be rejected, which no producer can afford. Thus, he will be forced to improve the quality of his product.

DEFINING THE QUALITY OF A LOT

Whereas an individual article is accepted on the basis of its conformance to specification, we need another criterion for acceptance of a lot containing a large number of articles. A perfectionist might say that a lot containing even one defective piece should be rejected, but we know from actual experience that in most cases, this is not practicable. If we want to insist on zero-per cent defective lots, we should be prepared to pay a comparatively heavy price for inspection, which may prove more expensive than accepting a few defective pieces in the lot. Therefore, except in the case of stores of critical nature, a certain percentage of defective articles are accepted in the lot. The lower the percentage defective, the better is the quality of the lot. The lot quality can also be expressed in terms of the number of defects counted, rather than the number of units on which the defects are found. Since the use of percentage defectives is more common, this term will be used for defining the quality of the lots in the subsequent discussion.

SAMPLING PLAN

A sampling plan lays down in brief, the sampling inspection procedure. It includes the number of samples to be taken, the size of each sample and the acceptance criteria. A typical sampling plan is given below:

Single Sample Size	..	50
Acceptance Number	..	2
Rejection Number	..	3

This indicates that one sample consisting of 50 units is to be inspected from the lot. If there are two or less number of defective units in the sample, the lot is to be accepted. If the defective units are three or more, the lot is to be rejected.

DETERMINING THE RISK IN SAMPLING INSPECTION

We have already seen that sampling inspection involves a certain amount of risk, both for the consumer and producer. The effective use of sampling inspection technique requires that these risks be clearly understood, so that the selection of a particular plan is based on a logical decision, rather than an arbitrary choice.

The risk in a particular sampling plan can be determined by considering the results of samples drawn from a large number of lots of various quality levels using the mathematical theory of probability. These results can be shown in the form of graphical representation called an OPERATING CHARACTERISTIC CURVE, generally known as OC curve. Let us consider the sampling plan where,

Sample Size	..	50
Acceptance Number	..	1
Rejection Number	..	2

Such a plan can be written in an abbreviated form, as 50 (1/2), *i.e.* sample size (Acceptance No./Rejection No.). The OC curve for this plan is shown in Fig. 1.

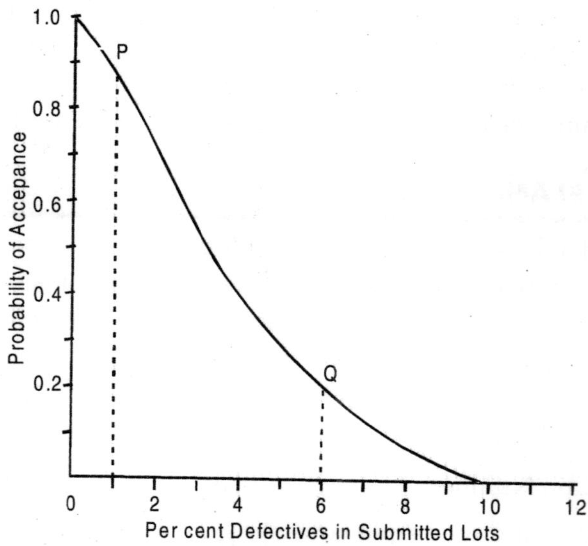

Fig. 1: Operative Characteristic Curve

The horizontal axis of the curve shows the actual percentage of defectives in the submitted lots, and the vertical axis gives the probability of their acceptance. Assuming that lots with 1% defectives are considered just acceptable, point P shows that a lot with 1% defectives has 0.9 probability of acceptance. It means that if a large number of lots of this quality were inspected by this plan, about 90% of the lots will be accepted and the remaining 10% rejected. This 10% rejection is referred to as producer's risk. Point Q on the OC curve shows that if the quality of the submitted lots is 6% defective, the probability of acceptance is reduced to 0.2 and the producer's risk increases to 80%. Now, looking from the consumer's point of view, it can be seen from point Q that even though the minimum acceptable quality of the lot is 1% defective, there is a 20% chance of a lot with 6% defectives being accepted. This is termed as consumer's risk.

Every sampling plan has its own consumer's and producer's risks, as indicated by its OC curve. An ideal sampling plan would be one, which accepts all the lots which are of quality better than the minimum acceptable standard and rejects all those which do not come up to the minimum standard. Such an ideal sampling plan is represented by the thick/bold OC curve in Fig. 2. This curve has 1.0 probability of acceptance up to

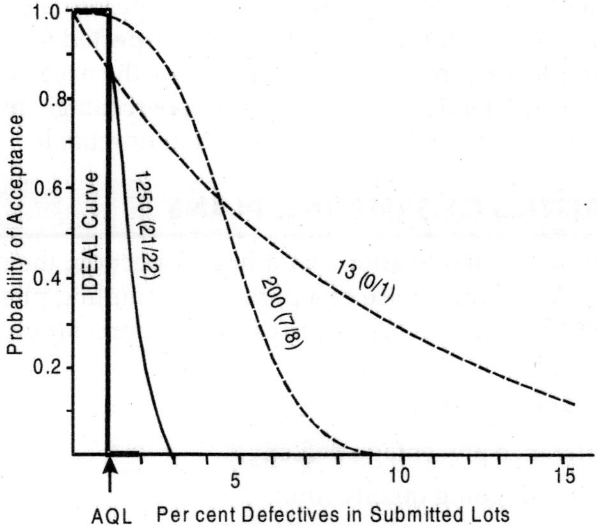

Fig. 2: OC Curves

minimum acceptable quality level, and zero probability of acceptance beyond this point. Therefore, there is no risk involved either for the consumer or the producer. But this ideal curve is unattainable in practice. The degree of risk can be reduced by increasing the sample size. Figure 2 shows in addition to the ideal curve three OC curves of sample size 13, 200 and 1250. It can be seen that as the sample size is increased, the OC curve approaches nearer the ideal curve. But an increase of sample size also increases the inspection cost, which is the price which has to be paid for the reduction of risk.

INFLUENCE OF LOT SIZE ON SAMPLING RISK

In the above discussion, we have not given any consideration to the size of the lot. This is because of the fact that the lot size has very little influence on the effectiveness of a sampling plan, or the risks involved. It is found that except in cases where the sample size is more than one-fifth of the lot size, the OC curve is DOE appreciably affected by variation in the lot size. In practice, the sample size is rarely more than one-fifth of the lot size and acceptance criteria. As such, for all practical purposes, the risk of sampling inspection is independent of the lot size, and the discriminating power of a sampling plan depends entirely upon the sample size and acceptance criteria. Thing brings out the fallacy of 'percentage inspection' which is sometimes mentioned in some specifications. If percentage inspection is followed, unnecessarily large samples may be inspected for large lots and too small a sample for a small lot may not provide the necessary protection against the risks involved. Further, the risks in percentage inspection vary the lot size, which makes this type of inspection unreliable.

CHARACTERISTICS OF SAMPLING PLANS

Once it has been decided to adopt sampling inspection, the next question which arises is about the choice of a particular sampling plan, *i.e.* Sample size and Acceptance no. This requires clear appreciation of the main statistical concept:

(a) Acceptable quality level

(b) Lot tolerance percentage defectives

(c) Average outgoing quality limit

ACCEPTABLE QUALITY LEVEL (AQL)

An AQL denotes percent nonconforming units or non-conformities when the lots of quality better than or equal to this are acceptable by the customer. Such lots when offered for inspection are almost certain to be accepted.

The degree of certainty is specified in terms of probability of acceptance or the risk of rejection. For example, an AQL of 2% defectives at 5% producer's risk means that if a series of lots containing 2% defectives is offered for inspection, 95% chance of the lots getting accepted and 5% chance of lots getting rejected. Generally, an AQL is the average process quality of the product.

LOT TOLERANCE

Lot tolerance refers to that quality level, which is almost certain of rejection. In the Quality Control literature, it is generally referred as Lot Tolerance Percent Defective (LTPD). Here, the degree of certainty is usually expressed in terms of consumer's risk. For example, if it is desired that a 6% defective lot should have a 90% chance of rejection and only 10% chance of acceptance, its lot tolerance should be 6% defective with 10% consumer's risk.

AVERAGE OUTGOING QUALITY LIMIT (AOQL)

Average outgoing quality refers to the quality of lots after they have been accepted. This is not the same thing as AQL, which is the lowest quality level of the lot that will generally be accepted. In case the lots of quality varying about AQL are submitted for sampling inspection, some of the accepted lots may have their quality higher than AQL. At the same time, it will be seen from an OC curve of a typical sampling plan that some of the lots having a quality level lower than AQL will also be accepted. Those lots, which are rejected by sampling inspection, will generally be screened by 100% inspection and all the defective units in these lots will be replaced by good ones. These lots thus accepted will be zero per cent defective or, in other words, will have the highest attainable quality level. Thus, the accepted stores will consist of lots of varying quality level, ranging from the quality worse than AQL, to zero per cent defective. When all these lots are considered together, their average quality level may be considerably different from the AQL. AOQL is the limiting value of AOQ. This limit means that the average quality of outgoing lots after acceptance inspection cannot be worse than AOQL, irrespective of the quality of submitted lots, provided it is ensured that all rejected lots are made 100% good. This condition, of course, cannot be met in the cases where inspection is destructive and 100% inspection is impossible. In all other cases where outgoing quality protection is required by the customer, it is made obligatory for the producer that all the rejected lots will be subjected to 100% inspection to eliminate defective pieces, which should be replaced by good pieces, so that the size of the lot remains unchanged. The concept of AOQL can be explained better by considering a specific sampling plan.

Suppose a certain store is being inspected in accordance with the following sampling plan:

Single Sampling

Sample Size	—	32
Acceptance No.	—	1
Rejection No.	—	2

The OC curve for the above plan is shown in Fig. 3. Let us consider what happens to the outgoing quality for the incoming lots of varying quality levels. If the incoming lots are zero per cent defective, all the lots will be accepted and the outgoing quality will also be zero per cent defective. If the incoming lots are 1% defective, it can be seen from the OC curve that 95% of the lots will be accepted and the remaining 5% lots will be rejected. These 5% rejected lots, according to agreement, will be screened by 100% inspection and the defective units in these lots will be replaced by good units. Thus, these 5% lots will be zero defective when they are accepted on resubmission. Let us say that a total of 100 lots of 1% defective incoming quality have been finally accepted. Out of these, 5 lots will be zero per cent defective and 95 lots will be 1% defective. Thus, the average outgoing quality of these 100 lots will be:

$$\frac{5 \times 0\% + 95 \times 1\%}{100} \text{ or } 0.95\% \text{ defective.}$$

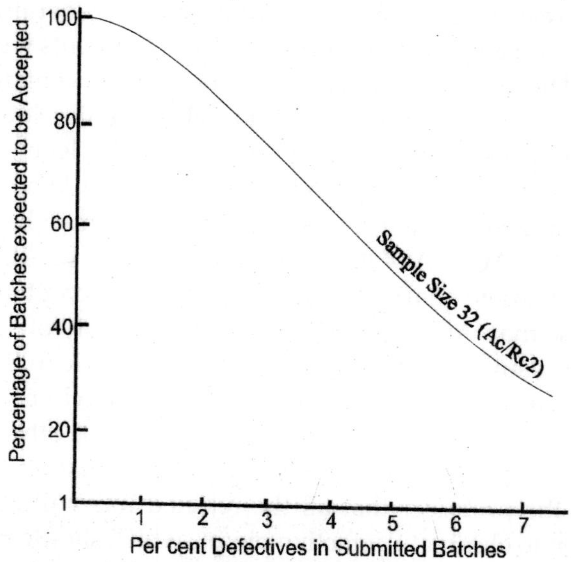

Fig. 3: OC Curve for Sample Size 32, Acceptance No. 1

It will be seen that the average outgoing quality can be obtained by multiplying the fractional probability of acceptance of a lot, with the percentage defectives in the incoming lots. In this case, the probability of acceptance is 0.95. Multiplying this with 1 (*i.e.* per cent defective), we get 0.95. Thus, whereas the incoming lots were 1% defective, the average quality of the accepted or outgoing lots is .95% defective. Now, let us see what happens if lots having 2% defectives are offered for inspection. From the OC curve, it is seen that the probability of acceptance of such lots is .88% and the remaining 12% will be rejected, which will again be 100% screened and all defectives in these lots will be replaced by good pieces.

The average outgoing quality of these lots will be

$$.88 \times 2 = 1.76\% \text{ defective.}$$

Similarly, the average outgoing quality can be calculated for other levels of incoming quality.

The results obtained are shown in Table A. The results in Col. 3 of the table been obtained by multiplying the values in Col. 1 with those in Col 2. The graph of the average outgoing quality level against incoming quality levels is shown in Fig. 4. It will be seen that initially as the per cent defectives in the incoming lots increases, the outgoing quality also deteriorates, *i.e.* it will have higher per cent defectives. The worst outgoing quality level (*i.e.* highest per cent defectives) is reached when the incoming quality is 5% defective. Thereafter, as the percentage of defectives in the submitted lots increases further, the average outgoing quality improves, *i.e.* outgoing lots will have fewer defectives. This is because of the fact that as the quality of the submitted lots deteriorates further, a greater number of lots will be rejected on first inspection and will be sorted out by 100% inspection to eliminate the defectives. Thus, they will be 0% defective when finally accepted. If the incoming quality goes beyond 5% defective, screened and resubmitted lots which are zero per cent defective, will more than compensate for the poor quality of the fewer lots which are directly accepted on first inspection. Thus, no matter what happens to the quality of the submitted lots, the average outgoing quality, as per this sampling plan, cannot be worse than 2.4% defective. This worst level of quality is known as the Average Outgoing Quality Limit (AOQL). Every sampling plan has its own AOQL, which can be used as one of the parameters for selecting a sampling plan.

Table A

Incoming quality (Per cent) defective	*Probability of acceptance of the lots*	*Average outgoing quality (Per cent) defective*
1	2	3
0	1.00	0
1	0.95	0.95
2	0.88	1.76
3	0.75	2.25
4	0.59	2.36
5	0.48	2.40
6	0.39	2.35
7	0.32	2.24
8	0.26	2.08
10	0.16	1.60
12	0.08	0.96

SELECTION OF SAMPLING PLANS

A sampling plan can be determined by selecting two of the five characteristics mentioned in Section 2. Although any two characteristics

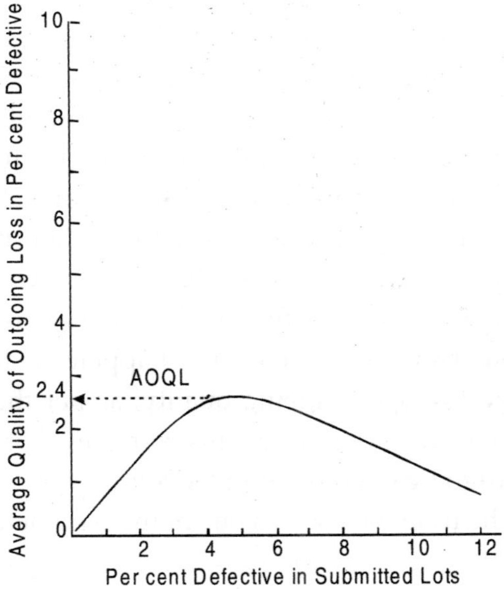

Fig. 4: Average Outgoing Quality Limit

can be chosen, such arbitrary choice sometimes leads to unnecessary risks and uneconomical sample size. Normally, one characteristic is chosen to meet the risk requirement of the customer and the other to provide risk protection to the producer. Alternatively, one characteristic is specified to meet the requirements of the purchaser or supplier and out of a number of sampling plans which may meet this particular requirement, the one which involves the least cost of inspection is selected. These two methods for the selection of sampling plans are discussed below.

RISK APPROACH

In this method, a sampling plan is selected by stipulating particular limits for the consumer's and producer's risk. Let us suppose that the average process quality of a product is 1% defective. It is mutually agreed between the producer and the purchaser, that AQL will be 1% defective at 5% producer's risk. It is also agreed that the lot tolerance will be 4% defective at 10% consumer's risk. Now, we have to select a plan, whose OC curve gives the required AQL and lot tolerance. Such a plan can be found from Poisson's exponential cumulative probability chart, shown in Fig. 5. The horizontal axis, marked in a logarithmic scale, shows the PN value, where 'P' is the fraction defective in the lot and 'N' is the sample size. The vertical scale shows the probability of occurrence of 'C' or less defective units in the sample. The curves shown on the graph pertain to various values of 'C', viz. C=0, C= 1, C = 2 etc.

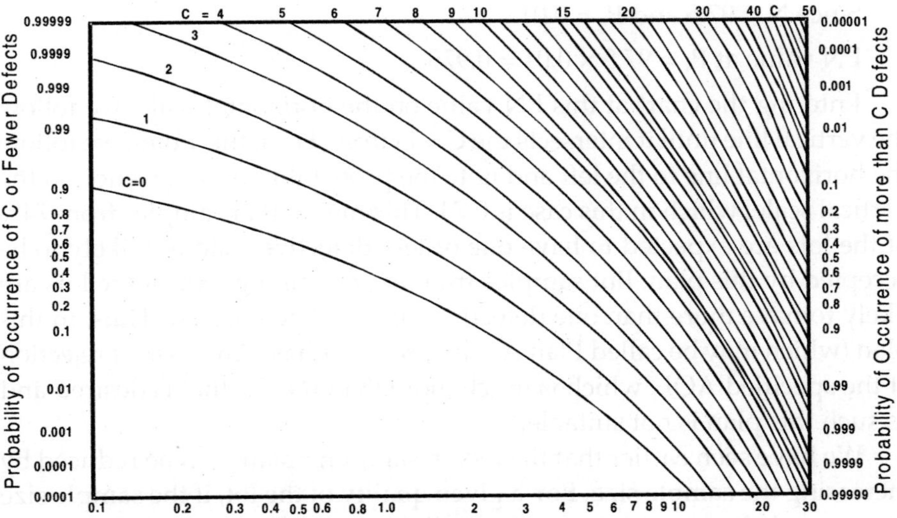

Fig. 5: Probability of Occurrence of C or Fewer Defects/Defectives

In this example, we have

Consumer's Risk (R_1) = 10% or 0.1

Lot Tolerance (P_1) = 4% defective or 0.04 fraction defective

Producer's Risk (R_2) = 5% or 0.05

AQL (P_2) = 1% defective, *i.e.* 0.01 fraction defective

To find a plan, we first assume a certain acceptance number C, such as C = 0, C = 1 or C = 2. Assumption of C = 0 generally gives a plan with too small sample size. Therefore, it is usual to assume C = 1 and then proceed to derive a sampling plan, as explained below.

In the above example, let us start with acceptance number C = 1, and first find the sample size which will meet the requirement of consumer's risk which stipulates that if a 4% defective lot is offered, the probability of acceptance should not be more than 0.1. Entering the chart in Fig. 5 at 0.1 probability of occurrence on the vertical scale, we go right until we meet the (C = 1) curve, and note the value at this point on the PN scale. In this case PN = 3.9, since P_1 is 0.04, sample size

$$(N) = \frac{3.9}{0.04} = 97.5$$

As the sample size has to be in whole numbers, we may use size 97 or 98, but for the purpose of further calculations, size 97.5 will be retained. Now that we have a plan which meets the consumer's risk, let us see whether it also meets the producer's risk requirement of $R_2 = 0.05$ at $P_2 = 0.01$

Since N = 97.5 and $P_2 = 0.01$

PN value at $P_1 = 97.5 \times 0.01 = 0.975$

Entering the chart at this PN value on the horizontal scale, we follow the vertical line until it intersects the C = 1 curve. From this point, we follow the horizontal line to the left and note the probability of occurrence on the vertical scale, which in this case is 0.74. This means that samples from 74% of the lots are expected to have one or less defectives and are likely to be accepted by this plan. But samples from the remaining 26% of the lots are likely to have more than one defectives and will be rejected. Thus, in this plan (which may be called Plan A), the producer has a 26% risk of rejection at the specified AQL, which is much more than the 5% that is desired and as such this plan is not suitable.

We have seen earlier that the risk in sampling plans can be reduced by increasing the sample size. For a given quality of the lot, if the sample size is increased, the acceptance number will also be correspondingly increased. Therefore, let us now consider plan B having the next higher acceptance number, *i.e.* C = 2, and find the sample size for the same consumer's risk, *i.e.* $R_1 = 0.1$ at $P_1 = 0.04$. Again, entering the chart at a probability of occurrence

0.1, we find that the PN value for the C = 2 curve is 5.3, since $P_1 = 0.04$, sample size N for plan

$$B = \frac{5.3}{0.04} = 132.5$$

The producer's risk for Plan B at 1% defective quality is calculated by the same method as for Plan A and it is found to be 0.15, which is still too high. Similarly, the sample size and producer's risk are calculated for other plans by successively increasing the acceptance number, until we get a plan which meets the producer's requirement. The result of this calculation is shown in Table B.

It can be seen from the table that Plan D with a sample size of 200 and an acceptance number 4, meet the risk requirements of both the consumer the producer, and as such this plan can be adopted. This method of determining a sampling plan is suitable only for large lot sizes. Where the size of lots is comparatively small, this approach gives disproportionately large sample sizes, which defeats the very purpose of sampling inspection, namely economy of inspection cost. For small lots, the following approach is more profitable:

Table B

	Consumer's risk					*Producer's risk*				
Plan	N	C	P_1	P_{1N}	R_1	N	C	P_2	P_{2N}	R_2
A	97.5	1	0.04	3.9	0.10	97.5	1	0.01	0.975	0.26
B	132.5	2	0.04	5.3	0.10	132.5	2	0.01	1.325	0.15
C	167.5	3	0.04	6.7	0.10	167.5	3	0.01	1.675	0.09
D	200	4	0.04	8.0	0.10	200	4	0.01	2.00	0.05

MINIMUM INSPECTION COST APPROACH

In this method, one of the characteristics of a sampling plan is chosen according to the requirements of the purchaser or the producer. Then, out of a number of plans which may meet this particular requirement, a choice is made on the basis of economic considerations to minimise the cost of inspection. In this consideration, it is generally assumed that all the rejected lots will be 100% inspected and that the total cost of inspection is proportional to the number of article inspected. Let us suppose that an economical sampling plan is required to be devised for a product which has a process average quality of 1% defective and is being offered in lots of 500 each. The purchaser requires that the lot tolerance should not exceed

4% defective at 10% consumer's risk. From Table B, it can be seen that all the four plans meet this requirement of consumer's risk. To determine the relative economics of these four plans, we shall see how many pieces per lot will be required to be inspected in each of the four plans. It should be appreciated that when a lot is accepted, the number of pieces inspected is the sample size, whereas when the lot is rejected, the entire lot will be equal to the lot size. The average number of pieces inspected per lot, is given by the following formulae:

(Sample size × proportion of lots accepted) + (lot size × proportion of lots rejected)

Applying this formula to the four plans of Table B, we get the results which are given in Table C.

Table C

Plan	Sample size	Acceptance number	Proportion of lots likely to be accepted	Proportion of lots likely to be rejected	Average number inspected per lot
A	97.5	1	0.74	0.26	97.5 x 0.74 + 500 x 0.26 = 202
B	132.5	2	0.85	0.15	132.5 x 0.85 + 500 x 0.15 = 187
C	167.5	3	0.91	0.09	167.5 x 0.91 + 500 x 0.09 = 197
D	200	4	0.95	0.05	200 x 0.95 + 500 x 0.05 = 215

It can be seen from Table C that the average number of pieces inspected per lot is the least in the case of Plan B. Therefore, from the inspection cost point of view, Plan B is preferable.

DOUBLE AND MULTIPLE SAMPLING PLANS

DOUBLE SAMPLING

In the sampling system discussed so far, a single sample of fixed size is inspected, and the lot is accepted or rejected on the basis of the sample. In the double sampling system, up to two samples may be taken from the lot to be sentenced. At first, one sample, which is of smaller size than that in single sampling, is inspected and certain decisions are taken on the basis of its result. If the quality of the first sample is sufficiently good, the lot is accepted straightaway. If it is sufficiently bad, the lot is rejected, without taking the second sample. If, however, the quality of the sample is a borderline case, a second sample is taken and the lot is sentenced on the basis of combined results of the first and the second sample. Double sampling permits economy in inspection when the quality of the submitted lots is appreciably above or below the acceptable quality level. The main advantage of double sampling is, the psychological factor that the manufacturer feels that his lot is given a second chance before it is rejected.

Specification and Working of a Double Sampling Plan

A double sampling plan is designated by five numbers given below:

First sample size	N_1
First acceptance number	C_1
First rejection number	C_2
Second sample size	N_2
Second acceptance number	C_3

It will be seen that the second rejection number is not mentioned above, since it is understood that it will be the next consecutive number to C_3. At first, a sample of size N_1 is inspected. If the number of defectives in this sample is equal to or greater than C_2, the lot is rejected. If the number of defectives is equal to or less than C_1 the lot is accepted. In case the number of defectives is more than C_1 but less than C_2, a second sample of size N_2 is inspected. If in both the samples are put together, the number of defectives is equal to, or less than, C_3, the lot is accepted, but if the defectives are more than C_3 the lot is rejected.

Devising a Double Sampling Plan

We have seen that there are five numbers which specify a double sampling plan, as against only two in the case of single sampling plans. This makes the choice of double sampling plans much more complicated. However, a method has been evolved, based on the work of Hamaker, Van Strik and Hill*, which considerably simplifies the derivation of double sampling plan to meet the requirements of the producer and the consumer. In this method, a single sampling plan is first designed by the method discussed earlier. Then, with the help of Table D, a double sampling plan is devised, whose OC Curve matches the OC curve of the particular single sampling plan. Let us suppose a double sampling plan is required for

AQL = 0.01 fraction defective at 5% producer's risk

LT = 0.04 fraction defective at 10% consumer's risk.

*I.D. HILL, "An Introduction to Sampling Inspection" Institution of Engineering Inspection, UK.

First, we derive a single sampling plan which meets this requirement. We have seen earlier that Plan D with sample size 200 and acceptance number 4 meets the above requirement. To find the suitable sampling plan which will meet these requirements, we use Table D. Looking against single sample acceptance no. 4, in the first column, we get a double sampling plan with the following features:

First Sample No. $N\mu = 0.4_n$ = (0.4) (200) = 80 {n is a single sample size which in this case is 200}

First Acceptance No. $C_1 = 0$

First Rejection No. $C_2 = 4$

Second Sample Size N_2 = .8n = .8 (200) = 160

Second Acceptance No. $C_3 = 5$

Table D

Single sample acc. no	First sample size	First sample acceptance no.	First sample rejection no.	Second sample size	Acc. no for combined sample	
	N_1	C_1	C_2	N_2	C_3	
0	*n*	0	1	—	—	
1	0.6*n*	0	2	0.6*n*	1	
2	0.4*n*	0	3	0.8*n*	2	
3	0.4*n*	0	4	0.8*n*	5	Where 'n' is the single sample size
4	0.4*n*	0	4	0.8*n*	5	
5	0.4*n*	1	5	0.8*n*	6	
6	0.4*n*	1	5	0.8*n*	7	
7	0.4*n*	1	6	0.8*n*	8	
8	0.4*n*	2	6	0.8*n*	9	
9	0.4*n*	2	7	0.8*n*	10	
10	0.4*n*	3	8	0.8*n*	11	
11	0.4*n*	3	8	0.8*n*	12	
12	0.4*n*	3	8	0.8*n*	14	
13	0.4*n*	3	9	0.8*n*	15	
14	0.4*n*	4	9	0.8*n*	16	
15	0.4*n*	4	10	0.8*n*	17	

The OC curves of the above double sampling plan and single sampling plan based on Table D, are shown in Fig. 6, from which it can be seen that they are almost identical. In this way, a double sampling plan to match any single sampling plan can be derived.

MULTIPLE SAMPLING

Multiple sampling is an extension of the double sampling system, where more than two samples may be inspected to arrive at a decision in the case of border line quality of the samples. The principle of multiple sampling is the same as for double sampling. A subsequent sample is taken only if the decision is not reached by the results of the earlier sample. Multiple sampling plans are seven stage plans, where up to a maximum of seven samples may be taken to reach a decision. In practice, it is very rare for the seventh sample to be taken, since a decision is usually reached at an earlier stage. In most multiple sampling plans, the successive samples are all of equal size, each of which is of much less size than the sample for the equivalent single sampling plan. Overall inspection is reduced. A typical multiple sampling plan is given in Table E.

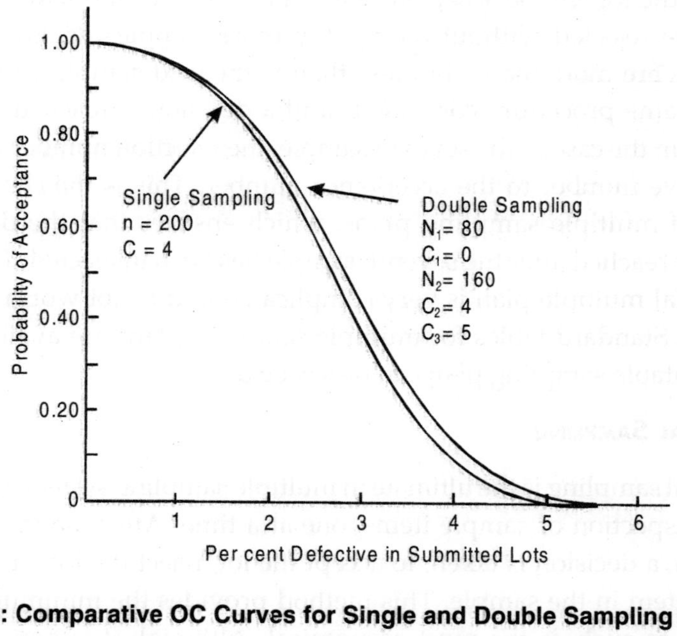

Fig. 6: Comparative OC Curves for Single and Double Sampling Plans

Table E

Sample no.	*Sample size*	*Cumulative acceptance no.*	*Cumulative rejection no.*
First	32	0	4
Second	32	1	6
Third	32	3	8
Fourth	32	5	10
Fifth	32	7	11
Sixth	32	10	12
Seventh	32	13	14

Here, it should be noted that the acceptance and rejection numbers are cumulative figures and are not for individual samples. For example, in the third sample, acceptance number 3 and rejection number 8 are for all the three samples combined. Thus, if there are only 3 defectives in the first 3 samples, the lot will be accepted, but if there are 8 or more defectives the lot will be rejected without taking any more samples. If, however, the defectives are more than 3 but less than 8, the next sample will be taken and the same procedure continued until a decision is reached. It will be seen that in the case of the seventh sample, the rejection number is the next consecutive number to the acceptance number. This is the characteristic feature of multiple sampling plans, which ensures that the decision is definitely reached after the seventh sample has been inspected. The design of a special multiple plan is very complicated and is not worth the effort involved. Standard tables for multiple sampling plans are available from which suitable sampling plan can be selected.

Sequential Sampling

Sequential sampling is the ultimate in multiple sampling system. It provides for the inspection of sample items, one at a time. After the inspection of each item, a decision is taken, to accept the lot, reject the lot, or to inspect the next item in the sample. This method provides the minimum sample size and, as such, is the most economical. Although it is more complex than single and double sampling, the economy in inspection cost may justify its use, especially where the samples are costly to obtain and the inspection is destructive. This system was developed by A. Wald in USA and G. A. Barnard in England. Barnard's system, which is comparatively simpler to administer, is discussed as follows:

Procedure for Sequential Sampling

In Barnard's system, a continuous score is maintained as the items in the sample are inspected one by one. If the item inspected is found acceptable, one point is added to the score. If the item is rejected, certain penalty points called 'b' are substracted from the score. The score initially starts from a handicap called H. When it rises to a certain target figure called 'T', the lot is accepted. If the score equals or falls below zero, the lot is rejected. Thus, a sequential sampling plan is specified by the following three numbers:

Handicap *i.e.* initial value of score — H
Penalty figure for each rejected item — b
Target figure for acceptance of lot — T

Table F

Item	*Quality*	*Score initial score H 15*
1st	Good	15+1 = 16
2nd	Good	16+1 = 17
3rd	Bad	17–5 = 12
4th	Good	12+1 = 13
5th	Good	13+1 = 14
6th	Good	14+1 = 15
7th	Good	15+1 = 16
8th	Good	16+1 = 17
9th	Good	17+1 = 18
10th	Good	18+1 = 19
11th	Good	19+1 = 20
12th	Good	20+1 = 21
13th	Good	21+1 = 22
14th	Good	22+1 = 23
15th	Good	23+1 = 24
16th	Good	24+1 = 25
17th	Good	25+1 = 26
18th	Good	26+1 = 27
19th	Good	27+1 = 28
20th	Good	28+1 = 29
21st	Good	29+1 = 30
22nd	Good	30+1 = 31
23rd	Good	31+1 = 32

Suppose a lot is being inspected by a sequential sampling plan in which H = 15, b = 5, and T = 32. The inspection results of the first 23 pieces of the sample are given in the second column of Table F. The third column shows the cumulative score. The score starts with the initial figure 15 (the H value). The first two pieces have been found acceptable. As such, one point for each good piece has been added in the score. The third piece has been found bad. Therefore, five points (*i.e.* penalty figure) have been deducted from the score. In this way, the score is maintained as shown in the table.

After the inspection of the 23rd item of the sample, the score reaches 32, which is the target figure T. As such, the lot is accepted at this stage. It may happen that the score does not reach the acceptance or rejection limit, even after a large number of pieces have been inspected. To avoid such a situation, a certain maximum sample size is specified by a mutual agreement between the purchaser and the supplier after which, if the score is H or less, the lot is rejected, whereas if it is more than H the lot is accepted. Alternatively, some agreements may provide for the application of the criteria for a corresponding multiple sampling plan, if no decision is reached up to a certain sample size. The aim is that in no case the sample size should increase beyond the maximum sample size for a corresponding multiple sampling plan.

28

Standard Sampling Tables

We have seen in the previous chapter that it is possible to design sampling plans to suit particular requirements of the purchaser and the supplier. However, in practice, it is not normally necessary to make these computations. Standard sampling tables have been published by various agencies in which one can always find a plan to meet most situations normally met within practice. Two of the most widely used sampling tables are discussed below:

DODGE AND ROMIG TABLES

Sampling plans in these tables are based on the specific AOQL and minimum inspection cost approach. An extract of Dodge and Romig tables for an AOQL of 2% defectives is given in Appendix 'A'. To determine a sampling plan from the Dodge and Romig tables, it is essential to know,

(a) The AOQL desired

(b) The process average quality

(c) The size of the lot.

The plan can then be chosen from the relevant AOQL table by looking at the lot size row under the specified process average quality column. The plan indicates,

The sample size,

The acceptance number and the Lot tolerance.

Let us suppose a plan is required for

AOQL = 2 defectives

Process average quality = 1% defective

Lot size = 1,500

Looking at a 2% AOQL table against the 1000–2000 lot size row, we find the following plan under the process average 0.81% to 1.20%:

Sample Size N = 65

Acceptance No. C = 2

Lot tolerance = 8.2% defective at 10% consumer's risk

Similarly, a sampling plan for any other requirement can be chosen. It should be noted that in all sampling plans based on AOQL, it is mandatory on the part of the producer that all the rejected lots be made 100% good.

MILITARY STANDARD TABLES

The armed forces in the USA and the UK, being among the largest consumers of industrial products in the world, have done considerable development work on sampling inspection. The latest Military Standard Sampling Tables have been published as Military Standard 105D in the USA, and DEF 131-A in the UK. Both these are based on sampling table which were originally published as Mil. Std. 105A, and incorporate certain modifications and improvements. These sampling tables have been designed from the consumer's point of view, to persuade the manufacturer to improve the quality of his product, rather than for sorting out good lots from the bad ones. These tables can be used if the lot size and the desired AQL is known. The sampling tables indicate the sample size and the acceptance number.

TABLES FOR SINGLE SAMPLING

Mil. Std. 105 D tables for single sampling plans are given in Appendix C. To select a sampling plan from these tables, the first thing to be chosen is the sample size code letter. This can be determined from the lot size by choosing a suitable Inspection Level. We have seen earlier, while discussing OC curves, that the larger the sample size, the lesser is the risk in sampling inspection. These tables have been so planned that when the lot size is large the sample size is comparatively larger than when the lot size is small, although not in the same proportion. To provide flexibility in the sample size, for a particular lot size, different inspection levels have been laid down, as shown in the table of sample size code letters given in Appendix B. Three general inspection levels I, II and III are provided which give different sample sizes according to the discrimination required. Normally, inspection level II is used to obtain the sample size from the lot size. This inspection level gives a reasonably good discrimination and an economical sample size. When lesser discrimination is required [*i.e.*, a greater risk of incorrect sentencing can be taken], inspection level I, which gives a smaller sample size, may be used. For better discrimination (*i.e.*, lesser sampling risk), inspection level III may be used, since it gives a comparatively larger sample size. Four additional special levels: S-1, S-2, S-3 and S-4 are also provided, when very small sample sizes are required and greater risks can be tolerated. In Military sampling tables, sample sizes are designated by code letters A, B, C, etc. After the sample code letter has been chosen by selecting an inspection level from Table I in Appendix B, the actual sampling plan can be obtained from the master Table IIA for single sampling plans given in Appendix C.

Let us suppose that a sampling plan is required for lot size 1,000, AQL 1% and inspection level II. Looking at Table I in Appendix B in the 501 to 1,200 lot size row, we get a code letter J under the column general inspection level II. Then, from the master Table IIA for single sampling given in Appendix C-l, we find that the sample size for code letter J is 80. Looking in this sample size row, under the AQL column 1.0, we get AC-2 and Re-3, which means acceptance number 2 and rejection number 3. Thus, our sampling plan will be:

Sampling Size — 80
Acceptance No. — 2
Rejection No. — 3

It will also be seen in the master table that, in some places, AC and Re numbers are not given. Instead, there are arrows point upwards or downwards. This indicates that for that particular AQL, the sample size given in column 2 is not compatible. Therefore, the table directs the reader by means of the arrow, to go above or below in the table to get a suitable plan. For example, let us say a plan is required for lot size 200 and AQL 1.25%. Table I in Appendix B gives for lot size 151 to 280 and inspection level II the code idler G. Looking in the code letter G row in the master Table II-A, for single sampling under the 0.25 AQL column, it is found that the acceptance and rejection numbers are not given. In their place the arrow points to the plan in the H code letter row, where the sample size is 50, the acceptance number zero and rejection No. 1 (the reader should note that the sample size should be taken from the same row which contains the acceptance and rejection numbers).

Preferred AQLs

The Mil. Std. tables are arranged for 26 fixed values of AQL, ranging from 0.01% (*i.e.*, one defective per 10,000 units) to 1,000 units) to (*i.e.*, 1,000 defects per 100 units). The AQLs more than 10% pertains only to the number of defects per 100 units, and cannot be applied to per cent defectives. These 26 values of AQL are so chosen that each value is approximately one and a half times as large as the previous one. While specifying AQL for sampling plans, one of these preferred AQLs should be used. Otherwise, these tables are not applicable. However, if due to any particular reason, an AQL other than the preferred values is to be specified, the sampling plan can be specially designed by methods discussed earlier.

Normal and Tightened Inspection

We have so far considered the normal inspection plans contained in Mil. Std. Table IIA. These plans have been designed mainly to encourage the producer to keep the quality of his product above AQL. If he is able to achieve this, the probability of acceptance of lots will be 0.90 to 0.99, depending upon the sample size and AQL. However, in these plans, the consumer's risk is too high if the quality of the product is considerably worse than the AQL. To safeguard the consumer's interest, there is a provision in Mil. Std. tables for switching to tightened inspection plans if the quality of the lots deteriorates. The master table for single sampling (tightened inspection) is given in Table IIB (Appendix C-2). The sampling plans in these tables provide for a reduced acceptance number for the same sample size, as compared to tables for normal inspection. It is recommended that inspection should be switched from a normal inspection plan to the tightened inspection plan, if 2 out of 5 consecutive lots are rejected. After the tightened inspection has been in force, there is a provision for switching back to the normal inspection if the quality of the lots improves. As per the Mil. Std. normal inspection can be re-instituted if 5 consecutive lots have been accepted under the tightened inspection plan.

Reduced Inspection

When the quality of the submitted lots is well above the AQL, there is a provision for reduced inspection to minimize the cost of inspection. The master table of sampling plans for reduced inspection is given in Table IIC (Appendix C-3). In these plans, the sample size is about two fifths of the sample size in the corresponding tables for normal inspection. The acceptance number is also appropriately reduced. Before introducing reduced inspection, it should be ensured that the quality of the product is consistently well above the AQL and is likely to remain so. As per Mil. Std. the following criteria are recommended for switching to reduced inspection:

(a) The preceding to lots have been on normal inspection and none has been rejected on original inspection.

(b) The total number of defectives in the samples from the preceding 10 lots is equal to or less than the applicable limit number given in Table VIII (Appendix C-4).

(c) The production is steady.

While reduced inspection is in operation, if any lot is rejected, the inspection should immediately be switched to the normal inspection plan. It will be noticed that unlike the normal and lightened inspection tables, the rejection number in reduced inspection plan is not the next number to the acceptance number. During reduced inspection, if the acceptance number has been exceeded but the rejection number has not been reached, the particular lot will be accepted, but inspection should immediately be switched to the normal inspection.

LOT TOLERANCE PROTECTION FOR THE CONSUMER

The sampling plans given in Mil. Std. have been designed for use where the store is produced in a continuing series of lots over a period of time. In such cases, procedure for tightened inspection can afford some protection to the consumer against acceptance of lots with very poor quality. If, however, a lot is of an isolated nature, it is desirable to limit the selection of sampling plans to those which provide a specified lot tolerance or Limiting Quality protection at the desired consumer's risk. Table VIA (Appendix C-5) gives the Limiting Quality (*i.e.*, the Lot tolerance) values at 10% consumer's risk. In this table, if a plan associated with a particular AQL does not give the required lot tolerance, the plan with a higher sample size, which gives the required lot tolerance, may be chosen.

AOQL FOR SAMPLING PLANS

The values of AOQL for the various plans in the Mil. Std. tables are given in Table V-A (Appendix C-6). Here again, if it is found that the sampling plan associated with a particular AQL does not give the required AOQL protection, the sampling plan with a higher sample size which gives the required AOQL may be chosen. It must, however, be appreciated that plans with higher sample sizes will increase the cost of inspection, which is the price that has to be paid for getting AOQL protection.

OC CURVES FOR SAMPLING PLANS

The Mil. Std. table also gives the OC Curves for sampling plans contained in the tables from which the probability of acceptance at any quality level of lots can be determined. A sample of OC curves for code letter G is given in Fig. 1.

DOUBLE SAMPLING TABLES

Like single sampling, standard tables for double sampling plans are also available, from which any desired plan can be selected. Master tables for double sampling plans for normal and tightened inspection, based on Mil. Std. 105D and British Defence specification 131-A, are given in Appendix D. In these tables, the first and the second sample size is the same for ease of operation and the selection of plans is made on the basis of lot size and AQL. For example, let us say a double sampling plan (normal inspection) is required for a lot size 800, and AQL 1.5% defective. Looking in the lot size 501-1200 row in Table I (Appendix B), we get sample size code letter J under inspection level 11. Then, from the master table for double sampling (normal inspection) given in table IIIA (Appendix D1), we get the following samples sizes for code letter J:

$$N_1 = 50$$
$$N_2 = 50$$

Continuing in the same row, we see under the 1.5% AQL column,

$C_1 = 1$ (First acceptance No.)
$C_2 = 4$ (First rejection No.)
$C_3 = 4$ (Second acceptance No.)

Here, the reader may wonder, at finding C_2 and C_3 the same. This may happen because C_2 is a rejection number for the first sample, whereas C_3 is an acceptance number for both samples combined. If in the first sample four defectives are found, the lot will be rejected.

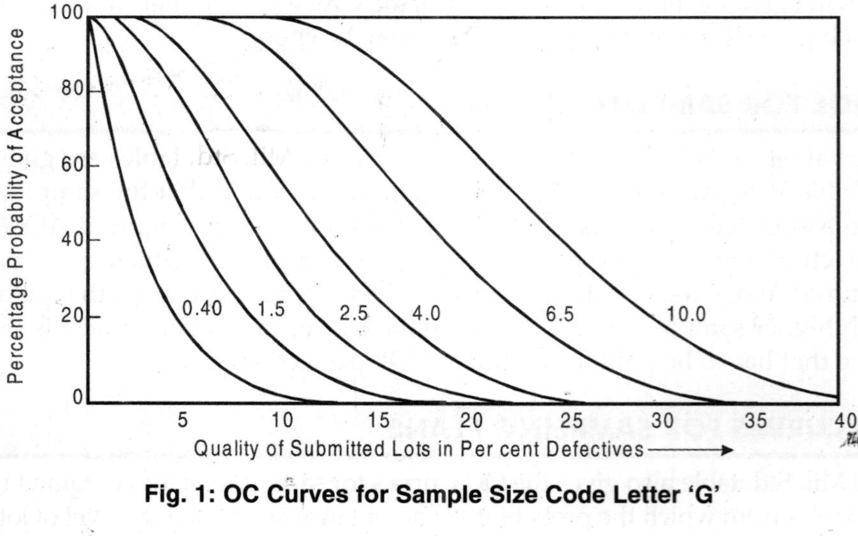

Fig. 1: OC Curves for Sample Size Code Letter 'G'

On the other hand, if only four defectives are found in both samples put together, the lot will be accepted. Double sampling tables can be used to select a sampling plan for any lot size and AQL. The sampling plans in this table are so designed that their OC curves are similar to the OC curves of corresponding single sampling plans for the same lot size and AQL.

MULTIPLE SAMPLING TABLES

Tables for multiple sampling plans recommended by British Defence Specification 131-A and Mil. Std. 105D are given in Appendix D-4. The sampling plan from these tables too is selected on the basis of lot size and AQL. First, the sample size code letter is found from Table I given in Appendix B, by choosing an inspection level and, subsequently, the actual sampling plan for that code letter is determined from the master table given in Appendix D. For example, for a lot size 4000 and AQL 0.65% defective, the multiple sampling plan given by the master table is shown in Table A.

Table A

Sample no.	*Sample size*	*Acceptance no.*	*Rejection no.*
I	50	//	3
II	50	0	3
III	50	1	4
IV	50	2	5
V	50	3	6
VII	50	4	6
VIII	50	6	7

Symbol (//) in the above table in place of the acceptance number for the first sample, indicates that acceptance cannot be given at this stage even if no defective is found and the next sample has got to be taken. This is because of the fact that only one sample of 50 pieces is considered inadequate to give reliable index of the quality of the lot. The master tables for multiple sampling have been so designed that their OC curves match the OC curves of corresponding single and double sampling plans for the same lot size and AQL. Although the average sample size in multiple sampling is somewhat less than that in double sampling, these plans are more complicated, difficult to administer and requires more data recording. Due to this reason, multiple sampling is employed only where highly trained inspection staff is available and a large number of lots are to be inspected.

STANDARD TABLES FOR SEQUENTIAL SAMPLING

Like other types of sampling, standard tables for sequential sampling are also available. Tables recommended by UK Defence Specification 131-A are reproduced as Appendix E. The plans are selected from the lot size and AQL. For example, for a lot size 200, and AQL of 1.5% defectives, the sequential plan as per Def 131-A is,

$$H = 22$$

$$b = 21$$

In these tables, target T is taken to be equal to 2 H. Thus, in this case, the score will start from 22, and target T for acceptance will be 44. To avoid the inspection of an unduly large number of units in the event of no decision being reached, the maximum sample size is also indicated in these tables for each plan. For the above plan, the maximum sample size is 56.

PRACTICAL APPLICATION OF SAMPLING INSPECTION

Sampling inspection is an important inspection tool, which can be employed for acceptance inspection as well as process control where conditions warrant its use. The decision, whether to use 100% inspection or sampling inspection, depends upon the end use of the product and economic considerations. As a general rule, 100% inspection is used for stores where a defective unit may cause danger to life or property, or when the store is of a complex nature and is expensive, such as weapons or vehicles and test is non-destructive. In such cases it is desirable to superimpose sampling inspection to sustain effectiveness of 100% inspection. On the other hand, sampling inspection is employed where 100% inspection causes fatigue and hold-ups in the flow of the product, or where the inspection is destructive. It makes sense to base decisions on choice of sampling versus 100% inspection on economic considerations, which involve the calculation of Break Even Point (BEP). BEP can be defined as the percentage ratio between the per unit cost of inspection and the cost of repair or replacement of a defective unit and the likely loss it can cause. The following formula can be used for the calculation of BEP:

$$\text{BEP} = \frac{\text{Cost of inspection per unit}}{\text{Cost of repair or replacement per defective unit}} \times 100$$

Since the cost of repair of defective units varies with the type of defect, it is usual to take per unit manufacturing cost of the product in the denominator of the above formula. For example, if the per unit cost of inspection of a component is Re.0.20 and the manufacturing cost of the component is Rs.4.00

$$\text{BEP} = \frac{0.02 \times 100}{4.00} = 5\%$$

The following criteria can then be used to decide, whether to use 100% inspection or sampling inspection:

(a) If the percentage of defective units in the store offered for inspection is less than or equal to BEP, sampling inspection will be most economical.

(b) If the percentage of defectives in the incoming lots is substantially more than BEP, 100% inspection should be preferred, since the elimination of defectives will more than pay for the extra cost of inspection.

(c) If the percentage defectives in the store is considerably less than the BEP, inspection may be eliminated altogether. However, before this decision is taken, it should be ascertained that the quality level is consistent. To guard against deterioration of quality in the future, it may be prudent to inspect a few samples occasionally, at irregular intervals. On the basis of the above criteria, it is seen that in most cases where the store is produced in large quantities, sampling inspection is found to be more economical. However, a price has to be paid for this economy in the form of risk of acceptance of a certain number of substandard stores or the rejection of stores of accpetance quality.

CHOOSING A SAMPLING PLAN

Having decided that sampling inspection will be employed, the next question is, what types of sampling plan is to be used. We have seen that there are four main types, namely, single, double, multiple and sequential sampling. Each of these has its own advantages and disadvantages which make it suitable for certain situations. The main factors which govern the choice are discussed below:

(a) Simplicity of Operation

The success of sampling inspection depends to a large extent on the ease of its operation. The more complicated a plan, the greater is the chance of its mis-application. Therefore, simpler sampling plans should be preferred. The single sampling plan is obviously the easiest to understand and administer. Double sampling is relatively more complicated. Multiple and sequential sampling are still more complex and should not be introduced unless highly trained staff and facilities for proper drawing of samples are available.

(b) Economy of Inspection

When sampling inspection is employed, the cost of bulk inspection is generally proportional to the average size of the samples which are inspected. To economise on the cost of inspection, obviously the type of plan which requires the least average sample size is preferable. In the case of single sampling, the sample size is constant, but for double, multiple and sequential samplings, the average size varies with the quality of the submitted lots. Average sample size curves for the above-mentioned types of sampling plans having similar operating characteristics are shown in Fig. 2. It can be seen that at any particular quality level the single sampling plan requires the maximum sample size and the sequential sampling requires the least average sample size. In the case of double and multiple sampling, the average sample size is in between that required by single and sequential sampling. It will also be seen that at border line quality level of lots, there is not much difference between the average sample size for the different types of sampling plan. Substantial economy in inspection cost is possible by use of double, multiple and sequential sampling, only when the quality of submitted lots is either considerably better or worse than AQL. Therefore, the expected quality of the submitted lots should be given due consideration while deciding the type of sampling plan to be used.

(c) Ease of Drawing Samples

Ease of drawing a sample is a major factor in deciding the type of plan which can be employed.

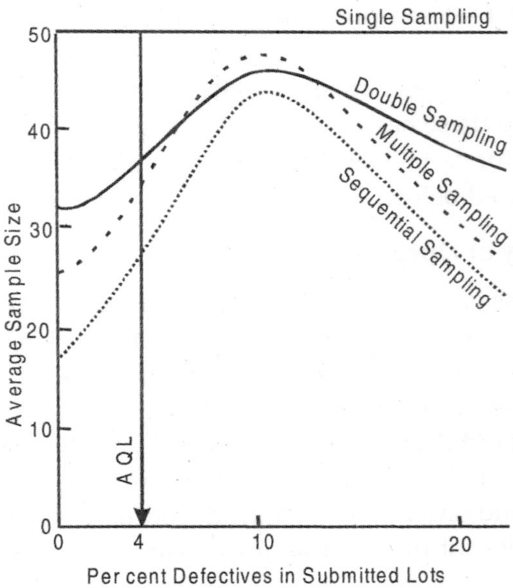

Fig. 2: Comparative Sample Size for Single, Double, Multiple and Sequential Sampling

(The procedure of drawing a sample is discussed later in this section.) Sometimes, drawing of sample is a simple affair and any number of samples can be picked up without any difficulty. In others cases, drawing of second and subsequent sample is much more difficult. When sampling inspection is employed as process control in continuous flow production, drawing of second may not be possible. Therefore, where picking up a sample forms a large part of inspection effort or where drawing of second sample is difficult, single sampling should be preferred.

(d) Testing Effort and Duration of Test

The time and effort required to test a sample will also have considerable influence in the choice of a sampling plan. When the test is of long duration and a number of pieces can be tested simultaneously, such as in environmental testing, single sampling plan should be preferred, because other types of sampling would involve undue delay. Single sampling should also be preferred where arrangements for test facilities require considerable time and effort, although actual testing needs very little time, such as the proof firing of ammunition. In the case of very expensive pieces of ammunition, however, this factor should be balanced against the cost of the sample items, to finally decide the type of sampling plan to be used. When the inspection of individual items involves elaborate testing and only one or two pieces can be tested at a time, the sampling plan requiring the least average sample size is more advantageous.

From the above considerations, it will be appreciated that no one type of sampling inspection can be considered superior to the others for all situations. Often, economy in inspection cost has to be sacrificed for the sake of simplicity and ease of operation. Whichever type of plan is chosen, it should be mutually agreed upon by the purchaser and the supplier. Once the type of sampling plan has been decided, the actual plan can be selected from standard tables or can be specially designed, as explained earlier.

Specifying AQL

AQL is one of the fundamental parameters for sampling inspection. So far, in the discussion, we have assumed that the AQL will be known. In actual practice, AQL has to be laid down before considering the employment of sampling inspection. There are no readymade rules or tables from which AQL may be determined. The choice of AQL will depend upon various considerations such as end-use, average quality of the process, and cost of inspection. From the definition of AQL, it is clear that it is the lowest quality of the lot which is considered acceptable. To meet this quality stipulation, the manufacturer has to ensure that the process average (*i.e.*, average quality level of the process) of the product is at least as good as the AQL. If an unduly high AQL (*i.e.*, very small per cent defective), is specified, the manufacturer may not be able to achieve it with his existing plan and machinery. He has then two alternatives, either to install new machinery or resort to 100% screening inspection before submitting the lot for acceptance inspection. Both these alternatives will increase the cost, which ultimately will have to be borne by the customer. Therefore, the first guideline for establishing AQL is that as far as possible it should not be higher than the process average quality of the product. This may be satisfactory from the producer's point of view, but it has also to be ensured that it meets the customer's requirement also. For this, the end-use and consequences of failure should be taken into account. If a defective article merely results in improper assembly, where it can easily be replaced, a comparatively lower AQL (higher per cent defectives) can be tolerated. On the other hand, if a defective article causes the failure of an important and expensive piece of equipment at a time or place where replacement is difficult, a higher AQL, *i.e.*, smaller per cent defectives) will have to be specified. Thus, the choice of AQL is a compromise between what is required by the consumer, and what can be attained with the available manufacturing process at a reasonable cost. Unless the product is of a critical nature, a purely economic approach can be employed which involves the calculation of BEP. (Break Even Point), as discussed earlier. The BEP then becomes the maximum limit for AQL from the economic point of view. As long as the AQL is equal to or less than BEP, sampling inspection will be more economical than 100% inspection. In some companies, for the sake of simplicity it is standard practice to have AQL equal lo BEP. For example, let us suppose that the per-unit cost of inspection of an article is 3.5 Paise (*i.e.*, Rs.0.035) and the cost of repair of replacement is Rs.2.00.

$$\text{BEP} = \frac{0.035}{2.00} = 0.0175 \quad \text{or } 1.75\%$$

Then, AQL can be laid down as 1.75%.

When using sampling tables in Def. 131-A, one of the preferred AQLs given in these tables should be chosen. Otherwise, a sampling plan cannot be selected from these tables. In the above example, the next lower AQL to 1.75% available in Def. 131-4 tables is 1.5%. Therefore, this value of AQL should be laid down rather than 1.75%. Although the above-mentioned procedure has the merit of simplicity, a more economical use of sampling inspection can be made by specifying AQLs which are appreciably higher (*i.e.*, lesser per cent defectives), then the BEP, as recommended in Table B.

Table B

Recommended Values

BEP	AQL
0.5% to 1.0%	0.25%
1.0% to 1.75%	0.65%
1.75% to 3%	1.0%
3% to 4%	2.5%
4% to 6%	4.0%
6% to 10%	6.5%
10% to 15%	10%

The above values have been recommended from the customer's point of view and should not be taken as hard and fast rules. The producer's ability to attain these levels, and the past experience with the product should be given due consideration while deciding AQL. When a product is to be manufactured for the first time, AQL cannot be laid down. The first few lots should be subjected to 100% inspection to ascertain the process average quality and the effect of a defective product on end-use. This period can also be used to finalise the inspection techniques. Sampling inspection can only be employed gainfully when the quality of the product has stabilised at an acceptable level. Then, the AQL can be worked out by the methods discussed above.

DRAWING OF SAMPLES

The whole concept of sampling inspection is based on the premise that the quality of the sample represents the quality of the lot. This will be valid only if each piece of the lot has equal chance of being included in the sample drawn for inspection or the sample is representative of the lot. Practically, it is not as simple as it looks. It is seen that when the sample pieces are picked up from the lot, inspectors have their own preferences. Some of them have a tendency to pick up more pieces from the centre than the corners. Others may take the pieces from sides and leave the centre. Therefore, a conscious attempt should be made to ensure that the sample drawn is really a random sample without any bias. The essential requirement for this is that the entire lot should be produced and displayed in such a manner that every piece is readily accessible, so that choice is not limited on account of inaccessibility. Sometimes, it is possible to allot a number to each article in the lot, either by physical marking or by its location. For example, when articles are arranged in rows of 20 each, number 86 may refer to the sixth article in the fifth row. In such cases, random numbers taken from standard tables can be used to draw the sample. A specimen table of random numbers is given in Appendix F.

The use of this table can be explained by considering a lot of 3000 articles which are arranged in such a way that a number from 2001 to 5000 can be allotted to each of the articles. Let us say that a sample of 13 articles is to be drawn. Choosing random numbers from the top of the table in Appendix F, we get the samples with the following numbers:

3502, 4731, 3645, 2090, 4844, 3586 4546,

4681, 4032, 2366, 2092, 4064, 3156

In this table, numbers like 0972 and 6731 which do not occur in the lot should be ignored, and the next applicable number should be taken. Rather than starting from the top of the tables, it is advisable to start from different positions in different tables, every time a sample is to be selected. The tables given in Appendix F, are four-figure tables. In case the numbers in the lot consist only of three figure numbers, the first three figures of numbers in the table may be taken to compile the sample. The numbers can also be selected by going in the reverse order either by rows or by columns. The main aim is that when the lot is being arranged or numbers are being allotted, it should not be known as to which numbers will be selected for the sample.

DISPOSAL OF THE REJECTED PRODUCT

In normal industrial situations, certain lots are bound to be rejected on the basis of sampling inspection. For the successful application of sampling inspection, it is important that a strict watch be kept over the rejected lots. It is not sufficient that the rejected lot is returned to the producer. An unscrupulous producer may resubmit the same as a new lot. According to the laws of probability, if a rejected lot is resubmitted a sufficient number of times, it is likely to be accepted. If this is allowed, it negates the very object of sampling inspection. Rejection of a lot does not mean that the whole lot is considered as scrap. It can be screened by 100% inspection and the defective pieces rectified or replaced. After this screening, the lot can be resubmitted for acceptance inspection. Such resubmitted lots should be clearly identified and inspected separately. It is recommended that the resubmitted lots are inspected as per sampling plans for tightened inspection. This may prevent the producer from resubmitting the rejected lot without proper screening. It is also recommended that the rejected articles which cannot be rectified, should be defaced or destroyed to avoid their getting mixed with the accepted lot, or lots under inspection. To avoid the cost of to and fro transportation, the rejected lot may be inspected 100% at receivers end and non-conforming units made good and the cost of inspection debited to the supplier Alternatively supplier's representative may come and do 100% inspection, when recheck with sampling plan becomes obligatory.

Appendix - A: Single Sampling Table for Average Outgoing Quality Limit (AOQL) = 2.0%

Lot Size	Process Average 0 to 0.04%			Process Average 0.05 to 0.40%			Process Average 0.41 to 80%			Process Average 0.8 to 1.20%			Process Average 1.21 to 1.60%			Process Average 1.61 to 2.00%		
	n	c	P_t%	*n*	c	P_t%	*n*	c	P_t%	*n*	c	P_t%	*n*	c	P_t%	*n*	c	P_t%
1-15	All	0	...	All	0	...	All	0	...	All	0	...	All	0	...	All	0	...
16-150	14	0	13.6	14	0	13.6	14	0	13.6	14	0	13.6	14	0	13.6	14	0	13.6
51-100	16	0	12.4	16	0	12.4	16	0	12.4	16	0	12.4	16	0	12.4	16	0	12.4
101-200	17	0	12.2	17	0	12.2	17	0	12.2	17	0	12.2	35	1	10.5	35	1	10.5
201-300	17	0	12.3	17	0	12.3	17	0	12.3	37	1	10.2	37	1	10.2	37	1	10.2
301-400	18	0	11.8	18	0	11.8	38	1	10.0	38	1	10.0	38	1	10.0	60	2	8.5
401-500	18	0	11.9	18	0	11.9	39	1	9.8	39	1	9.8	60	2	8.6	60	2	8.6
501-600	18	0	11.9	18	0	11.9	39	1	9.8	39	1	9.8	60	2	8.6	60	2	8.6
601-800	18	0	11.9	40	1	9.6	40	1	9.6	65	2	8.0	65	2	8.0	85	3	7.5
801-1000	18	0	12.0	40	1	9.6	40	1	9.6	65	2	8.1	65	2	8.1	90	3	7.4
1,001-2,000	18	0	12.0	41	1	9.4	65	2	8.2	65	2	8.2	95	3	7.0	120	4	6.5
2,001-3,000	18	0	12.0	41	1	9.4	65	2	8.2	95	3	7.0	120	4	6.5	180	6	5.8
3,000-4,000	18	0	12.0	42	1	9.3	65	2	8.2	95	3	7.0	155	5	6.0	210	7	5.5
4,001-5,000	18	0	12.0	42	1	9.3	70	2	7.5	125	4	6.4	155	5	6.0	245	8	5.3
5,000-7,000	18	0	12.0	42	1	9.3	95	3	7.0	125	4	6.4	185	6	5.6	280	9	5.1
7,001-10,000	42	1	9.3	70	2	7.5	95	3	7.0	155	5	6.0	220	7	5.4	350	11	4.8
10,001-20,000	42	1	9.3	70	2	7.6	95	3	7.0	190	6	5.6	290	9	4.9	460	14	4.4
20,000-50,000	42	1	9.3	70	2	7.6	125	4	6.4	220	7	5.4	395	12	4.5	720	21	3.9
50,000-100,000	42	1	9.3	95	3	7.0	160	5	5.9	290	9	4.9	505	15	4.2	955	27	3.7

Appendix - B: Sample Size Code Letters (Mil. Std. 105D, Table 1)

Lot or Batch Size	*Special Inspection Levels*				*General Inspection Levels*		
	S-1	S-2	S-3	S-4	I	II	III
2 to 8	A	A	A	A	A	A	B
9 to 15	A	A	A	A	A	B	C
16 to 25	A	A	B	B	B	C	D
26 to 25	A	B	B	C	C	D	E
51 to 90	B	B	C	C	C	E	F
91 to 150	B	B	C	D	D	F	G
151 to 280	B	C	D	E	F	G	H
281 to 500	B	C	D	E	F	H	J
501 to 1200	C	C	E	F	G	J	K
1201 to 3200	C	D	E	G	H	K	L
3201 to 10000	C	D	F	G	J	L	M
10001 to 35000	C	D	F	H	K	M	N
35001 to 150000	D	E	G	J	L	N	P
150001 to 500000	D	E	G	J	M	P	O
500001 to over	D	E	H	K	N	Q	R

Appendix C-1: Master Table for Normal Inspection – Single Sampling (Mil. Std. Table II-A)

Sample Size Code Letter	Sample Size	Acceptable Quality Levels (normal inspection)																																																			
		0.010		0.015		0.025		0.040		0.065		0.10		0.15		0.25		0.40		0.65		1.0		1.5		2.5		4.0		6.5		10		15		25		40		65		100		150		250		400		650		1000	
		Ac	Re	Ac	Re	Ac	Re	Ac	Re	Ac	Re	Ac	Re	Ac	Re	Ac	Re	Ac	Re	Ac	Re	Ac	Re	Ac	Re	Ac	Re	Ac	Re	Ac	Re	Ac	Re	Ac	Re	Ac	Re	Ac	Re	Ac	Re	Ac	Re	Ac	Re	Ac	Re	Ac	Re	Ac	Re	Ac	Re
A	2	↓		↓		↓		↓		↓		↓		↓		↓		↓		↓		↓		↓		↓		↓		0	1	↓		↓		1	2	2	3	3	4	5	6	7	8	10	11	14	15	21	22	30	31
B	3	↓		↓		↓		↓		↓		↓		↓		↓		↓		↓		↓		↓		↓		0	1	↑		↓		1	2	2	3	3	4	5	6	7	8	10	11	14	15	21	22	30	31	44	45
C	5	↓		↓		↓		↓		↓		↓		↓		↓		↓		↓		↓		↓		0	1	↑		↓		1	2	2	3	3	4	5	6	7	8	10	11	14	15	21	22	30	31	44	45	↑	
D	8	↓		↓		↓		↓		↓		↓		↓		↓		↓		↓		↓		0	1	↑		↓		1	2	2	3	3	4	5	6	7	8	10	11	14	15	21	22	30	31	44	45	↑		↑	
E	13	↓		↓		↓		↓		↓		↓		↓		↓		↓		↓		0	1	↑		↓		1	2	2	3	3	4	5	6	7	8	10	11	14	15	21	22	30	31	44	45	↑		↑		↑	
F	20	↓		↓		↓		↓		↓		↓		↓		↓		↓		0	1	↑		↓		1	2	2	3	3	4	5	6	7	8	10	11	14	15	21	22	↑		↑		↑		↑		↑		↑	
G	32	↓		↓		↓		↓		↓		↓		↓		↓		0	1	↑		↓		1	2	2	3	3	4	5	6	7	8	10	11	14	15	21	22	↑		↑		↑		↑		↑		↑		↑	
H	50	↓		↓		↓		↓		↓		↓		↓		0	1	↑		↓		1	2	2	3	3	4	5	6	7	8	10	11	14	15	21	22	↑		↑		↑		↑		↑		↑		↑		↑	
J	80	↓		↓		↓		↓		↓		↓		0	1	↑		↓		1	2	2	3	3	4	5	6	7	8	10	11	14	15	21	22	↑		↑		↑		↑		↑		↑		↑		↑		↑	
K	125	↓		↓		↓		↓		↓		0	1	↑		↓		1	2	2	3	3	4	5	6	7	8	10	11	14	15	21	22	↑		↑		↑		↑		↑		↑		↑		↑		↑		↑	
L	200	↓		↓		↓		↓		0	1	↑		↓		1	2	2	3	3	4	5	6	7	8	10	11	14	15	21	22	↑		↑		↑		↑		↑		↑		↑		↑		↑		↑		↑	
M	315	↓		↓		↓		0	1	↑		↓		1	2	2	3	3	4	5	6	7	8	10	11	14	15	21	22	↑		↑		↑		↑		↑		↑		↑		↑		↑		↑		↑		↑	
N	500	↓		↓		0	1	↑		↓		1	2	2	3	3	4	5	6	7	8	10	11	14	15	21	22	↑		↑		↑		↑		↑		↑		↑		↑		↑		↑		↑		↑		↑	
P	800	↓		0	1	↑		↓		1	2	2	3	3	4	5	6	7	8	10	11	14	15	21	22	↑		↑		↑		↑		↑		↑		↑		↑		↑		↑		↑		↑		↑		↑	
Q	1250	0	1	↑		↓		1	2	2	3	3	4	5	6	7	8	10	11	14	15	21	22	↑		↑		↑		↑		↑		↑		↑		↑		↑		↑		↑		↑		↑		↑		↑	
R	2000	↑		↑		1	2	2	3	3	4	5	6	7	8	10	11	14	15	21	22	↑		↑		↑		↑		↑		↑		↑		↑		↑		↑		↑		↑		↑		↑		↑		↑	

⇩ = Use first sampling plan below arrow. If sample size equals or exceeds the lot or batch size, do 100 percent inspection.

⇧ = Use first sampling plan above the arrow.

Ac = Acceptance number

Re = Rejection number

Appendix C-2: Master Table for Normal Inspection – Single Sampling (Mil. Std. Table II-B)

Sample Size Code Letter	Sample Size	Acceptable Quality Levels (tightened inspection)																									
		0.010	0.015	0.025	0.040	0.065	0.10	0.15	0.25	0.40	0.65	1.0	1.5	2.5	4.0	6.5	10	15	25	40	65	100	150	250	400	650	1000
		Ac Re	Ac Re	Ac Re	Ac Re	Ac Re	Ac Re	Ac Re	Ac Re	Ac Re	Ac Re	Ac Re	Ac Re	Ac Re	Ac Re	Ac Re	Ac Re	Ac Re	Ac Re	Ac Re	Ac Re	Ac Re	Ac Re	Ac Re	Ac Re	Ac Re	Ac Re
A	2	⇩	⇩	⇩	⇩	⇩	⇩	⇩	⇩	⇩	⇩	⇩	⇩	⇩	⇩	⇩	⇩	⇩	⇩	1 2	2 3	3 4	5 6	8 9	12 13	18 19	27 28
B	3	⇩	⇩	⇩	⇩	⇩	⇩	⇩	⇩	⇩	⇩	⇩	⇩	⇩	0 1	0 1	⇩	⇩	1 2	2 3	3 4	5 6	8 9	12 13	18 19	27 28	41 42
C	5	⇩	⇩	⇩	⇩	⇩	⇩	⇩	⇩	⇩	⇩	⇩	⇩	⇩	⇩	⇩	⇩	1 2	2 3	3 4	5 6	8 9	12 13	18 19	27 28	41 42	⇧
D	8	⇩	⇩	⇩	⇩	⇩	⇩	⇩	⇩	⇩	⇩	⇩	0 1	0 1	⇩	⇩	1 2	2 3	3 4	5 6	8 9	12 13	18 19	27 28	41 42	⇧	⇧
E	13	⇩	⇩	⇩	⇩	⇩	⇩	⇩	⇩	⇩	⇩	0 1	⇩	⇩	⇩	1 2	2 3	3 4	5 6	8 9	12 13	18 19	27 28	41 42	⇧	⇧	⇧
F	20	⇩	⇩	⇩	⇩	⇩	⇩	⇩	⇩	⇩	0 1	⇩	⇩	⇩	1 2	2 3	3 4	5 6	8 9	12 13	18 19	⇧	⇧	⇧	⇧	⇧	⇧
G	32	⇩	⇩	⇩	⇩	⇩	⇩	⇩	⇩	0 1	⇩	⇩	⇩	1 2	2 3	3 4	5 6	8 9	12 13	18 19	⇧	⇧	⇧	⇧	⇧	⇧	⇧
H	50	⇩	⇩	⇩	⇩	⇩	⇩	⇩	⇩	⇩	⇩	⇩	1 2	2 3	3 4	6 6	8 9	12 13	18 19	⇧	⇧	⇧	⇧	⇧	⇧	⇧	⇧
J	80	⇩	⇩	⇩	⇩	⇩	⇩	⇩	0 1	⇩	⇩	1 2	2 3	3 4	5 6	8 9	12 13	18 19	⇧	⇧	⇧	⇧	⇧	⇧	⇧	⇧	⇧
K	125	⇩	⇩	⇩	⇩	⇩	0 1	0 1	⇩	⇩	1 2	2 3	3 4	5 6	8 9	12 13	18 19	⇧	⇧	⇧	⇧	⇧	⇧	⇧	⇧	⇧	⇧
L	200	⇩	⇩	⇩	⇩	0 1	⇩	⇩	⇩	1 2	2 3	3 4	5 6	8 9	12 13	18 19	⇧	⇧	⇧	⇧	⇧	⇧	⇧	⇧	⇧	⇧	⇧
M	315	⇩	⇩	⇩	⇩	⇩	⇩	⇩	1 2	2 3	3 4	5 6	8 9	12 13	18 19	⇧	⇧	⇧	⇧	⇧	⇧	⇧	⇧	⇧	⇧	⇧	⇧
N	500	⇩	⇩	0 1	0 1	⇩	⇩	1 2	2 3	3 4	5 6	8 9	12 13	18 19	⇧	⇧	⇧	⇧	⇧	⇧	⇧	⇧	⇧	⇧	⇧	⇧	⇧
P	800	⇩	⇩	⇩	⇩	⇩	1 2	2 3	3 4	5 6	8 9	12 13	18 19	⇧	⇧	⇧	⇧	⇧	⇧	⇧	⇧	⇧	⇧	⇧	⇧	⇧	⇧
Q	1250	⇩	0 1	⇩	⇩	1 2	2 3	3 4	5 6	8 9	12 13	18 19	⇧	⇧	⇧	⇧	⇧	⇧	⇧	⇧	⇧	⇧	⇧	⇧	⇧	⇧	⇧
R	2000	0 1	⇧	⇩	1 2	2 3	3 4	5 6	8 9	12 13	18 19	⇧	⇧	⇧	⇧	⇧	⇧	⇧	⇧	⇧	⇧	⇧	⇧	⇧	⇧	⇧	⇧
S	3150		⇧	1 2								⇧	⇧	⇧	⇧	⇧	⇧	⇧	⇧	⇧	⇧	⇧	⇧	⇧	⇧	⇧	⇧

⇩ = Use first sampling plan below the arrow. If sample size equals or exceeds the lot or batch size, do 100 percent inspection.

⇧ = Use first sampling plan above the arrow.

Ac = Acceptance number

Re = Rejection number

Appendix C-3: Master Table for Normal Inspection – Single Sampling (Mil. Std. Table II-C)

Sample Size Code Letter	Sample Size	Acceptable Quality Levels (reduced inspection) 0.010	0.015	0.025	0.040	0.065	0.10	0.15	0.25	0.40	0.65	1.0	1.5	2.5	4.0	65	10	15	25	40	65	100	150	250	400	650	1000
		Ac Re	Ac Re	Ac Re	Ac Re	Ac Re	Ac Re	Ac Re	Ac Re	Ac Re	Ac Re	Ac Re	Ac Re	Ac Re	Ac Re	Ac Re	Ac Re	Ac Re	Ac Re	Ac Re	Ac Re	Ac Re	Ac Re	Ac Re	Ac Re	Ac Re	Ac Re
A	2	⇩	⇩	⇩	⇩	⇩	⇩	⇩	⇩	⇩	⇩	⇩	⇩	⇩	⇩	0 1	⇩	⇩	1 2	2 3	3 4	5 6	7 8	10 11	14 15	21 22	30 31
B	2	⇩	⇩	⇩	⇩	⇩	⇩	⇩	⇩	⇩	⇩	⇩	⇩	⇩	0 1	⇧	⇩	0 2	1 3	2 4	3 5	5 6	7 8	10 11	14 15	21 22	30 31
C	2	⇩	⇩	⇩	⇩	⇩	⇩	⇩	⇩	⇩	⇩	⇩	⇩	0 1	⇧	⇩	0 2	1 3	1 4	2 5	3 6	5 8	7 10	10 13	14 17	21 24	⇧
D	3	⇩	⇩	⇩	⇩	⇩	⇩	⇩	⇩	⇩	⇩	⇩	0 1	⇧	⇩	0 2	1 3	1 4	2 5	3 6	5 8	7 10	10 13	14 17	21 24	⇧	⇧
E	5	⇩	⇩	⇩	⇩	⇩	⇩	⇩	⇩	⇩	⇩	0 1	⇧	⇩	0 2	1 3	1 4	2 5	3 6	5 8	7 10	10 13	14 17	21 24	⇧	⇧	⇧
F	8	⇩	⇩	⇩	⇩	⇩	⇩	⇩	⇩	⇩	0 1	⇧	⇩	0 2	1 3	1 4	2 5	3 6	5 8	7 10	10 13	⇧	⇧	⇧	⇧	⇧	⇧
G	13	⇩	⇩	⇩	⇩	⇩	⇩	⇩	⇩	0 1	⇧	⇩	0 2	1 3	1 4	2 5	3 6	5 8	7 10	10 13	⇧	⇧	⇧	⇧	⇧	⇧	⇧
H	20	⇩	⇩	⇩	⇩	⇩	⇩	⇩	0 1	⇧	⇩	0 2	1 3	1 4	2 5	3 6	5 8	7 10	10 13	⇧	⇧	⇧	⇧	⇧	⇧	⇧	⇧
J	32	⇩	⇩	⇩	⇩	⇩	⇩	0 1	⇧	⇩	0 2	1 3	1 4	2 5	3 6	5 8	7 10	10 13	⇧	⇧	⇧	⇧	⇧	⇧	⇧	⇧	⇧
K	50	⇩	⇩	⇩	⇩	⇩	0 1	⇧	⇩	0 2	1 3	1 4	2 5	3 6	5 8	7 10	10 13	⇧	⇧	⇧	⇧	⇧	⇧	⇧	⇧	⇧	⇧
L	80	⇩	⇩	⇩	⇩	0 1	⇧	⇩	0 2	1 3	1 4	2 5	3 6	5 8	7 10	10 13	⇧	⇧	⇧	⇧	⇧	⇧	⇧	⇧	⇧	⇧	⇧
M	125	⇩	⇩	⇩	0 1	⇧	⇩	0 2	1 3	1 4	2 5	3 6	5 8	7 10	10 13	⇧	⇧	⇧	⇧	⇧	⇧	⇧	⇧	⇧	⇧	⇧	⇧
N	200	⇩	⇩	0 1	⇧	⇩	0 2	1 3	1 4	2 5	3 6	5 8	7 10	10 13	⇧	⇧	⇧	⇧	⇧	⇧	⇧	⇧	⇧	⇧	⇧	⇧	⇧
P	315	⇩	⇩	⇧	⇩	0 2	1 3	1 4	2 5	3 6	5 8	7 10	10 13	⇧	⇧	⇧	⇧	⇧	⇧	⇧	⇧	⇧	⇧	⇧	⇧	⇧	⇧
Q	500	0 1	0 1	⇩	0 2	1 3	1 4	2 5	3 6	5 8	7 10	10 13	⇧	⇧	⇧	⇧	⇧	⇧	⇧	⇧	⇧	⇧	⇧	⇧	⇧	⇧	⇧
R	800	⇧	⇧	0 2	1 3	1 4	2 5	3 6	5 8	7 10	10 13	⇧	⇧	⇧	⇧	⇧	⇧	⇧	⇧	⇧	⇧	⇧	⇧	⇧	⇧	⇧	⇧

⇩ = Use first sampling plan below the arrow. If sample size equals or exceeds the lot or batch size, do 100 percent inspection.

⇧ = Use first sampling plan above the arrow. Ac = Acceptance number Re = Rejection number

If the acceptance number has been exceeded, but the rejection number has not been reached, accept the lot, but reinstate normal inspection.

Appendix C-4: Limit Numbers for Reduced Inspection (Mil. Std. 105D Table VIII)

Number of sample units from last 10 lots or batches	Acceptable Quality Level																									
	0.010	0.015	0.25	0.040	0.065	0.10	0.15	0.25	0.40	0.65	1.0	1.5	2.5	4.0	6.5	10	15	25	40	65	100	150	250	400	650	1000
20 - 29	*	*	*	*	*	*	*	*	*	*	*	*	*	*	*	0	0	2	4	8	14	22	40	68	115	181
30 - 49	*	*	*	*	*	*	*	*	*	*	*	*	*	*	0	0	1	8	7	13	22	36	63	105	178	277
50 - 79	*	*	*	*	*	*	*	*	*	*	*	*	*	0	0	2	3	7	14	25	40	63	110	181	301	
80 - 129	*	*	*	*	*	*	*	*	*	*	*	*	0	0	2	4	7	14	24	42	68	105	181	397		
130 - 199	*	*	*	*	*	*	*	*	*	*	*	0	0	2	4	7	13	25	42	63	115	177	301	490		
200 - 319	*	*	*	*	*	*	*	*	*	*	0	0	2	4	8	14	22	40	68	115	181	277	471			
320 - 499	*	*	*	*	*	*	*	*	*	0	0	1	4	8	14	24	39	68	113	169						
500 - 799	*	*	*	*	*	*	*	*	0	0	2	3	7	14	25	40	63	110	181							
800 - 1249	*	*	*	*	*	*	*	0	0	2	4	7	14	24	42	64	105	181								
1250 - 1999	*	*	*	*	*	*	0	0	2	4	7	13	24	40	60	110	169									
2000 - 3149	*	*	*	*	*	0	0	2	4	8	14	22	40	68	115	181										
3150 - 1999	*	*	*	*	0	0	1	4	8	14	24	38	67	111	186											
5000 - 7999	*	*	*	0	0	2	3	7	14	25	40	63	110	181												
8000 - 12499	*	*	0	0	2	4	7	14	24	42	68	105	181													
12500 - 19999	*	0	0	2	4	7	13	24	40	69	110	169														
20000 - 31499	0	0	2	4	4	14	22	40	68	115	181															
31500 - 49999	0	1	4	8	14	24	38	67	111	186																
50000 - Over	2	3	7	14	25	40	63	110	181	301																

Denotes that the number of sample units from the last ten lots or batches is not sufficient for reduced inspection for this AQL. In this instance, more than ten lots or batches may be used for the calculation, provided that the lots or batches used are the most recent ones in sequence, that they have all been on normal inspection, and that none has been rejected while on original inspection.

Appendix C-5: Limiting Quality (In Percent Defective) for which P_a = 10 Percent (For Normal Inspection, Single Sampling) (Mil. Std. 105D, Table VI–A)

Code Letter	Sample Size	Acceptable Quality Level															
		0.010	0.015	0.025	0.040	0.065	0.10	0.15	0.25	0.40	0.65	1.0	1.5	2.5	4.0	6.5	10
A	2															68	
B	3														54		
C	5													37			58
D	8												25			41	54
E	13											16			27	36	44
F	20										11			18	25	30	42
G	32									6.9			12	16	20	27	34
H	50								4.5			7.6	10	13	18	22	29
J	80							2.8			0.48	6.5	8.2	11	14	19	24
K	125						1.8			3.1	4.3	5.4	7.4	9.4	12	16	23
L	200					1.2			2.0	2.7	3.3	4.6	5.9	7.7	10	14	
M	315				0.73			1.2	1.7	2.1	2.9	3.7	4.9	6.4	9.0		
N	500			0.46			0.78	1.1	1.3	1.9	2.4	3.1	4.0	5.6			
P	800		0.29			0.46	0.67	0.84	1.2	1.5	1.9	2.5	3.5				
Q	1250	0.18			0.31	0.43	0.53	0.74	0.94	1.2	1.6	2.3					
R	2000			0.20	0.27	0.33	0.46	0.59	0.77	1.0	1.4						

Appendix C-6: Average Outgoing Quality Limit Factors for Normal Inspection (Single Sampling) Table V–A

Code Letter	Sample Size	0·010	0·015	0·025	0·040	0·065	0·10	0·15	0·25	0·45	0·65	1·0	1·5	2·5	4·0	6·5	10	15	25	40	65	100	150	250	400	650	1000
A	2															18			42	69	97	160	220	330	470	730	1100
B	3														12			28	46	65	110	150	220	310	490	720	1100
C	5													7·4			17	27	39	63	90	130	190	290	430	660	
D	8												4·6			11	17	24	40	56	82	120	180	270	410		
E	13											2·8		·	6·5	11	15	24	34	50	72	110	170	250			
F	20										1·8			4·2	6·9	9·7	16	22	33	47	73						
G	32									1·2			2·6	4·3	6·1	9·9	14	21	29	46							
H	50								0·74			1·7	2·7	3·9	6·3	9·0	13	19	29								
J	80							0·46			1·1	1·7	2·4	4·0	5·6	8·2	12	18									
K	125						0.29			0.67	1.1	1.6	2.5	3.6	5.2	7.5	12										
L	200					0.18			0.42	0.69	0.97	1.6	2.2	3.3	4.7	7.3											
M	315				0.12			0.27	0.44	0.62	1.67	1.4	2.1	4.7	4.7												
N	500			0'074			0'17	0'27	0'39	0'63	0'90	1'3	1'9	4'7													
P	800		0'046			0'11	0'17	0'24	0'40	0'56	0'82	1'2	1'9														
Q	1250	0·029			0·067	0·11	0·16	0·25	0·36	0·52	0·75	1·2															
A	2000			0·042	0·069	0·097	0·16	0·22	0·33	0·47	0·73																

Notes for the exact AOQL the above value must be multiplied by $\left(1 - \frac{\text{Sample Size}}{\text{Lot or Batch Size}}\right)$ (See 11.4)

Appendix D-1: Master Table for Normal Inspection–Double Sampling (Mil. Std. 105D, Table III-A)

Sample Size Code Letter	Sample	Sample Size	Cumulative Sample Size	Acceptable Quality Level (normal inspection)																									
				0.010	0.015	0.025	0.040	0.065	0.10	0.15	0.25	0.40	0.65	1.0	1.5	2.5	4.0	6.5	10	15	25	40	65	100	150	250	400	550	1000
				AC Re	AC Re	AC Re	AC Re	AC Re	AC Re	AC Re	AC Re	AC Re	AC Re	AC Re	AC Re	AC Re	AC Re	AC Re	AC Re	AC Re	AC Re	AC Re	AC Re	AC Re	AC Re	AC Re	AC Re	AC Re	AC Re
A	First Second			⇩	⇩	⇩	⇩	⇩	⇩	⇩	⇩	⇩	⇩	⇩	⇩	⇩	⇩	●	⇩	⇩	●	●	●	●	●	●	●	●	●
B	First Second	2 2	2 4	⇩	⇩	⇩	⇩	⇩	⇩	⇩	⇩	⇩	⇩	⇩	⇩	⇩	●	⇧	⇩	0 2 1 2	0 3 3 4	1 4 4 5	2 5 6 7	3 7 8 9	5 9 12 13	7 11 18 19	11 16 26 27	17 22 37 38	25 31 56 38
C	First Second	3 3	3 6	⇩	⇩	⇩	⇩	⇩	⇩	⇩	⇩	⇩	⇩	⇩	⇩	●	⇧	⇩	0 2 1 2	0 3 3 4	1 4 4 5	2 5 6 7	3 7 8 9	5 9 12 13	7 11 18 19	11 16 26 27	17 22 37 38	25 31 56 57	⇧
D	First Second	5 5	5 10	⇩	⇩	⇩	⇩	⇩	⇩	⇩	⇩	⇩	⇩	⇩	●	⇧	⇩	0 2 1 2	0 3 3 4	1 4 4 5	2 5 6 7	3 7 8 9	5 9 12 13	7 11 18 19	11 16 26 27	17 22 37 38	25 31 56 57	⇧	⇧
E	First Second	8 8	8 16	⇩	⇩	⇩	⇩	⇩	⇩	⇩	⇩	⇩	⇩	●	⇧	⇩	0 2 1 2	0 3 3 4	1 4 4 5	2 5 6 7	3 7 8 9	5 9 12 13	7 11 18 19	11 16 26 27	17 22 37 38	25 31 56 57	⇧	⇧	⇧
F	First Second	13 13	13 26	⇩	⇩	⇩	⇩	⇩	⇩	⇩	⇩	⇩	●	⇧	⇩	0 2 1 2	0 3 3 4	1 4 4 5	2 5 6 7	3 7 8 9	5 9 12 13	7 11 18 19	11 16 26 27	⇧	⇧	⇧	⇧	⇧	⇧
G	First Second	20 20	20 40	⇩	⇩	⇩	⇩	⇩	⇩	⇩	⇩	●	⇧	⇩	0 2 1 2	0 3 3 4	1 4 4 5	2 5 6 7	3 7 8 9	5 9 12 13	7 11 18 19	11 16 26 27	⇧	⇧	⇧	⇧	⇧	⇧	⇧
H	First Second	32 32	32 64	⇩	⇩	⇩	⇩	⇩	⇩	⇩	●	⇧	⇩	0 2 1 2	0 3 3 4	1 4 4 5	2 5 6 7	3 7 8 9	5 9 12 13	7 11 18 19	11 16 26 27	⇧	⇧	⇧	⇧	⇧	⇧	⇧	⇧
J	First Second	50 50	50 100	⇩	⇩	⇩	⇩	⇩	⇩	●	⇧	⇩	0 2 1 2	0 3 3 4	1 4 4 5	2 5 6 7	3 7 8 9	5 9 12 13	7 11 18 19	11 16 26 27	⇧	⇧	⇧	⇧	⇧	⇧	⇧	⇧	⇧
K	First Second	80 80	80 160	⇩	⇩	⇩	⇩	⇩	●	⇧	⇩	0 2 1 2	0 3 3 4	1 4 4 5	2 5 6 7	3 7 8 9	5 9 12 13	7 11 18 19	11 16 26 27	⇧	⇧	⇧	⇧	⇧	⇧	⇧	⇧	⇧	⇧
L	First Second	125 125	125 250	⇩	⇩	⇩	⇩	●	⇧	⇩	0 2 1 2	0 3 3 4	1 4 4 5	2 5 6 7	3 7 8 9	5 9 12 13	7 11 18 19	11 16 26 27	⇧	⇧	⇧	⇧	⇧	⇧	⇧	⇧	⇧	⇧	⇧
M	First Second	200 200	200 400	⇩	⇩	⇩	●	⇧	⇩	0 2 1 2	0 3 3 4	1 4 4 5	2 5 6 7	3 7 8 9	5 9 12 13	7 11 18 19	11 16 26 27	⇧	⇧	⇧	⇧	⇧	⇧	⇧	⇧	⇧	⇧	⇧	⇧
N	First Second	315 315	315 630	⇩	⇩	●	⇧	⇩	0 2 1 2	0 3 3 4	1 4 4 5	2 5 6 7	3 7 8 9	5 9 12 13	7 11 18 19	11 16 26 27	⇧	⇧	⇧	⇧	⇧	⇧	⇧	⇧	⇧	⇧	⇧	⇧	⇧
P	First Second	500 500	500 1000	⇩	●	⇧	⇩	0 2 1 2	0 3 3 4	1 4 4 5	2 5 6 7	3 7 8 9	5 9 12 13	7 11 18 19	11 16 26 27	⇧	⇧	⇧	⇧	⇧	⇧	⇧	⇧	⇧	⇧	⇧	⇧	⇧	⇧
Q	First Second	800 800	800 1600	●	⇧	⇩	0 2 1 2	0 3 3 4	1 4 4 5	2 5 6 7	3 7 8 9	5 9 12 13	7 11 18 19	11 16 26 27	⇧	⇧	⇧	⇧	⇧	⇧	⇧	⇧	⇧	⇧	⇧	⇧	⇧	⇧	⇧
R	First Second	1250 1250	1250 2500	⇧	⇧	0 2 1 2	0 3 3 4	1 4 4 5	2 5 6 7	3 7 8 9	5 9 12 13	7 11 18 19	11 16 26 27	⇧	⇧	⇧	⇧	⇧	⇧	⇧	⇧	⇧	⇧	⇧	⇧	⇧	⇧	⇧	⇧

⇩ = Use first sampling plan below the arrow. If sample size equals or exceeds the lot or batch size, do 100 percent inspection.

⇧ = Use first sampling plan above the arrow. Ac = Acceptance number Re = Rejection number

● = Use corresponding single sampling plan (or alternatively, use double sampling plan below, where available).

Appendix D-2: Master Table for Normal Inspection–Double Sampling (Mil. Std. 105D, Table III-A)

Sample Size Code Letter	Sample	Sample Size	Cumulative Sample Size	Acceptable Quality Levels (Tightened Inspection)																									
				0.010	0.015	0.025	0.040	0.065	0.10	0.15	0.25	0.40	0.65	1.0	1.5	2.5	4.0	6.5	10	15	25	40	65	100	150	250	400	650	1000
				AC Re	AC Re	AC Re	AC Re	AC Re	AC Re	AC Re	AC Re	AC Re	AC Re	AC Re	AC Re	AC Re	AC Re	AC Re	AC Re	AC Re	AC Re	AC Re	AC Re	AC Re	AC Re	AC Re	AC Re	AC Re	AC Re
A																		⇩			⇩	•	•	•	•	•	•	•	•
B	First Second	2 2	2 4														⇩	•		⇩	0 2 1 2	0 3 3 4	1 4 4 5	2 5 6 7	3 7 11 12	6 10 15 16	9 14 24 24	15 20 34 35	23 29 52 53
C	First Second	3 3	3 6													⇩	•		⇩	0 2 1 2	0 3 3 4	1 4 4 5	2 5 6 7	3 7 11 12	6 10 15 16	9 14 24 24	15 20 34 35	23 29 52 53	⇧
D	First Second	5 5	5 10												⇩	•		⇩	0 2 1 2	0 3 3 4	1 4 4 5	2 5 6 7	3 7 11 12	6 10 15 16	9 14 24 24	15 20 34 35	23 29 52 53	⇧	
E	First Second	8 8	8 16											⇩	•		⇩	0 2 1 2	0 3 3 4	1 4 4 5	2 5 6 7	3 7 11 12	6 10 15 16	9 14 24 24	15 20 34 35	23 29 52 53	⇧		
F	First Second	13 13	13 26										⇩	•		⇩	0 2 1 2	0 3 3 4	1 4 4 5	2 5 6 7	3 7 11 12	6 10 15 16	9 14 24 24	⇧	⇧	⇧			
G	First Second	20 20	20 40									⇩	•		⇩	0 2 1 2	0 3 3 4	1 4 4 5	2 5 6 7	3 7 11 12	6 10 15 16	9 14 24 24	⇧						
H	First Second	32 32	32 64								⇩	•		⇩	0 2 1 2	0 3 3 4	1 4 4 5	2 5 6 7	3 7 11 12	6 10 15 16	9 14 24 24	⇧							
J	First Second	50 50	50 100							⇩	•		⇩	0 2 1 2	0 3 3 4	1 4 4 5	2 5 6 7	3 7 11 12	6 10 15 16	9 14 24 24	⇧								
K	First Second	80 80	80 160						⇩	•		⇩	0 2 1 2	0 3 3 4	1 4 4 5	2 5 6 7	3 7 11 12	6 10 15 16	9 14 24 24	⇧									
L	First Second	125 125	125 250					⇩	•		⇩	0 2 1 2	0 3 3 4	1 4 4 5	2 5 6 7	3 7 11 12	6 10 15 16	9 14 24 24	⇧										
M	First Second	200 200	200 400				⇩	•		⇩	0 2 1 2	0 3 3 4	1 4 4 5	2 5 6 7	3 7 11 12	6 10 15 16	9 14 24 24	⇧											
N	First Second	315 315	315 630			⇩	•		⇩	0 2 1 2	0 3 3 4	1 4 4 5	2 5 6 7	3 7 11 12	6 10 15 16	9 14 24 24	⇧												
P	First Second	500 500	500 1000		⇩	•		⇩	0 2 1 2	0 3 3 4	1 4 4 5	2 5 6 7	3 7 11 12	6 10 15 16	9 14 24 24	⇧													
Q	First Second	800 800	800 1600	⇩	•		⇩	0 2 1 2	0 3 3 4	1 4 4 5	2 5 6 7	3 7 11 12	6 10 15 16	9 14 24 24	⇧														
R	First Second	1250 1250	1250 2500	•	⇧	⇩	0 2 1 2	0 3 3 4	1 4 4 5	2 5 6 7	3 7 11 12	6 10 15 16	9 14 24 24	⇧															
S	First Second	2000 2000	2000 4000		0 2 1 2																								

⇩ = Use first sampling plan below the arrow. If sample size equals or exceeds the lot or batch size, do 100 percent inspection.
⇧ = Use first sampling plan above the arrow. Ac = Acceptance number Re = Rejection number
● = Use corresponding single sampling plan (or alternatively, use double sampling plan below, where available).

Appendix E: TABLE I-A—Sequential Sampling Plans for Normal Inspection (Master Table)

Sample size code letter	Maximum sample size		Acceptable Quality Levels (normal inspection)															
			0.010	0.015	0.025	0.040	0.065	0.10	0.5	0.25	0.40	0.65	1.0	1.5	2.5	4.0	6.5	10
A B C			⇩	⇩	⇩	⇩	⇩	⇩	⇩	⇩	⇩	⇩	⇩	⇩	⇩ •	⇩ • ⇧	• ⇕	⇩
D	14	H b	⇩	⇩	⇩	⇩	⇩	⇩	⇩	⇩	⇩	⇩	⇩	8 16	⇧	⇩	6 5	4 2
E	21	H b	⇩	⇩	⇩	⇩	⇩	⇩	⇩	⇩	⇩	⇩	13 26	⇧	⇩	9 8	8 5	6 3
F	35	H b	⇩	⇩	⇩	⇩	⇩	⇩	⇩	⇩	⇩	20 40	⇧	⇩	14 13	10 7	9 5	8 3
G	56	H b	⇩	⇩	⇩	⇩	⇩	⇩	⇩	⇩	32 64	⇧	⇩	22 21	16 12	15 9	11 5	10 3
H	91	H b	⇩	⇩	⇩	⇩	⇩	⇩	⇩	50 100	⇧	⇩	34 33	26 20	22 14	17 8	16 6	13 4
J	140	H b	⇩	⇩	⇩	⇩	⇩	⇩	80 160	⇧	⇩	33 54	40 32	34 23	28 14	24 10	20 7	17 5
K	224	H b	⇩	⇩	⇩	⇩	⇩	125 250	⇧	⇩	86 85	64 53	54 36	43 22	37 16	31 11	28 8	22 5
L	350	H b	⇩	⇩	⇩	⇩	200 400	⇧	⇩	137 136	103 86	86 59	69 36	60 27	51 19	43 13	36 8	⇧
M	560	H b	⇩	⇩	⇩	315 630	⇧	⇩	216 215	162 136	136 93	109 58	94 42	80 30	58 21	56 14	⇧	⇧
N	875	H b	⇩	⇩	500 1000	⇧	⇩	343 342	260 219	216 149	174 93	150 68	127 48	108 34	89 22	⇧	⇧	⇧
P	1400	H b	⇩	800 1400	⇧	⇩	348 547	410 346	345 238	278 150	239 109	203 77	173 55	142 36	⇧	⇧	⇧	⇧
Q	2205	H b	1250 2500	⇧	⇩	856 855	651 542	532 373	434 235	374 171	318 121	270 86	223 58	⇧	⇧	⇧	⇧	⇧
R	3500	H b	⇧	⇧	1370 1369	1026 868	862 597	694 376	598 273	508 194	432 139	356 93	⇧	⇧	⇧	⇧	⇧	⇧

⇩ = Use first sampling plan below the arrow.
⇧ = Use first sampling plan above the arrow.
● = Use corresponding single sampling plan (or alternatively, use sequential plan below)
++ = Use corresponding single or double sampling plan (or alternatively, use sequential plan below)
H = Handicap
b = Penalty

Appendix F: Random Sampling Numbers

3502	7917	0413	3519	0452	6846	2273	2666	6076	9139
4731	6400	8494	3125	2159	3845	8686	2433	0425	8646
3645	2366	4959	8056	1027	0145	4512	3884	9967	4152
0972	7392	9152	4878	2812	5239	4348	2393	5698	7591
6731	0826	0569	7684	8345	5746	4716	4496	7273	6584
2090	7773	5140	4479	0620	9475	2548	5139	7407	5418
1240	6879	0932	0475	8720	2538	1192	6895	6318	3744
9881	4092	0941	9385	9224	4721	5697	4634	9924	9627
0385	7008	3748	4631	6793	4287	4197	2981	9157	5425
6749	0478	2800	3673	8972	2986	0440	3496	6187	3493
1182	7202	8139	7904	9002	2959	3971	0095	2533	0063
4844	4064	8417	8030	5932	7360	9764	4294	7998	8889
0539	8431	0548	0449	0767	4673	7987	5911	8097	9887
3586	6609	5875	3433	7734	5172	2704	5903	4945	8648
1181	5165	9210	7996	6767	2216	1643	2564	4119	1359
5387	1346	1018	1127	6931	3195	7673	8264	6450	0085
5989	3156	6067	6107	0632	5242	7278	6766	3396	2620
8464	3570	1408	3983	8630	5263	1555	3965	7899	1845
9076	3642	6516	8357	5246	4722	9570	2285	1734	6897
4546	7733	2972	4218	4454	0543	9362	7150	0114	5499
4681	4643	9668	4848	5122	8853	7859	0547	1308	7074
7133	0918	9972	8534	7739	7413	1293	2421	9498	2120
4032	7763	0223	5684	6649	7409	0287	6966	2577	6749
7577	6685	9597	6599	5015	8760	8358	5822	7608	8624
7082	2564	2973	8099	9440	2427	0870	2865	1468	5345
9370	5856	3462	3271	4712	4496	4514	0982	3346	5644
8765	6645	6118	4057	6475	3134	2262	1318	3405	2087
0066	0120	4235	9529	7757	0785	1369	2905	1598	6827
4903	8158	1828	6462	5312	5894	9069	7328	3964	4503
2355	7680	2724	2753	8139	5941	4074	8218	0102	6213
8381	9616	9113	5150	0277	7013	3436	4365	9597	5359

Random Sampling Numbers (Contd...)

5866	1501	7193	8308	6299	5673	1559	3218	4843	5222
1975	3597	8887	8198	0271	3747	8049	0928	5526	5775
3217	7211	1160	5324	8708	4195	6299	5615	6022	3763
5777	6920	4474	6719	7697	0450	1313	7118	8765	4599
0930	3390	2166	8359	5053	0428	9089	5903	3810	7577
6793	4878	5303	2016	8037	1727	4877	3842	4341	0361
5992	3943	6409	8104	3309	9195	1830	0989	2667	1363
1623	8860	4642	3088	4349	8772	1695	6300	5967	0594
2978	2995	2849	4874	0193	3506	2201	6117	3409	0049
7982	9672	4167	2972	2462	1421	2570	0850	2307	4363
8176	9154	0789	7354	6935	8714	4937	3820	9785	9181
0116	7350	7072	8774	4007	2068	7608	4901	8729	9047
2459	9070	5872	0533	2588	2137	2677	7694	6841	2465
8896	8536	914	1278	2945	0008	1957	0590	6640	1122
4917	2534	7520	1517	5120	3609	1374	5914	2566	7043
9258	8548	3209	6117	7776	0181	4454	9281	0969	3689
9089	8521	5191	5532	3277	6227	9094	3000	8110	0272
4129	9337	6469	6713	7864	8935	5794	9113	1782	5832
1406	9641	8954	8229	3745	0674	9825	1638	4291	0400

29

Test of Significance

MAKING ESTIMATES FROM SAMPLE OBSERVATIONS

In the statistical quality control techniques discussed so far, the quality of a lot or production run was assessed on the basis of the quality of a sample drawn from the lot. This is based on the assumption that every random sample truly represents the lot (called population in statistical language) from which it is drawn. This, in actual fact, is not the case. In practice, various samples drawn from the same lot show some difference in quality from each other and consequently, from the lot. Thus, estimation of the quality of a lot from its sample involves a certain degree of risk or error. For example, suppose a batch of articles is known to be 5% defective. If a number of random samples of 100 pieces each are drawn from the batch, it is not certain that every sample will contain five defective pieces. Some samples may show four, three or even less number of defectives, whereas others may show five, six or even more defectives. Thus, from a sample which has three defectives, if we estimate that the batch is 3% defective we shall be making an erroneous estimate. Such risk in estimation is called 'Sampling Error'. Unless the possible extent of the sampling error or inaccuracy is known, the estimate is of no practical value. Fortunately, certain statistical methods have been developed, by which the extent of 'Sampling Error' can be known, which makes it easier to take decisions. Some of the simpler methods which aid in interpreting the sampling results are discussed in this chapter.

DIFFERENCE BETWEEN POPULATION AND SAMPLE CHARACTERISTICS

We have seen above that since every sample does not truly reflect the population, estimates of characteristics such as 'mean', 'standard deviation' or fraction defective based on sample result will show some difference from the corresponding characteristics of the population. To avoid confusion, population characteristics, such as mean or fraction defective etc. are called PARAMETERS, and their estimates taken from samples are called STATISTICS. The differences among samples are called, 'sampling errors'. Obviously, the greater the sampling errors, the lesser the sample will agree with the population. These errors can be minimised by enlarging the sample size. The larger the sample size, the greater will be the accuracy of its results. However, the sample size cannot be increased indefinitely. Otherwise, it will defeat the very object of sampling. Therefore, a certain amount of sampling error has to be accepted.

SAMPLING DISTRIBUTION AND STANDARD ERROR

Sampling errors are governed by chance causes. If a population is, more or less, normally distributed, the corresponding sample statistic will also follow normal distribution. Thus, it is possible to assign limits within which the sample statistic might vary from the population parameter. These limits can be determined in terms of the standard deviation of the sample statistic, which is also called 'Standard Error'. To illustrate the concept of sampling distribution and standard error, let us suppose that there is a large lot of bullets, whose mean weight is to be determined. Since it is impractical to weigh every bullet, we take (say) 70 samples of 40 bullets each, and find the mean weight of bullets in each sample. It will be found that the mean weight in different samples will vary. If we make a frequency distribution of mean weight of different samples, we shall get a distribution closely resembling the shape of a 'normal' curve. This is called the sampling distribution of the means. It can be proved that the true mean of a population and the mean of its sampling distribution are the same. In other words, the sample means are normally distributed about the population mean. The dispersion of sample means is indicated by their standard deviation which is also called 'Standard Error' since it is a measure of sampling error.

CALCULATION OF STANDARD ERROR

In the above illustration, we had assumed that a large number of samples were drawn to obtain the sampling distribution, from which the standard error (*i.e.* standard deviation) of sample means could be directly calculated. In actual practice, the drawing of a large number of samples is not feasible, and an estimate of the population parameter is made from the results of one or two samples only. This is possible, because the standard error can be derived from the sample observations. Here we must note the distinction between the standard error and the standard deviation of sample means. The standard deviation of the parameter is a measure of the variation of individual items in the population. However, the two are closely related. For samples of comparatively large size (greater than 30), the standard error of the mean can be calculated from the standard deviation of the population by the following formula:

$$\sigma_x = \frac{\sigma_p}{\sqrt{n}} \qquad \text{...(i)}$$

Where

- σ_x is the standard error of sample means.
- σ_p is the standard deviation (SD) of the population observations.
- n is the sample size.

Generally, the true standard deviation of the population is not known. However, it can be estimated from the standard deviation of individual items in the sample drawn from the population by using the following relationship:

$$\sigma_p = \sigma_s \times \frac{\sqrt{n}}{\sqrt{n-1}} \qquad \text{...(ii)}$$

Where

- σ_p is the estimated SD of the population.
- σ_s is the SD of individual items in a sample of size n.

Substituting σ_p from (ii) in formula (i) we get

$$\sigma_{\bar{x}} = \sigma_s \frac{\sqrt{n}}{\sqrt{n-1}} \times \frac{1}{\sqrt{n}} = \frac{\sigma_x}{\sqrt{n-1}}$$

In this way standard error can be obtained from the standard deviation of individual items in a sample. In the above relationship, if the sample size n is large, $\sqrt{n-1}$ can be substituted by $\sqrt{n}$ because there will be practically no difference between the two.

CONFIDENCE INTERVALS

When we make an estimate of the quality characteristic of a lot by studying a sample, we cannot give a single value of estimate with any degree of certainty. We have seen above that various samples drawn from the same lot will generally give different estimates of the quality characteristic of the lot. Therefore, it will be risky to give a single value of an estimate based on the result of one sample.

For example, consider a case where it is found from a random sample of 50 packets drawn from a lot, that the mean weight of the contents is 98 grams. Can we infer from this that the mean weight of packets in the whole lot is 98 grams? This is the best estimate if have data only of one sample. However, this may not be true estimate, because if we draw another sample from the same lot, it may show a slightly different mean weight of the contents. How can we arrive at a reasonable estimate? For this, we must study how the sample means vary. We have seen in the earlier discussion that the distribution of sample means follows the Normal Curve. From the area property of the Normal Curve, we know that 99.7% of all values fall within ±3 standard deviations from the mean value of the distribution. Thus, if μ is the mean value of the distribution (which will also be the mean value of the lot) and σ_x is the standard deviation (*i.e.* the standard error) of the sample means, the mean values of samples may vary between $\mu - 3\sigma_{\bar{x}}$ to $\mu + 3\sigma_{\bar{x}}$. Thus, under random sampling, the sample mean can differ from the actual mean of the lot by a maximum of $3\sigma_{\bar{x}}$. Looking at it in another way, we can say that if X_1 is the mean value of a particular sample drawn at random from the lot, μ (the mean value of the lot) may lie anywhere between $X_1 - 2\sigma_{\bar{x}}$ to $X_1 - 3\sigma_{\bar{x}}$. Thus from the mean value of a sample, we can determine an interval in which the lot (or population) mean must lie. Such an interval is called a Confidence Interval. Since this interval is based on $\pm\ 3\sigma$ which has the probability of 99.7%, (corresponding to area under normal curve) it is called the confidence interval with a 99.7% degree of confidence. Which implies that in case of repeated estimation on the basis of sampling, if we assert that lot mean μ lies within $\pm 3\sigma_{\bar{x}}$ of sample mean, we are likely to be right in 997 cases out of 1,000 and only in three cases, our assertion may prove wrong. Although we have discussed the confidence intervals with relation to 'population mean', the above confidence interval equally applies to other characteristics, provided the population is normally distributed with respect to the relevant characteristic.

TEST OF SIGNIFICANCE

We have seen in the above discussion that certain limits can be set, beyond which the sample results are not expected to vary due to sampling errors.

These limits or intervals give us an important aid in the interpretation of the sampling data. This can best be explained by an example. Suppose, in a heat treatment shop, the existing process of heat treatment of a particular steel gives a mean tensile strength of 40 tons per square centimeter. A change in the heat treatment process is suggested, which, it is claimed, will give greater tensile strength. To test the efficacy of the new process, say four test bars are heat-treated according to the new procedure. The mean tensile strength given by the new process is found to be 44 Tons/cm^2. Now the question arises: whether the increase of strength noticed with the new process is due to sampling error or it represents a real increase as claimed by the process engineer. We can assume that the standard deviation (σ_p) of the mean tensile strength will be same with the modified process as with the old process which was 1.2 TSCM.

We have seen earlier that we can say with 99.7% confidence that a random sample mean will not differ from the true mean by more than $3\sigma_{\bar{x}}$. In this case, since σ_p is 1.2 TSCM, we can expect a maximum difference of 3×1.2 *i.e.* 3.6 Tons/cm^2, *i.e.* 1.8 TSCM due to sampling errors. Whereas we find that the actual difference between the existing mean (40 TSCM) and the mean of sample treated by modified process (44 TSCM), is 4 TSI. Since there is a very high probability (99.7%) that difference due to sampling errors will not exceed 3.6 TSCM, we can conclude that this represents a real or significant change, that is, there has, in fact, been an increase in the tensile strength due to the new process of heat treatment. If the change in the mean tensile strength was less than 3.6 TSCM, then it would have been difficult for us to come to a reasonably sure conclusion, because such a change could as well have occurred due to normal sampling error. In such a case, we might have to carry out further trials before accepting or rejecting the modified process.

NULL HYPOTHESIS AND TEST OF SIGNIFICANCE

In the above illustration, we are in fact testing the truth of our belief, namely that the mean tensile strength given by the new process is the same as that given by the old one. A statement of belief or conjecture with respect to the nature of the population is called a Hypothesis in the statistical language. The test of significance discussed above is also called the Test of Hypothesis as it enables us to verify or refute the hypothesis. A hypothesis formulated for the test is called 'Null Hypothesis'. Usually, a null hypothesis is stated in the form: the population parameter has a particular value, *e.g.*, 'the mean diameter of bearings in the batch is 25.00 mm', or 'the particular lot of bulbs is 4% defective'. A null hypothesis is formulated in such terms that it can readily be tested by study of a sample drawn at random from the population in question.

Hypothesis testing involves the following procedure: First, a confidence interval for the sample statistic commensurate with the desired degree of confidence is determined. Then, a random sample is drawn from the subject population. If the sample statistic observed value of sample statistic is found to be outside the confidence interval, it is said to be significant, and the 'null hypothesis' is rejected, or deemed as untrue. On the other hand, if the observed value is found to be within the above-stated confidence interval, it is said to be insignificant. In such a case the Null Hypothesis cannot be rejected, and it is accepted 'ipso facto' due to lack of evidence to the contrary. It should be noted that when the sample result is significant, we can reject a null hypothesis with a high degree of confidence, but when the test shows acceptance of the null hypothesis, it should not be taken as the conclusive proof of its truth. All it shows is that the observed value of the sample could also occur due to sampling errors. The concept of test of significance as applied to hypothesis testing is illustrated in the following paragraphs.

CRITERIA FOR TEST OF SIGNIFICANCE

In the discussion so far, we have taken the limits of confidence interval to be $\pm 3\sigma$ for which the probability is 99.7%. Although theoretically, sample statistics may vary to the extent of $\pm 3\sigma$ from the population parameter, in Quality Control practice, it is not advisable to adopt these limits as the criteria for the test of significance for all situations, because such wide limits may mask the real or significant changes. The usual practice is to adopt $\pm 2\sigma$ as the criterion for the test of significance, for which the probability of occurrence is .955 (refer to area under normal curve between $\pm 2\sigma$ in Appendix 'A' to Chapter X. (The Z value in Appendix 'A' should be taken as 50% of 0.955.) This means that we can be 95.5% confident that the sample statistic will not fall beyond $\pm 2\sigma$. Thus, when this criterion is adopted, there is a 4.5% risk of our conclusions being proved wrong, but this small risk is accepted, rather than taking the chance of a real change going undetected. If, for any particular situation, a greater degree of confidence is required, the test of significance criteria with somewhat wider limits can be adopted. For instance, if we want criteria for a test of significance where we can be 99% confident of our conclusions being proved right, we can adopt the limits where the probability of occurrence is 0.99. From the table of areas under the normal curve in Appendix 'G', the limits corresponding to area of 0.99 is $\pm 2.58\sigma$. In this way, limits for any desired degree of confidence can be adopted as the criteria for the test of significance. Each set of limits or intervals is associated with a particular degree of confidence and the risk of conclusions being proved wrong. Some of the confidence intervals with their associated degree of risk are shown below:

Confidence Interval	*Degree of Confidence*	*Degree of Risk*
$\pm$ 3.2σ	99.9%	0.1%
$\pm$ 3.0σ	99.7%	0.3%
$\pm$ 2.58σ	99.0%	1.0%
$\pm$ 2.00σ	95.5%	4.5%

For further discussion in this chapter, we shall use $\pm$ 2σ as the criteria for test of significance, which will nominally be referred to as 95% confidence interval associated with 5% risk. (The exact value of the 95% confidence interval is $\pm$ 1.96σ, which is slightly less than $\pm$ 2σ, but the latter value makes calculations easier and, in any case, has a slightly lesser degree of risk.)

The test of significance discussed above can be used for interpretation of results of comparatively large samples (where the sample size is more than 30) drawn from a population which is more or less normally distributed. These conditions are met in most situations in quality control practice. The application of this simple test of significance is illustrated by practical examples discussed in the following pages.

TEST OF SIGNIFICANCE FOR THE MEAN

A sizeable quantity of rexine is to be accepted on the basis of the results of a sample containing 37 rolls of 25 metres each. One of the clauses of the specification states that the average number of surface defects shall not exceed 15 per 25 metre length. On examination of 37 rolls of rexine in the sample, a total of 592 defects were detected, giving an average of 16 defects per 25 metre length. The standard deviation of the number of defects in the inspected rolls was found to be $4 = \sqrt{15}$. A decision is required whether the quality of rexine with respect to the surface defects is acceptable.

The sample result taken on its face value indicates that the quality of rexine with respect to surface defects, does not meet the specification. On the other hand, the manufac turer maintains that his lot taken as a whole will meet the quality requirement and insists that the excessive numbers of defects found in the inspected sample could be due to sampling variations. It was, therefore, decided to apply the statistical test of significance for which the Null Hypothesis is 'the defects in the rexine do not exceed 16 per 25 metres length'. For this, the standard error was calculated, as shown below:

$$\sigma_{\bar{x}} = \frac{\sigma_x}{\sqrt{n-1}}$$

Where $\begin{cases} \sigma_S \text{ is the standard deviation of defects in the sample.} \\ \sigma_{\bar{x}} \text{ standard deviation of the sample means.} \end{cases}$

Since $\sigma_S = 3$

$n = 37$

$$\sigma_{\bar{x}} = \frac{3}{\sqrt{37-1}}$$

$$= 0.5$$

Taking 95% confidence interval, *i.e.* ± 2σ as the criteria for the test of significance, the maximum expectec' variation of the sample average from the true average of the lot will be ± 2 (0.5) or ± 1. Thus, if the true average of the whole lot is 15 defects per 25 metre length, the sample average may vary between 14 and 16 defects. Since, in this particular case, the sample average is 16, which can very well occur due to sampling variations, we cannot reject the null hypothesis on the basis of the result of the sample. This of course, does not imply that the true average number of defects per 25 metre length is definitely 15 or less. All it means is that the inspected sample does not provide sufficient evidence to reject the claim of the manufacturer about the quality of the lot. If the sample average were 17 instead of 16, we could be sure that the lot average was more than 15, and would have been justified in rejecting the lot. In this case, since the sample average is 16, which could have also occurred due to sampling variations, we may either –

(a) inspect further samples or the whole quantity, or

(b) take the word of the manufacturer and accept the lot.

CONFIDENCE INTERVAL FOR ONE-SIDED RISK

In random sampling, there are equal chances for the sample value to be greater or lesser than the corresponding population parameter. Consequently, when we use 95% confidence interval as the criteria of significance, the 5% risk of our conclusion proving wrong comprises of a 2.5% risk of overestimation and a 2.5% risk of underestimation. In the example discussed above, we were estimating the number of defects and therefore we had to guard against underestimation only, since overestimation of defects involves no risk for the purchaser. Thus the actual risk is reduced to 2.5% only. In other words, the ± 2σ interval becomes a 97.5% confidence interval. In such cases, where we are concerned with only one-sided risk, *i.e.* either overestimation or underestimation, the correct 95% confidence interval is $\pm 1.65\sigma$. But for the sake of simplicity and ease of calculation, it may be prudent to use a ± 2σ confidence interval in most situations. In any case it is safer to use those limits, because in the case of one-sided estimation, the risk is reduced. Therefore, $\pm 2\sigma$ limits have been used in all the problems discussed in this chapter.

TEST OF SIGNIFICANCE FOR PROPORTIONS DEFECTIVES

We have seen in the discussion on control charts for attributes, that for some of the products, quality is expressed in terms of proportion defective or per cent defective. When a sample of such a product shows a quality level which is different from the usual one, it will be essential to know whether the change in quality level is real, or it can be attributed to sampling variations. Take, for instance, the case of a company where the average rejection rate for a particular type of castings was 20%. The process engineer made certain changes in the material composition and furnace temperature. As a trial, 400 components were cast according to the new process schedule, out of which 60 components were rejected, giving a rejection rate of 15%. It is desired to know whether this apparent improvement in the quality of the process is real, or due to sampling variations. In such situations also, the statistical test of significance can be applied, as explained below.

In this case, the null hypothesis adopted was "the quality level with the new process is same as with the old one." The standard error (*i.e.* standard deviation) of the per cent defective is given by,

$$^{\sigma}\bar{P}_c = \sqrt{\frac{\bar{P}_c(100 - \bar{P}_c)}{n}}$$

Where
- $^{\sigma}\bar{P}_c$ — is the standard error of per cent defective.
- $\bar{P}_c$ — is the average per cent defective.
- n — is the sample size.

In this particular situation, $\bar{P}_c$ is 20, and n is 400, therefore,

$$^{\sigma}\bar{P}_c = \sqrt{\frac{20\,(100 - 20)}{400}} = 2$$

Taking $\pm$ 2 standard errors, *i.e.* $\pm\ 2^{\sigma}\bar{P}_c$ as the criteria for the test of significance, we can expect that the percentage of defectives in different samples may vary by 2×2, *i.e.* 4% from the average percentage defective of 20%. In the sample under consideration, which is 15% defective the variation is 5% which is more than what can be explained by sampling errors. Therefore, the null hypothesis is rejected. From this, it can be concluded that the quality of the new process is, indeed, better than that of the old process.

COMPARISON OF PRODUCT QUALITY

Inspectors are often called upon to evaluate the products from different sources in order to see whether one is better than the other. The difference in the quality of samples drawn from different sources may sometimes be so little that it is difficult to say whether the observed difference is due to sampling errors or represents a real difference in the quality of two products. Here again, the test of significance can enable us to arrive at a decision. Although the basic approach to test the difference in the quality of two lots or groups is the same, the formula to derive the standard error is slightly different, as is explained below.

TEST OF SIGNIFICANCE FOR DIFFERENCE IN MEASUREMENT DATA

Let us consider two product groups A and B, in which an important quality characteristic is normally distributed about the mean values *a* and *b* respectively. Now, if one sample is drawn from each group and we compute the difference between the two sample means, it may not be (a-b), though it will be very near this value. If a large number of pairs of samples are drawn (each pair comprising of one sample from each group) and the difference of sample means in each pair is tabulated, it will be found to be normally distributed about the central value (a-b). If the standard deviations of the two groups are known, we can determine the standard error of difference of sample means by using the following relation, provided the two samples are independent:

$$\sigma_d = \sqrt{\frac{\sigma^2_A}{n_A} + \frac{\sigma^2_A}{n_B}}$$

Where

- σ_d is the standard error of difference of the sample means.
- σ_A and s_B are the standard deviations of groups A and B respectively.
- n_A and n_B are the sample sizes drawn from groups A and B, respectively.

Once the standard error is known, the following test of significance can be applied:

The observed difference in the means of two samples is significant if it exceeds $2 \times \sigma_d$.

In the test developed above, it is assumed that the standard deviation of the two groups is known, which will seldom be the case in actual practice. However, a reasonable estimate of the standard deviation can be made if a fairly large sample (say exceeding 50) is taken. Then, the standard deviation of the sample can be taken to be approximately equal to the standard deviation of the whole lot. Application of this test is illustrated by the following case study.

A large order for the supply of bulbs with a specified mean life of 100 hours was being negotiated with two firms, A and B. A sample of 72 bulbs from firm A, when tested, gave a mean life of 102 hours and a standard deviation of 12 hours. Another sample of 67 bulbs from firm B gave a mean life of 98.5 hours and standard deviation of 10 hours. The purchase department wanted to know whether there was any difference in the quality (in terms of mean life) of the bulbs being offered by the two firms.

To apply the statistical test of significance the null hypothesis adopted in this case was: 'the mean life of bulbs supplied by the two firms is the same'. The standard error of the difference was calculated as under:

$$\sigma_d = \sqrt{\frac{\sigma^2_A}{n_A} + \frac{\sigma^2_B}{n_B}}$$

Since, $\sigma_A = 12$

$n_A = 72$

$\sigma_B = 10$

$n_B = 67$

$$\sigma_d = \sqrt{\frac{12^2}{72} + \frac{10^2}{67}} = \sqrt{\frac{144}{72} + \frac{100}{67}}$$

= 1.9 hours.

Taking ± 2σ as the criterion for the test of significance, we can expect that the difference up to 2 x 1.9 *i.e.* 3.8 hours can occur due to chance or sampling error. The observed difference in the mean life of two samples was 102 – 98.5 *i.e.* 3.5 hours. Since the observed difference was less than 3.8 hours, it could easily have occurred due to sampling errors and thus the null hypothesis could not be rejected. Therefore, it was assumed that there is no appreciable difference in the quality of the bulbs offered by the two firms.

TEST OF SIGNIFICANCE FOR DIFFERENCE IN PER CENT DEFECTIVE

The test of significance for comparing two samples can also be employed when their quality is expressed in terms of proportion or per cent defective. The formula for standard error in such cases is given by,

$$\sigma_d = \sqrt{\frac{P_1(100 - P_1)}{n_1} + \frac{P_2(100 - P_2)}{n_2}}$$

Where

σ_d, is the estimate of st. dev. Of difference between two per cent defectives
P_1 is the per cent defective in sample no. 1 of size n_1.
P_2 is the per cent defective in sample no. 2 of size n_2.

The application of the test of significance involving a difference in the quality of the two samples is best explained by considering a specific example:

A company had to install a certain number of additional process machines for their expansion programme. The choice of machines was to be made from the machines manufactured by two different firms. It was decided to study the actual performance of the two machines before the final decision was taken. Trial production figures for the two machines are given below:

	Total no. of items produced	*No. found defective*	*Percentage defective*
Machine A	950	47	5%
Machine B	998	70	7%

The trial production from each machine given above can be treated as a sample of the expected production from the respective machines. On a cursory look, it appears that machine A can maintain better quality than machine B. But the management wanted to guard against sampling errors and be sure of the true capability of each type of machine. It was, therefore, decided to apply the statistical test of significance. The null hypothesis adopted in this case was: 'the two types of machines have the same quality capability'. The standard error was calculated as follows:

$$\text{Standard Error } \sigma_d = \sqrt{\frac{P_1(100-P_1)}{n_1} + \frac{P_2(100-P_2)}{n_2}}$$

Since,

$P_1 = 5\%$

$n_1 = 950$

$P_2 = 7\%$

$n_2 = 998$

$$\sigma_d = \sqrt{\frac{5\,(100-5)}{950} + \frac{7\,(100-7)}{998}}$$

$$= \sqrt{\frac{475}{950} + \frac{651}{998}}$$

$$= 1.06\%$$

Taking $\pm\ 2\sigma_d$ as the criteria for significance, we may expect a maximum variation of 2 x 1.06% or 2.12% in the difference of the per cent defectives of samples from two machines having the same quality capability. The actual observed difference in the percentage defective of the samples from two machines was (7–5) *i.e.* 2%. Since the observed difference was less than 2.12%, the null hypothesis could not be rejected. That is, it could not be definitely said that the quality capability of machine A was better than that of machine B. However, since the acceptance of the null hypothesis by the test of significance is not a conclusive proof, it was decided to study another batch of trial production from each machine. The study of second batch confirmed the earlier conclusion that there was no appreciable difference in the quality capability of the two machines. The mean quality capability of both machines was found to vary around 6% defective. The choice between the machines was, therefore, made purely on the basis of price and delivery considerations.

TEST OF SIGNIFICANCE FOR SMALL SAMPLES

The methods of test of significance discussed so far were based on two assumptions, *viz.*

(a) The standard deviations of individual items in a sample are close to the population standard deviation and can, therefore, be used in its place for the calculation of standard error.

(b) The distribution of sample statistics is normal. Because of this, it is possible to assign limits within which the difference between the sample statistics and the population parameters are likely to lie.

Those assumptions do not hold good when the size of the sample is small (say less than 30). Although larger samples are preferable because they give a better picture of the population, there are certain situations, where the drawing of large samples is not practicable. Statistical tests of significance for such cases have also been developed, but they are more complex in character and are beyond the scope of this work. The interested reader is advised to refer to any book on advanced statistics for such problems.

30

Statistical Tolerancing

One of the most difficult jobs during the design of a product is the fixing of tolerances of the components and assemblies. Product tolerances are governed by two conflicting factors. The need for proper functioning and interchangeability requires close tolerances. On the other hand ease and economy of manufacture require that the tolerances should be as wide as possible. It is the tolerance of a component which largely decides the process of manufacture. Very close tolerances may require use of expensive machinery and special tooling and instruments, thereby increasing the cost of manufacture. Designers have a very difficult choice. Generally, sufficient data on loading and stress conditions is not available. Therefore, they tend to be over-cautions in specifying strength limits and tolerances. By tradition and training, they keep a good safety margin to avoid the risk of malfunctioning or failure for which they will be directly blamed. The result is that, in most cases, the tolerances are closer than they are really necessary. In recent years, a technique called 'Statistical tolerancing' which is based on variance analysis has been developed to provide a rational basis for the solution of tolerancing problems. The general principal and application of this technique is discussed in this chapter.

VARIANCE ANALYSIS

Variance, in statistical language, refers to the squared standard deviation. For example, if the standard deviation of resistance in a batch of heater elements is 3 ohms, the variance would be $(3)^2$ or 9 ohms. The advantage of using variance rather than simple standard deviation is that certain calculations become easier when squares are taken. One of the important variance relationships, which is used in statistical tolerancing, is given below:

Resultant variance = Sum of contributory variances.

Suppose the values in a data can be influenced by two independent factors F_1 and F_2 which cause variations with a standard deviation of σ_1 and σ_2, respectively. Then, the standard deviation σ_T, of the overall resultant variation due to the combined effect of F_1 and F_2 is given by,

$$(\sigma_T^2) = (\sigma_1)^2 + (\sigma_2)^2$$

The above formula in general form can be written as,

$$(\sigma_T)^2 = (\sigma_1)^2 + (\sigma_2)^2 + (\sigma_3)^2 + \; .. \; .. \; .. \; (\sigma_n)^2$$

Where $\sigma_1, \sigma_2, \sigma_3$ .. .. σ_n are the standard deviation caused by factors F_1, F_2, F_3 .. .. F_n, respectively. Thus, when two or more factors are acting in a random manner and causing variation in a product, their individual variances can be simply added together to find the combined variance.

For example, let us suppose that variation in the resistance of heater elements is mainly caused by two factors, difference in length, and difference in diameter of element wire. It is found that the standard deviation due to the diameter is 4 ohms, and that due to difference in length is 3 ohms. Since individual elements will have random combinations of length and diameter, the standard deviation of the overall variation will be as given below:

Overall variance = Variance due to length + Variance due to diameter

$$(\sigma_T)^2 = (3)^2 + (4)^2$$

$$= 9 + 16 = 25 \text{ ohms.}$$

Resultant Standard Deviation $(\sigma_r) = \sqrt{25} = 5$ ohms

It should be noted that unlike the variance, the resultant standard deviation is not equal to the sum of individual standard deviations. This is why variance is used in preference to the standard deviation in such applications.

A TOLERANCING PROBLEM

Tolerancing, if it is properly planned, should commence from the system and end with the components. In a typical mechanical system, tolerances for the assemblies are decided on the basis of mating clearances required for the smooth functioning of the system. Having specified the tolerances for the assembly, the tolerances for individual components are worked out in such a way, that in the case of random assembly of components, specified assembly tolerances can be achieved. To illustrate the problem, let us suppose that levers A and B having a width of 15.0 mm each are to be assembled together and fitted in housing H as shown in Fig. 1. For proper clearance, it is desired that the tolerance on the combined width of both levers should not exceed 0.6 mm.

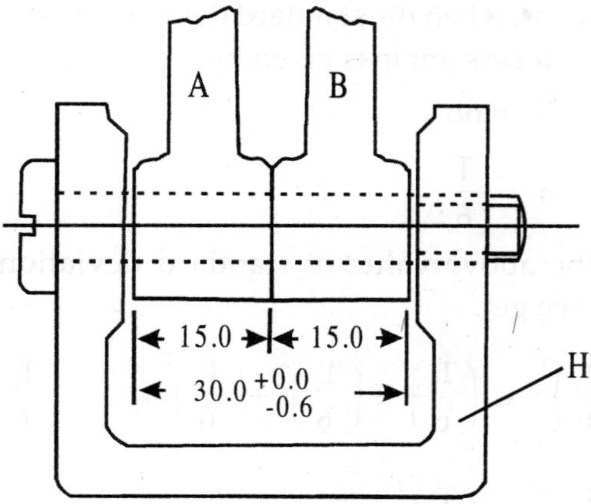

All dimensions are in mm.

Fig. 1

The problem is, how much tolerance on the width of individual levers should be specified? At first consideration, it may appear obvious that the tolerance of levers A and B should be such that their sum does not exceed the desired combined tolerance of 0.6 mm. This may suggest an individual tolerance of 0.3 mm each. This method of tolerancing is based on the reasoning that even if both the levers having maximum or minimum width are mated together, the specified combined tolerance will still not be exceeded. A question which is likely to arise in the mind of some readers is that under the conditions of random assembly, how often will both the mating levers have maximum or minimum width? Obviously, such occurrences will be very rare. From this, it appears that the tolerance of individual components can be increased to some extent as compared to the values obtained by the above method, without the risk of exceeding the combined tolerances on assembly. This still leaves the question as to how much can the tolerances be increased without appreciably affecting the assembly or operating clearance. It is to answer this question that statistical tolerance analysis can be employed.

STATISTICAL TOLERANCE ANALYSIS

We have seen in the discussion on variance analysis that when two factors cause a variation, the resultant variance is given by the sum of the variances caused by the individual factors. When variance analysis is applied to the product variability, we get a useful relationship which can be used as a basis for statistical tolerancing.

It will be recalled that the tolerance which can be maintained by a process with the standard deviation σ is given by 6σ. This is termed as the natural tolerance. Thus, when the standard deviation is known, the product tolerance from the process angle is given by,

$$\text{(Tolerance)} \qquad T = 6\sigma$$

$$\text{or} \qquad \sigma = \frac{T}{6}$$

Substituting the above value of standard deviation in the general variance equation we get,

$$\left(\frac{T_t}{6}\right)^2 = \left(\frac{T_1}{6}\right)^2 + \left(\frac{T_2}{6}\right)^2 + \left(\frac{T_3}{6}\right)^2 \ldots \ldots \left(\frac{T_n}{6}\right)^2$$

$$\left(\frac{T_t}{6}\right)^2 = \left(\frac{T_t}{6}\right)^2 \quad [(T_1)^2 + (T_2)^2 + (T_3)^2 \ldots \ldots \ldots (T_n)^2]$$

Multiplying both sides by 6^2

$$(T_t)^2 = (T_1)^2 + (T_2)^2 + (T_3)^2 \ldots \ldots \ldots T_n$$

$$\text{or} \qquad T_t = \sqrt{T_1^2 + T_2^2 + T_3^2 \ldots \ldots \ldots T_n^2}$$

Where T_t is the overall tolerance for the 'Total' and T_1, T_2, T_3, etc. are the contributory individual tolerances.

Thus, when individual tolerances are known, the combined statistical tolerance can be obtained by taking the square root of the sum of the squared individual tolerances. Let us see how this relationship can be applied to a tolerancing problem discussed above, where the required combined tolerance of the width of levers in Fig. 17.1 is 0.6 mm.

Earlier, it was suggested that the individual tolerance of the levers may be 0.3 mm each. The combined statistical tolerance for 0.3 mm individual tolerance is given by,

$$T_C = \sqrt{(0.3)^2 + (0.3)^2} \qquad \text{Where } T_C \text{ is the Combined Tolerance}$$

$$= \sqrt{0.09 + 0.09}$$

$$= \sqrt{0.18}$$

$$= 0.42 \text{ mm}$$

It can be seen that the combined tolerance which would be achieved by random assy with 0.3 mm individual tolerance is much less than 0.6 mm, which was conjectured. Thus, there is a scope to increase the tolerance of individual levers without exceeding the combined tolerance, or any adverse effect on assembly.

Let us increase the individual tolerance to 0.4 mm and calculate the combined tolerance.

$$T_c = \sqrt{(0.4)^2 + (0.4)^2}$$
$$= \sqrt{0.32}$$
$$= 0.5 \text{ mm}$$

Since this is still less than the allowed tolerance of 0.6 mm, the individual tolerance can safely be fixed at 0.4 mm. The advantage of statistical analysis of tolerances would now be apparent. By allowing the increased tolerance of individual mating parts without exceeding the combined tolerance, it provides economy in production cost.

In the above example, the optimum tolerance of individual parts was obtained by trial and error. Where the mating parts are to have equal tolerances, the maximum component tolerance can also be obtained from the required combined tolerance by the use of the following formula:

$$T_t = \frac{T_c}{\sqrt{n}}$$

Where $\begin{cases} T_i \text{ is the individual tolerance of each part.} \\ T_c \text{ is the stipulated combined tolerance of assembly} \\ n \text{ is the no. of parts in the assembly} \end{cases}$

In the above example, the required assembly tolerance is 0.6 mm. Applying this formula, the maximum component tolerance T_i is given by,

$$T_i = \frac{0.6}{\sqrt{2}}$$
$$= 0.42 \text{ mm}$$

TOLERANCING OF PARTS WITH UNEQUAL TOLERANCES

In the example discussed above, the determination of tolerances was comparatively simple, since there were only two components having equal tolerances. Where the number of components forming an assembly are more and have different tolerances, the problem is a little more complicated and many adjustments have to be made before compatible tolerances are obtained, though the basic principle remains the same. To illustrate the technique, let us suppose that an electrical assembly contains 5 components connected in series. From a functional point of view, it is desired that the resistance in the circuit should not vary more than ± 5 ohms from the specified value which, in other words, means, that the circuit tolerance should not exceed 10 ohms. From production considerations, it is found that the following tolerances can be easily maintained on the components.

T_1 = 5 ohms.
T_2 = 3 ohms.
T_3 = 6 ohms.
T_4 = 2 ohms.
T_5 = 7 ohms.

Where T_1, T_2, T_3, T_4, T_5, are the tolerances of component nos. 1, 2, 3, 4 and 5 respectively.

The overall circuit tolerance with the above values is given by,

$$\text{Circuit Tolerance } (T)_c = \sqrt{(5)^2+(3)^2+(6)^2+(2)^2+(7)^2}$$
$$= \sqrt{25+9+36+4+49}$$
$$= \sqrt{123}$$
$$= 11.1 \text{ ohms.}$$

Since this is more than the permissible tolerance of 10 ohms, we have to reduce the tolerance of some of the components. The next question is how to select the tolerance which is to be reduced. For this, let us study the effect of change in component tolerance on the circuit tolerance. In this case, changing T_4 from 2 to 1 ohms may be very expensive and would reduce the circuit tolerance from $\sqrt{123}$ to $\sqrt{123}$ ohms, whereas reducing T_5 from 7 to 6 ohms would have a much greater effect by reducing circuit tolerance from $\sqrt{123}$ to $\sqrt{110}$ ohms. Therefore, a reduction of T_5 may be preferred to the reduction of any other tolerance. In this case, it is seens that even with the reduction of T_5, from 7 to 6 ohms. The circuit tolerance remains above the permissible limit. Next, we may consider reduction of T_3, T_1 or even further reduction of T_5 depending upon which is practicable and cheaper to reduce. Let us say it is decided to reduce T_3 to 5 ohms. With T_5 already reduced to 6 ohms, the circuit tolerance can be recalculated as shown below:

$$T_c = \sqrt{(5)^3+(3)^3+(5)^2+(2)^2+(6)^2}$$
$$= \sqrt{25+9+25+4+36}$$
$$= \sqrt{99}$$
$$= 9.95 \text{ ohms (approximately).}$$

As the circuit tolerance is less than the permissible limit, the readjusted tolerance values of the components may be considered acceptable. Thus, the following component tolerance may be approved:

T_1 = 5 ohms

T_2 = 3 ohms

T_3 = 5 ohms

T_4 = 2 ohms

T_5 = 6 ohms

In this example, the tolerances were for electrical resistances. These could equally well have been in linear dimensions for mechanical assemblies or in terms of any other units. As long as component tolerances are accumulative, the procedure of fixing the component tolerances will be the same as discussed above.

It should also be noted that the method of tolerance analysis is valid only if the components are produced by the processes which are under a reasonable state of statistical control. This condition will normally be met if the manufacturing plant has a well-organised quality control system.

TOLERANCES FOR FITS AND CLEARANCES

We have so far discussed the tolerances in accumulative assemblies, where the assembly dimensions were dependent upon the sum of the varying dimensions of the components. Fits and clearances of two mating components, on the other hand, depend upon the difference between the dimensions of the mating parts. Since the dimensions of mating parts can vary within their permissible tolerances, the mating clearance will also vary accordingly and will have its own resultant tolerance which can be obtained from the tolerance analysis formula,

$$T_c = \sqrt{(t_1)^3 + (t_2)^2}$$

Where T_c is the tolerance of the clearance.
t_1 and t_2 are tolerance of mating components.

Adjustment of the tolerances of mating components to achieve the desired clearance on assembly is illustrated by a specific example of mating hole and shaft whose dimensions are given below:

Drawing dimensions of the hole = 25.08 ± .03 mm

Drawing dimensions of the shaft = 25 – 00 ± .03 mm

Mean clearance when the components are aimed at nominal dimensions

$\{ = 25.08 - 25.00 = .08$ mm

Minimum possible clearance *i.e.*, when a hole of minimum size is mated with a shaft of maximum size

$\{ = 25.05 - 25.03 = .02$ mm

Maximum possible clearance, *i.e.* when a hole of maximum size is mated with a shaft of minimum size

$\{ = 25.11 - 24.97 = .14$ mm

Theoretical tolerance in clearance the mean value

$\{ \pm .06$ mm

It is important to note here that even though the clearance itself is the difference of two mating dimensions, the tolerance of clearance is equal to the sum of tolerances of mating dimensions. However, the theoretical tolerance of clearance calculated above classically is rarely met in practice, because components of extreme dimensions rarely mate under the conditions of random assembly. A more realistic tolerance in clearance is given by the formula, based on variance analysis.

$$T_c = \sqrt{(t_1)^2 + (t_2)^2}$$

$$T_c = \pm\sqrt{(t_1)^2 + (t_2)^2}$$

$$= \pm\sqrt{(.03)^2 + (.03)^2}$$

$$= \pm\sqrt{(.0009 + .0009)}$$

$$= \pm .04 \text{ mm (approximately).}$$

Thus, practically the minimum and maximum clearances well be as given below:

Minimum clearance = 0.08 – 0.04 = 0.04 mm
Minimum clearance = 0.08 + 0.04 = 0.12 mm

If, however, the theoretical clearance limits viewed classically of .02 mm and .14 mm are acceptable in the final product, the individual tolerances of shaft and hole can be relaxed to achieve economy in production. Let us see the expected clearance if the shaft and hole tolerance is increased from ± 0.3 mm to ± .04 mm.

Expected clearance $T_c = \pm\sqrt{(0.4)^4 + (0.4)^4}$

$$= \pm\sqrt{.0032}$$

$$= \pm 0.056 \text{ mm}$$

With this tolerance on clearance from the mean value,
Minimum expected clearance = .08 – .056 = .024 mm
Maximum expected clearance = .08 + .056 = .136 mm

As these clearances are still within the acceptable limits of 0.02 and 0.14, the relaxed tolerances of the hole and the shaft can be approved.

COMBINED ACCUMULATIVE AND CLEARANCES TOLERANCES

Having studied the accumulative and clearance tolerances individually, we are now in a position to discuss the tolerancing of assemblies involving both accumulative and clearance tolerances. Suppose levers L and M are assembled together and are fitted in fork N as shown in Fig. 2.

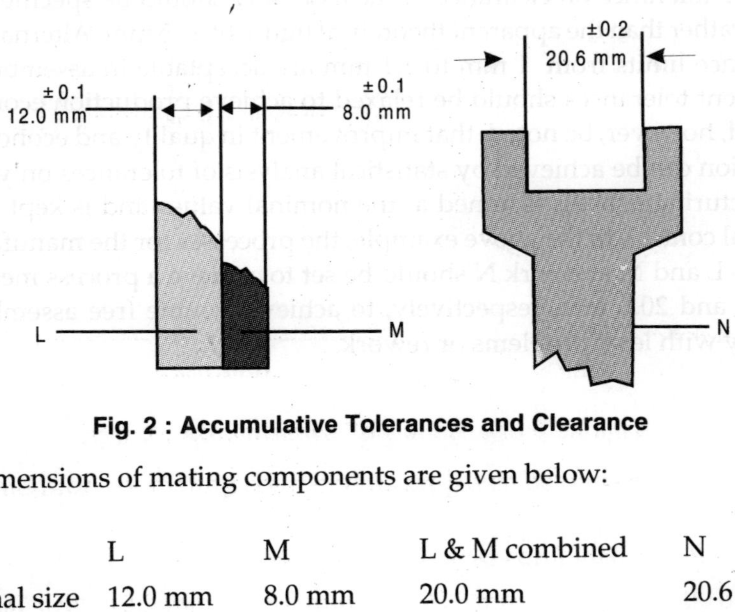

Fig. 2 : Accumulative Tolerances and Clearance

Dimensions of mating components are given below:

	L	M	L & M combined	N
Nominal size	12.0 mm	8.0 mm	20.0 mm	20.6 mm
Tolerance	± .2 mm	± .1 mm		± .2 mm

Mean clearance at the nominal size = 20.6–20.0 = .6 mm

Apparent theoretical minimum clearance would be when both L and M are at the maximum and N is at the minimum, as such

Theoretical minimum clearance = 20.4 – (12.2 + 8.1)

= 20.4 – 20.3 = 0.1 mm

Similarly, the apparent theoretical maximum clearance will be obtained when L and M are at the minimum and N is at the maximum and as such,

Apparent theoretical maximum clearance = 20.8 – (11.8 + 7.9)

= 20.8 – 19.7 =1.1 mm

Apparent theoretical tolerance in clearance from mean value of .6 mm = ± .5 mm. Expected clearance on random assembly is given by:

$$T_c = \pm\sqrt{(.2)^2 + (.1)^2 + (.2)^2}$$

$$= \pm\sqrt{.04 + .01 + .04}$$

$$= \pm\sqrt{0.9}$$

$$= \pm .3$$

Thus, the tolerance on clearance of the assembly should be specified as ± 0.3 mm rather than the apparent theoretical figure of ± .5 mm. Alternatively, if clearance limits from .1 mm to 1.1 mm are acceptable in assembly, the component tolerances should be relaxed to achieve production economy. It should, however, be noted, that improvement in quality and economy in production can be achieved by statistical analysis of tolerances only if the manufacturing process is aimed at the nominal values and is kept under statistical control. In the above example, the processes for the manufacture of levers L and M and fork N should be set to achieve a process means of 12.0, 8.0 and 20.6 mm, respectively, to achieve trouble free assembly or assembly with least problems or rework.

31

ABC Analysis

GENERAL CONCEPT

ABC analysis is primarily a materials control technique for reducing inventory costs. In recent years, however it has found increasing use in quality control applications too. It is generally seen that in any store having a large number of products, there are a few items of stock which represent the bulk of the value in monetary terms. These are termed as 'A' items. There are also a large number of other items of trivial value which collectively account for only a small fraction of the stock value. These are termed as 'C' items. The intermediate range of items of moderate value are referred to, as 'B' items. With this as the basis, it can be easily deduced that 'A' items are the ones which are required to be closely watched. If these are controlled, the bulk of the inventory will remain under control. This leads to the economy of effort, in that, rather than trying to control every item (which may be a formidable task), attention is concentrated on 'A' items which are likely to result in substantial reduction in inventory costs. Next in order of priority should be 'B' items. 'C' items can be loosely controlled as they are not going to make appreciable difference in the stock value.

APPLICATION IN QUALITY CONTROL

Although this technique was originally developed for material control, it has been found that it can be applied to other fields of management, including quality control, with equal effectiveness. It has been found that most industrial activities are subject to a large number of influencing factors, but the vital factors are only a few which exert major influence. There may be many other factors whose total effect on the activity is relatively very small. Then, there may be intermediate range of factors which collectively exert moderate influence. Thus, according to the degree of influence, the factors can be grouped into A, B and C categories. In quality control, the ABC analysis is generally applied for analysis of rejects and defect data.

REJECT DATA ANALYSIS

Application of ABC analysis in quality control is illustrated by the following example. In a company manufacturing compressor units, it was decided to carry out reject data analysis to find the components which were responsible for rejection of the compressors during final inspection. Final inspection records for the last one year were examined and the number of times each defective component had caused the rejection of the compressor unit was noted. This record was tabulated in the descending order of incidence of rejects caused by defective components as shown in Table A. Out of a total of 1,000 rejects, the percentage contribution by each component and the cumulative percentage is shown in Cols. 4 and 5, respectively. The analysis of Table A shows that the first 5 components had together caused over 60% of all rejects. These five components can, therefore, be designated as 'A' components. The next 9 components have together contributed to about 30% of all the rejects and as such, these can be designated as 'B' components. The last 16 components have together caused less than 10% of all the defects. These are, therefore, designated as 'C' components. It should be noted that there is no fixed border line between A and B as well as between B and C items. The first 4 or 6 components could as well have been termed as 'A' components, or the list of 'B' could have been extended up to the 16th component. As long as the basic concept is understood, the exact line of demarcation is immaterial.

From the following analysis, it can be seen that if the quality of the first 5 or 6 components can be improved, by redesign or better process control, the incidence of rejects in the final inspection can be reduced by 60%. It is also obvious that excessive effort spent in the improvement of the quality of the last 16 components may not be worth the results, which at best can reduce the reject rate by only 10%. Thus, it can be seen that the ABC analysis is a valuable tool for the quality manager, as it considerably narrows down the area for application of quality improvement programmes and ensures effective utilisation of the limited resources of a quality control organisation.

Table A: ABC Analysis of Reject Data

Sl. no.	Part no.	No. of rejects caused	Percentage of total rejects	Cumulative percentage of rejects
1	H-16	151	15.1	15.1
2	H-34	139	13.9	29.0
3	T-38	126	12.6	41.6
4	T-64	103	10.3	51.9
5	T-82	87	8.7	60.6
6	S-51	73	7.0	67.6
7	T-07	56	5.6	73.2
8	T-14	43	4.3	77.5
9	H-23	31	3.1	80.6
10	H-36	27	2.7	83.3
11	H-71	23	2.3	85.6
12	T-29	19	1.9	87.5
13	T-62	18	1.8	89.3
14	S-30	16	1.6	90.9
15	G-71	13	1.3	92.2
16	H-21	11	1.1	93.3
17	H-18	9	0.9	94.2
18	H-45	9	0.9	95.1
19	H-76	7	0.7	95.8
20	T-06	6	0.6	96.4
21	T-52	6	0.6	97.0
22	H-62	5	0.5	97.5
23	S-21	5	0.5	98.0
24	T-41	5	0.5	98.5
25	H-82	4	0.4	98.9
26	H-39	4	0.4	99.3
27	T-64	3	0.3	99.6
28	T-20	2	0.2	99.8
29	H-68	1	0.1	99.9
30	H-24	1	0.1	100.0

32

Value Analysis

Value Analysis is an organised method of cost reduction of a product by attacking its basic design. Its approach is similar to that of method study. The difference is that whereas method study concentrates on improving the method of manufacture, the value analysis questions the product design itself, with a view to evolving a cheaper design system that can perform the intended function. In the search for cheaper design, quality is not sacrified, rather, it often leads to improvement in quality. Value Analysis as a formalised technique, is of recent origin. It was first put forward by L. D. Miles in the early 1950s based on his work with General Electric. During the short span of 20 years, its effectiveness has been proved beyond doubt and a new discipline, namely Value Engineering has come into being.

VALUE ANALYSIS AND QUALITY MANAGEMENT

A natural question which may arise in the mind of the reader is that "If value analysis is a cost reduction technique, what has a quality engineer to do with it." To answer this, we must refer to the overall aim of quality management which is 'maximum user satisfaction at minimum cost'. When viewed against this aim, the utility of value analysis becomes obvious. A successful value analysis study results in reduced cost for the same quality or improved quality with the same cost or both. Either way, it increases the quality contribution (the difference between value and cost of quality) and thus furthers the overall aim of quality management. This is an additional tool with the quality engineer, which is particularly useful in improving the reliability of an equipment.

VALUE OF A PRODUCT AND PROFIT

What is the value of a product? The value of a product to a customer, can be determined by the price which he is willing to pay. This value can be termed as the EXCHANGE VALUE. The exchange value is comprised of two elements, namely USE VALUE and ESTEEM VALUE.

USE VALUE

It is the price which a customer is willing to pay for the performance of a function or rendering of a service. For determining this value, it is essential that the function or functions which the product is intended to perform must be identified. This is not as easy as it sounds. In fact, as will be seen later, half the problem of value analysis is solved when the function is correctly identified.

ESTEEM VALUE

It is the price which is offered by the customer in excess of the use value for the properties or features of the product which make him want to own it. It may be difficult to exactly pinpoint the characteristics which contribute to the esteem value. Often, it is the cumulative effect of styling, surface finish and getup, and sometimes the attractiveness of the packing.

The above values are from the customer's viewpoint. When looked at from the producer's point of view, there is another kind of value known as the COST VALUE (also called intrinsic value) which is the sum of material, labour and other costs which are to be incurred to produce it. Value Analysis is mainly concerned with the reduction of the cost value of the product while maintaining or increasing its use and esteem values. Since the difference between exchange value (*i.e.* use value + esteem value) and the cost value represents profit, value analysis aims to increase profit by better design.

SELECTION OF PROJECTS FOR VALUE ANALYSIS

Although value analysis can be applied to any product and will result in some reduction of cost, the overall savings will vary according to the product and the total quantity involved. For instance in a product of 'which only a few pieces', are to be manufactured, even if value analysis results in 25% reduction in cost, the total saving will not be much unless the product is very expensive. On the other hand, in case the product which is to be manufactured in large numbers on a continuing basis, even 5% reduction in cost will amount to substantial savings in the long run. Since the value analysis itself costs money (due to the time of engineers and executives spent on it), the project selected should be such where the expected savings will justify investment in value analysis.

COMPOSITION OF VALUE ANALYSIS TEAM

Value analysis is not a one-man job. It is essentially a creative activity. The more the number of brains working on it, the better is the chance that one of them will hit upon the right solution. In fact, for its success, it owes a lot to the team approach. In addition to one or two professional value engineers, the team should comprise of design engineers, and representatives from production, quality control and sales. The aim is to bring as many fresh minds to attack the problem as possible. At the same time, too big a team becomes unwieldy and difficult to manage. Generally, a team composed of 6 to 10 persons is considered adequate. Of these, two or three may be wholetime members, who could form the core and the others could be co-opted for value analysis sessions, as and when required. The leader of the team however should preferably be a professional value analyst.

VALUE ANALYSIS PROCEDURE

After Miles introduced this technique in the early nineteen fifties, other workers in the field have contributed a lot towards its refinement and ease of application. In the UK, considerable work on this subject has been done by WL. Gage, management teacher and consultant. In his book "Value Analysis", he suggests a procedural drill composed of twelve questions given below. Answers to these questions help in the evolution of a cheaper and possibly better product.

1. What is it?
2. What does it cost?
3. How many parts?
4. What does it do?
5. How many required?
6. Which is the primary function?
7. What else will do?
8. What will that cost?
9. Which three of the alternative ways of doing the job show the greatest difference between cost and use value?
10. Which ideas are to be developed?

11. What other functions and specific features must be incorporated?
12. What do we do to sell our ideas and forestall road-blocks?

Answering each of the above-mentioned questions forms a step in the value analysis procedure. Action to be taken at various steps is briefly discussed below:

Selection of Product for Analysis

1. Here the product to be analysed is identified. Considerations for selection of the product have already been discussed. Products suitable for analysis are:
   (a) Products to be made in large numbers
   (b) Multi-component equipment

Obtaining Cost of Product

2. Obtaining overall cost of product may be difficult, as exact apportioning of overheads may present some problems. At this stage, the direct cost of the product, *i.e.* cost of material plus cost of labour will serve the purpose.

Recording Number of Components

3. The larger the number of components, the greater is the chance that value analysis will show results. Generally, the reduction of components brings savings in the cost, besides improving reliability. (see Chapter XX).

Identification of the Function/Functions

4. Identification of the function is to look for the purpose, which the product is intended to meet. Often, there are more than one functions. All these must be listed. While listing the functions, they must be reduced to the simplest expression comprising of just a verb-noun combination, such as,

A stove, 'provides heat'.

A clutch, 'transmits motion' and 'interrupts motion'.

A soldier's shoe, 'protects feet', and 'supports weight'.

Assessment of Quantity Required

5. Assessment of quantity of the product required, will give an indication of the possible savings which may be expected, and thus help to decide whether its analysis is justified. It will also set a limit to the effort which can be expended on the project.

The first five steps mentioned above pertain to the information gathering stage, during which the problem is stated. This part of work is normally carried out by the whole-time value engineers, who are members of the team. The problem is actually solved in the next seven steps in which the whole team participates.

Determination of the Primary Function

6. A product may have a number of functions, but all of them are not likely to have the same importance. Since all the functions cannot be considered simultaneously, an order of priority has to be laid down. We must, therefore, identify the primary function out of the list complied in step 4. For instance, for a soldier's shoe, the primary function is to 'protect feet'. This example is comparatively simple and the primary function can be straight away identified. In some multi-function products, it may not be so easy to determine the primary function. In such cases, one must put oneself in the position of a customer, who is asked to name one function which he would like to sacrifice last. This would be the primary function.

Finding Alternative Methods of Achieving Primary Function

7. This is the most crucial stage of the value analysis exercise. It is here that the creative ability of the group is utilised to find solution to the problem. Generally, it takes the form of brain storming session. The problem is stated by the leader of the team and ideas for alternative methods of performing the function are invited. For the success of the exercise, it is essential that relaxed atmosphere is created for free and uninhibited expression of ideas. The participants should be encouraged to put forward any idea however outrageous which comes to their mind. An idea which may be absurd in itself may still be useful, because it can trigger off some one else's mind to put forth an idea which will work. Comment or criticism of the ideas should be strictly forbidden at this stage. Otherwise, participants will be afraid to give expression to their ideas due to fear of redicule. All ideas generated during the brainstorming session should be listed for evaluation which should be done later.

Estimation of Costs of the Alternatives

8. Out of the ideas generated in the brainstorming sessions, the feasible ideas should be shifted and their costs should be obtained. The cost estimate should be based on material and labour costs without overheads. There is no need to go through elaborate costing procedures. For the purpose of this exercise an approximate estimate of cost will do. This part of job is normally carried out by the core staff of the team.

Determination of Three Cheapest Alternatives

9. The alternatives discussed in steps 7 and 8 should not be examined for determining which three are the cheapest and show promise with

due regard to the efficient performance of the primary function. These alternatives should be arranged in the order of their cost the cheapest being at the top.

Decision on the Alternatives to be Developed

10. Out of the three cheapest alternatives considered in step 9, a decision should now be taken regarding the alternative which is to be developed. It is not necessary that the cheapest alternative would always be the first choice. If the second cheapest alternative involves lesser changes, and the difference in the cost of this and the cheapest alternative is not much the second cheapest alternative may be preferred as it would be easier to implement.

Incorporation of Other Functions and Features

11. From step 6 onwards, we have pursued the achievement of only the primary function. Step 4 may have revealed certain other functions also. All these functions must be critically examined for their contribution to the use value. Those which do not substantially contribute to the use value may be discarded. Depending upon their contribution, a list should now be made of functions which are considered essential and those considered desirable. Efforts should then be made to incorporate all the essential functions and as many of the desirable functions as possible, at the same time keeping track of the costs which would be added to the product. At this stage, consideration should also be given to the esteem features, because these are equally important for the stability of some of the products.

It sometimes happens that incorporation of additional functions and features results in so much increase in the cost that it no longer remains cheaper than the existing product. In such cases a decision may have to be taken to develop another idea. This will be continued until a satisfactory solution is found.

ARRANGING ACCEPTANCE OF THE NEW PRODUCT

12. Although value analysis exercise would have been conducted with the full blessings of the management, it does not follow that the new product emerging out of the value analysis will automatically be accepted. For this, the management will have to be convinced that the proposed product will result in overall savings. Where the value analysis team has been carried out on an existing product, the value analysis team has to prepare a detailed case showing.

- Product cost comparison.
- Capital expenditure in the change.

- Improvements in quality were achieved.
- Anticipated savings.

A working model of the proposed product is of considerable help in convincing the management about the soundness of the new idea.

APPLICATION OF VALUE ANALYSIS

Value analysis or value engineering, as it is sometimes called, has a very wide application in industry. Its application is not limited to the already established products. It can be applied even before a product comes into being. In fact, the maximum benefit is obtained by applying value analysis when the product is on the drawing board or in prototype stage. For short-run projects, this is the only time when it can be applied.

33

Defect Diagnosis and Prevention

Some of the most taxing quality problems are those which are connected with defect investigation. In spite of meticulous planning and proper process controls, certain defects may still be revealed during assembly or in final inspection. To prevent these defects from recurring, they have to be investigated to find out the underlying cause, so that efforts can be made for its elimination. The causes of certain defects are fairly obvious and can directly be identified. In fact, the 'analysis' element in any process control of system is a form of defect investigation, in the sense that based on the defects observed, the causative factor is identified, which in turn gives a clue to the corrective action required. However, there are other defects which cannot be readily explained. There may be so many possible causes that it may be difficult to spot with any degree of certainty the factor which has caused a particular defect. In such cases, formal defect studies may be carried out to find the real cause and the remedial measures required. An organised method of defect investigation is discussed in this chapter.

WHICH DEFECTS SHOULD BE INVESTIGATED?

A quality enthusiast may say that every single defect must be investigated to assure defect-free production. Unfortunately, this may not be practicable nor economically desirable. Defect studies cost money in the form of the time of engineers and technicians test facilities and the products destroyed in testing, and, therefore, unless the expected benefits from the prevention of defects are likely to exceed the cost of the defect study, it will not be economically justifiable. Further, the resources at the disposal of the quality manager will normally be limited. Therefore, he will have to undertake defect studies on a selective basis.

The defects may be broadly grouped into two classes, namely, sporadic and chronic. A sporadic defect generally signifies that some new factor has entered into the process, and unless this factor is identified and eliminated, the process will remain out of control. Therefore, such defects have to be investigated on priority. On the other hand, chronic defects are the various types of defects which have been occurring in a certain percentage of the product, due to unknown causes. As these defects also cause losses to the company, their incidence has to be minimised, where possible. Generally, chronic defects comprise a large number of different types of defects of varying magnitude. Since all of these cannot be taken up for investigation, simultaneously, it is advisable to concentrate on the 'vital few' rather than the 'trivial many'. To identify the 'vital few', the resultant losses due to different defects may be evaluated. The defects showing highest losses merit first attention. There may be certain defects which result in serious failures of equipment in service. Though direct losses (such as warranty claims) due to these defects may not be appreciable, the loss in customer's goodwill may be considerable. Therefore, the quality manager should be on the alert for such defects which will not figure as major defects in a purely financial analysis.

MANAGEMENT APPROVAL

Having identified the major defects which merit investigation, the quality manager should then make an assessment of the time, resources and cost required for the investigation for each defect. The cost of the study should be compared with the expected savings due to the elimination of defects. If the defect study appears to be justified, the proposal must be presented to the management for their approval. This approval is essential for two reasons. Firstly, for the sanction of necessary funds. Secondly, most defect studies require the active collaboration of other departments, such as engineering and production, which will be more readily forthcoming if the programme has been approved by the management.

DEFINING RESPONSIBILITY

A defect study, like any other activity, requires proper planning and organisation to be fruitful. The object of a defect study and its responsibility should be clearly defined. The task is generally entrusted to a team rather than an individual. The team may be composed of personnel from quality control, engineering production, or wherever expertise is available. For proper direction and coordination, a study coordinator is also named, who coordinates the activities of the team and keeps the management informed about the progress of the study.

CONDUCT OF DEFECT STUDY

Once the study team is formed and the objective of the study has been explained to them, the first question which arises is how to go about it and where to start? Although there is no cut-and-dried method of defect investigation, which will be valid for all situations, the general approach to the organised study of defects in different products and processes is, more or less the same. The main steps of this approach are discussed below:

Study of the Product and Data Collection

Before a defect in any product can be investigated, the investigation team must acquire thorough knowledge of the product. Some members of the team may have a general idea about the product, but that is not enough (otherwise there will not have been the need for a formal investigation). What is required is an in-depth study of the product, covering its functions, quality characteristics, operation, method of manufacture and the salient features of the process involved. While studying the product, the relevant data such as final inspection results, process control data, material inspection results and the records of material or process changes, if any, should also be collected.

IDENTIFICATION OF DEFECTIVE COMPONENT/PROCESS

In the initial stages, a defect is generally referred to by its symptom or apparent departure from the specified quality standard. In a complex equipment or a product, the defective system or the process stage has to be identified before the basic cause can be found. For instance, if an engine gives less power when checked at the test bench, the defect will be referred to as 'insufficient power'. Now, insufficient power may be caused by the malfunctioning of any of the following units:

Cylinder and piston unit

Fuel system

Ignition system

Clutch assembly

The actual defective system may be identified by the study of other symptoms and their correlation with the defects in various systems. Alternatively, the assemblies or the system may be replaced one by one until the defect is removed, which will reveal the defective system. Once the defective assembly or system has been identified, the same process of analysis and elimination may be followed further, until the ultimate defective component or assembly is identified.

In the same manner, for the defect in a product involving a number of processes, the process causing the defect has to be identified. For instance, surface defects in certain components may be due to defective material, faulty casting, improper heat treatment, or poor metal finishing. To narrow down the investigation, it is essential to identify the process responsible for the defect.

ANALYSIS OF PROCESS

Having identified the defect-causing process, the next step is to pinpoint the basic cause to which the defect can be attributed. Only then can remedial measures be considered. For this, the process has to be analysed to consider all variable factors which could have caused the defect. For a component having only a few quality characteristics, it may be easy to examine the various features and arrive at the feature/features responsible for causing the defect. In other cases where there are a number of variables, it may involve extensive measurement/testing. In particularly complex processes, special tests may have to be designed for which the service of a statistician or a quality consultant may be required.

Prof. Kaoru Ishikawa of Japan developed a cause-and-effect diagram, depicting the variables to facilitate the analysis of a process. Slightly modified form of Ishikawa diagram applied to an electroplating process is shown in Fig. 1. In the diagram, the thick lines indicate main activities or operations. The lines branching off from these represent sub-activities or factors influencing the main operations. If these factors have subfactors, further branches are attached to the factor lines. In this way, this process of subdivision is continued until all factors are covered. The main advantage of the Ishikawa diagram is that all the relevant factors can be examined in proper relation to each other and to the product as a whole.

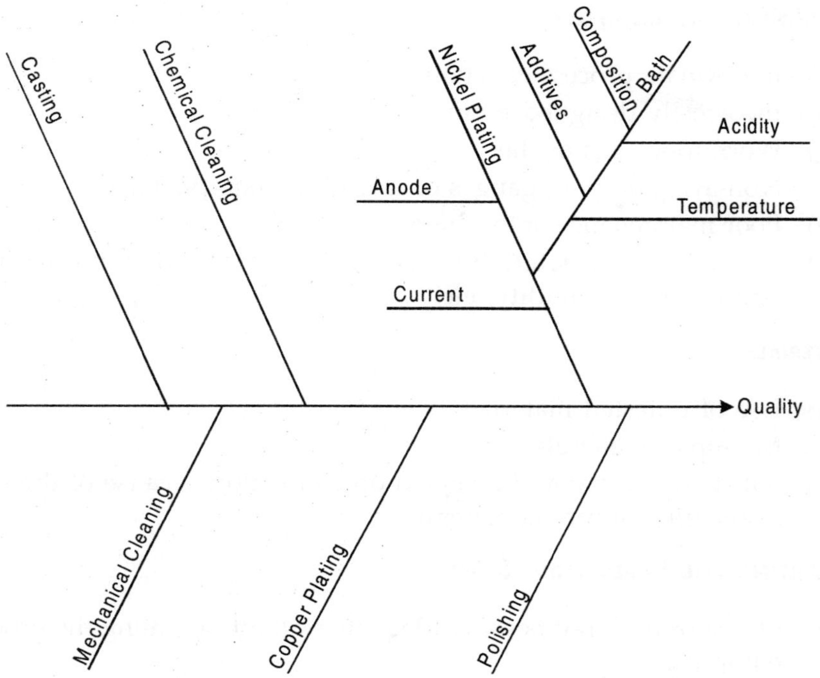

Fig. 1: Ishikawa Diagram of Nickel Plated Components

At one stage of the analysis, the cause will be traced to non-conformance of certain quality characteristics. For instance, the tolerance on a particular dimension may not have been maintained. Although this may appear to be the basic cause, the analysis should not stop here. It must be carried further to find out the ultimate reason for non-conformance. In the above instance, the ultimate reason may be the inadequate process capability of the machine, a worn jig, poor setting or any other cause out of the host of possible reasons. During this stage of analysis the investigators should be on the lookout for the typical causes of non-conformance given below:

Design and Specification

(a) Vague or insufficient manufacturing particulars or illegible drawing prints
(b) Impracticable design or incompatible component and assembly tolerance
(c) Obsolete drawing being used

Machinery and Equipment

(a) Inadequate process capability
(b) Incorrectly designed tooling
(c) Worn tools, jigs or dies
(d) Non-availability of gauges or measuring equipment
(e) Poor maintenance of machines
(f) Equipment affected by environmental conditions such as temperature, humidity, etc.

Materials

(a) Use of untested materials
(b) Mix-up of materials
(c) Substandard material accepted on concession because of the non-availability of correct material

Operating and Supervisory Staff

(a) Operator does not possess adequate skill for operating the process equipment.
(b) Operator does not understand the manufacturing drawing or instructions relating to the process.
(c) Machine setter does not know how to correctly set the machine.
(d) Careless operator and inadequate supervision.
(e) Undue rush by the operator to achieve quantity targets.

Process Control and Inspection

(a) Inadequate process controls
(b) Non-availability of proper test equipment
(c) Test equipment out of calibration
(d) Vague inspection/testing instructions
(e) Inspectors do not possess the necessary skill.
(Above list is not exhaustive).

EVALUATION OF REMEDIAL MEASURES

If the analysis of the defect-causing process has been carried out in sufficient depth, the cause itself will suggest the remedy. Some of the remedies, such as replacement of an obsolete drawing or calibration of equipment may be quite simple and can straight a way be applied. In other cases, deciding a remedial measure may require considerable thought and deliberation. For instance, if it is found that the process capability of the machine is such that it is unable to hold the specified tolerance, it may not be easy to replace the machine. First efforts should be made to service the machine, which may improve the process capability to some extent. In addition to this remedy, certain other measures such as the following may also be considered before final decisions are arrived at:

(a) Alternative method of manufacture
(b) 100% inspection of the affected component before assembly to screen the defective components. (This shall be only short term remedy)
(c) Redesign of the component to provide for wider tolerances.

During this stage, consultation with all the concerned departments will also be required to obtain their views on the various possible methods of avoiding defects. The actual decision on the remedial measures to be adopted, will depend upon the practicability and economics of various alternatives. After an agreement is reached on the most suitable remedy, the necessary recommendation must be made to the management to obtain their approval for the implementation of the proposed measures.

IMPLEMENTATION OF CORRECTIVE MEASURES

After corrective measures have been applied, the quality of the product, with particular reference to the defect under study, must be carefully monitored to see whether the defect has been eliminated or minimised. During this stage, further changes in the process or its controls may be called for. This process of the adjustment of remedial measures and study of their effect must be continued until the objectives of the study have been fully achieved.

34

Reliability Design, Evaluation and Control

Reliability is a characteristic which refers to the ability of a product to perform its intended function when required to do so. Special interest in reliability has been generated because of the increasing incidence of failure in complex equipment. It is only in the last few decades that this important quality parameter has been quantified in precise terms, so that it can be objectively evaluated. Since the reliability refers to the behaviour of the product at a point of time in future, it cannot be measured or tested with certainty. At best, an estimate of the likelihood of its functioning satisfactorily can be made, based on the past experience with that, or other similar products.

DEFINING RELIABILITY

If an equipment works satisfactorily whenever it is operated, we say that it is a reliable equipment. For example, a new car generally runs perfectly and does not give any trouble. In this case, we say that the car is reliable. On the other hand, another car which is, say 10 to 15 years old, may give frequent troubles, so much so that we may be afraid to take it on a long run, lest it should break down on the way. When the car is, in such a condition, we say it is unreliable. Between these extremes of almost complete reliability and unreliability, there will be varying degree of reliability which can best be expressed in terms of the probability of its functioning normally when called upon to do so.

While considering reliability, it must be appreciated that no machine or equipment, however well designed and manufactured, can continue to function satisfactorily for an indefinite period. For example, a car which may be highly reliable when it is new, will have comparatively less reliability after a few years. Thus, to be meaningful, reliability must be related to a point in the life of an article. The useful life of articles which continuously wear out or deteriorate during operation or ageing is related to the time. The examples are running machinery, where the wear is generally proportional to the period of operation. There are other articles such as ammunition items, which, although meant for one-time use, still suffer deterioration during storage. The useful life of such articles also is expressed in terms of time. On the other hand, there are articles such as electrical switches where the wear or deterioration is of a cyclic nature. That is, there is a certain amount of wear or deterioration in every cycle of operation, which is not related to the period of operation. In such cases, the useful life is generally expressed in terms of the number of cycles of operation. With this as the background, now we can formally define reliability.

"The reliability of a product is the probability of its performing its intended function over its specified life."

If N articles are operated under normal conditions for a period of time *t*, out of which n articles fail during this period, the reliability of the articles for time *t* is given by,

$$R(t) = \frac{N-n}{N}$$

For example, if 100 items were tested and two of them failed, we can say reliability is 0.98.

A reliability of 0.98 means that there is a 98% chance that the article will function normally when operated. The lower the reliability of a product, the lesser are the chances of its functioning normally. Since the reliability is a probability, it can only vary between 0 and 1. Thus, a reliability 0 for a product indicates the certainty of its not working as intended and a reliability 1 means that it is certain to work as required.

FACTORS AFFECTING RELIABILITY

Complexity of a Product

Simple products are always much more reliable than complex ones. The reason is obvious. The greater the number of components along with their linking mechanisms, the more are the chances that one of them will fail, thereby preventing the product from performing its intended function. Take the simple case of the good old kitchen hearth. As long as there are enough logs in the hearth, one can be sure of its heating capability. Compare it with the modern cooking range, with its numerous heating elements, switches, thermostats and connecting wiring. Any of these components or their connections could fail and the cooking range will be useless until it is repaired. It will be seen later in this chapter that as the number of components increases, the reliability of the total system decreases in geometric progression. One of the reasons of complexity of the equipment is the incorporation of automatic functions in the product. Although automation eases the human burden, it makes the equipment less reliable. Firstly, more components have to be added to provide additional functions, which bring in their own unreliability. Secondly, in a manually operated device the human controlling agency can provide necessary adjustments to meet the requirements of unforeseen situations, whereas in automatic devices, only those adjustments are possible which are already programmed into it. In case a new factor emerges, there is no easy way by which the device can be suitably adjusted. This, of course, does not mean that we should not have automatic devices. Automation represents technological advancement, since well-designed automatic devices save time and effort and often perform specified functions much better than the human agency. The problem of reliability in automatic devices has been mentioned merely to bring out the need for greater vigilance in design to ensure that reliability does not suffer. If proper attention is given to this aspect, it is possible to design automatic devices with a fairly high degree of reliability.

COMPONENT RELIABILITY

It is said that the strength of a chain is actually the strength of its weakest link. The same applies to the reliability of a complete equipment or a system, which is governed by the reliability of the components. This is what makes reliability control much more difficult than the control of any other quality parameter. Even one small component of poor quality getting into the assembly, can have a disproportionately adverse effect on the overall reliability of the equipment. The worst part of it is that an unreliable component cannot be easily detected in the final inspection and may be revealed only when a failure takes place in actual service.

MANUFACTURING PROCESS

Although the inherent reliability of a product is determined by its design, the extent to which it is actually achieved depends upon the process of manufacture. A product with a high designed reliability may yet have an early failure because of certain factors introduced during its manufacture. The manufacturing drawings only lay down the important dimensions and characteristics of the product. There are a number of other features such as surface finishes, radius of curvature of edges and corners, welding and brazing details, etc. which are left to the manufacturer and are provided for according to the general engineering practice followed in the manufacturing concern. Nevertheless, these characteristics can have an appreciable effect on the reliability of the equipment. An electronic device using high quality components may have low reliability, merely because poor quality solder is used. Seemingly, inconsequential features such as tool marks or an insufficient radius at the change of section in a stressed component which may not have any immediate functional effect, may, however, cause early failure because of the stress concentration in the affected part.

ENVIRONMENTAL CONDITIONS

Every device or mechanism is subjected to certain environmental conditions which may have a marked influence on its functioning and operating life. Some environmental factors such as temperature, humidity, corrosive atmosphere, vibration and shock, may cause rapid deterioration of the product and thereby adversely affect its reliability. Therefore, these factors have to be given due consideration during the design of a product to ensure that it can withstand environmental hazards and achieve the required standard of reliability.

OPERATION AND MAINTENANCE

The way a machine or device is operated and maintained, is another factor which determines the reliability that will be achieved in actual service. As is well known to any vehicle owner, bad driving habits and indifferent preventive maintenance takes a heavy toll and can render even the best of vehicles unreliable. Since this factor depends upon the user, the designer of the product does not have much control over it. At best, efforts can be made to educate the user by providing detailed instructions on usage and maintenance.

RELIABILITY AND FAILURE OF A PRODUCT

We have seen earlier that the reliability of a product depends upon the incidence of its failure. The study of reliability is, in fact, the study of the failure pattern of a product. For this, we must first define a failure. When a product is unable to perform the function for which it is meant, it is said to have failed. Failure may be partial or complete. For instance, if a 10-ton crane can lift only up to 5 tons load due to a leak in its hydraulic system, it can be termed as a case of partial failure. On the other hand, when a car breaks down and does not run at all, it is a complete failure. Whether the inability of the product is partial or complete, of a temporary or permanent nature, from the point of view of reliability, it will count as a failure, since, at that particular time, the product is unable to perform its intended function. It is the failure-proneness of the product which determines its reliability. Therefore, for the proper appreciation and evaluation of reliability, it is essential to study the rate and pattern of failures in the product.

FAILURE RATE

Suppose ten pieces of an article were subjected to a life test and the first five pieces failed at intervals shown below:

Item no.	*Time of occurrence of failure*
1.	25 hours
2.	45 hours
3.	70 hours
4.	92 hours
5.	128 hours

The test was terminated after the fifth piece failed. The failure rate which is generally designated by Greek letter (Lambda), is given by the following relation:

$$\text{The failure rate } (\lambda) = \frac{\text{No. of items which failed.}}{\text{Total test hours of all items.}}$$

In the above example, the first item ran for 25 hours, the second for 45 hours, the third for 70 hours and the fourth for 92 hours. All the remaining six items were run for 128 hrs.

$$\text{Thus} \qquad (\lambda) = \frac{5}{25 + 45 + 70 + 92 + 6 \times 128}$$

$$= \frac{5}{1000}$$

$$= 0.005 \text{ per hour}$$

The failure rate of 0.005 means that if it remains constant, five items out of every 1,000 being operated are likely to fail every hour. The failure rate can also be defined as the probability of failure in a unit time of an item which is still working. The failure rate of 0.005 in the above case indicates that for every item which is being operated there is a probability of 0.005 that it will fail during the next hour. Since the failure rate gives an indication of the probability of failure of a product, it can be used as a measure of reliability.

The higher the failure rate, the lower is the reliability and vice versa. From this, it should not be assumed that the failure rate and hence the reliability of a product always remains constant. The reliability not only differs from product to product, but it may also vary during different stages of the product life.

PATTERN OF FAILURES

The pattern of the failures can be studied by subjecting a large number of units of a product to the life test till all the pieces have failed. Generally, the pattern of failures which is normally observed in most of the industrial products is shown in Fig. 1.

It will be seen that there is a relatively high rate of failure in the early phase of life represented by T_1, due to the failure of weak or substandard components. This period is some times referred to as the "running in" or "burning in" period. As the units with weak components are eliminated by their failure, the rate of failure drops off rapidly. In the next phase represented by period T_2, the failure rate is fairly low and stable, on account of failures due to random causes. This is the normal operating period or the useful life of a device. In the next phase represented by T_3, the failure rate again begins to rise. This increase in the failure rate is generally attributable to the wearing out of parts. As more and more parts wear out, the failure rate rises at an increasing rate till all the pieces have failed. The failure pattern graph of any article can provide very useful information to the quality engineer regarding its behaviour in service.

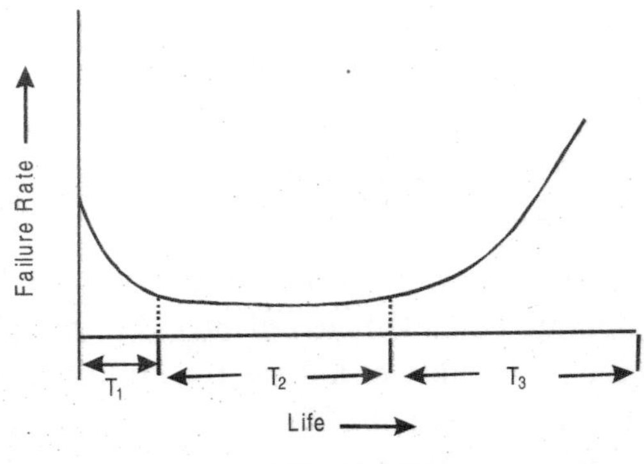

Fig. 1: Pattern of Failures

MEAN TIME TO FAILURE (MTTF)

In reliability problems, sometimes, it is more convenient to express the failure-proneness in terms of mean time to failure (MTTF) rather than failure time. To understand the concept of MTTF, let us suppose a device is being subjected to a life test in such a way that every time it fails,

IN TERMS OF TIME OR NUMBER OF OPERATIONS

it is replaced with a new one. If the device has a constant failure rate of 0.005 per hour, then we can expect it to fail on the average of five times in every 1,000 hours. In other words, the mean time to failure will be 1000/5 = 200 hours. From this, it can be seen that the MTTF is the reciprocal of the failure rate. In quality control practice, MTTF is generally designated by θ. The relationship of MTTF and the failure rate (λ) is algebraically given by,

$$\theta = \frac{1}{\lambda}$$

Where $\begin{cases} \theta \text{ is MTTF} \\ \lambda \text{ is the constant failure rate.} \end{cases}$

As we have discussed earlier, the failure rate and hence the MTTF remains approximately constant throughout the useful life of most of the industrial products where reliability is of major importance. Therefore, it may be more convenient to specify the reliability of such products by MTTF, rather than by reliability itself. The reliability value has the disadvantage of being always related to a particular planned life, which may not always meet the user's requirements. On the other hand, MTTF is independent of the life and is a better index for the comparison of the reliability of different products.

CALCULATION OF RELIABILITY

Once the failure rate or the MTTF is known, the reliability for any duration of time or number of cycles of operation can be easily calculated by using the following formula:

$R(t) = e^{\lambda t}$ where $\begin{cases} R(t) \text{ is the reliability for the duration } t. \\ \lambda \text{ is the failure rate} \\ e \text{ is the base for Naperian Logarithms,} \\ \text{which has a value of 2.72} \end{cases}$

For example, if the constant failure rate of a particular item is 0.005 per hour, its reliability for a 100-hour life can be determined as follows:

$$\text{Failure rate} = 0.005 \text{ per hour}$$
$$\text{Specified life } (t) = 100 \text{ hour}$$
$$R(t) = e^{-\lambda t}$$

Substituting the values of t and λ, we get,

$$R(100) = e^{-0.005 \times 100}$$
$$= e^{-0.5}$$
$$= .606 \begin{cases} \text{From the table of exponential functions} \\ \text{given in Table A, we find } e^{-0.5} = 0.606. \end{cases}$$

This means that there is a probability of 0.606 that the item will not fail during the first 100 hours of its operation. When the life of a product is expressed in terms of a number of cycles instead of time, the failure rate is also given in the same terms as is illustrated in the following example:

In a reliability test for a particular switch, five failures were observed over a total of 100,000 operations, which gave a failure rate of 0.00005 per cycle of operation. Let us suppose the planned life of this switch is 6,000 operations. The reliability of the switch for its intended life can be determined as follows:

$$\lambda = 0.00005 \text{ per cycle t } t = 6000 \text{ cycles}$$
$$R(t) = e^{-\lambda t}$$

Substituting values of t and λ,
we get

$$R(6000 \text{ cycles}) = e^{-0.00005 \times 6000}$$
$$= e^{-0.30} = \frac{1}{e^{0.30}}$$
$$= 0.74. \text{ (from Table A)}$$

Which means that there are 74% chances that the switch will not fail in 6,000 operations. To simplify the calculation of reliability, standard tables based on exponential distribution are available from which the reliability for any particular time period can be read against the known failure rate on MTTF. One such tabulation is given in Table (B). Suppose a sample of 5 switches were tested for 100,000 operations and a total of 10 failures were noticed, giving an average of 2 failures per 100,000 operations. If we want to know the reliability of the switch for 1000 operations. We see from Table 1, against 2 failures per 1000,000 (2nd too row) under column of 1000, reliability value of 98.0%. Similarly reliability for any failure data can be obtained from Table B.

Table-A

x	e^x	e^{-x}	θ° (gd x)	cosh x (sin θ)	Sinh x (tan θ)	tanh x (sin θ)	log cosh x	log sinh x
.1	1.1052	.9048	5.720	1.0050	.1002	.0997	.0022	1.0007
.2	1.2214	.8187	11.384	1.0201	.2013	.1974	.0086	1.3039
.3	1.3499	.7408	16.937	1.0453	.3045	.2913	.0193	1.4836
.4	1.4918	.6703	22.331	1.0811	.4108	.3799	.0339	1.6136
.5	1.6487	.6065	27.524	1.1276	.5211	.4621	.0522	1.7169
.6	1.8221	.5488	32.483	1.1855	.6367	.5370	.0739	1.8093
.7	2.0138	.4966	37.183	1.2552	.7586	.6044	.0987	1.8800
.8	2.2255	.4493	41.608	1.3374	.8881	.6640	.1263	1.9485
.9	2.4596	.4066	45.750	1.4331	1.0265	.7163	.1563	0.0114
1.0	2.7183	.3679	49.605	1.5431	1.1752	.7616	.1884	0.0701
1.1	3.0042	.3329	53.178	1.6685	1.3356	.8005	.2223	0.1257
1.2	3.3201	.3012	56.476	1.8107	1.5095	.8337	.2578	0.1788
1.3	3.6693	.2725	59.511	1.9709	1.6984	.8617	.2947	0.2300
1.4	4.0552	.2466	62.295	2.1509	1.9043	.8854	.3326	0.2797
1.5	4.4817	.2231	64.843	2.3524	2.1293	.9051	.3715	0.3282
1.6	4.9530	.2019	67.171	2.5775	2.3756	.9217	.4112	0.3758
1.7	5.4739	.1827	69.294	2.8283	2.6456	.9354	.4515	0.4225
1.8	6.0496	.1653	71.228	3.1075	2.9422	.9468	.4924	0.4687
1.9	6.6859	.1496	72.987	3.4177	3.2682	.9562	.5337	0.5143
2.0	7.3891	.1353	74.584	3.7622	3.6269	.9640	.5754	0.5595
2.1	8.1662	.1225	76.037	4.1443	4.0219	.9705	.6175	0.6044
2.2	9.0250	.1108	77.354	4.5679	4.4571	.9757	.6597	0.6491
2.3	9.9742	.1003	78.549	5.0372	4.9370	.9801	.7022	0.6936
2.4	11.023	.0907	79.633	5.5569	5.4662	.9837	.7448	0.7377
2.5	12.183	.0821	80.615	6.1323	6.0502	.9866	.7876	0.7818
2.6	13.464	.0743	81.513	6.7690	6.6947	.9890	.8305	0.8257
2.7	14.880	.0672	82.310	7.4735	7.4063	.9910	.8735	0.8696
2.8	16.445	.0608	83.040	8.2527	8.1919	.9926	.9166	0.9134
2.9	18.174	.0550	83.707	9.1146	9.0596	.9940	.9597	0.9571
3.0	20.086	.0498	84.301	10.068	10.018	.9951	1.0029	1.0008
3.1	22.198	.0450	84.841	11.121	11.076	.9959	1.0462	1.0444
3.2	24.533	.0408	85.336	12.287	12.246	.9967	1.0894	1.0880
3.3	27.113	.0369	85.775	13.575	13.538	.9973	1.1327	1.1316

(Contd...)

Table-A *(Contd...)*

x	e^x	e^{-x}	θ^o *(gd x)*	*cosh x* *(sin θ)*	*Sinh x* *(tan θ)*	*tanh x* *(sin θ)*	*log cosh x*	*log sinh x*
3.4	29.964	.0334	86.177	14.999	14.965	.9978	1.1761	1.1751
3.5	33.115	.0302	86.541	16.573	16.543	.9982	1.2194	1.2186
3.6	36.598	.0273	86.870	18.313	18.285	.9985	1.2628	1.2621
3.7	40.447	.0247	87.168	20.236	20.211	.9988	1.3061	1.3056
3.8	44.701	.0224	87.437	22.362	22.339	.9990	1.3495	1.3491
3.9	49.402	.0202	87.681	24.711	24.691	.9992	1.3929	1.3925
4.0	54,598	.0183	87.903	27.308	27.290	.9993	1.4363	1.4360
4.1	60.340	.0166	88.104	30.178	30.162	.9995	1.4797	1.4795
4.2	66.686	.0150	88.281	33.351	33.336	.9996	1.5231	1.5229
4.3	73.700	.0136	88.447	36.857	36.843	.9996	1.5665	1.5664
4.4	81.451	.0123	88.591	40.732	40.719	.9997	1.6099	1.6098
4.5	90.017.	.0111	88.728	45.014	45.003	.9997	1.6533	1.6532
4.6	99.484	.0101	88.849	49.747	49.737	.9988	1.6968	1.6967
4.7	109.95	.0091	88,957	54.978	54.969	.9998	1.7402	1.7401
4.8	121.51	.0082	89.055	60.759	60.751	.9999	1.7836	1.7836
4.9	134.29	.0074	89.146	67.149	67.141	.9999	1.8270	1.8270
5.0	148.41	.0067	89.227	74.210	74.203	.9999	1.8705	1.8704

BUILDING RELIABILITY IN THE PRODUCT

The reliability of a product, like other quality parameters is dictated by the customer's or user's requirements. Unfortunately, this aspect is often overlooked at the design stage. The product is generally designed to meet functional requirements and it is hoped that if good quality components are used the reliability of the product will be automatically ensured. This 'hope for the best' approach can prove very costly in the long run. It is some time seen that when the final product goes in the hands of the users, it is found to have much too high a failure rate which is not acceptable to the users. It is at this stage that some effort is made to evaluate the reliability of the product and ad hoc modifications and changes are made in the product with a view to improving reliability. The incorporation of major changes at this stage, when tooling and process have already been set, is extremely expensive, besides upsetting delivery schedules. How much easier and economic would it be, if the reliability were properly evaluated at the design stage itself, when the design could have been easily adjusted

Table-B: Reliability in Terms of Probability of Survival

Failures 100,000 hr.*	Mean time to failure	5	10	20	50	100	200	300	500	1000	2000	3000	5000	7500	10,000	15,000
		Hours of Operation														
		Probability, Percent, of Survial, P														
1	100,000	99.995	99.99	99.98	99.95	99.9	99.8	99.7	99.5	99.0	98.0	97.0	95.1	92.8	90.5	86.1
2	50,000	99.990	99.98	99.96	99.90	99.8	99.6	99.4	99.0	98.0	96.1	94.2	90.5	86.1	81.9	74.1
3	33,000	99.985	99.97	99.94	99.85	99.7	99.4	99.1	98.5	97.0	94.2	91.4	86.1	79.9	74,1	63.8
4	25,000	99.980	99.96	99.92	99.80	99.6	99.2	98.8	98.0	96.1	92.3	88.7	81.7	74.1	67.0	54.9
5	20,000	99.975	99.95	99.90	99.75	99.5	99.0	98.5	97.5	95.1	90.5	86.1	77.9	68.7	60.7	47.2
6	16,700	99.970	99.94	99.88	99.70	99.4	98.8	98.2	97.0	94.2	88.7	83.5	74.1	63.8	54.9	40.7
7	14,300	99.965	99.93	99.86	99.65	99.3	98.6	97.9	96.6	93.2	86.9	81.1	70.5	59.2	49.7	35.0
8	12,500	99.960	99.92	99.84	99.60	99.2	98.4	97.6	96.1	92.3	85.2	78.7	67.0	54.9	44.9	30.1
9	11,100	99.955	99.91	99.82	99.55	99.1	98.2	97.3	95.6	91.4	83.5	76.3	63.8	50.9	40.7	25.9
10	10,000	99.95	99.9	99.8	99.5	99.0	98.0	97.0	95.1	90.5	81.9	74.1	60.7	47.2	36.8	22.3
20	5,000	99.90	99.8	99.6	99.0	98.0	96.1	94.2	90.5	81.9	67.0	54.9	36.8	22.3	13.5	5.0
30	3,330	99.85	99.7	99.4	98.5	97.0	98.0	97.0	95.1	90,5	81.9	74.1	60.7	47.2	36.8	22.3
40	2,500	99.80	99.6	99.2	98.0	96.1	92.3	88.7	81.9	67.0	44.9	30.1	13.5	5.0	1.8	0.2
50	2,000	99.75	99.5	99.0	97.5	95.1	90.5	86.1	77.9	60.7	36.8	22.3	8.2	2.4	0.7	0.1
60	1,670	99.70	99.4	98.8	97.0	94.2.	88.7	83.5	74.1	54.9	30.1	16.5	5.0	1.1	0.3	
70	1,430	99.65	99.3	98.6	96.6	93.2	86.9	81.1	70.5	49.7	24.7	12.3	3.0	0.5	0.1	
80	1,250	99.60	99.2	98.4	96.1	92.3	85.2	78.7	67.0	44.9	20.2	9.1	1.8	0.3		
90	1,110	99.55	99.1	98.2	95.6	91.4	83.5	76.3	63.8	40.7	16.5	6.7	1.1	0.1		
100	1,000	99.5	99.0	98.0	95.1	90.5	81.9	74.1	60.7	36.8	13.5	5.0	0.7			
200	500	99.0	98.0	96.1	90.5	81.9	67.0	54.9	36.8	13.5	1.8	0.3				
300	333	98.5	97.0	94.2	86.1	74.1	54.9	40.7	22.3	5.0	.03					
400	250	98.0	96.1	92.3	81.9	67.0	44.9	30.1	13.5	1.8						
500	200	97.5	95.1	90.5	77.9	60.7	36.8	22.3	8.2	0.7						
600	167	97.0	94.2	88.7	74.1	54.9	30.2	16.6	5.0	0.3						
700	143	96.6	93.2	86.9	70.5	49.7	24.7	12.3	3.0	0.1						
800	125	96.1	92.3	85.2	67.0	44.9	20.2	9.1	1.8							
900	111	95.6	91.4	83.5	63.7	40.7	16.5	6.7	1.1							
1000	100	95.1	90.5	81.9	60.7	36.8	13.5	5.0	0.7							

*In place of hours, any time unit may be used, so long as the units are alike for the 3 terms involved: Average number of failures per period (λ); Mean time to (or between) failure (s) (m); and operating time (t). In place of a. time period, a time-related basis may also be used, such as "number of actuations" or "number of flexures" until failure. For example, relay life might be expressed in terms of failure-free actuations and wire life may be measured by the number of flexures that the wire can withstand before breaking.

to provide high inherent reliability.

DESIGN OF RELIABILITY

Before undertaking the actual design of a product, a desired standard of reliability should be established, based on the end use. This standard should find a place in the design or target specifications, so that it is given due consideration at every stage of the development of the product. For the actual design of reliability in a product, there are two fundamental rules:

1. Use as few parts as possible.
2. The reliability of each part should be as high as is economically feasible.

It should be easy to appreciate the first rule. If there are fewer parts in a system, there will be fewer things to go wrong, which means that the reliability of the system will be higher than if there were more parts. Unfortunately, the present trend is in the opposite direction. The need for multifunction capability and automation in modern equipment requires increasing numbers of parts, which tend to reduce the system reliability. Due to this reason there is an increasing need to improve the reliability of individual components as envisaged in the second rule of reliability design.

RELIABILITY OF PARTS IN SERIES

Suppose a system consists of a number of parts, each of which is vital for the functioning of the system, in the sense that the failure of one part results in the failure of the whole system. The parts in such a system can be considered to be in series as shown in Fig. 2.

If the reliability of each part be r_1, r_2, r_3 .... r_n, the reliability (R_s) of the whole system is given by:

$$R_s = r_1 \times r_2 \times r_3 \times \ldots\ldots\ldots\ldots r_n \quad \ldots\ldots\ldots\ldots (i)$$

Parts in Series

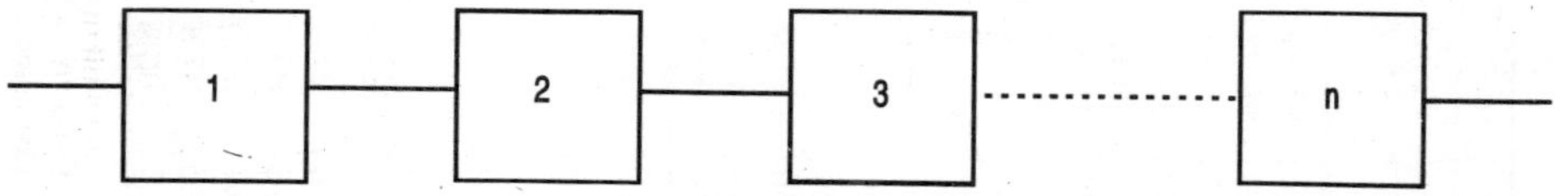

Fig. 2

Let us consider the example of a warning system, which consists of a switch, a sensor unit and a lamp. For, simplicity's sake let us assume that each of the three parts has a reliability of 0.9. The reliability of the whole warning system is given by,

$$R_s = 0.9 \times 0.9 \times 0.9$$

$= 0.73.$

Now let us suppose that a system comprises of 20 parts each with 0.9 reliability. The reliability of such a system will be,

$$R_s = (0.9^{20})$$
$$= 0.12$$

0.12 Reliability means that there are only 12% chances that the system would work, which is a statistical way of saying that the system is useless. Now a system with 20 parts is very simple according to the modern standards. A radio or domestic refrigerator has more than 100 vital parts, a car, more than 1000 and a large aircraft over a million. How can a reasonable level of reliability for such complex systems be achieved? Firstly, every effort must be made to reduce the number of parts in the system. To achieve this end the Value Analysis Technique discussed in chapter 18, have been found to be very useful. Secondly, we should have components with as high reliability as possible. In the above example we had assumed component reliability to be 0.9. Luckily, with the technological progress made in the last few decades it is now possible to achieve much higher level of reliability and components with 0.999 reliability have become quite common. Let us study the reliability of a system using parts with a reliability of 0,999. Suppose the system has 400 parts in series, its reliability will be $(0.999)^{400}$ or 0.67%. Now a system where the chances of successful operation are 67% or 2 out of 3, cannot be called very reliable. Therefore, in addition to using components with high individual reliability, certain other measures are also required to improve system reliability. Some of these are discussed in the following paragraphs.

DERATING

All systems are designed to withstand certain loads or stress conditions. A safe working load or stress is specified after allowing for a safety margin which caters for unknown factors and occasional unintended overloading. The rate of deterioration of the system generally bears some relation with the loading. This is particularly true for systems having electronic components. The reliability of such systems will be higher if the components are operated at lower than the rated voltage and current values, *i.e.* the components are derated. This of course, would involve the use of heavier and more expensive components than are really necessary, from functional points of view, but this price may have to be paid to achieve an acceptable level of reliability.

CONTROL OF ENVIRONMENTS

Certain parts and materials are greatly affected by environments. For instance, deterioration in optical and electrical parts is accelerated by heat and humidity. To check the rate of deterioration and consequently improve reliability, it may be necessary to control the temperature and humidity under which the system is operated. The cooling of transformers and provision of built-in air conditioners in large radars are examples, where reliability is improved by controlling environments.

BURNING-IN OR RUNNING-IN

We have seen in Fig. 1 that the failure rate in an early part of the product life is relatively higher than that in the middle part. If he application is critical, we may consider running-in the device for the initial period and eliminating the early failures before it is handed over to the customer or put to actual use.

Redundancy

When every thing discussed above has been done and the required reliability of the system has still not been achieved, we may consider duplication of one or more elements of the system, so that if one fails, the alternative element is available takes over to perform the function and thereby avoid the failure of the whole system. This technique is called REDUNDANCY. Automatic switching of the emergency light in an operation theater, the starting handle and the spare tyre in the car are all examples of redundancy. Redundancy may be active or standby. In active redundancy, the spare item is automatically brought into use, once the original item fails. For this a device may have to be incorporated in the design which senses the failed unit and brings the spare unit into action. Automatic emergency lights are an example of active redundancy. In standby redundancy, the spare item such as a car tyre is brought into use manually and the system does not function during the changeover period. The reliability of a system using redundancy can be determined if the reliability of individual elements is known.

Suppose a particular component in the system is found to be unreliable and it is decided to use two similar elements in parallel so that if one fails, the other can carry on the function. Let the two elements be designated as No. 1 and No. 2 as shown in Fig. 3 and their reliability be R_1, and R_2 respectively. The system will fail only if both the elements fail, the probability of which can be calculated as follows:

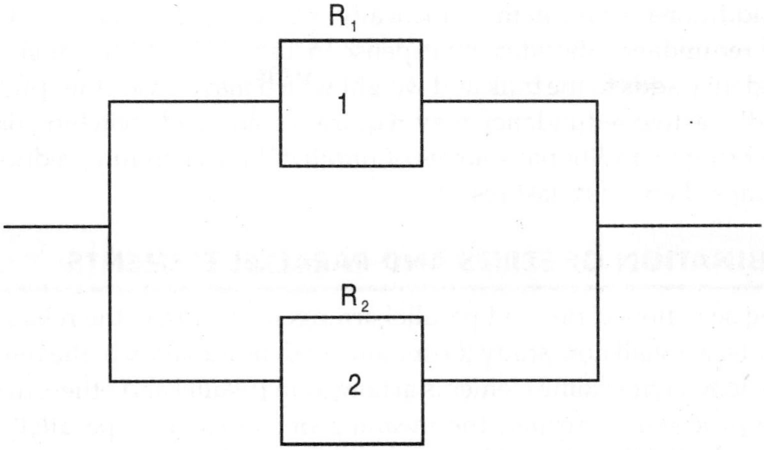

Fig. 3: Parts in Parallel

Probability (F_1) that element No. 1 fails = $1 - R_1$

Probability (F_2) that element No. 2 fails = $1 - R_2$

Probability that both No. 1 and No. 2 fail = $F_1 \times F_1$ 'See Multiplication theorem of probability in chapter 24.

The system will continue to work satisfactorily until both the elements fail.

Therefore, reliability (R_c) of the combined unit of two elements is given by

$$(R_c) = 1 - (F_1 \times F_2).$$

The same equation can be written in the following general form when there are K elements in parallel.

$$R_c = 1 - (F_1 \times F_2 \times F_2 \ldots\ldots\ldots\ldots F_k)$$

$$= 1 - (1 - R_1)(1 - R_2)(1 - R_2)\ldots\ldots\ldots\ldots(1 - R_k)\ldots\ldots\ldots\ldots\text{(ii)}$$

For example, if three elements are in parallel and each has a reliability of 0.80, the reliability R_C of the combined unit is given by,

$$R_C = 1\ (1–0.8)\ (1\text{-}0.8)\ (1\text{-}0.8)$$

$$= 1–0.2 \times 0.2 \times 0.2$$

$$= 1 - 0.008$$

$$= 0.992.$$

From the above, it can be seen that theoretically, we can raise the reliability to any desired level by means of redundancy, provided we can afford to have additional spare items. Practically, however, there is a limit to the use of redundancy. Besides the expense incurred on additional elements, redundancy adds to the bulk and weight which may cause other problems. Secondly, active redundancy may require sensing and switching devices, which bring in additional sources of unreliability. Therefore, redundancy is attempted only as a last resort.

COMBINATION OF SERIES AND PARALLEL ELEMENTS

Having seen how series and parallel arrangements affect the reliability of elements, we shall now study the method of determination of the reliability of a system having some elements arranged in parallel and others in series. Before proceeding further, the meaning of 'series' and 'parallel' in the context of reliability should be clearly understood. As already mentioned, components can be considered in series when a failure in any of them can cause a failure of the whole system. Components are considered in parallel when they provide an alternative method of performing a function. Figure 4 shows a system LMN in which some elements are in series and some are in parallel. The reliability of each element is shown in Fig. 4. To determine the overall reliability of system LMN, we should proceed as follows:

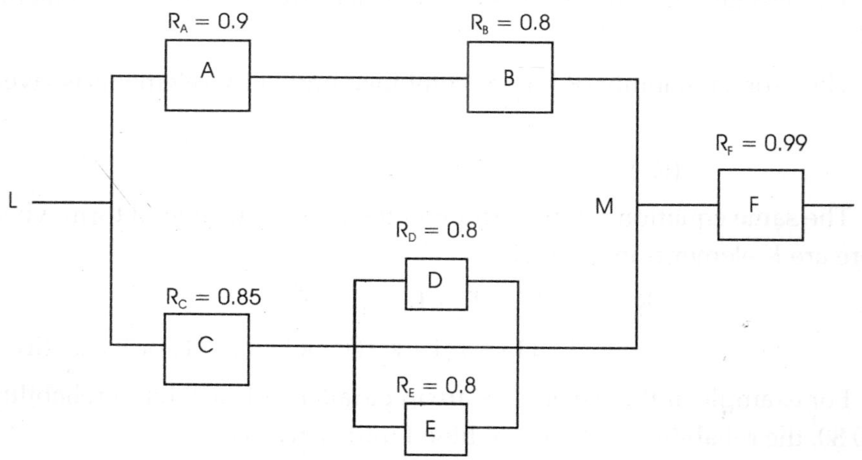

Fig. 4

(a) Look for the elements arranged in series within the parallel network and calculate the reliability of the combined equivalent unit with the help of equation ...(i)

(b) Calculate the reliability of each parallel arrangement by using equation ...(ii)

The above drill is to be repeated until the entire network is solved as illustrated below:

In the upper branch of the network, elements A and B are in series. The reliability of the combined unit A - B is given by:

$$R_{AB} = R_A \times R_B \qquad \text{From equation} \qquad ...(i)$$
$$= 0.9 \times 0.8$$
$$= 0.72$$

Next, let us take up the smallest parallel arrangement D - E. Their combined reliability is given by

$$R_{DE} = 1 - (1 - R_D) \times (1 - R_E) \qquad \text{From equation} \qquad ...(ii)$$
$$= 1 - (1 - 0.8) \times (1 - 0.8)$$
$$= 1 - 0.2 \times 0.2 = 1 - 0.04$$
$$= 0.96$$

Now, the lower branch can be considered to have C and (DE) in series and their combined reliability R_{CDE} can be obtained as follows:

$$R_{CDE} = R_C \times R_{DE}$$
$$= 0.85 \times 0.96$$
$$= 0.816$$

Next, we can calculate the reliability of subsystem LM having two parallel branches AB and CDE.

$$R_{LM} = 1 - (1 - R_{AB}) \times (1 - R_{CDE})$$
$$= 1 - (1 - 0.72) \times (1 - 0.816)$$
$$= 1 - (0.28) \times (0.184)$$
$$= 1 - 0.05$$
$$= 0.95$$

Finally, the reliability of the whole system LMN having subsystem LM and element F in series can be worked out.

$$R_{LMN} = R_{LM} \times R_F$$
$$= 0.95 \times 0.99$$
$$= 0.94$$

In this manner, the reliability of a system having any combination of series and parallel elements can be calculated.

PLACING OF REDUNDANCY

We have already discussed that during the design of a system, if it is found that the reliability is not up to the required standard, the redundancy of one or more components may be incorporated in the design. We shall now study the methods of connecting the spare elements to the system to obtain maximum improvement in system reliability.

Let us suppose that it is intended to incorporate redundancy for components A and B in a system. Two alternative methods of connecting the components are shown in Fig. 5. In Fig. 5(a), spare components A and B are connected in series and the combined unit A-B is connected in parallel with unit A-B. On the other hand, in Fig. 5(b), each of the spare components is connected in parallel with its original counterpart. Let us calculate the combined reliability in both cases.

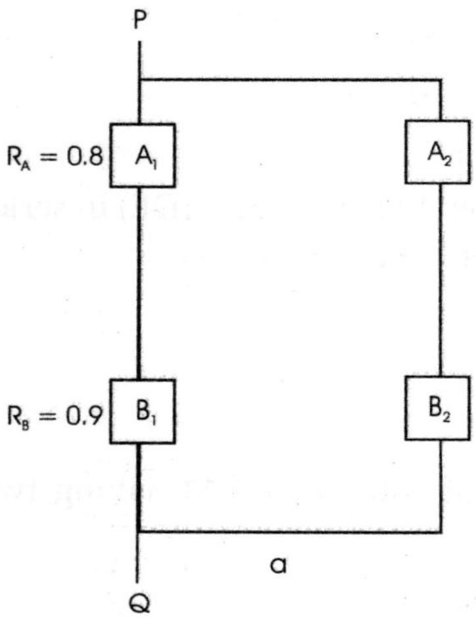

Fig. 5 (a)

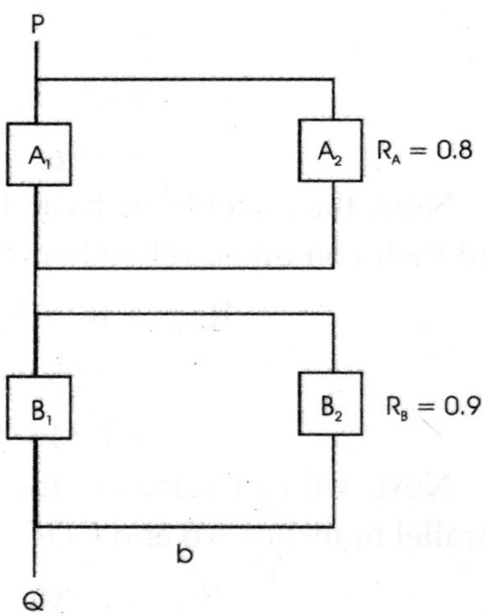

Fig. 5 (b)

Since the reliability of spare and original components are the same, the reliability of each parallel branch in Fig. 5(a) is given by,

$$R_{A1B1} = R_{A2B2} = R_A \times R_B$$
$$= 0.8 \times 0.9$$
$$= 0.72$$

The combined reliability of both parallel branches in Fig. (a) using equation (ii) is given by,

$$R_{AB} = 1 - (1 - 0.72)\,(1 - 0.72)$$
$$= 1 - 0.28 \times 0.28$$

$$= 1 - 0.078$$
$$= 0.922, \text{ say } 0.92$$

Now, let us see the combined reliability of elements A and B in Fig. 5(b). In this figure, elements A_1 and A_2 are connected in parallel. Their combined reliability R_A is given by,

$$R_A = 1 - (1 - R_{A1}) \times (1 - R_{A2})$$
$$= 1 - (1 - 0.8)\ (1 - 0.8)$$
$$= 1 - 0.2 \times 0.2$$
$$= 1 - 0.04$$
$$= 0.96$$

Similarly, the combined reliability of B and B; in Fig. 5(b) is given by,

$$R_B = 1 - (1-0.9) \times (1 - 0.9)$$
$$= 1 - 0.1 \times 0.1$$
$$= 1 - 0.01$$
$$= 0.99$$

Now the two parallel sets A_1 A_2 and B_1 B_2 can be considered to be in series in Fig. 5(b), and the combined reliability of both sets can be obtained as follows:

$$R_{AB} = R_A \times R_B$$
$$= 0.96 \times 0.99$$
$$= 0.95$$

From the above, it can be seen that overall reliability is higher if each spare component is connected in parallel with its original component, rather than when the group of spare components together as a unit is connected in parallel with the corresponding unit of original components. However, in practice, it may not always be possible to connect every spare component in such a manner. Further, extra connections and switching or fixing arrangements may bring in their own unreliability, which may neutralise the advantage of individual coupling. Therefore, in actual practice, the placing of spare components in the system is generally a compromise between individual coupling and group coupling, depending upon the ease of switching or fitting.

EVALUATION OF RELIABILITY

PROBLEMS OF RELIABILITY TESTING

Unlike other quality parameters, the reliability of a product cannot be directly measured or checked. At best, an estimate of the reliability of the product lot can be made by testing a few pieces, as is done in the case of sampling inspection. Reliability testing generally involves running the product units under test for the duration of their expected life. The proportion of the units which fail during the test gives an indication of reliability of the product. The product units subjected to reliability test have to be written off, as at the end of the test either the units would have failed or be in the last stage of their useful life. In case the product is expensive the cost of test pieces may place a limit on the number of pieces which can be tested. Further, the life of a product may be thousands of hours, or even more. To test the product for this duration may be impracticable due to the limited time available. This problem may be overcome by adopting one of the following approaches:

(a) Accelerated Testing

A device may operate intermittently in actual life. Testing time can be reduced by operating the device more or less continuously. In such cases, care must be taken to see that continuous operation does not lead to undue rise in temperature which may cause premature failure of the device. While testing devices which are subject to this tendency, adequate rest periods must be allowed for the device to cool down.

(b) Test of Increased Severity

Sometimes, it may be possible to carry out the test under more severe conditions than are met in actual service. This may be achieved by increasing the loading or imposing harsher environmental conditions such as temperature, pressure, vibrations, etc. If the device does not fail during a relatively brief exposure to these conditions, it may be possible to predict the life by extrapolations. However, this approach can only be adopted if a proper correlation has previously been established between the actual observed life and the life under specified severe conditions.

(c) Testing a Larger Number of Pieces

We have seen earlier that the failure rate during the useful period of life of a product is generally constant. Instead of testing a few pieces for the entire period of specified life, a larger number can be tested for a comparatively shorter time, until a few failures have occurred. The failure rate can then be determined from the total hours logged by all pieces under test, as explained earlier in this chapter.

INTERPRETATION OF TEST RESULTS

Accuracy of reliability evaluation depends upon our ability to correctly interpret the result of the reliability tests. Suppose one device is tested and it fails before the specified period of life. It tells us very little. We do not know whether the life given by the device is typical of the product in general, or it was an odd bad piece in the lot. However, because of the various problems enumerated above, we want to test as few pieces as possible. It is, therefore, essential that the reliability tests are carefully planned to obtain maximum information from the pieces which are tested.

The probability of survival of any particular number of product units can be obtained from the binomial expansion, as given below:

$$= (R+F)^n + \frac{n}{1}R^{n-1}\, F + \frac{n(n-1)R^{n-2}}{1\times 2} F^2 + \frac{n(n-1)(n-2)}{1\times 2\times 3} R^{n-3}F^3 + \ldots\ldots F^n$$

Where
- R is the reliability of the product.
- F is the probability of failure which is equal to (1–R).
- n is the number of units tested.

In the above expansion, the first term gives the probability of all units surviving, *i.e.* zero failures. The second, third and subsequent terms give the probability of 1, 2 and more failures, respectively. For example, if ten units of a product having a reliability of 0.9 are being tested, the probability of getting various numbers of failures are shown in Table C.

Table C

Number of failure(s)	*Probability*
0	$R^n = 0.9^{10} = 0.35$
1	$\frac{nR^{n-1}}{1} F = 10\,(0.9)^9 \times (0.1)^1 = 0.39$
2	$\frac{n(n-1)R^{n-2}}{1\times 2} F^2 = \frac{10\times 9}{2} (0.9)^8 \times (0.1)^2 = 0.19$
3	$\frac{n(n-1)(n-2)R^{n-3}}{1\times 2\times 3} F^3 = \frac{10\times 9\times 8}{2} (0.9)^7\ (0.1)^3 = 0.06$

Reliability R = 0.9

Probability of failure F = (1–R) = 0.1

Number of units (n) = 10

In the above example, we had assumed the reliability of the product to be 0.9. In actual fact, it would not be known to us and may have any value from 0 to 1. Let us work out the probability of zero failures for various values of reliability, using the formula,

Probability of zero failures = R^n

For ten units under test, the probability of zero failures for various values of reliability is given in Table D.

Table D

Reliability of product	*Probability of zero failures in a sample of 10 units*
0.95	$(0.95)^{10} = 0.59$
0.90	$(0.90)^{10} = 0.35$
0.85	$(0.85)^{10} = 0.20$
0.80	$(0.80)^{10} = 0.11$
0.75	$(0.75)^{10} = 0.06$
0.70	$(0.70)^{10} = 0.03$

OPERATING CHARACTERISTIC

The data in Table C can also be presented in a graphical form as shown in Fig. 6, where the horizontal axis represents the actual reliability of the product and the vertical axis represents the probability of getting 0 failures. A keen reader would have already guessed that Fig. 6, is in fact, an operating characteristic curve similar to those discussed in Chapter 27. Let us see what the OC curve tells us. It will be seen from point 'P' that if the actual reliability of the product is 0.85, there is a 0.20 probability of getting zero failures in the sample of ten units which is tested. In other words, there is a probability of (1.0–0.2) or (0.80 of getting 1 or more failures in the sample. Thus, if we do get '0' failures, we can be 80% confident that the reliability of lot from which the sample came is 0.85 or more, and there is only 20% chance that the reliability of the product is less than 0.85. The confidence level goes on increasing as we move towards the right of the OC curve. For instance, confidence level for 0.70 reliability is 97%, which means that if 0 failure occurs in a sample of ten units we can be 97% confident that the reliability of the product is 0.70 or better. The OC curve in Fig. 21, is for '0' failures. Similar OC curves for up to 1, 2 or greater number of failures can be plotted by using the following relationships.

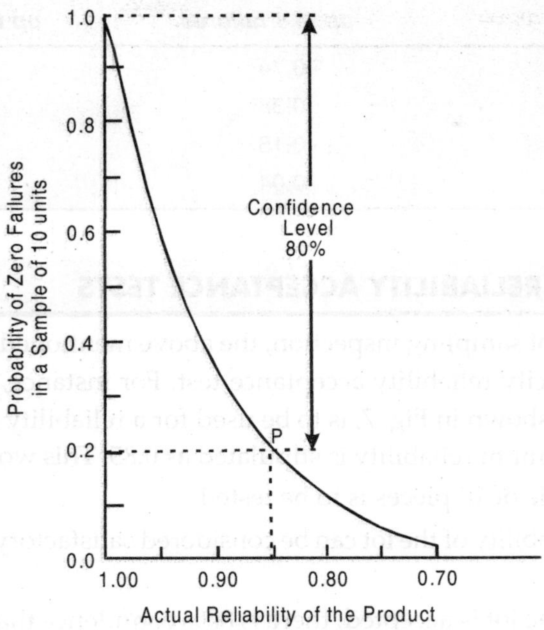

Fig. 6

Probability of getting

1 or less failures = $R^n + nR^{n-1}F$ *i.e.* probability of getting 0 failures plus the probability of getting 1 failure.

Probability of getting

2 or less failures = $R^n + nR^{n-1}F + \frac{n(n-1)}{1 \times 2} R^{n-2}F^2$ and so on.

For a given sample size n, the probability of getting up to the specified number of failures for various values of reliability, can be calculated by substituting corresponding values of reliability as was done for deriving values in Table E. In the above example, having sample size 10, the probabilities of getting up to one failure, and up to two failures for various levels of product reliability are given in Table E. These figures can then be used to plot the OC curves as shown in Fig. 7.

Table E

Product reliability	*Probability of getting up to 1 failures*	*Probability of getting up to 2 failures*
0.90	0.74	0.93
0.80	0.38	0.68
0.70	0.15	0.38
0.60	0.04	0.17

SPECIFYING RELIABILITY ACCEPTANCE TESTS

As in the case of sampling inspection, the above mentioned OC curves can be used to specify reliability acceptance test. For instance, let us suppose that the curve shown in Fig. 7, is to be used for a reliability acceptance test for which minimum reliability is stipulated as 0.85. This would imply that,

(a) A sample of 10 pieces is to be tested.

(b) The reliability of the lot can be considered satisfactory if zero failures occur.

(c) When the lot is accepted, there is 80% confidence that the reliability is 0.85 or better. Associated with this is a 20% risk, that the reliability may be less than 0.85. This can be treated as the consumer's risk at 0.85 reliability (compare it with the lot tolerance in sampling inspection).

Now, let us look at it from the producer's point of view. Even if he has ensured that actual reliability of the product is 0.85, the probability of occurrence of zero failures in a sample of 10 as seen from point Q is only 0.59. This means that there is (1 – 0.59) or 0.41 probability of one or more failures occurring. Therefore, there is 41% risk of the lot getting rejected, even though the reliability is 0.85 (Compare it with the producer's risk at AQL in sampling inspection). If the producer's risk is considered too high, we have to increase the sample size which will give a curve with reduced risk. Alternatively, if a larger sample is not feasible due to cost considerations, the consumer may be persuaded to agree to a test with a lower confidence level such as represented by OC curves for one or less failure shown in Fig. 7. Confidence level in such a case would be reduced to 54% associated with a consumers risk of 46%. On the face of it, this risk may appear to be high, but it may have to be taken in certain situations.

A reliability acceptance test like sampling plan can be derived by specifying the following characteristics, as illustrated in Fig. 7.

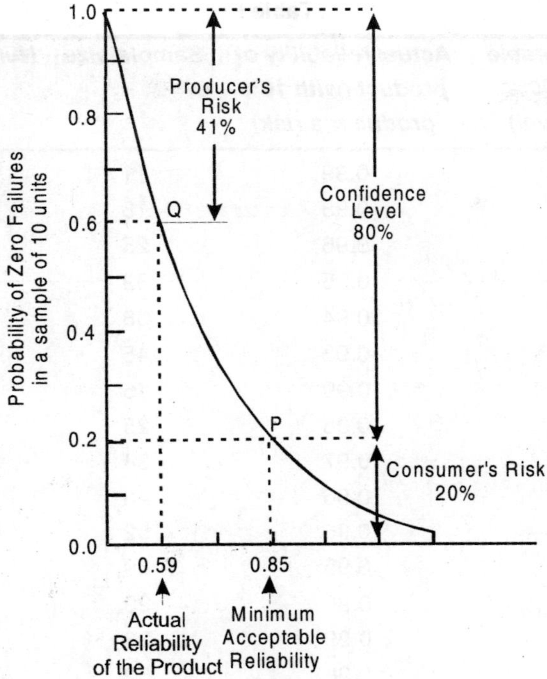

Fig. 7

(a) Minimum acceptable reliability

(b) Confidence level at minimum acceptable reliability

(c) Actual reliability of the product

(d) Producer's risk at actual reliability

Calculation of reliability acceptance tests based on the above-mentioned characteristics is quite tedious and beyond the scope of this text. However, to provide some guidance to the quality control staff Table F has been provided from which a suitable test plan can be selected for various values of minimum acceptable reliability. This table has been compiled for 90% confidence level and 10% producer's risk.

Suppose we want to plan a test which should demonstrate minimum reliability of 0.8 at 90% confidence level. At the same time, if manufacturer is able to achieve an actual reliability of 0.95, his product should have only 10% risk of rejection. Looking in the 0.80 reliability block, we find that against 0.95 actual reliability, the sample size is 32 and, the number of failures allowed is three. This gives us the test plan where 32 pieces are to be tested for the specified life. If three or less failures occur, it can be assumed with 90% confidence that the reliability of the product is at least 0.80.

Table F

Minimum acceptable reliability (at 90% confidence level)	Actual reliability of product (with 10% producer's risk)	Sample size	Number of failures allowed
0.80	0.99	11	0
	0.98	18	1
	0.96	25	2
	0.95	32	3
	0.94	38	4
	0.93	45	5
0.85	0.99	15	0
	0.98	25	1
	0.97	34	2
	0.96	43	3
	0.95	52	4
	0.95	60	5
0.90	0.99	23	0
	0.99	38	1
	0.98	52	2
	0.97	65	3
	0.97	78	4
	0.97	91	5
0.95	0.998	45	0
	0.993	77	1
	0.990	105	2
	0.987	132	3
	0.985	158	4
	0.983	184	5
0.97	0.999	60	0
	0.996	130	1
	0.994	180	2
	0.992	220	3
	0.991	270	4
	0.991	310	5
0.99	0.999	230	0
	0.999	390	1
	0.998	530	2
	0.997	670	3
	0.997	800	4
	0.997	930	5

USE OF SAMPLING TABLES

Standard sampling table can also be used to obtain a test plan for any desired confidence level, and producer's risk. Suppose a lot of 250 condensers is to be checked for reliability. Specification calls for a minimum of 0.88 reliability at 90% confidence level. The manufacturer maintains that he has ensured 0.99 reliability for his product and he cannot accept more than 5% risk for his product getting rejected.

Now reliability of 0.88 means that for every item there is 0.12 probability of failure. If we take the probability of survival of the lot as a whole, 12% of the condensers are likely to fail in reliability test. This, for the purpose of sampling inspection, can be taken to mean that there may be up to 12% defectives in the lot. Similarly, 0.99 reliability can be taken to mean 1% defectives. This gives us the following characteristics based on which we can select a suitable plan from standard sampling tables.

(a) Lot size—250

(b) Minimum acceptable reliability 0.88, *i.e.* Lot tolerance 12% defective

(c) Confidence level 90%, *i.e.* consumer's risk = 10%

(d) Actual reliability 0.99, *i.e.* AQL = 1% defective

(e) Producer's risk = 5%

From the table of sample size code letters given in Appendix B in chapter 28 we can obtain the sample size. Looking in 151 to 280 lot size row under general inspection level II, we get code letter G.

From the OC Curves of code letter G given in Fig. 8, we should find a curve which meets the above requirements. We see that OC Curve for AQL 1.5% defective, (second curve from left) cues 12% defective line at less than 10% probability of acceptance and 1% defectives line at more than 95% probability of acceptance. Thus, this curve meets all the requirements of reliability specification. The actual sampling plan can then be obtained from the master table for single sampling (normal inspection) reproduced in Appendix C. For code letter G, we find sample size 32 and under AQL 1.5% defective we find acceptance number 1 and rejection number 2. This gives us the following test plan.

A sample of 32 condensers out of the lot should be subjected to the reliability test. If the number of failures is one or less, the lot should be assumed to have the minimum specified reliability. If the number of failures is 2 or more, the reliability of the condensers in the lot is expected to be less than 0.88. As such, the lot may be rejected. In this manner, reliability test plan for any other requirements can be derived from the sampling tables.

RELIABILITY CONTROL DURING MANUFACTURE

Like other quality characteristics, reliability is actually built into the product during its manufacture. The extent to which the inherent reliability of the design is achieved, depends upon the care taken during the processing of the product. Process controls discussed in earlier chapters will generally control this aspect also. However, certain minor features such as tool marks, radii at the change of sections, or the quality of soldered joints which are likely to be overlooked during processing, being un-important, may have a marked influence on the reliability of the end-product. Therefore, special checks and controls must be instituted to watch this aspect for products where a high degree of reliability is required. The management of reliability is of relatively recent origin. Sufficient data on failure mechanisms is not available, as the detailed effects of various contributory factors have not yet been studied. Under these circumstances, it is possible that some of the quality characteristics affecting reliability may be overlooked during manufacture. To guard against such a possibility, it is advisable that a certain percentage of the finished product is specifically tested for reliability, so that any flaw or weakness observed in the manufacturing process can be rectified by suitable corrective action.

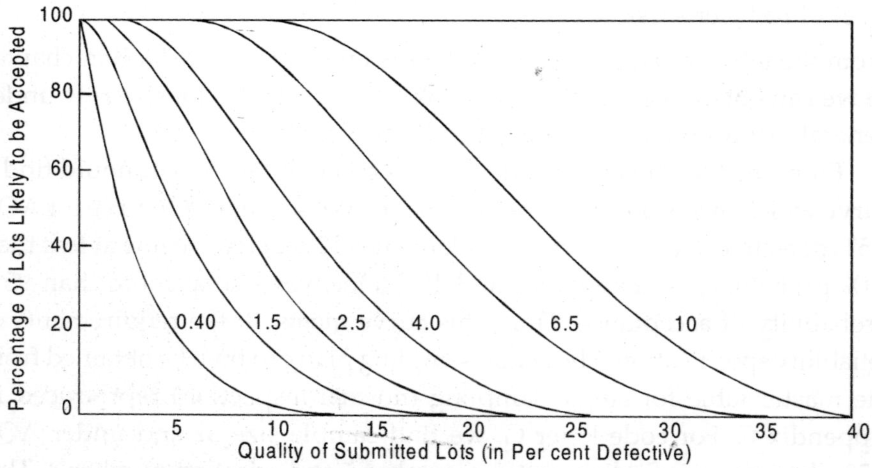

Fig. 8: OC Curves for Sample Size Code Letter 'G'

RELIABILITY IMPROVEMENT BY USER EXPERIENCE

The evaluation of reliability during design and manufacture is based on the tests conducted under simulated conditions. However, methodically and painstakingly one may try, simulated conditions cannot accurately represent actual operating conditions. Therefore, it is important that the reliability of product during actual service should be monitored, wherever possible. Left to the user, they will report only those cases where abnormally low reliability has been encountered. To be able to draw meaningful deductions, data about devices which have behaved normally is as important as that for devices which have had early or frequent failures. Special programmes may have to be instituted for the feedback of authentic data from the actual users, particularly for those products which have been newly designed or marketed. All the reported failures of the product should be thoroughly investigated to arrive at the basic cause of the failure. In case the manufacturing process is to be blamed, necessary corrective measures must immediately be taken. If the cause points to the weakness of design, immediate steps should be taken to see if the weakness can be overcome by some modification of the existing product. In particularly serious cases, the affected components may have to be replaced free of cost for all the products already sold, to save the quality reputation of the company. Accurate feedback from the users is of immense value, not only for the improvement of reliability in the current product, but also for the design of future products of similar type.

35

Maintainability

We have seen in the previous chapter that despite every effort to improve the reliability in a complex system, a certain number of failures cannot be altogether avoided. Even if it were theoretically possible to attain near 1.0 reliability, it may not be advisable to strive for it, because improvement beyond a certain value may be extremely expensive. Having accepted that a certain number of breakdowns will occur, the main interest of the user would then be to see that the equipment is put back into service as early as possible. The characteristic of the equipment which enables it to be restored to its normal efficiency is termed as MAINTAINABILITY. Like reliability, maintainability can also be quantified in terms of probability. Maintainability can be defined as "the probability of a system being restored to normal operational efficiency within a given time, if the specified maintenance is carried out."

It will be seen from the definition that since maintainability is related to the "given maintenance time", obviously if the given maintenance time is increased, *i.e.*, if greater time is allowed for the repair, the probability of its being restored to normal function will increase. In this respect, maintainability can be compared to reliability, which is dependent upon specified life. The difference is that if the specified life is increased, the reliability will be decreased.

MAINTENANCE TIME

Since maintenance time is an important constraint of maintainability, let us analyse its composition. The main activities which are carried out between the occurrence of failure and the time by which the system is put back in service, are given below:

(a) Reporting of failure
(b) Sending the equipment to the workshop or sending a repair team to the equipment
(c) Inspection of the equipment to locate the cause of failure
(d) Arranging tools and spares
(e) Actual repairs of the equipment
(f) Final testing to assess the effectiveness of repairs
(g) Sending the equipment back to the works site if it had been moved earlier.

It will be seen that among the activities mentioned above, only (c), (e) and (f) are related to the quality of the equipment as such. For instance, the equipment may be awaiting repairs for days or even months, due to the non-availability of spares, for which it will be unfair to blame the maintainability of the equipment. Due to this difficulty, the maintainability expressed in terms of probability as given in the above definition, is not of much use in quality control practice.

MEAN TIME TO REPAIR

Another term used in the context of maintainability is the mean time to repair (MTTR). Suppose we have a number of equipments and every time a failure occurs, a record is kept as to how long it took to repair the equipment. (Here, the repair time should include inspection, actual repair and final testing.) After data on a sufficient number of failures has been collected, we could then calculate the mean repair time per failure, as shown below:

$$\text{MTTR} \; \frac{\text{Total Number of Hours spent on Repairs}}{\text{Number of Equipments}}$$

The shorter the MTTR, the earlier the equipment will be put back into operational condition. Thus, the MTTR can be used as an index of maintainability.

DESIGNING FOR EASE OF MAINTENANCE

Maintainability, like other quality parameters, is primarily built into the design of the product. The main factors which affect maintainability are ease of fault location and ease of repairs.

FAULT LOCATION

The location of a fault in a system is essential before it can be repaired. Fault location can be made easier if this aspect is given due consideration during the design of the system. Some of the measures which can facilitate the location of faults are given below:

(a) Meters or lights can be provided on the instrument panels, which indicate that a particular system or sub-system has failed.

(b) Where feasible, viewing windows or detachable cover should be provided, through which the functioning of the mechanism can be seen.

(c) In electronic equipment, as far as possible, test points should be provided in important stages, where the functioning of a sub-system can be checked by means of test equipment.

(d) For particularly fault-prone units in a system, alternative units should be provided, which can be quickly brought into the circuit to check whether the subject unit is faulty.

(e) A proper colour or number code should be adopted for wiring in the electronic equipment. This will enable easy tracing of circuits.

(f) Special test equipment, where required, should be designed to enable quick location of faults in the system.

(g) Well-illustrated instruction manuals should be prepared, in which various fault location drills are properly explained.

REPAIR OF EQUIPMENT

Once the fault has been located, repair or replacement of the defective component of assembly has to be carried out to make the equipment fit for normal operation. Here again, the designer can facilitate the task of the maintenance engineer by suitably adjusting the design. Some of the points which should be considered during design, are as follows:

(a) The parts can be speedily repaired only if they are easily accessible. In order to make a system compact, there will be a great temptation to cram the parts together. However, a thought must be given to the difficulty which may be faced while replacing the parts when they become defective. If a mechanic has to remove a number of assemblies to get at the defective part, the repair time would needlessly be increased. Therefore, the parts and assemblies should be laid out in such a manner that they are readily accessible. Where the parts are masked by shields or covers, detachable window plate may be provided to facilitate access.

(b) Fixing and coupling devices of assemblies or units of the system should be such that they are not jammed due to corrosion or other chemical action.

(c) Bolts, nuts and other fastening devices should not be fitted in such places where these are likely to fall into the system during their removal.

(d) Electronic systems, as far as possible, should comprise of separate units or modules which can quickly be plugged in or removed.

(e) Special maintenance and repair tools should be designed where required, and detailed repair manuals should be provided to facilitate repairs.

(f) System should be so designed that preventive maintenance can be easily carried out.

Improving Maintainability of an Equipment

When a new system is designed, the designer has practically no means of predicting the frequency and nature of repairs, which will be required for the equipment. Maintenance problems will generally be known only after the equipment has been in service for a certain period, that too only if there is a proper channel for feedback of repair data from the user to the designer. Generally, mechanics and maintenance engineers are practical people who do not keep detailed records of repairs unless they have been specifically instructed to do so. Therefore, special efforts are required to be made by the quality engineers to collect the repair data. Special forms and questionnaires, eliciting information about repairs could be designed, which the user's maintenance engineers may be asked to send at periodic intervals. The repair data so obtained could then be used to provide innovations for improving maintainability of the equipment.

36

5 'S' Practices

INTRODUCTION

Japanese companies are known for their clean and orderly work environment. Japan has limited land area, and they do not have the luxury of spread-out factories. Yet, any visitor to a Japanese facility may observe that it is not generally crowded or cluttered. In fact, one is likely to see a great deal of space for free movement, a neat and clean workplace and a clear view of all work areas. So, how have they achieved this? The secret is often the adoption of 5 'S' practices.

The rationale for the adoption of 5 'S' is that well-organised and neat workplaces, standardisation and the discipline to implement quality standards are the fundamental requirements for producing high-quality products, avoiding waste and achieving the high productivity necessary for competitiveness. Some persons attribute the 'Japanese Miracle' to the culture of Japan. Although national culture does influence behaviour and work environments in general, 5 'S' is a structured management tool like many others and has been successfully employed in a number of countries, including India. The Indian industry can greatly benefit from this important tool of TQM.

WHAT IS 5 'S' ?

The concept of 5 'S' has evolved from the first letters of five Japanese words which are related to order, neatness and workplace standardization. 5 'S' practices consist of the following five simple steps:

1. Seiri (sort)
2. Seiton (systematic arrangement)
3. Seiso (shine and inspect)
4. Seiketsu (standardize)
5. Shitsuku (sustain and self-discipline)

These steps are explained in the paragraphs below.

1. Seiri (sort)

The first principle of 5 'S' is Seiri. Seiri means that you should sort out (and put away) what you do not need. Any workplace can get cluttered with parts, work-in-progress tools, jigs, shelves and cabinets, chairs, desks, documents, etc. This impedes the free flow of personnel, trolleys etc., and may cause safety hazards due to pinch points and sharp corners. Thus, the 'Seiri' principle requires that you should clearly distinguish the items which are needed at the workplace and those which are not needed. The items which are not needed immediately could be classified into two categories – Those which are not required at all, and those which may be needed occasionally. The first category should then be examined to see if these are required by some one else and, if not, they should be disposed off. The second category should be kept in a storage place from where they can be taken out when needed, but are otherwise out of the way. You may be surprised how much space becomes available for productive work using 5 'S' approach. Consultants of the FICCI Quality Forum during consultancy in a steel cold rolling unit were able to free space of about 1,500 sq. mtrs. in the plant where an additional equipment could be installed, thus avoiding construction of another shed.

Implementation of Seiri would require the following activities:

- Establish criteria for identifying necessary and unnecessary items.
- Take photographs of stored items before undertaking a 5 'S' exercise. This can serve as a reference point to assess the progress of 5 'S'.
- Discard unnecessary items.
- Decide on the retention period for records and the frequency of disposal of records beyond the specified period.
- Take photographs after the first sorting, which can be used for review.
- Organize first review of records and weed out unwanted documents.
- Discard out-dated notices, calendars and other display items.

2. Seiton (systematic arrangement)

The second principle of 5 'S' is Seiton, which requires that all items necessary for production should be kept according to a fixed arrangement, based on which they can easily be retrieved and used. In other words, we must follow the proverb "A place for everything and everything in its place." Implementation of Seiton would require following activities:

- Establish criteria for the classification of necessary items into different groups, depending on frequency of usage, on special safety requirements for storage, and so on.
- Decide on storage locations for items of various categories. Items required daily should be kept near the workplace. Those required infrequently should be kept in a separate store.
- Consumable materials and components should be kept in suitable containers, which should be properly labelled/marked.
- The names and quantities of stored items should be listed, and the person responsible for replenishment should be clearly identified.
- All moving parts, components and items which are prone to dust, should be visible and easily accessible.
- Tools and jigs should be kept on shadow boards marked with the outlines of the tools for ease of storage and retrieval.
- The 'home' position of heavy equipment should be marked on the floor.
- Gangways should be clearly marked and it should be ensured that no material or equipment encroaches on the gangway space.
- Signboards and labelling should be clearly visible.
- All files should be appropriately categorized and stored in separate drawers, cabinets, etc. Their location should be marked on the file covers.
- Files and their locations should be indexed for easy retrieval.
- Hazardous materials should be clearly marked and separated, and precautions for their proper handling, use and disposal should be clearly displayed.

3. Seiso (shine and inspect)

A spick-and-span environment and a well-ordered workplace will raise the spirits and morale of the work team, since nobody likes to work in a chaotic or and filthy workplace. Following the first two principles of 5 'S' would already have cleared a lot of floor and shelf space. Now look for dust, filth, grime and foreign matter lying on the shelves, floor and equipment. All this must be cleaned. The 5 'S' team has to determine what to clean, how to clean it, and who will do the cleaning on a regular basis.

The areas to be cleaned, should include machinery, aisles, office and meeting rooms, canteens, etc. Cleaning methods should be determined for all cases, including cleaning equipment and materials. All this cleaning-related equipment should be kept at specified 5 'S' stations so that they do not clutter other places. The responsibility for cleaning should be clearly defined along with a cleaning schedule and cleaning check-sheets. As far as possible, users of any equipment or workplace should do their own cleaning so that they can take pride in keeping their equipment and workplace spick and span. "Seiso" also means regular inspection. Once the equipment is cleaned, it will be easier to inspect and the inspector can more readily notice any leakage, seepage or other abnormal conditions, so that immediate corrective action can be taken. Implementation of "Seiso" would require following activities:

- Identify various types of foreign matter such as dust, soot, oil and other filth around workplaces.
- Examine the causes of generation of such foreign matter and take appropriate measures to reduce its accumulation.
- Develop a plan of what is to be cleaned and how. The areas to be cleaned might include machinery, passageways, stores, offices, toilets, canteen, etc.
- Particular care should be taken to clean around machines, on walls, on ceilings, under racks and stands, in various nooks and corners, etc., which may be difficult to access.
- Establish a proper drainage system to facilitate washing and cleaning by water, if appropriate.
- Plan the cleaning of fans, air conditioners and their filters, lights, switches, notice boards, etc.
- Define frequency of cleaning and allocate responsibility for cleaning and its verification.
- Every group or department in an organization should have a 5 'S' station. Each 5 'S' station should have at least the following items:
  - Broom, hand brush, vacuum cleaner and mop
  - Dust pan, bag of wiping rags
  - Cleaning liquid, and
  - A large trash bin
- After cleaning, inspect for any leakage or seepage of fluids from machines so that appropriate corrective measures can be taken.
- Inspect electrical fittings, wiring and switches to ensure that they are functional and secure.

- Inspect faucets and toilet fittings for proper functioning.

4. Seiketsu (standardize)

With the application of the first three principles of 5 'S', we have removed all unwanted things and organised all the required equipment and materials in proper order. Clear labels and locations have been assigned to equipment, both in the shop floor and in storage areas. We have also ensured that everything is clean and in good condition. Thus, we have created a fine-looking workplace, but will it remain so?

Left to themselves, things go back to haphazard or chaotic conditions. It is a fundamental law of nature that all systems and physical conditions tend to degrade with time, unless conscious efforts are made to maintain these in the desired conditions. For this, we must develop and apply standards for maintaining conditions for S-1 to S-3. A few examples of standards are provided below.

(a) Standards for S-1

- What items are needed for various workplaces.
- Responsibility and frequency of checking for unwanted things.
- Procedures for disposal of unwanted items.

(b) Standards for S-2

- Types of signboards and identification labels.
- Marking of gangways and dangerous areas.
- Types of protective clothing to be used.

(c) Standards for S-3

- Areas and equipment to be cleaned and the responsibility thereof.
- Methods of cleaning and provision of cleaning materials.
- Inspection methods and check sheets.

5. Shitshuke (sustain and self-discipline)

A number of cultures include a strong sense of the dignity of labour – no job is considered "below the dignity" of anyone. For instance, it is quite common for householders to clean their own homes, and for workers to clean their own workplaces. In other cultures, it can be quite different. In India, for instance, even in the lower-middle-class houses, maids are expected to perform 'menial' chores like cleaning. In offices, clerks expect someone else to clean and maintain their work environments. Therefore, an organization in a culture like India needs a great deal of effort to change worker mindsets and embed a 5 'S' culture. Listed below are some activities, which can be undertaken to promote and sustain 5 'S' cultures:

- Organize awareness campaigns in the company by explaining the benefits of 5 'S'. Images of organizations that have implemented 5

'S' can be shown and contrasted against disorganized and shabby work environments where such ideas have not been implemented. Once employees realize that they too can achieve good work environments, they would welcome such an initiative.

- Arrange training programmes for employees in various departments on how 5 'S' can be implemented in their specific department.
- Organise competitions among departments for the implementation of 5 'S' programmes, and award prizes to winning departments.
- Invite suggestions for innovative ideas for implementing 5 'S' and publicly recognize the authors of good ideas.
- Publicize 5 'S' success stories in the in-house magazine or during 5 'S' training programmes.
- Recognize individuals who have made major contributions as 5 'S' champions.

Visual Management Systems

Clean and tidy workplaces are one aspect of 5 'S'. The other aspect is a visual management system. Visual management does not simply mean sign boards, labelling and marking of specified areas. A more important aspect of visual management is that all employees must have a clear picture of the performance of the organization. Although computers and ERP systems enable executives and managers to be aware of ongoing activities, most shop-floor workers and supervisors in Indian factories are not 'in the loop' in this respect. Therefore, there is a need for staff in general to see important data about the factory facility where they work. This may be achieved by having display boards containing the following informations:

- Monthly or weekly production status
- Daily 'defect' status on a department-by-department basis for the past week
- Machine availability statistics
- Inventory levels
- Delivery commitments and fulfilment statistics
- Production targets etc.

This will enable staff to get fully involved in improving their performance and achieving organizational goals.

BENEFITS OF 5 'S'

The implementation of 5 'S' in an organization provides a number of benefits for the organization as well as individual employees. Some benefits are listed as follows:

Benefits for the Organization

a) Better utilisation of space, equipment and other resources.
b) Reduction of wastage of materials, time and money.
c) Reduction of non-value-added activities.
d) Improvement in safety and work environments.
e) Improvement in quality and productivity.
f) Improved awareness of standards and work culture.
g) Easy retrieval of documents.
h) Improvement in punctuality, commitment and discipline.

Benefits for Individual Employees

a) Improvement in general ambience and quality of work life.
b) Reduced fatigue due to easy access to work items.
c) Improved efficiency and effectiveness.
d) Stress reduction.
e) Development of an organized and disciplined attitude to work.

PLANNING FOR 5 'S'

Like any other concept, the implementation of 5 'S' in any organization requires careful planning and organised activity. Guidelines for planning various 5 'S' activities are provided in the following sections:

Management of 5 'S' Programme

Like all other quality initiatives, the full commitment of top management is vital for the success of 5 'S'. To start 5 'S' in an organization, there must be a champion at a senior level of the organization who should be passionate about the subject. It need not be the Quality Manager because this is one activity which needs to be carried on a daily basis by all departments in the organization. Unless all heads of departments or groups take ownership for 5 'S' in their group, it can never be implemented. Some elements of 5 'S' such as general cleanliness of office buildings, production shops and service areas like canteen and toilets may be outsourced with proper control. However, all other activities have to be carried out by the personnel of various departments and offices.

The first step in the implementation programme is that the champion should convince the top management about the benefits of a 5 'S' programme and request them to approve it as a formal project, provide adequate resources and take a leadership role in its implementation.

Once a 5 'S' project is approved, a meeting needs to be organised under the chairmanship of the CEO in which heads of all departments need to participate. In this meeting, the champion could be asked to make a presentation to explain the salient activities of 5 'S' and their benefits to the organization and the role of heads of departments and other key functionaries. In this meeting it may be helpful to show photographs of existing conditions in various departments so that everyone can see how these adversely affect quality, efficiency, productivity and morale of the persons working in this environment.

When a general consensus has been achieved to implement 5 'S' in the organisation, a central steering committee needs to be constituted under the CEO to oversee the 5 'S' campaign. Since actual action will take place in all departments, they need to set up a task force in their respective departments implementing 5 'S' and make it a way of life.

Implementation Methodology

The actual implementation of 5 'S' is likely to require the following steps:

- An audit of the current condition in all the areas, based on which 5 'S' activities can be planned.
- Effective implementation would require facilitators–at least one in every department. Facilitators should be selected based on their dynamism and standing in their groups to fulfill the role of opinion makers.
- Organising the training of facilitators in all the five 5 'S' activities.
- Detailed plan should be worked out for 5 'S' in different areas by the facilitators and approved by departmental task groups.
- The 5 'S' campaign should be formally launched by the CEO, where he, along with other senior officers, take up the broom to demonstrate their commitment and encourage staff to take 5 'S' seriously.
- A first assessment should be carried out after trial implementation for a week, wherein all problems that are encountered, could be discussed and corrective measures taken.
- At this point, all departments should be given one month to fully implement 5 'S'.
- An audit of the 5 'S' programme for various groups should be carried out, preferably by an outside consultant, and a detailed report should be provided so that everyone can take corrective measures.
- Inter-group competitions should be planned for implementation of 5 'S', with well-defined criteria and mechanisms for assessment.
- Prizes should be awarded to two or three groups which have shown the best performance.
- The implementation of 5 'S' should be continuously improved until it gets embedded in the organisational culture.

37

Quality Circles

BASIC PHILOSOPHY

The quality problems are the products of industrial age. During the pre-industrial age, the craftsmen personally understood the needs of the customers, designed the product and crafted it himself or through his apprentices under close supervision. Thus, there was no communication gap and he had no difficulty in delivering the products of the desired quality. With the industrialisation came the increasing distance between the user and the actual maker of the product needing written specifications of product. The need of specialisation broke up the manufacturing job into design, process engineering, tooling and actual production. In these environments, it is understood that all creative and innovative ideas for quality improvement can come from the designer and the process engineer, whereas production worker can provide only his muscle power. Japanese were the first to realise that creative power was not limited to the designers and engineers only. The shop floor worker who actually manufactured the product could also contribute significantly in the quality improvement programme. However, for this to happen, proper environment and motivation has to be provided. It was Dr. Ishikawa, a Japanese quality expert, who introduced the concept of Quality Circle, which stressed the participation of maximum number of people engaged in industry in Quality Control programmes. It was a unique Japanese answer to the challenge of quality upon which their economic future depended. It disseminated the message of quality down below and, in fact, it reversed the normal flow of ideas. Quality consciousness grew bottom and spread horizontally, of course with full support and encouragement from the top. What is remarkable about the game is that the basic rules were not made by the Japanese. It was based upon the SQA techniques as learnt from the Americans. But a practical way of implementing this knowledge, suiting the genius of their people, was certainly a Japanese 'Invention'.

WHAT IS QUALITY CIRCLE?

Quality Circle is a small group of members working together who meet voluntarily with a view to analysing and resolving work related problems. The meetings are informal in nature, but are held regularly. The group consists of 7 to 10 persons from one group in an organization who meet at least once a week for one hour. All of them work under the same management. At the meetings, they speak only about their work and problems pertaining to it, not the administrative or personal problems. The whole organisation is voluntary by nature. Nevertheless, all the members are highly motivated in their work.

OBJECTIVES OF QUALITY CIRCLES

(a) To improve quality and productivity of the products.
(b) To promote consciousness among workers about quality, safety and cost of production.
(c) To give opportunity to the employees to learn new techniques of identifying technical problems in the area of their production, thereby improving their knowledge.
(d) To allow employees to solve the problems in their work area, thereby giving job satisfaction.
(e) To improve employee motivation.
(f) To inspire more effective team work and develop leadership among some employees who have the potential.
(g) To improve communications within the organisation and develop healthy superior-subordinate relationship.
(h) To develop a complete coherent problem solving methodology within the organisation.

FUNCTIONING OF QUALITY CIRCLES

(a) Ideally, the members of a particular circle come from the same work area or who perform similar work so that the problems they select are familiar to all of them, and it is easy to find solutions with their experience and knowledge. Alternatively, a circle may also be constituted with members from different connected work areas. In such case, they may look at the problem from all angles, so that it is easy for them to arrive at optimum solutions. Whichever may be the formation of a circle, the membership is strictly voluntary.

(b) An ideal size of a circle is 5 to 10 members. The size must never be so large that each member does not get sufficient time to participate and contribute in the meetings.

(c) The number of circles in a given work area may be more than one, if the response for working in Quality Circle is more than 15, but any one person cannot be a member of more than one circle. To avoid duplication of activities in the same work area, good coordination should be maintained between the leaders of these circles and the facilitator.

(d) As a thumb rule, the meetings should take place once a week and each meeting should be for approximately one hour. It is preferable to conduct the meetings in a separate room in the same work area or very close to the work area. Circle meetings may be held during or after office/factory hours, depending on the convenience and discretion of circle members.

STRUCTURE OF QUALITY CIRCLES

Basic Elements

The basic elements which constitute the structure of Quality Circles are as follows:

(a) Top management,
(b) Steering committee,
(c) Coordinator,
(d) Facilitators,
(e) Leaders,
(f) Members, and
(g) Non-members.

Top Management

The executives at the highest level who extend all the necessary support to the activities of the Quality Circles, and through their personal presence at the presentations and other major activities of Quality Circles make their support visible to all. The top management has an important role to play to ensure the success of implementation of the QC concept in the organisation.

They should be fully convinced and committed to Quality Circles. Their broad functions in the promotion of Quality Circles are given below:

(a) Demonstrate unequivocally its understanding and faith in the concept of Quality Circles.

(b) Make a provision in the annual budget for meeting the expenditure of operation of Quality Circles.
(c) Encourage healthy growth through competition between Quality Circles by instituting an award to the division/department which performs best in propagation of Quality Circles as well as to the Quality Circles which make the best presentations at any centrally organised convention or conference.
(d) Give necessary guidance to employees at different levels for making the Quality Circle movement a self-sustained success.
(e) Include propagation of Quality Circles as one of the Corporation objectives.
(f) Attend management presentation of various circles.
(g) Respond to the Circle recommendations in a positive way without any delays.
(h) Verify the implementation of circle recommendations without any undue delays.
(i) Depute the members to outside seminars/workshops, and
(j) Periodically review the QC activities on a regular basis.

STEERING COMMITTEE

As soon as a decision is made to implement Quality Circles programme, the steering committee comprising the chief executive, divisional heads of departments and the coordinator is constituted. The chief executive and the coordinator act as chairman and secretary of the steering committee, respectively. The meetings are convened at least once in two or three months.

FUNCTIONS

(a) Promote Quality Circles in the organisation;
(b) Develop working methodology and give the guidelines relating to Quality Circle operations with respect to the facilities to be provided, for example, place, date and time of conducting the meetings, type of rewards for motivation;
(c) Establish the programme objectives and resources;
(d) Provide policy guidelines and direction;
(e) Nominate coordinator and facilitators;
(f) Attend various presentations of the studies carried out by Quality Circles;
(g) Obtain feedback from facilitators and review Quality Circles activities;
(h) Provide necessary provisions in the annual budget;

(i) Grade the project reports of Quality Circles for awards; and
(j) Review the overall working of Quality Circles.

Coordinator

The coordinator coordinates the activities of Quality Circles throughout the organisation and carries out such functions as would make the operation of Quality Circles smooth, effective and self-sustained.

Functions

(a) Register Quality Circles in the unit/division;
(b) Has liaison with the facilitators for ensuring regularity of Circle meetings, mid-term presentations, etc. and to analyse 'activity level charts'.
(c) Convene Steering Committee meetings and circulate record notes thereof;
(d) Convene monthly leaders' meetings and circulate record notes thereof;
(e) Organise systematic documentation of Quality Circle case studies and publish their compilation annually;
(f) Organise top-management presentations in coordination with the facilitators;
(g) Gives assistance to Circles, whenever asked for;
(h) Conduct opinion surveys to assess intangible gains from time to time;
(i) Publish newsletter on Quality Circle activities in local language;
(j) Prepare training material for facilitators and leaders in conjunction with training departments;
(k) Organise training programmes for facilitators and leaders in collaboration with training departments;
(l) Organise lectures, seminars, conferences, exhibitions, etc. on Quality Circles;
(m) Publish periodicals, pamphlets, etc. for the promotion of Quality Circles;
(n) Provide display boards of Quality Circles in the shops, areas where Quality Circles are functioning;
(o) Expose all employees at the grassroots and different levels of executives to the concept of Quality Circle through audio-visuals and lectures;
(p) Disseminate knowledge by circulating information and news on Quality Circles from journals/books;
(q) Develop schemes for the recognition of Quality Circles for the contributions made by them;

(r) Organise presentations of Quality Circle case studies in sister units for mutual exchange of ideas; and
(s) Organise conventions of Quality Circles.

Facilitator

The facilitator is usually a senior officer of the department where Quality Circles are working and is nominated by the management. He does not only guide the Quality Circle activities in his area, but also enthuses others to get involved in these activities. Because of the crucial role that the facilitator plays in making Quality Circles operation a success, his selection shall be done carefully.

Functions

(a) Attend Quality Circle meetings, at least for brief periods;
(b) Guide Circles in the proceedings of meetings;
(c) Coordinate with the training officer for organising necessary training programmes in SQC techniques, QC Working procedures, etc. for Quality Circle leaders and members;
(d) Provide necessary facilities and act as a catalyst for the Circle members.
(e) Coordinate and obtain the support and assistance from other functional areas whenever required by the Quality Circles;
(f) Act as an intermediary in resolving Quality Circle problems;
(g) Work closely with the Steering Committee;
(h) Ensure that each Quality Circle keeps a record of its activities by way of maintaining registers, follow-up for implementation of completed project.
(i) Arrange for periodical management presentations and to schedule meetings of Quality Circles;
(j) Communicate the Steering Committee decisions regarding the implementation of recommendations submitted by Quality Circles, search for new ideas, and publicise the achievements of the Quality Circles in his area.
(k) Collect and arrange dissemination of literatures relating to Quality Circle activities elsewhere;
(l) Arrange periodical get-togethers of Circle members with the top executives of the organisation; and
(m) Strengthen and promote participative culture within the organisation.

LEADER

Leader is chosen by the members of a Quality Circle among themselves. Members may also themselves decide to have a leader by rotation. The deputy leader may also be chosen by the Quality Circle so as to ensure that Circle meetings and other activities would go on uninterruptedly even if the leader is not present. Initially, the supervisor may be a leader and another worker as deputy leader.

FUNCTIONS

(a) Conduct Circle meetings regularly;
(b) Maintain registers regarding the proceedings of the Circle meetings, problem selections, etc.
(c) Train the members with the assistance of the facilitator/ coordinator;
(d) Maintain a high degree of cohesiveness of his team with a sense of identity;
(e) Involve every member in the Circle meetings/activities;
(f) Set Circle goals and improve performance towards the same;
(g) Chalk out action plans and delegate responsibility to Circle members;
(h) Bring about a consensus approach in problem solving;
(i) Prepare the project report and present to the departmental heads and Steering Committee;
(j) Appraise the progress of the work with the facilitator and the concerned departmental head;
(k) Interact with other functional areas in problem-solving;
(l) Review progress vis-a-vis goals and objectives set for themselves;
(m) Arrange for mid-term and top management presentations; and
(n) Catalyze non-members to join existing Circles or start new ones.

MEMBERS

Members are the basic element of the structure of Quality Circles. Members of Quality Circle are a small group of people from the same work area or doing similar type of work, who voluntarily form a Quality Circle. Once a Circle is formed, they remain as permanent members of the Circle, unless they leave the work area for good. The members should contribute actively to the effective functioning of their Quality Circle, aiming at better performance of their work area in every way on an ongoing basis.

FUNCTIONS

(a) Meet regularly (one hour in a week) and actively participate in Quality Circle meeting;

(b) Contribute ideas for problem solving;
(c) Assist the leader in data gathering record-keeping, interacting with people from other areas;
(d) Catalyze generation of cohesive team working in the work area;
(e) Strive for the highest standards of performance of the Circle;
(f) Involve in the improvement of the total performance of the organization; and
(g) Take part in the mid-term and top management presentations.

TRAINING FOR QUALITY CIRCLE ACTIVITIES

The objective of training for Quality Circle activities is to prepare the concerned people for playing their roles effectively for the successful functioning of Quality Circles. People are to be trained for their specific roles and hence emphasis need to be laid on the role of each person involved in the Quality Circle function.

The success of the Circle activities depends on the training received by the concerned people in:

(a) Proper understanding of the concept and philosophy;
(b) Translating effectively the philosophy into practice;
(c) Proper application of simple statistical quality control techniques;
(d) Improving communication capability; and
(e) Developing leadership qualities and building up individuals.

Training is primarily given to the facilitators and leaders, who in turn train Circle members. The following aspects should be covered for training of facilitators and Circle leaders:

(a) For Facilitator

i. Quality Circle—its genesis, concept and philosophy
ii. Role of facilitator, functions of leaders, members and steering committee
iii. Quality control techniques used in Quality Circle activities, and
iv. Problems encountered by Quality Circles and their solutions

(b) For Leader

i. Introduction of Quality Circles
ii. Identification of problems—brainstorming
iii. Selection of the priorities—Pareto analysis
iv. Identification of the causes for the problems—cause and effect diagram
v. Collection and presentation of data

vi. Identification of the solutions and selecting the best—brainstorming and cost
vii. Benefit analysis
viii. Delegation of responsibility
ix. Effective conduct of meetings
x. Record-keeping and follow-up action
xi. Review of progress against goals
xii. Management presentations

LIMITATIONS OF QUALITY CIRCLES

While Quality Circle is an excellent technique for motivating the employees and improving quality of products and the work culture in a company, it is not a panacea for all problems in an organisation. It is not a substitute for the main tasks of the management which is planning, organising, employing and allocating resources including human resource, directing, controlling, checking, review and prepare budget. Quality Circle is not a substitute for Task force that is employed to solveing specific problems. It is not even directly responsible for improvement of quality, although this is one of its main objectives. It is not a substitute for shop councils, nor does it exclude the role of individual suggestions for job or quality improvement. Quality Circle is not an agency for diverting its own problems by the management. It is neither pro nor against Union or Management.

Quality Circle is meant for improving the work, for which it should constantly strive. It should aim at making the work more meaningful and effective, and thereby more ethically satisfying for the persons involved in doing it. It is a people's movement for improvement of work culture that includes improvement of quality and productivity as its main objective.